Rethinking Democratic Innovation

Rethinking Democratic Innovation

Cultural Clashes and the Reform of Democracy

Frank Hendriks

OXFORD
UNIVERSITY PRESS

OXFORD
UNIVERSITY PRESS

Great Clarendon Street, Oxford, OX2 6DP,
United Kingdom

Oxford University Press is a department of the University of Oxford.
It furthers the University's objective of excellence in research, scholarship,
and education by publishing worldwide. Oxford is a registered trade mark of
Oxford University Press in the UK and in certain other countries

Published in the United States of America by Oxford University Press
198 Madison Avenue, New York, NY 10016, United States of America

British Library Cataloguing in Publication Data
Data available

Library of Congress Control Number: 2023932342

ISBN 978–0–19–284829–1

DOI: 10.1093/oso/9780192848291.001.0001

Printed and bound by
CPI Group (UK) Ltd, Croydon, CR0 4YY

Dedicated to the memory of Evert Jan Hendriks (1930–2020)

Picasso's famous Guernica has grown to become the image of violence and war victims in the twentieth century. Well: Victory Boogie Woogie by Mondriaan is the image of the victory of joy and freedom.

Hans Locher, former director Gemeentemuseum, Kunstmuseum Den Haag

…Removing the dividing lines not only made it possible to fully appreciate the colors, much more importantly, it created space for a new world… Victory Boogie Woogie poignantly depicts multicultural, democratic society.

Hans Goslinga, journalist newspaper Trouw

Preface and acknowledgements

It's naive political solutionism to expect that one product of what has become a kind of global democracy innovation industry—be it internet voting, assemblies of randomly chosen citizens, or what have you—will get us out of our difficulties.

Jan-Werner Müller[1]

How democracies revive

The democracy section in the bookshop or library sometimes feels like the vanitas section in the art museum, where paintings of rotting fruit, burnt candles, bleached skulls, and the like are meant to remind the viewer of the transience of life. Recent books on democracy have ominous titles such as *How Democracies Die, How Democracy Ends, Death by a Thousand Cuts, The End of Representative Politics.*[2] The message is penetrating: democracy has been at the forefront of world history only for a relatively short while, and may well fade into the background again; various signs of decline and back-sliding should give us cause for serious concern; rekindling democracy is very difficult, and perhaps a fight against the inevitable course of all life.

It was to be expected that a subsequent series of books would take on a different tone. More recently, under titles such as *Hope for Democracy, Mending Democracy, Let the People Rule, Democracy Rules,* various paths towards the revitalization of democracy have been discerned.[3] The tone of these books

[1] Müller, J.W., *Democracy Rules*, Penguin Books, 2021, p. xiv.

[2] Levisky S. and D. Ziblatt, *How Democracies Die*, New York, Crown, 2018; Runciman, D., *How Democracy Ends*, Profile books, 2018; Qvortrup, M., *Death by a Thousand Cuts: The Slow Demise of Democracy*, De Gruyter, 2021; Tormey, S., *The End of Representative Politics*, Cambridge, Polity Press, 2015. On democratic malaise and decline see also Beek, U. van (ed.), *Democracy under Threat: A Crisis of Legitimacy*, Palgrave Macmillan, 2019; Diamond, L. and M.F. Plattner (eds), *Democracy in Decline?*, Baltimore, John Hopkins University Press, 2016; Foa, R.S. and Y. Mounk, The Democratic Disconnect, *Journal of Democracy*, 2016, 27, 3, pp. 5–17; Flinders, M., The Problem with Democracy, *Parliamentary Affairs*, 2015, 69, 1, pp. 181–203; Ercan, S.A. and J.P. Gagnon, Crisis of Democracy: Which Crisis? Which Democracy?, *Democratic Theory*, 2014, 1, 2, pp. 1–10; Papadopoulos, Y., *Democracy in Crisis?*, Basingstoke, Palgrave Macmillan, 2013. Furthermore, see recurring updates of the *Democracy Report* and the *Democracy Index*. See V-Dem, Democracy Reports, <https://www.v-dem.net/democracy_reports.html>, n.d.; Economist Intelligence Unit, Democracy Index, <https://www.eiu.com/n/campaigns/democracy-index-2021/>, n.d.

[3] Gastil, J. and K. Knobloch, *Hope for Democracy: How Citizens Can Bring Reason Back into Politics*, Oxford, Oxford University Press, 2020; Hendriks, C.M., S.A. Ercan, and J. Boswell, *Mending Democracy: Democratic Repair in Disconnected Times*, Oxford, Oxford University Press, 2020; Matsusaka, J., *Let the*

is more hopeful, without denying the serious problems of democracy. The present volume fits more into this series of books (the hopeful) than into the previously mentioned category (the ominous). Still, there are important differences to bear in mind. The books mentioned illustrate how divergent lines of thought can be.

The democratic improvements that Jan-Werner Müller, author of *Democracy Rules*, hopes to see developing pertain to the macro-infrastructure of democracy: political parties and the public media foremost. Particularly striking is his defence of political parties, which would provide 'the most plausible political machinery to counter the two secessions'—the secession of the lower as well as the highest end of the income spectrum—that plague democracy in his view.[4] In contrast, Carolyn Hendriks, Selen Erkan, and John Boswell focus on the micro-fabric of democracy beyond formal democratic institutions—a fabric that is arguably wearing thin. In *Mending Democracy* the authors call attention to the unassuming and often overlooked repair work undertaken by everyday actors threading and maintaining connections in the delicate fabric of democracy. They call for a connective turn in deliberative-democracy thinking, which is for them still 'the most prominent and vibrant reservoir of hope'.[5]

John Gastil and Katherine Knoblauch also look at deliberative democracy for improvements, but other than Carolyn Hendriks et al. they pin their *Hope for Democracy* on a formalized institution for deliberation: the Citizens' Initiative Review, a randomly-selected group of citizens assembled to review propositions for direct legislation. Such interventions of the deliberative-democracy persuasion are reviewed just briefly, and mainly doubtfully, in Jan-Werner Müller's *Democracy Rules*.[6] They are largely overlooked by John Matsusaka's *Let the People Rule*, which primarily focuses on ways to make direct democracy work for the good of the people, particularly through the referendum—a plebiscitary instrument of mass voting that contrasts with the deliberative-democracy interventions and connective repairs advocated in *Hope for Democracy* and *Mending Democracy*. Matsusaka also points to the friction with representative democracy. In his view, referendums would neutralize the political middlemen who aggravate the dealignment of citizen

People Rule: How Direct Democracy Can Meet the Populist Challenge, Princeton, Princeton University Press, 2020; Müller, J.W., *Democracy Rules*, Penguin Books, 2021.

[4] Müller, J.W., *Democracy Rules*, Penguin Books, 2021, p. 182. While an increasing number of citizens at the lower end of the income spectrum no longer vote or participate in any other form of politics, the most privileged find refuge in their gated communities and tax havens.

[5] Hendriks, C.M., S.A. Ercan, and J. Boswell, *Mending Democracy: Democratic Repair in Disconnected Times*, Oxford, Oxford University Press, 2020, p. 9.

[6] Müller, J.W., *Democracy Rules*, Penguin Books, 2021, p. 86 et seq.

preferences and public policies—the very middlemen that Müller hopes to see reform.[7]

The aforementioned works are recent exponents of a much broader debate on democratic revitalization, where divergent and often contrasting approaches are emerging. This book is about how such divergent approaches manifest themselves, what tensions accompany them, and about whether such tensions can also be made productive. Could different approaches complement and correct each other in ways that are good for democracy? Could it be that combined approaches are needed to address a larger part of the democratic revitalization puzzle, while separate approaches are confined to more limited areas of concern? This book ultimately provides an affirmative answer, without sidestepping the complexities and challenges of combining approaches that are often defined in contrast to one another.

This book explores both the possibilities and limitations of hybrid democratic innovation (HDI), understood as a form of innovation that thrives on exploiting, not eliminating, oppositions. Underlying the broader debate are two fundamental, recurring dichotomies. One dichotomy is all too familiar, yet still relevant: the opposition between, on the one hand, approaches aimed at improvements in representative—politically controlled, top-down arranged—democracy, and, on the other hand, more or less direct—citizen directed, bottom-up propelled—democracy. The other dichotomy is as fundamental as it is dynamic: the opposition between approaches that seek innovations through deliberative—talk-centric—democracy on the one hand, and plebiscitary—direct-voting oriented—democracy on the other.

The deliberative–plebiscitary opposition is particularly tense. Plebiscitary democrats have doubts about the intensive talk sessions for which, in their view, deliberative democrats have inflated expectations. Deliberative democrats, on the other hand, have problems with the swift voting practices that plebiscitarians aim for. Yet there are good reasons to look for ways to make such tensions productive and connective, as I set out to do in this book, picking up on recent developments in both theory and practice—*inter alia* reflecting on the deliberative referendum in Ireland and Participatory Budgeting-new style in Antwerp, Belgium, both remarkably creative combinations of instruments, embedded in representative democracy.

In the present study of competing counterparts and possible connections between them, the plebiscitary–deliberative opposition comes first, while connected to this the direct–representative dichotomy comes into play. Or

[7] Matsusaka, J., *Let the People Rule: How Direct Democracy Can Meet the Populist Challenge*, Princeton, Princeton University Press, 2020, p. 5.

x Preface and acknowledgements

to put it differently, the deliberative–plebiscitary frontline is foregrounded against the backdrop of the direct–representative dichotomy. In my view, we thus push against a new frontier in democratic-innovations research and practice, where there is much still to discover, discuss, and ponder.

On a personal note

The search for productive links between approaches that do not automatically seek each other out is something of a constant in my work. When I wrote my dissertation in the 1990s at Leyden University in the Netherlands, I was stunned by the invisible but nevertheless tangible iron curtain between scholars of Public Administration (PA) and Political Science (PS) who were in fact direct neighbours on the same office floor. The dissertation's starting point was clearly in PA-inspired policy science—it was an attempt to understand why competing policy views amount to cross-fertilization and policy learning in one place but not so much in another. Ultimately, I learned that political institutions, particularly the democratic systems in place, accounted for much of the difference. Hence, the title of the resulting book: *Public Policy and Political Institutions*.[8] In following years, democratic institutions and reforms thereof became increasingly central to my research, manifested in another monograph: *Vital Democracy*.[9] A respected PA-colleague felt that I had gone to 'the other side' voicing the opinion, shocking to my mind, that studying the dynamics of democratic institutions is a PS-thing, not a PA-thing.

I felt and still strongly feel that studying this should be both a PS- and a PA-endeavour, as I hope is reflected in the present volume.[10] My understanding of democratic institutions and the refurbishing thereof (Part I of the book) combines theories of democracy and cultural dynamics that I find dispersed in PS and PA. In further rethinking innovations in democratic governance (Part II of the book), I extend and apply the PS-dominated democratic-innovations literature in addition to the PA-dominated governance-innovations literature.[11] Referring to Fritz Scharpf's well-known dichotomy, the former is focused more on input-legitimacy (getting the right societal engagement),

[8] Hendriks, F., *Public Policy and Political Institutions*, Aldershot, Edward Elgar, 1999.
[9] Hendriks, F., *Vital Democracy: A Theory of Democracy in Action*, Oxford, Oxford University Press, 2010.
[10] In that sense I agree strongly with Peters, B.G., J. Pierre, E. Sørensen, and J. Torfing, Bringing Political Science back into Public Administration Research, *Governance*, 2022, pp. 1–22. I should add that exchange in the opposite direction is highly desirable as well.
[11] See 'Introduction and overview' for a more detailed synopsis of both parts.

the latter more on output-legitimacy (getting the right things done).[12] Based on the research I have seen and done for this book, I contend that both broad types of legitimacy should be upheld if liberal democracy wants to survive as well as thrive.

This amounts, *inter alia*, to a partly appreciative, partly critical assessment of the prominence in democratic-innovations discourse of deliberative-democracy thinking. I understand why it has grown so strongly in political theory, particularly since the 1990s in the Anglo-American world, where democratic and political debate has become more adversarial and bellicose than ever, and where established institutions support rather than mitigate this. However, coming from the Netherlands, the European Rhineland, the European Union—all contexts in which consensual, round-table, talk-centric forms of democracy are far more entrenched—I can see why some would prefer to put more emphasis on getting things done aside from getting people talking, and would at times long for 'a little less conversation, a little more action'.[13]

In some settings, more deliberation may be needed but often different instruments outside the deliberative-democracy toolbox need to be upgraded and deployed as well—not merely as servants to the purpose of 'deliberative systems' but for the sake of vital democracy in more encompassing terms.[14] In some domains, especially in the Anglo-American sphere, plebiscitary polling may have got out of hand, while in other parts little of this has been put to the test at all. In both instances, there is good reason for new ways of aggregating individual votes and views to be explored, critically as well as with open-minds, and to be assessed in terms of added democratic value. In this sense, new plebiscitary instruments should be treated no differently to new deliberative tools. Accordingly with this, I have done my utmost to keep an open mind towards the potential of diverging approaches to democratic betterment, without going native in any particular direction.

[12] Scharpf, F.W., *Governing in Europe: Effective and Democratic?*, Oxford, Oxford University Press, 1999.
[13] As inspiredly sung about by Elvis Presley, 1968: Wijdeven, T. van de and F. Hendriks, A Little Less Conversation, a Little More Action: Real-Life Expressions of Vital Citizenship, in J.W. Duyvendak, F. Hendriks, and M. van Niekerk (eds), *City in Sight*, Amsterdam, Amsterdam University Press, 2009, pp. 121–41; Hendriks, F. and Th.A.J. Toonen (eds), *Polder Politics: The Re-Invention of Consensus Democracy in the Netherlands*, Aldershot, Ashgate, 2010. The original argument of Fritz Scharpf was also to take output legitimacy more seriously in the hyper-complex EU-context. See Scharpf, F.W., *Governing in Europe: Effective and Democratic?*, Oxford, Oxford University Press, 1999.
[14] More on deliberative systems in chapters to come, particularly Chapters 3, 6, and 9.

Words of thanks

As a paragon of investigating diverging thought styles even-handedly, I am first of all grateful to the memory of Dame Mary Douglas, the British anthropologist who pioneered the cultural theory that I combine with democratic theory in this book to rethink democratic innovation. Through her work and personal communication, I learned that engaging with competing biases, attempting to understand them side by side, does not necessarily gravitate to a grey middle, but can actually enhance full-colour qualities. My gratitude for sharing valuable experience and inspiration in this sphere also extends to Michael Thompson, Steven Ney, Virginie Mamadouh, Richard Ellis, Brendon Swedlow, John Gastil, Perri 6, and last but not least, Marco Verweij, who keeps me on my toes in this like no other.

I could not have developed the ideas for this book without a large number of other people that I have worked with in research on democracy in flux, the civic side as well as the political side, throughout the years. These include Marcel Boogers, Claartje Brons, Wieke Blijleven, Leon van den Dool, Gerard Drosterij, Erkan Ergün, Laurens de Graaf, Merlijn van Hulst, Daan Jacobs, Niels Karsten, Koen van der Krieken, Ammar Maleki, Tamara Metze, Julien van Ostaaijen, Linze Schaap, Marieke van der Staak, Charlotte Wagenaar, Ted van de Wijdeven, Sabine van Zuydam. I am fortunate to collaborate with Krista Ettlinger, Caroline van Ham, Kristof Jacobs, Stella Koenen, Ank Michels, Josje den Ridder, Martin Rosema, Take Sipma, Julia Starrenburg, Jelle Turkenburg, Irene Witting, and Charlotte Wagenaar in the research project on hybrid democratic innovations called REDRESS.

Elements of this book were discussed in conferences, seminars, and smaller-scale meetings and exchanges. I am grateful for helpful comments and insights from, *inter alia*, Renske Doorenspleet, Roel During, Jurgen Goossens, Martijn Groenleer, Haye Hazenberg, Alex Ingrams, Patrick Kenis, Ira van Keulen, John Loughlin, Anders Lidström, Quinten Mayne, Jos Raadschelders, Mike Saward, Graham Smith, Mariangela Veikou, Stavros Zouridis, and participants in recent ECPR, TAD, and NIG conferences where elements of this book were discussed. For the chapter on the Irish case of the Citizens' Assembly-plus-referendum I gratefully received vital input and feedback from David Farrell, besides important pointers from Theresa Reidy, Jos Elkink, and Colm Walsh. For the chapter on Participatory Budgeting-new style in Antwerp I was fortunate to receive invaluable input and feedback from Inge van Nieuwenhuyze, Hanne Bastiaensen, and Joop Hofman. Any remaining errors of fact or judgement are solely my responsibility.

I thank Tilburg University for giving me time and support to work on the completion of this book through a research sabbatical in the Spring of 2022, and I thank Ghent University, Belgium (Bram Verschuere) and Roskilde University, Denmark (Eva Sørensen) for short but powerful research visits in this period.

I am grateful to Dominic Byatt and Jade Dixon at Oxford University Press for their trust and support in the book project, to anonymous reviewers commissioned by the publisher who provided very useful and generous feedback, and to research assistant Nikolai Lehre for great help getting all texts and references in line with OUP's requirements.

Some of the chapters have been previously published in international journals, and have been revisited and somewhat rearranged to fit the flow of this book. I am indebted to the journals concerned, the anonymous reviewers they commissioned, and the publishing houses behind them for permission to reprint here from the following:

Hendriks, F., Democratic Innovation beyond Deliberative Reflection, *Democratization*, 2019, 26, 3, pp. 444–64.

Hendriks, F., Key Values for Democratic-Governance Innovation: Two Traditions and a Synthesis, *Public Administration*, 6 April 2021.

Hendriks, F., Purity and Democracy: Beauty Ideals and Pollution Reduction in Democratic Reform, *Administrative Theory & Praxis*, 2011, 33, 1, pp. 45–62.

Hendriks, F., Unravelling the New Plebiscitary Democracy: Towards a Research Agenda, *Government & Opposition*, 2021, 56, 4, pp. 615–39.

Finally, my gratitude goes to my amazing wife Barbet, and our equally amazing daughters Eva and Meike who do not cease to inspire me and put up with me, even when I am writing a book.

Contents

List of Figures

List of Tables

List of Boxes

List of Abbreviations

AV	alternative voting
C2D	Centre for Research on Direct Democracy
CA	Citizens' Assembly
CCC	*Convention Citoyenne pour le Climat* (Convention on Climate Change)
CIR	Citizen Initiative Review
COP	council of the participatory budget
CPR	common pool resources
EEE	economy, efficiency, and effectiveness
EIU	Economist Intelligence Unit
EP	European Parliament
FFM	*Frankfurt Fragt Mich*
FPTP	first past the post
HDI	hybrid democratic innovation
IEM	Iowa Electronic Market
OECD	Organisation for Economic Co-operation and Development
NERC	Natural Environment Research Council
NPD	New plebiscitary democracy
NPG	New Public Governance
NPM	New Public Management
PA	public administration
PB	Participatory Budgeting
PB-ns	Participatory Budgeting-new style
PM	prime minister
PR	Proportional Representation
PS	political science
QV	quadratic voting
SES	social-economic status
STV	Single Transferable Vote

Rethinking: An overview

Understanding and advancing democratic repair

In a prequel to this book, *Vital Democracy*, I distinguished and compared four general models of democracy—pendulum, consensus, participatory, and voter democracy—looking at their cultural underpinnings, their associated styles of democratic leadership and citizenship, as well as their institutionalized strengths and weaknesses. Focusing on democratic forms and expressions, I discussed how democracy was arranged, mixed, and mingled in various countries and regions of the world.[15]

In the present volume, I continue the investigation by looking more closely at plans, proposals, and methods specifically geared towards changing the face of democracy—democratic reforms and innovations—including the ways they compare, compete, and potentially connect. Relevant research has advanced, and the general interest and perceived urgency of improving democratic governance have further increased following discussions about democratic decline and backsliding.[16] Against this backdrop, I will discuss and compare, *inter alia*, mobilized and random mini-publics, and other instruments to get citizens involved in democratic deliberation, offline and online (digital) referendums, and other plebiscitary arrangements designed to heed the voice of the people (Part I). Reflecting on historical distinctions and current variations, I move to the promising though challenging field of hybrid democratic innovation (HDI), national-level expressions of this as well as local-level expressions (Part II)—the next section contains a detailed overview of chapters.

Rethinking Democratic Innovation is the culmination of intensive engagement with studies of democratic revitalization, in-depth studies as well as comparative studies, drawing on a substantial and growing international research base, as well as reflecting on extensive comparative research conducted by myself or under my supervision.[17] This book reflects both

---

[15] Hendriks, F., *Vital Democracy, A Theory of Democracy in Action*, Oxford, Oxford University Press, 2010.

[16] See previous references to studies of democratic malaise, decline, and (near) death of democracy in the Preface and acknowledgements.

[17] See the underlying research and collaborations mentioned in the Preface and acknowledgements; see following chapters for specific references to sources used.

continued investigation and a rethinking of discussions and cases of democratic regeneration that I have engaged with since the early 1990s. Since then, important developments have played out to varying degrees in varying contexts, *inter alia*:

- the reinvention of participatory democracy in various guises, including online 'clicktivism', and hands-on collaborative democracy on the intersection of government and society;
- the 'deliberative turn' and the quest for communicative rationality and collective reflection;
- the reinvention of referendums, direct democracy, and the advent of a 'new plebiscitary democracy' radicalizing longer-existing methods such as referendum, initiative, recall, petitioning, and polling (in often digital ways).[18]

The overarching aim of this new book is to *rethink* democratic innovation and debates about longer-standing reform in a fresh and systematic way that is critical yet constructive, through a combination of democratic and cultural theory. The book contributes to present-day debates about democratic 'innovation', often focused on participatory and deliberative instruments, and connects this to longer-standing debates about improving democracy through 'reform'.[19] Democratic innovation is the contemporary headline concept, but, as I will explain, it is essentially intertwined with the long lines of democratic-reform debate.

Adding a cultural perspective to democratic theory, this book contributes to a deeper understanding of democratic innovation, the layered quality of it, the variety of justifications for interventions, and the perceptions thereof. Revisiting Mary Douglas's seminal take on culture as anomaly management and pollution reduction—'dirt is matter out of place'—democratic innovations and related reforms are understood as expressions of culturally-informed cleaning; they are seen as attempts to polish up, or rub out, what

---

[18] Recent overviews in Elstub, S. and O. Escobar (eds), *Handbook of Democratic Innovation and Governance*, Cheltenham, Edward Elgar, 2019; Bächtiger, A., J. Dryzek, J. Mansbridge, and M.E. Warren (eds), *The Oxford Handbook of Deliberative Democracy*, Oxford, Oxford University Press, 2018; Morel, L. and M. Qvortrup (eds), *The Routledge Handbook to Referendums and Direct Democracy*, Abingdon, Routledge, 2018.

[19] Elstub, S. and O. Escobar (eds), *Handbook of Democratic Innovation and Governance*, Cheltenham, Edward Elgar, 2019, p. 3; Smith, G., Reflections on the Theory and Practice of Democratic Innovations, in S. Elstub and O. Escobar (eds), *Democratic Innovation and Governance*, Cheltenham, Edward Elgar, 2019, p. 572; Fishkin, J., *Democracy and Deliberation: New Directions for Democratic Reform*, New Haven, Yale University Press, 1991. Also see March, J.G. and J.P. Olsen, Organizing Political Life: What Administrative Reorganization Tells us about Government, *American Political Science Review*, 1983, 77, pp. 281–96; Hendriks, F., Democratic Reform between the Extreme Makeover and the Reinvention of Tradition: The Case of the Netherlands, *Democratization*, 2009, 12, 2, pp. 243–68.

is assumed to be proper and in place, or improper and out of place, in democratic governance.[20]

While inherently desirable in itself, a deeper *understanding* of current democratic-innovations discourse (Part I) is also a stepping stone to *advancing* this discourse realistically (Part II)—recognizing that democratic cleaning will never be finished, but can yet be done in ways that are more rather than less fertile. The devil and its angelic counterpart is not only in the detail of democratic design, but emphatically also in the mixture of instruments and their embedding in wider institutional contexts.

Interest in mixed models of advancing democracy has emerged in various places. A case in point is the quest for a 'deliberative referendum' that adds to representative democracy by combinations of plebiscitary and deliberative processes. Recent experiences with Citizens' Assemblies-plus-referendums, more or less embedded in parliamentary procedure, provide interesting cases to ponder over. Another field to look into is the dynamic field of Participatory Budgeting, which, under the influence of digitalization, has become more and more a mixture of deliberative participation and plebiscitary voting, more or less embedded in systems of local government. Reflecting on such practices, this book looks into the scope for hybrid innovation and possible extensions.[21] Relatedly, the book takes a fresh look at the values or 'guiding lights' for improving democratic governance, integrating two influential though separate strands of literature: one focusing on democratic innovations, the other on governance innovations.[22]

In rethinking democratic innovation, this book not only speaks to the older democracies, often under prolonged reform pressure, in Europe, North America, and Australasia, but also to the newer democracies or newly-democratizing countries, facing calls for democratic change from one side and attempts to lure them away to alternative governing systems from another. For the many present-day champions, developers, moderators, and researchers of democratic innovation—operating in public, professional, and academic arenas—this book is meant to be helpful in both understanding and advancing their worlds of action.

My approach to rethinking democratic innovation is different from, but not necessarily in conflict with the approach developed by Michael Saward in his 2021 book *Democratic Design*. The main difference is in the starting

---

[20] 'Dirt is matter of out place' became a shorthand description among anthropologists for the central message of Douglas, M., *Purity and Danger*, London, Routledge & Kegan Paul, 1966. More about this in Chapter 2.

[21] See specifically Chapters 7 and 8.

[22] See specifically Chapter 6.

points taken, not in the arrival at democratic design as a process of mixing and mingling of democratic ingredients and principles. Saward writes that in my previous book, *Vital Democracy*, I pointed 'the way towards a greater openness as to the possibilities and potential for hybrid designs'. He adds 'that what is needed now is for us to travel further down that road'.[23] However, instead of starting with coherent models of democracy in mind, Saward proposes to step back from such first-order models as he calls them, and to shift the focus to the second-order work on the 'raw stuff of designs'—that is, the numerous potential components of first-order models. Saward recognizes at least 115 democratic practices and devices and more than 40 democratic principles that can be mixed and mingled in democratic design, adding that these are just indicative and far from exhaustive lists.

Although I recognize that potentially very many specific materials and ingredients are on the table of democratic (re)design—and that Saward displays them meticulously—my approach to the processes and interactions in democratic innovation is decidedly different, working from cohesive clusters to real-world mixtures of ingredients, from theoretical ideal types to empirical real types.[24] In my thinking, this does not foreclose but rather facilitates the identification of varied, mixed, and mingled democratic designs. Understanding the patterns helps to appreciate the specifics as well as the modifications and potential innovations.[25] Another advantage is that working from cohesive clusters of ingredients to particular mixtures more closely approximates the reality of democratic innovation—more often developing from already existing concepts downwards and sideways than from all the potential ingredients upwards to a brand new design. The working memory of the human mind has its inevitable limitations, and tends to work with clusters, cues, and shortcuts. This is not to say that (re)design thinking that starts from the countless nuts and bolts is in any way wrong or less valuable. Different starting points in such thinking can very well co-exist and enrich each other.

---

[23] Saward, M., *Democratic Design*, Oxford, Oxford University Press, 2021, p. 7.

[24] In using theoretical 'ideal types' of democratic form and reform to gauge and understand the empirical 'real types', the real-existing mixtures of innovations *in situ*, I am deeply influenced by the Weberian method of analysis and interpretation (*Verstehen*); see Bruun, H.H., *Science, Values and Politics in Max Weber's Methodology*, Aldershot, Ashgate, 2012. See also my contribution to a blog series initiated by Jean-Paul Gagnon on how to approach democracy: Hendriks, F., Selection: the key to studying democracy and innovation, The Loop, <https://theloop.ecpr.eu/selection-the-key-to-studying-democracy/>, 24 January 2022.

[25] For a strong focus on the varieties and hybrids in democratic practice see also Felicetti, A., Learning from Democratic Practices: New Perspectives on Institutional Design, *The Journal of Politics*, 2021, 83, 4 pp. 1589–601.

Book overview

The overarching aim of this book, *rethinking* democratic innovation including its relation to longer-standing democratic reform, bifurcates into interconnected parts on *understanding* (Part I, Chapters 1–5) and *advancing* democratic innovation (Part II, Chapters 6–9). In broad strokes the chapters contain the following.

Chapter 1—The layered quality of democratic innovation and reform. This chapter demarcates the central topic of the book: wilful attempts to improve the functioning of democracy through interventions framed as democratic innovations or, in more historical terms, democratic reforms. Using the metaphor of the 'reform cake', Chapter 1 characterizes democratic innovation as the currently most visible top layer of the reform cake, connecting to and resting on underlying layers of reform, prepared and developed earlier, which need to be appreciated to understand the reform cake in general, and the more recent democratic-innovations discourse in particular. Although varying subthemes have been associated with democratic innovation and reform throughout the years, the main theme—improving democracy—is fundamentally similar.

Chapter 2—A cultural perspective on purity and democracy. Whereas Chapter 1 introduces the locus of the book, Chapter 2 overlays this with a distinctive focus: a cultural take on ideational variety and social interplay in the quest for democratic betterment. Taking the broader concept with the longest historical lines as a point of departure—democratic reform— Chapter 2 reveals how this can be understood on a deeper level when using and expanding a conceptual framework inspired by the anthropologist Mary Douglas. In this framework, cultural biases and institutional preferences, particularly preferences for cleaning and reforming democracy, strongly interact. Functional arguments for democratic cleaning cannot be fully understood without also appreciating the cultural logics behind them. Processes of institutionalization—'polishing up' what is culturally constructed as proper in democracy—and de-institutionalization—'rubbing off' what is believed to be improper in democracy—are fundamental to democratic reform, and by extension also to more recent expressions framed as democratic innovation.

Chapter 3—Democratic innovation beyond deliberative reflection. This chapter takes a closer look at the currently most conspicuous democratic-innovations discourse, which since the 1990s has been increasingly coloured by variants of deliberative democracy. While sharp in perceiving some ills of and cures for democracy, the deliberative-democracy discourse of innovations is also biased in particular ways. For good measure, the chapter proposes to broaden the focus on current variations in ways that include instruments for deliberative reflection (relevant as they are), but also looks beyond these to new action-oriented (in addition to talk-oriented) and new plebiscitary or aggregative (in addition to deliberative and integrative) models of change at the same time. A case is made for paying more attention to concretization (getting things done in public affairs) in addition to reflection (getting public opinion refined). A number of illustrative cases of innovation beyond deliberative reflection are discussed.

Chapter 4—Exploring the new plebiscitary democracy. This chapter explores the emerging, hitherto underconceptualized, new plebiscitary democracy, which reinvents and radicalizes longer-existing plebiscitary methods (initiative, referendum, recall, primary, petition, poll) with new tools and applications (mostly digital). The new plebiscitary democracy comes with a comparatively thin conception of democracy, invoking the bare notion of a *demos* whose aggregated will is to steer actors and issues in public governance in a straight majoritarian way. The chapter fleshes out an empirically informed typology, distinguishing between new plebiscitary methods that are developed bottom-up versus top-down, and that are issue-oriented versus leader-oriented. Various specimens are discussed. As systematic research into the various guises, drivers, and implications of the new plebiscitary democracy is largely missing, and much less advanced than research into the deliberative turn, a gap-filling research agenda is being teased out.

Chapter 5—Between counters and talkers: Grasping the full matrix. Chapter 5 revisits the contrast between deliberative and plebiscitary formats discussed in Chapters 3 and 4 from the angle of democratic-cum-cultural theory discussed in Chapter 2. From this theoretical angle, the chapter continues to look at what is budding, often experimentally, in the area between the two poles. At first sight, much of this seems to be played out in the lower half of the theoretical matrix—where bottom-up visions of aggregative voting and counting ('healthy aggregation') coexist with bottom-up visions of integrative talk and collaboration ('smart sourcing'). On closer inspection, however, citizen-focused concepts of innovation always compete and chafe with visions championing power distance in democracy—political representation, delegation, mandate, leadership. We need the full matrix of citizen-oriented and representative democracy to understand the interplay, which will help in advancing democratic innovation.

Chapter 6—Key values for democratic-governance innovation. This chapter marks the beginning of Part II, which broadens the argumentation from understanding to advancing innovation. In answering the fundamental question of which values or 'goods' are to serve as guiding lights for improving democratic governance, this chapter draws on two relevant, yet divergent, strands of literature: the democratic-innovations literature and the governance-innovations literature. The result is an integrative framework of key values—inclusiveness, efficaciousness, appropriateness, resilience, and counterbalance—related normative dimensions and key questions that together can serve as a sensitizing framework for evaluation and design thinking. For realistically applying the values framework, acknowledging the fundamental value diversity, tensions, and trade-offs between key values, the chapter explores a pragmatic road ahead, stressing the importance of open, prudent, context-sensitive, situated conversations.

Chapter 7—The deliberative referendum: Reflections on a national-level hybrid. In this chapter and the next attention shifts to real-life attempts to connect democratic innovations across the deliberative–plebiscitary divide, anchored in representative systems. Chapter 7 concentrates on national-level practices, with special attention to the Irish 'deliberative referendum' on abortion that sequenced two strongly contrasting instruments: a deliberative mini-public and a binary referendum. Confronting this case with the values framework set out in Chapter 6, and with relevant mirror cases, the Irish process is understood as a comparatively successful case of HDI, which helped to break a long-standing stalemate and navigate a cultural minefield. The mixed and balanced process catered to different values and audiences and was relatively well-integrated into the established system, compared to, for instance, a similar process in Iceland.

Chapter 8—Participatory Budgeting-new style: Reflections on a local-level hybrid. This chapter explores local-level hybrids, with special attention to smaller-scale deliberation and larger-scale voting in what is dubbed 'Participatory Budgeting-new style' (PB-ns). This is examined through the lens of the Citizens' Budget of Antwerp, a Belgian city with a reputation for creative design in this field, while recognizing more or less similar processes in other cities around the world. In view of the values framework, Antwerp's *Burgerbegroting* is seen as a relatively multifunctional instrument that largely—although not perfectly—does what it is expected to do in this particular context. The thoughtful and persistent effort to mix and balance different design principles and to connect with the local context is what makes Antwerp's citizens' budget exemplary. As in the previous chapter, a separate text box is dedicated to institutional variations on the same theme.

Chapter 9—Conclusion: The hybrid-innovations hypothesis. Chapter 9 continues and concludes with forward-looking reflections on HDIs that capi-
talize on tensions between opposites. This feeds into the hybrid-innovations
hypothesis, which posits that more versatile and connective democratic innovations stand a better chance of high performance on a broader spectrum
than democratic innovations that fall short of these qualities. The most
advanced hybrid innovations couple diverging forms of bottom-up pressure,
and keep representative democracy connected and on its toes. Hybrid democratic innovation may be desirable as well as possible, as this book contends,
but it also comes with challenges and questions reflected on in this final
chapter. A strategy of change based on connecting opposites requires great
effort, cognitive agility to rethink democratic innovation, and a good deal of
practical wisdom to effectuate it. Done properly, it is my proposition that this
is valuable and worth our while.

PART I
UNDERSTANDING VARIATION

1
The layered quality of democratic innovation and reform

This chapter sets out to clarify the layered quality of democratic innovation and democratic reform as discursively distinctive but essentially similar concepts. There is a layer cake, aptly called 'reform cake', which can serve as a useful metaphor for explaining this point. The more recent discourse on democratic innovations, in this reform-cake metaphor, is the currently most visible upper and outer layer of the cake. But it rests on and is infused by underlying layers, built-up earlier, which need to be appreciated to understand the reform cake in general and the more recent democratic-innovations discourse in particular. In reflecting on the unfolding quest for democratic repair, and on theoretical concepts that are helpful in capturing contemporary initiatives and developments, this chapter refers back to the landmark study of OECD countries in democratic flux edited by Cain, Dalton, and Scarrow[1]—a forceful reminder of the historically defined, layered quality of democratic reform, or democratic innovation as it is nowadays also called.

What's in a name? The dynamics of distinctions

Democratic innovation and democratic reform are essentially similar concepts, associated with distinctive accents in different waves of discursive practice. As will be elaborated below, both concepts relate to plans, proposals, methods, and interventions consciously and purposefully advanced to change democratic governance for the better. Both concepts imply protagonists that have developed ideas for democratic repair that are recommended to democratic governance for operationalization and implementation. Both concepts are inspired by the conviction that democratic governance should

---

[1] Cain, B.E., R.J. Dalton, and S.E. Scarrow (eds), *Democracy Transformed: Expanding Political Opportunities in Advanced Industrial Democracies*, Oxford, Oxford University Press, 2003.

Rethinking Democratic Innovation. Frank Hendriks, Oxford University Press. © Frank Hendriks (2023).
DOI: 10.1093/oso/9780192848291.003.0001

and can be improved. Norms for improvement and ideas for change vary within and between the realms of democratic innovation and reform, as will be extensively shown in this book, but that does not take away this common ground.

Democratic innovation is a contemporary label that has become conventionally associated with a particular subset of ideas for change, namely those in which advancing citizen participation is key. In an early and seminal work advancing this label, Smith defines democratic innovations as 'institutions that have been specifically designed to increase and deepen citizen participation in political decision-making.'[2] In a more recent formulation, Elstub and Escobar put a similar emphasis on the role of citizens: 'democratic innovations are processes or institutions that are new to a policy issue, policy role or level of governance, and developed to reimagine and deepen the role of citizens in governance processes by increasing opportunities for participation, deliberation and influence.'[3] The field of democratic innovation, in their view, accommodates both participatory and deliberative traditions, which are both citizen-centred. They rightly note that the deliberative tradition shares much with its participatory counterpart, but is in general more 'talk-centric' and less 'vote-centric'—at least compared to the sub-current focusing on voter participation in referendums and initiatives.[4] We should add that the deliberative tradition is also more 'reflection-oriented' than 'action-oriented', compared to the sub-current in participatory democracy that focuses on direct action, local initiatives, do-it-ourselves-democracy, and the like.[5]

Smith distinguished four broad categories of democratic innovations, all citizens-oriented: popular assemblies (town-meetings, participatory budgeting); mini-publics (randomized citizens' assemblies); direct legislation (referendums, initiatives); and e-democracy (basically denoting the digital versions of the former). Elstub and Escobar added collaborative governance (partnerships of participating citizens with societal stakeholders and governmental policymakers) to the list, which then enlists five families of

[2] Smith, G., *Democratic Innovation: Designing Institutions for Citizen Participation*, Cambridge, Cambridge University Press, 2009, p. 2. I will come back to this definition, exploring the potential for broadening, in Chapter 3 and Chapter 6.
[3] Elstub, S. and O. Escobar (eds), *Handbook of Democratic Innovation and Governance*, Cheltenham, Edward Elgar, 2019, p. 11.
[4] Elstub, S. and O. Escobar (eds), *Handbook of Democratic Innovation and Governance*, Cheltenham, Edward Elgar, 2019, pp. 2–3.
[5] Wijdeven, T. van de and F. Hendriks, A Little Less Conversation, a Little More Action: Real-Life Expressions of Vital Citizenship, in J.W. Duyvendak, F. Hendriks, and M. van Niekerk (eds), *City in Sight*, Amsterdam, Amsterdam University Press, 2009, pp. 121–41; Parker, S., *Taking Power Back: Putting People in Charge of Politics*, Policy Press, 2015.

innovations: mini-publics; participatory budgeting; referenda and initiatives; collaborative governance; digital participation. Other works on democratic innovations distinguish a similar subset of democratic change models, with slight variations of between-category demarcations.[6]

Interestingly, earlier works and wider-ranging debates on democratic reform have addressed such citizen-oriented models just as well—albeit on a broader plane that also comprises models of political and electoral reform, new and alternative ways of selecting and unseating democratic leadership.[7] Apart from discursive convention, there is no logical reason for not also labelling the citizen-oriented formats distinguished by proponents of the 'democratic innovations' frame as 'democratic reforms'—as various authors have done. Likewise, there is no fundamental basis for saying that electoral or political reform in a democratic setting—say a conversion from winner-take-all to proportional representation, or a scheme for introducing digital primaries for selecting democratic leadership—cannot be viewed or analysed as attempts at 'democratic innovation'—as if these could never be innovative in a democratic sense. Such models of change are usually not shortlisted in contemporary works on democratic innovation, but that is something else. This is the result of socially constructed conventions and shared academic interest's characteristic of a particular period in time—roughly speaking the first decades of the present century, especially the 2010s; just as previous episodes in the unfolding quest for democratic betterment also had their accentuated distinctions.[8]

---

[6] Smith, G., *Democratic Innovation: Designing Institutions for Citizen Participation*, Cambridge, Cambridge University Press, 2009; Geissel, B. and K. Newton (eds), *Evaluating Democratic Innovations: Curing the Democratic Malaise?*, Abingdon, Routledge, 2012; Geissel, B. and M. Jaos (eds), *Participatory Democratic Innovations in Europe: Improving the Quality of Democracy?*, Barbara Budrich Verlag, 2013; Michels, A.M.B., Innovations in Democratic Governance, *International Review of Administrative Sciences*, 2011, 77, 2, pp. 275–93.

[7] Fishkin, J., *Democracy and Deliberation: New Directions for Democratic Reform*, New Haven, Yale University Press, 1991; Cain, B.E., R.J. Dalton, and S.E. Scarrow (eds), *Democracy Transformed: Expanding Political Opportunities in Advanced Industrial Democracies*, Oxford, Oxford University Press, 2003; Hendriks, F. and A. Michels, Democracy transformed? Reforms in Britain and the Netherlands (1990–2010), *International Journal of Public Administration*, 2011, 34, 5, pp. 307–17; Fournier, P., H. van der Kolk, R.K. Carty, A. Blais, and J. Rose, *When Citizens Decide: Lessons from Citizens' Assemblies on Electoral Reform*, Oxford, Oxford University Press, 2011; Levy, R., *Deliberative Voting: Reforming Constitutional Referendum Democracy, Public Law*, July 2013, pp. 555–74; Heijstek-Ziemann, K., Exploring the impact of mass cultural changes on the patterns of democratic reform, *Democratization*, 2014, 21, 5, pp. 888–911.

[8] Jacobs, K. and M. Leyenaar, A Conceptual Framework for Major, Minor and Technical Electoral Reform, *West European Politics*, 2011, 34, 3, pp. 495–513; Geurtz, C., Immune to reform? Understanding democratic reform in three consensus democracies: the Netherlands compared with Germany and Austria, PhD dissertation, Tilburg University, 2012; Zieman, K., *Democratic Reforms and Legitimacy in Established Western Democracies*, PhD Thesis, Leiden University, 2014.

The general phenomenon—the dynamics of accentuated distinctions—is significant for a book that combines democratic with cultural theory to better understand the quest for democratic improvement. My approach here is to take accentuated distinctions in discourse on democratic betterment seriously—for, as the Thomas-theorem teaches, if people define a situation as real it is real in its consequences—but also to investigate them critically. I have contemplated using unifying language—renaming it all democratic renewal for instance—but this would obscure an essential quality of the phenomenon: the tendency to draw lines, to suggest rifts and contrasts, to distinguish the new(er) from the old(er), the presumed *avant-garde* from the alleged out-of-date.

While investigating the dynamics of distinctions—suggested rifts and contrasts in the quest for democratic betterment—I will not gloss over continuities and similarities in present-day discourse on democratic innovation and longer-standing debate on democratic reform. For instance, we can draw a direct line from referendums and initiatives—a subcategory of present-day 'democratic innovation' for Smith, Elstub and Escobar, and others—to reform advanced by the Progressive Movement in the USA and more conservative forces in Switzerland in what Dalton, Cain, and Scarrow called the first wave of 'democratic reform' (the direct-democracy wave of the late nineteenth and early twentieth centuries). We can also draw a direct line from what they call the second wave of 'democratic reform' (the participatory revolution of the 1960s and beyond)—to participatory budgeting and related participatory 'democratic innovations'.[9]

The layer cake of democratic reform and innovation

The layered quality of democratic innovation and reform bears resemblance to that of a layer cake.[10] There is a somewhat famous cake, appropriately named reform cake, which can serve as a useful metaphor to bring this

---

[9] Dalton, R.J., B.E. Cain, and S.E. Scarrow, New Forms of Democracy?, in B.E. Cain, R.J. Dalton, and S.E. Scarrow (eds), *Democracy Transformed*, Oxford, Oxford University Press, 2003, pp. 1–22; Dalton, R.J., B.E. Cain, and S.E. Scarrow, Democratic Publics and Democratic Institution, in B.E. Cain, R.J. Dalton, and S.E. Scarrow (eds), *Democracy Transformed*, Oxford, Oxford University Press, 2003, pp. 250–75; Smith, G., *Democratic Innovation: Designing Institutions for Citizen Participation*, Cambridge, Cambridge University Press, 2009; Elstub, S. and O. Escobar (eds), *Handbook of Democratic Innovation and Governance*, Cheltenham, Edward Elgar, 2019.

[10] Cf. Torfing, J., L.B. Anderson, C. Greve, and K. Klausen, who also compare the successive governance paradigms to the competing and co-existing layers of a cake, *Public Governance Paradigms: Competing and Co-Existing*, Cheltenham, Edward Elgar, 2020.

layered quality home. The more recent discourse on democratic innovations, in this reform-cake metaphor, is the currently most visible upper layer of the cake. But it rests on and is infused by underlying layers, built-up earlier, which need to be appreciated to understand the reform cake as a whole and specifically the more recent democratic-innovations discourse. Although different subthemes have been associated with democratic innovation and reform throughout the years, the main theme, improving democracy, is fundamentally similar.

Both labels nod to the newer, the better, the more advanced in democracy. On a linguistic level, it might be argued that the concept of innovation gives a somewhat stronger nod in this direction than the term reform. While the latter term stresses the revamping of form, the former adds the subtle suggestion of inventiveness and a cutting edge. Being a democratic reformer, revamping democratic form, does not perhaps sound too bad, but being a democratic innovator, taking democracy on the road to innovation, may sound even better to those who want to see democratic governance change in this day and age. Nevertheless, I tend to agree with Newton, who wrote that the exact dividing line between democratic reform and innovation is not readily seen or drawn—in contradiction to Edmund Burke, the eighteenth-century political philosopher, who suggested that innovation implies more radical change than reform.[11] Jill Lepore also invoked a contrast between more rash innovators—not afraid of radical changes and big leaps to newer, higher, and faster—and moderate reformers, cautious not to give too much power to the masses in public and private life.[12]

Looking at attempts to improve democratic governance under the banners of innovation and reform, however, the contrast is not so sharp at all. Some might even turn the whole argument around by saying that the biggest thing in contemporary democratic-innovations discourse, the deliberative mini-public, is decidedly cautious and small (microscopic), whereas reform of a country's electoral system is comparatively large and potentially far-reaching in scope (macroscopic). Yet, while this may be true for a particular democratic innovation compared to a particular democratic reform, I do not see a solid basis for turning this into a general rule either—for it will not be

[11] Newton, K., Curing the Democratic Malaise with Democratic Innovations, in B. Geissel and K. Newton (eds), *Evaluating Democratic Innovations: Curing the Democratic Malaise?*, London, Routledge, 2012, pp. 3–20.
[12] Lepore, J., *These Truths: A History of the United States*, New York, W.W. Norton, 2018, p. 363 et seq.; p. 737 et seq.

hard to find a counterexample categorized as a democratic innovation (e.g. Participatory Budgeting in Porto Alegre) that implies more of a qualitative break with the status quo compared to a particular proposal categorized as democratic reform (e.g. increasing the number of municipal council seats by 5 per cent).

In other words, whether a democratic innovation or reform is far-reaching or radical—or not—is an empirical question rather than a name-related given. Democratic innovations and reforms both aspire to significant change for the better, but to what extent and in which way this is actually achieved is open to both research and debate. Neither significant change (democratic transformation) nor better quality (democratic betterment) can be taken for granted, whether a model of change is labelled a democratic innovation or a democratic reform. Such labels are not self-evident accolades, although it is part of the game to suggest as much.

In short, my take on democratic innovation, democratic reform, and the fundamental connection between the two can be summarized in the following memorandums of understanding:

- Democratic innovations and democratic reforms are evenly understood as procedures and practices (institutions in Graham Smith's formulation) specifically and expressly developed and advanced with the aim of improving the quality of democratic governance in the public realm (advancing democracy in corporate governance is beyond the scope of this book).
- Democratic innovation as a contemporary label has become primarily associated with a specific subset of institutions in which improving citizen participation is key to improving democratic governance. However, we must bear in mind that the association is neither fundamentally nor practically exclusive. Focusing on the improvement of citizen participation does not preclude attention to changing relationships in representative democracy. Those advocating electoral or political reform with democratic intent cannot be stopped from presenting this as democratic innovation, as they sometimes do.
- Democratic reform is a longer-standing label associated with a wide range of institutions aimed at improving democratic governance, including those in which citizen participation is key, but emphatically also those in which representative politics is central. Compared

to the contemporary democratic-innovations label, the democratic-reform label is associated more often with political and electoral reform, but again the relation is neither fundamentally nor practically exclusive. As indicated, democratic reform has also been associated with citizen-focused models of change, and those advocating such models cannot be stopped from using the democratic-reform label in such cases.

Democratic innovation is central to the title of this book, reflecting my ambition to engage with and respond to contemporary discourse, but it must be clear, as I hope it is by now, that I connect this discourse to longer-standing debate on the reform of democracy. The reform cake illustrates this metaphorically (Box 1.1).

Accompanying concepts are democratic design, democratic transformation, and democratic betterment.[13] Democratic design is a wider umbrella concept that not only covers initiatives for the improvement of the quality of democratic governance in already democratized settings—as centralized here—but also the development of plans for the democratization of non-democratic regimes (e.g. the democratic design of post-Apartheid South -Africa); the latter is not the central topic of this book. Democratic transformation is the empirically discernible change of democratic institutions, possibly resulting from initiatives as centralized here (wilful and focused initiatives to introduce deliberative forums, referendums, etc.), in addition to other and wider changes in democracy such as the growing reliance on new and social media; the latter is relevant context but it is not the central topic of this book. Democratic betterment is a normative concept summarizing the ambition of democratic innovations and reforms alike to further democratic values or goods; how and to what extent this is achieved are questions for empirical and comparative research.

---

[13] B.E. Cain, R.J. Dalton, and S.E. Scarrow (eds), *Democracy Transformed*, Oxford, Oxford University Press, 2003, pp. 250–75; Goodin, R.E., *The Theory of Institutional Design, Theories of Institutional Design*, Cambridge, Cambridge University Press, 1998; Saward, M., *Democratic Design*, Oxford, Oxford University Press, 2021. See my earlier remarks on Saward's approach to democratic design in 'Rethinking: an overview'.

Box 1.1: Slicing the democratic reform cake

To understand the relation between present-day democratic-innovation discourse and longer-standing democratic-reform discourse, I use the metaphor of the democratic reform cake: a layered cake with an upper layer that is most visible at the present time—practices of democratic betterment that are framed as democratic innovations—resting on and infused by underlying layers of democratic reform discourse.

In a contemporary, relatively broad categorization of democratic innovations, used by Elstub and Escobar, the outer-layer consists of: (a) referendums and initiatives; (b) digital participation; (c) deliberative mini-publics; (d) participatory budgeting; (e) collaborative governance.[a] There are slightly different formulations, but these are rarely more-encompassing. Rather, various authoritative works on democratic innovation centralize a particular variant, the deliberative mini-public.[b] In many ways, the deliberative mini-public is the attention-grabbing centerpiece of the democratic reform cake, which, however, consists of much more.

Under the currently most visible upper layer, there are at least two layers of previous and wider-ranging democratic-reform discourse that need to be acknowledged. First, there is an underlying layer of so-called reforms also focused on direct, participatory, civil society-oriented democracy, with a key role assigned to active democratic citizenship. Examples include plans and initiatives to institutionalize neighbourhood councils, town-meetings, hearings, stakeholder summits, interactive design sessions and round tables; to establish provisions for public consultation, petitioning, direct legislation; to organize deliberative polling and empowered participation framed as democratic reforms.[c] As said, there is a direct line from current deliberative and participatory 'innovations' to citizen-oriented reforms championed from the 1960s onwards, as there is a direct line from referendums and initiatives as current democratic 'innovations' to underlying direct-democracy 'reforms' advanced at the end of the nineteenth century by progressives and conservatives on both sides of the Atlantic.[d]

Second, there is a layer of democratic reforms primarily focused on restructuring representative, party-political, election-oriented democracy, often in formal-institutional terms, with a key role assigned to elected and answerable democratic leadership by political actors and parties. Examples include proposals to change electoral systems, rules, and boundaries; to accelerate party finance reform and campaign regulation; to centralize or decentralize political leadership and accountability mechanisms; to restructure cabinets, parliaments, regional and local councils; to institutionalize alternative ways of (de)selecting candidates for party leadership and political office, recalls, primaries, subnationally elected mayors and governors.[e] While this has also been labelled democratic reform, it has a markedly different focus than the layer of democratic reform focused on furthering active citizenship.

In an illustrative, non-exhaustive way, Figure 1.1 connects schemes and proposals for democratic improvement to the layers of democratic-reform discourse underlying the currently most visible top layer of democratic innovations. The figure visualizes the reform-cake metaphor—inevitably a simplification.

In Chapter 2, I will take a theoretical knife to cut the democratic reform cake along conceptual lines.

[a] Elstub, S. and O. Escobar (eds), *Handbook of Democratic Innovation and Governance*, Cheltenham, Edward Elgar, 2019.

[b] Goodin, R., *Innovating Democracy: Democratic Theory and Practice after the Deliberative Turn*, Oxford, Oxford University Press, 2008; Grönlund, K., A. Bächtiger, and M. Setälä (eds), *Deliberative Mini-Publics, Involving Citizens in the Democratic Process*, Colchester, ECPR Press, 2014; Gastil, J. and K. Knobloch, *Hope for Democracy: How Citizens Can Bring Reason Back into Politics*, Oxford, Oxford University Press, 2020; OECD, *Innovative Citizen Participation and New Democratic Institutions: Catching the Deliberative Wave*, Paris, OECD Publishing, 2020.

[c] Deliberative polling, empowered participation, participatory budgeting were discussed in the context of democratic reform as well as later in the context of democratic innovation. See Fishkin, J., *Democracy and Deliberation: New Directions for Democratic Reform*, New Haven, Yale University Press, 1991; Fung, A., *Empowered Participation: Reinventing Urban Democracy*, Princeton, Princeton University Press, 2004; Ganuza, E. and G. Baiocchi, The Long Journey of Participatory Budgeting, in S. Elstub and O. Escobar (eds), *Handbook of Democratic Innovation and Governance*, Cheltenham, Edward Elgar, 2019, pp. 77–98. For other democratic reforms mentioned see, among others, Cronin, T. E., *Direct Democracy: The Politics of Initiative, Referendum and Recall*, Cambridge, Harvard University Press, 1989; Berry, J., K. Portney, and K. Thomson, *The Rebirth of Urban Democracy*, Washington, DC, The Brookings Institution, 1993; Box, R.C., *Citizen Governance*, Thousand Oaks, Sage, 1998; Thomas, J.C., *Public Participation in Public Decisions*, San Francisco, Jossey-Bass Publishers, 1995.

[d] Dalton, R.J., B.E. Cain, and S.E. Scarrow, New Forms of Democracy?, in B.E. Cain, R.J. Dalton, and S.E. Scarrow (eds), *Democracy Transformed*, Oxford, Oxford University Press, 2003, pp. 1–22; Dalton, R.J., B.E. Cain, and S.E. Scarrow, Democratic Publics and Democratic Institution, in B.E. Cain, R.J. Dalton, and S.E. Scarrow (eds), *Democracy Transformed*, Oxford, Oxford University Press, 2003, pp. 250–75.

[e] For overviews of democratic reforms extending to this realm, see Cain, B.E., R.J. Dalton, and S.E. Scarrow (eds), *Democracy Transformed: Expanding Political Opportunities in Advanced Industrial Democracies*, Oxford, Oxford University Press, 2003; Rahat, G., *The Politics of Regime Structure Reform in Democracies*, New York, State University of New York, 2008; Hendriks, F. and A. Michels, Democracy Transformed? Reforms in Britain and the Netherlands (1990–2010), *International Journal of Public Administration*, 2011, 34, 5, pp. 307–17; Leyenaar, M. and R. Hazan, Reconceptualizing Electoral Reform, *West European Politics*, 2011, 34, 3, pp. 437–55; Jacobs, K. and M. Leyenaar, A Conceptual Framework for Major, Minor and Technical Electoral Reform, *West European Politics*, 2011, 34, 3, pp. 495–513; Zieman, K., *Democratic Reforms and Legitimacy in Established Western Democracies*, PhD Thesis, Leiden University, 2014.

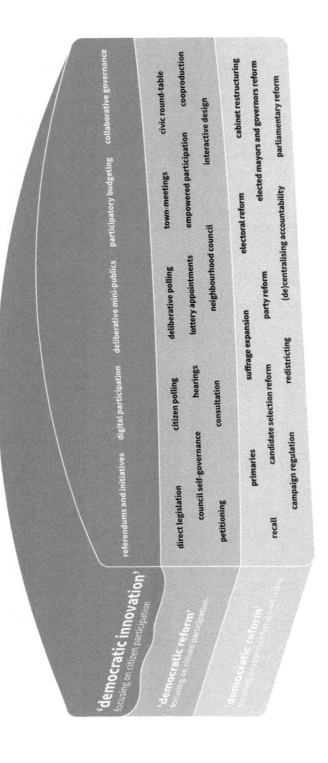

Figure 1.1 The democratic reform cake

'democratic innovation'
focusing on citizen participation

'democratic reform'
focusing on citizen participation

'democratic reform'
focusing on representative institutions

referendums and initiatives   digital participation   deliberative mini-publics   participatory budgeting   collaborative governance

direct legislation   citizen polling   deliberative polling   town-meetings   civic round-table

council self-governance   hearings   lottery appointments   empowered participation   cooproduction

petitioning   consultation   neighbourhood council   interactive design

suffrage expansion   electoral reform   cabinet restructuring

primaries   candidate selection reform   party reform   elected mayors and governors reform

recall   redistricting   (de)centralising accountability   parliamentary reform

campaign regulation

The unfolding quest for democratic betterment

Countries with fairly well-developed democratic institutions are commonly the focus of attention of studies in democratic reform and innovation. There must be some pre-existing democratic form in order to consider democratic reform or innovation beyond this form. This study is no different. Cases and investigations that inform this book are primarily derived from experience in countries listed as 'full democracies' on the democracy index produced by the Economist Intelligence Unit (EIU; 23 nations on the 2020 edition), as well as a number of countries now listed as 'flawed democracies' (such as the USA, France, Italy, Belgium).[14] What the countries dealt with in this book on democratic innovation and related reform have in common is significant experience with representative democracy, as well as notable debate about improving or supplementing democratic governance.

In their landmark study of the changing modes of democratic governance, Cain, Dalton, and Scarrow focused on eighteen continuously democratic OECD countries. For this type of country, they distinguished two histori-cal waves of democratic reform.[15] The first wave made itself known at the end of the nineteenth century, continuing into first decades of the twentieth century. In the so-called Progressive era, democratic reformers in the USA questioned the idea of representative democracy by trustees, and advanced various instruments of direct democracy: recall, referendum, initiative. They were partly stirred by populists and others criticizing the workings of Amer-ican democracy, and its capture by colluding industrial and political elites; partly inspired by the new provisions for direct democracy developed in the Swiss federation in the course of the nineteenth century. These ideas were advanced by Swiss radicals, but subsequently also discovered as an instru-ment of self-governance by conservative cantons. Related ideas for advancing direct democracy were promoted around the same time in Germany, Britain, the Netherlands, and other countries. A few decades later, the undemocratic use of plebiscitary instruments by fascists and Nazis gave direct democracy a bad name—even though Hitler's top-down plebiscites were in fact a far cry from Swiss-style citizen-triggered direct-democracy instruments. This which meant that by the middle of the twentieth century many democratic

---

[14] Economist Intelligence Unit, *Democracy Index 2020: In Sickness and in Health*, <www.eiu.com>, n.d.
[15] Cain, B.E., R.J. Dalton, and S.E. Scarrow (eds), *Democracy Transformed: Expanding Political Oppor-tunities in Advanced Industrial Democracies*, Oxford, Oxford University Press, 2003.

politicians and scholars returned to a more Madisonian, or Burkean, view of representative democracy by trustees.[16]

The second wave of democratic reform, according to Cain, Dalton, and Scarrow, picked up in the final third of the twentieth century. It began with university students and young professionals calling for more participatory democracy in line with a new, 'postmaterialist' political culture—demands that were soon picked up by wider segments of society: new social and political movements mainly, although not exclusively, on the progressive side of the political spectrum. From the 1960s onwards, a participatory wave swept the shores of the Atlantic, favouring mass participation, grassroots mobilization, and direct action. Carole Pateman's *Participation and Democratic Theory*, published in 1970, was an important intellectual companion to this wave.[17] This wave of democratic reform was clearly discernable in a wide range of established democracies. Many of the democratic innovations of today build on and extend ambitions and ideas advanced in this second wave of democratic reform.

The end picture of the democratic reform arena painted by Dalton et al. is currently still recognizable—albeit up to a certain point.[18] They ultimately distinguish three general modes—representative, direct, and advocacy democracy—which have demanded and received attention from democratic reformers at various moments in time. Paying due attention to representative democracy, they point at proposals for electoral and party reform, candidate selection, and deselection, which are too often glossed over in present-day research on democratic innovations—while it is a fundamental layer of the democratic reform cake.

In direct democracy, their second mode, 'citizens both participate in the discussion and deliberation about policies, and then make the final policy choice: it is unmediated participation in both policy formation and policy decision'.[19] Direct democracy comprises calls for direct voting in

[16] Dalton, R.J., B.E. Cain, and S.E. Scarrow, New Forms of Democracy?, in B.E. Cain, R.J. Dalton, and S.E. Scarrow (eds), *Democracy Transformed*, Oxford, Oxford University Press, 2003, p. 7; Kriesi, H. and D. Wisler, The Impact of Social Movements on Political Institutions: A Comparison of the Introduction of Direct Legislation in Switzerland and the United States, in M. Giugni, D. McAdam, and C. Tilly (eds), *How Social Movements Matter*, Minneapolis, University of Minnesota Press, 1999, pp. 42–65. For more on a new wave of plebiscitary democracy, see Chapter 4.

[17] Pateman, C., *Participation and Democratic Theory*, Cambridge, Cambridge University Press, 1970. See also Inglehart, R., *Culture Shift in Advanced Industrial Society*, Princeton, Princeton University Press, 1990.

[18] Dalton, R.J., B.E. Cain, and S.E. Scarrow, New Forms of Democracy?, in B.E. Cain, R.J. Dalton, and S.E. Scarrow (eds), *Democracy Transformed*, Oxford, Oxford University Press, 2003, pp. 9–11; Dalton, R.J., B.E. Cain, and S.E. Scarrow, Democratic Publics and Democratic Institution, in B.E. Cain, R.J. Dalton, and S.E. Scarrow (eds), *Democracy Transformed*, Oxford, Oxford University Press, 2003, pp. 252–6.

[19] Dalton, R.J., B.E. Cain, and S.E. Scarrow, New Forms of Democracy?, in B.E. Cain, R.J. Dalton, and S.E. Scarrow (eds), *Democracy Transformed*, Oxford, Oxford University Press, 2003, p. 10.

recalls, referendums, and voter initiatives associated with their first wave of democratic reform (at the end of the nineteenth and the start of twentieth centuries), as well as a second coming of voting-based direct democracy (from the 1980s onwards). However, their formulation also refers to elements of participatory and deliberative democracy, which according to many observers evolved into quite distinctive sub-species, particularly after the so-called 'deliberative turn' from the 1990s onwards, which implied a marked turn to small-group participation, talk-centric, and deliberative reflection in mini-publics on the one hand, and a turn away from mass participation, mass voting, and direct action on the other.[20]

Advocacy democracy is presented as a third mode, 'in which citizens directly participate in the process of policy formation or administration (or participate through surrogates such as environmental groups and other public interest groups), although the final decisions are still made by elites'.[21] In the theory and practice of public administration, concepts like interactive policymaking, network governance, and many verbal variants on the same theme, have become more commonly used frames to describe such practices—newly developed in some countries from the 1990s onwards, reformulated in other countries with a longer-existing tradition of state-society cooperation.[22] Regardless of the exact wording, advocacy democracy (or interactive, networked governance) is in fact a relevant piece of the democratic reform cake, not automatically or habitually acknowledged in democratic-innovations discourse.[23] It builds on changing modes of public governance first and then on public participation—which implies the participation of societal institutions and actors including citizens.

It is clear that advancing advocacy democracy is something other than advancing what Dalton et al. call direct democracy—in their formulation this is a broad church of rather different believers in democracy of a more or less direct sort. The question is, however, whether the distinction between

---

[20] Mutz, D.C., *Hearing the Other Side: Deliberative Versus Participatory Democracy*, Cambridge, Cambridge University Press, 2006; Chambers, S., Rhetoric and the Public Sphere: Has Deliberative Democracy Abandoned Mass Democracy?, *Political Theory*, 2009, 2, 3, pp. 323–50. For more about this, see Chapter 3.

[21] Dalton, R.J., B.E. Cain, and S.E. Scarrow, New Forms of Democracy?, in B.E. Cain, R.J. Dalton, and S.E. Scarrow (eds), *Democracy Transformed*, Oxford, Oxford University Press, 2003, pp. 10–11.

[22] Torfing, J., G. Peters, J. Piere, and E. Sørensen, *Interactive Governance*, Oxford, Oxford University Press, 2012; Hendriks, F. and Th.A.J., Toonen, (eds), *Polder Politics: The Re-Invention of Consensus Democracy in the Netherlands*, Aldershot, Ashgate; Kriesi, H. and A.H. Trechsel, *The Politics of Switzerland*, Cambridge, Cambridge University Press, 2008; Loughlin, J., F. Hendriks, and A. Lidström (eds), *The Oxford Handbook of Local and Regional Democracy in Europe*, Oxford University Press, 2010.

[23] This may change, now that Elstub, S. and O. Escobar (eds), *Handbook of Democratic Innovation and Governance*, Cheltenham, Edward Elgar, 2019, also recognize collaborative governance as democratic innovation. In Smith, G., *Democratic Innovation: Designing Institutions for Citizen Participation*, Cambridge, Cambridge University Press, 2009 collaborative governance was not shortlisted as such.

advocacy democracy and direct democracy still captures the most prominent alternatives to representative democracy available to democratic change
agents at the present time.

Drawing on more recent developments and investigations, I will propose a different way of conceptualizing the democratic reform cake in the
chapters to come. Therein, the opposition of plebiscitary versus deliberative
(or more generally aggregative versus integrative) instruments of democratic change will be foregrounded against the background of the distinction
between citizen-oriented versus representative-oriented (more direct versus
more indirect) ambitions and preferences. New expressions of democratic
innovation, including digital variants that could not have been described by
Cain et al. compiling their work in 2003, find their place on this conceptual
map. Meanwhile, the analysis of democratic reform by Cain et al. remains
a forceful reminder of the historically defined, layered quality of democratic
reform and democratic innovation as it is called nowadays.

In Chapter 2, I will elaborate on an alternative way of conceptualizing
the democratic reform cake, informed by a combination of democratic and
cultural theory. The general picture as presented in Figure 1.1—an upper
layer of citizen-oriented innovations, a foundation of representative-political
reforms, and lots in between—will serve as a metaphorical starting point, to
be refined along theoretical lines.

2
A cultural perspective on purity and democracy

While the previous chapter introduced the locus of the book in a general sense, the current chapter overlays this with a distinctive focus: a cultural take on ideational variety and interplay in the quest for democratic betterment. Taking the broader concept with the longest historical lines as the point of departure—democratic reform— Chapter 2 reveals how the ideational variety and interplay can be understood on a deeper level when using and expanding a conceptual framework inspired by the anthropologist Mary Douglas. Taking her cultural approach to the realm of democratic betterment aids a better grasp of the plural and dynamic interplay between cultural biases and institutional preferences for reform. Functional accounts of democratic reform cannot be fully understood without also appreciating the cultural logics behind them. Processes of institutionalization—'polishing up' what is culturally constructed as proper in democracy—and de-institutionalization—'brushing away' what is believed to be improper in democracy—are fundamental to democratic reform, and by extension also to more recent expressions framed as democratic innovation.

Introduction: Reform as cleaning

Notions of purity and cleanliness are often invoked in discussions about democratic form and reform. We are urged to help 'clean-up' our democracy, to 'tidy' what has become messy, and to 'polish-up' what needs to shine (again). Some people warn us, however, that we cannot expect democracy to be 'clean' or 'pure' on a permanent basis. 'Democracy, like lavatory cleaning, is an uphill task: no sooner have we got it all clean and tidy than someone comes in and pisses all over it.'[1] Michael Thompson may be putting it a bit graphically here, but he has a point, an essential one: just as you can keep

---

[1] Quote taken from the volume by Thompson, M., G. Grendstad, and P. Selle (eds), *Cultural Theory as Political Science*, London, Routledge, 1999, p. 18.

Rethinking Democratic Innovation. Frank Hendriks, Oxford University Press. © Frank Hendriks (2023).
DOI: 10.1093/oso/9780192848291.003.0002

cleaning a toilet because it keeps losing its tidied properties, you can keep polishing democracy; it is like a beauty ideal that demands ceaseless maintenance because reality never quite lives up to it.

With his cleaning metaphor, Michael Thompson proves himself a dedicated follower of the British anthropologist Mary Douglas, whose seminal thesis on cleaning behaviour and pollution reduction is condensed into six words: 'dirt is matter out of place'.[2] Unclean is what does not square with the cherished order. Cleaning means to restore this cherished order, to make distinctions, to polish and shine the one—the proper—and to brush away and distance the other—the improper. Douglas interprets the underlying pattern as culturally-defined cleaning—a combination of polishing up the acquainted and brushing away the alien. Whitewashing and removing foreign stains are two sides of the same coin.

In debates on democratic reform, the language of house-cleaning resurfaces time and again with reformers referring to cleansing, clearing, purging, putting the house in order, or—pitching it a little stronger—making a clean sweep.[3] Where one particular conception of democracy is polished up, deviant notions of democracy are brushed away, usually at the same time.

One example, among many, is presented by the heated debate on the referendum in representative democracy. In my own country, the Netherlands, the referendum has traditionally been defined as 'out of place' in its representative democratic system. Ruijs de Beerenbrouck, former Prime Minister, famously dubbed the referendum 'this plant of foreign soil'. His warning, voiced in 1918 and later often repeated, was clear: the referendum was to be kept out, taking it on 'would be a dangerous trial'.[4] Many rounds of debate

[2] The central text here is Douglas, M., Purity and Danger, London, Routledge & Kegan Paul, 1966. Douglas's approach to culturally inspired cleansing has, however, been developed further in a series of publications, which I have also used for this article: Douglas, M., Natural Symbols, London, Berrie & Rockliff, 1970; Douglas, M., Cultural Bias, London, Royal Antropological Institute, 1978; Douglas, M., How Institutions Think, Syracuse, Syracuse University Press, 1986; Douglas, M., Risk and Blame: Essays in the Sociology of Perception, New York, Routledge, 1992; Douglas, M., Thought Styles: Critical Essays on Good Taste, New York, Sage, 1996; Douglas, M. and A.B. Wildavsky, Risk and Culture: An Essay on the Selection of Technical and Environmental Dangers, Berkeley, University of California Press, 1982; Douglas, M. and S. Ney, Missing Persons: A Critique of Personhood in the Social Sciences, Berkeley, University of California Press, 1998.
[3] See March, J.G. and J.P. Olsen, Organizing Political Life: What Administrative Reorganization Tells us about Government, American Political Science Review, 1983, 77, pp. 281–96; Cain, B.E., R.J. Dalton, and S.E. Scarrow, Democracy Transformed: Expanding Political Opportunities in Advanced Industrial Democracies, Oxford, Oxford University Press, 2003; see also Hendriks, F., Democratic Reform between the Extreme Makeover and the Reinvention of Tradition: The Case of the Netherlands, Democratization, 2009, 12, 2, pp. 243–68.
[4] Full quote in Dutch: 'Deze plant van vreemde bodem te enten op onze constitutie ware een gevaarlijke proefneming. Als de Staten-Generaal hebben gesproken, is voor een nadere beslissing van het kiezersvolk geen plaats'. ('To graft this plant of foreign soil on our constitution would be a dangerous trial. When the Houses of Parliament have spoken, there is no further decision room for the electorate').

on the Dutch referendum later, journalist Hans Goslinga wrote a critical editorial for the daily newspaper *Trouw*. Writing in 2016, in the run-up to the first citizen-initiated, corrective referendum at the national level, he echoed Ruijs de Beerenbrouck's words, using the adjective 'impure' no less than four times in connection with the referendum. According to him it is 'an anomaly' that threatens to be 'rummaged into the constitution'. For Goslinga, and many others, there is no place for referendums and other instances of direct democracy in a representative, parliamentary democracy.[5] Interestingly, in another line of thinking direct democracy is not the contaminated but rather the pure thing. Here, pure democracy would be 'democracy in which the power is exercised directly by the people rather than through representatives'.[6] In this line of thinking, getting closer to the etymological essence of '*demos-kratia*' (the people that rule) would not be the impure course of action, but rather purely democratic.

How to make sense of such diverging notions of cleanliness, and of the various courses of action that they inspire? To understand cleaning behaviour in real life, Mary Douglas teaches us, we should first get a grip on the notions of order that inspire pollution reduction. This means that, in order to understand cleaning behaviour in the home of democracy, we should first bring into sharp focus the relevant notions of democratic order: the democratic 'beauty ideals' that inspire attempts at pollution reduction.

Inspired by Douglas's cultural theory, on the one hand, and theories of democratic design, on the other, I distinguish four such ideals: pendulum democracy, consensus democracy, participatory democracy, and voter democracy.[7] I delve into the inherent tensions between them, which can be made more or less productive as the real world of democracy illustrates. Different democratic ideals inspire different forms of democratic cleaning, but none of them can bring cleanliness on a permanent basis. The implication of this—and the related value of mixed and hybrid democracy—is discussed further on in this chapter and in this book.

---

[5] Goslinga, H., Het referendum deugt van geen kanten, *Trouw*, <https://www.trouw.nl/nieuws/het-referendum-deugt-van-geen-kant~b0096128/>, 3 April 2016. More on the Dutch referendum debate in Hendriks, F., K. van der Krieken, and C. Wagenaar, *Democratische zegen of vloek? Aantekeningen bij het referendum*, Amsterdam University Press, 2017; Meer, T. van der, C.C.L. Wagenaar, and K. Jacobs, The Rise and Fall of the Dutch Referendum Law (2015–2018): Initiation, Use and Abolition of the Corrective, Citizen-Initiated and Non-Binding Referendum, *Acta Politica*, 2020.

[6] Merriam-Webster, among many similar dictionary descriptions. Cronin, T. E., *Direct Democracy: The Politics of Initiative, Referendum and Recall*, Cambridge, MA, Harvard University Press, 1989.

[7] For extensive treatment and background see Hendriks, F., *Vital Democracy: A Theory of Democracy in Action*, Oxford, Oxford University Press, 2010.

Dirt is matter out of place

Mary Douglas has been recognized as one of the 1000 'Makers of the Twentieth Century', and her book *Purity and Danger* has been classed among the hundred most influential works of non-fiction since the Second World War.[8] In *Purity and Danger*, Douglas analysed what she saw as the essence of culture: polishing, tidying, keeping things in order—some cherished order. What corresponds with this cherished order—defined as 'in order', proper, wholesome, or even holy—will be maintained and 'polished up' as much as possible. What deviates from it will be perceived as 'out of order', impure, improper, or generally as misfitting and will be distanced and 'brushed away' as much as possible. In this sense, every culture, in one way or another, is engaged in pollution reduction and anomaly management. It can be traced in non-Western communities studied by traditional anthropology, but it can just as well be traced in Western societies, even in a heightened way according to some.[9] Pollution reduction can take the terrifying shape of ethnic cleansing or totalitarian purification,[10] but also the rather prosaic shape of desk clearing or gardening. And, as I will argue in this chapter, pollution reduction also pervades the praxis of democratic reform. Interestingly, in this domain competing notions of purity, and thereby inspired cleaning practices, work alongside each other. The previous example of the referendum in the Netherlands—with some approaching it as 'dirt out of place', and some as 'pure democracy' to be cherished—will be complemented with many other instances in this book.

But let us look first at a small example that succinctly illustrates Douglas's original thesis in *Purity and Danger*. In the Netherlands, there is a public agency called Fauna Protection. For years it fought against the introduction of a variant of the black grouse in the national park *De Hoge Veluwe*. It even took the matter to court. Their argument was that this new variant would endanger the purity of other types of grouse found in areas adjacent to *De Hoge Veluwe*. Crossbreeding would 'pollute' the guarded classification, the cherished order of grouse. Fauna Protection rested its case only when such crossbreeding turned out to be virtually impossible. Living

[8] Douglas, M., *Purity and Danger*, London, Routledge & Kegan Paul, 1966; Fardon, R., *Mary Douglas: An Intellectual Biography*, London, Routledge, 1999.
[9] Labrie, A., Purity and Danger in fin-de-siècle Culture, *Psychoanalytische Perspectieven*, 2002, 20, 2, pp. 261–74.
[10] Arendt, H., *The Origins of Totalitarianism*, Berlin, Schocken Books, 1951; Mann, M., *The Dark Side of Democracy: Explaining Ethnic Cleansing*, Cambridge, Cambridge University Press, 2005; Scurr, R., *Fatal Purity: Robespierre and the French Revolution*, New York, Metropolitan Books, 2006.

areas of grouse could be kept apart, the cherished classifications could be maintained.

This calls to mind Douglas's cultural analysis of the rules of avoidance derived from the Bible book *Leviticus*, the third book of the Old Testament, which is also sacred to Judaism and Islam. Many people know and obey dietary rules inspired by *Leviticus*, rules stipulating what is halal and what is haram, what is kosher and what is not. Rules of avoidance bestowed by *Leviticus*, however, go beyond this. Cloths must be either wool or linen, not both wool and linen; that would be impure. Cattle must be held like with like, not criss-cross; the instrumental effect of a rule such as 'do not mix wool and linen' is less important than its metaphorical value, according to Douglas. As a *pars pro toto*, it exemplifies on a small scale how things should be on a large scale, in the world of social affairs.

In later work, Mary Douglas kept refining the central thesis of *Purity and Danger*, still her most cited and best-known single publication. First, she pluralized her concept of cultural bias. *Purity and Danger* had focused on rules of avoidance that she would later describe as strongly 'hierarchical'. However, not all cultures are like that, Douglas conceded. Therefore, she set out to develop a more diverse typology of cultures, the so-called grid-group typology, distinguishing four basic cultural biases: hierarchy, individualism, egalitarianism, and atomism.[11] Secondly, she dynamized her cultural-bias theory, collaborating with public policy scholars such as Aaron Wildavsky and Michael Thompson who introduced the idea of competitive interplay between cultures. 'They compete for members, compete for prestige, compete for resources. What had started as a static mapping of cultures upon organisations was thereby transformed into a dynamic theoretical system.'[12] Finally, she gave *Leviticus* a new reading, separating the inherent literary qualities of the work from its religious and cultural impact.[13]

---

[11] The following are also used as shorthand: outlooks on life, ways of life, world views, cultural biases, solidarities. See Thompson, M., R. Ellis, and A. Wildavsky, *Cultural Theory*, Boulder, Westview Press, 1990; Hood, C., *The Art of the State: Culture, Rhetoric, and Public Management*, Oxford, Oxford University Press, 1998; Wildavsky, A., Democracy as a Coalition of Cultures, *Society*, 1993, 31, pp. 80–3; Verweij, M. and M. Thompson (eds), *Clumsy Solutions for a Complex World: Governance, Politics and Plural Perceptions*, Basingstoke, Palgrave Macmillan, 2006.

[12] Douglas, M., *A history of grid and group cultural theory*, <https://fliphtml5.com/lxsr/vpej/basic>, 2006, p. 8.

[13] The details of her new reading of *Leviticus* are generally more of interest to Bible scholars than to scholars of democracy, political power, and social interactions in real life. After her reanalysis of *Leviticus*, Douglas was no less convinced that pollution reduction is a major force in social and political life (evident in her other publications after 1999). However, understanding the language and actions of social and political life is one thing, Douglas would argue, and understanding the composition of *Leviticus* as ancient literature quite another. 'General pollution theory still stands, but its application to the Bible is limited', she concluded in Douglas, M., *Leviticus as Literature*, Oxford, Oxford University Press, 1999, p. viii.

Democratic house cleaning

Purity and Danger developed a Durkheimian thesis: 'classification under-writes all attempts to co-ordinate activities, anything that challenges the habitual classifications is rejected'.[14] In a necessary sequel, as she called it, Douglas began to think and write in terms of *Natural Symbols*.[15] In thinking about the state, for example, people often invoke metaphors referring to the human body: the overall 'body' politic, the vital 'organs' of the state, the parliament as the 'heart', the police as the strong 'arm', etc.

Following Douglas, Simon Schama pointed to another powerful symbol: the 'home' or the 'house', which needs to be maintained and fitted out for 'proper' consociation. Writing about cultural manifestations in the seventeenth-century Dutch Republic, Schama elaborated on the (in)famous cleanliness and spotlessness of the typical Dutch home. The almost ceaseless spring-cleaning activities going on in the Dutch house and its adjacent streets, reported on by many astounded foreign visitors, could hardly be explained by material circumstances. They could be explained better from a cultural than from a functional perspective, Schama suggested, closely following Douglas. In the newly established Dutch Republic, divorced from Catholicism as well as centralized Habsburg rule, fanatical house cleaning mainly satisfied cultural needs. In a very practical way, it exemplified the importance of distinction, crucial for a brand-new polity like the Dutch Republic, which very much needed to reinvent and refurbish the intrinsic, while distancing the extrinsic as much as possible. The clean home was both a fundamental building block and a powerful metaphor for the Dutch town, the Dutch province, and the Dutch Republic—emphatically in this sequence, as the cherished order was (re)designed in a bottom-up fashion, very much in opposition to the centralized and top-down Roman-Catholic and Habsburgian institutions.[16]

Inspired by Douglas and Schama, I used a cultural perspective to explain the more recent history of democratic reform in the Netherlands, which quite typically has been presented as tidying the 'House of Thorbecke'. This often-used metaphor refers to the constitutional structure signed off by the liberal statesman Johan Rudolph Thorbecke in the mid-nineteenth century. Thorbecke's constitutional principles—most prominently the constitutional

---

[14] Douglas, M., *A history of grid and group cultural theory*, <https://fliphtml5.com/lxsr/vpej/basic>, 2006, p. 2.

[15] Douglas, M., *Natural Symbols*, London, Berrie & Rockliff, 1970.

[16] Schama, S., *The Embarrassment of Riches: An Interpretation of Dutch Culture in the Golden Age*, Berkeley, University of California Press, 1987.

monarchy, ministerial responsibility, parliamentary accountability, co-governance in a decentralized unitary state—continue to underpin the Dutch system up to the present day. Although the Thorbeckean system has been adapted incrementally, politicians and parties have regularly come to the fore to demand more radical makeovers. The frequent calls for democratic reform in the Netherlands cannot be explained very well, let alone fully, by a dismal state of the 'House of Thorbecke', but rather and largely by the cultural orientations of its inhabitants and their interplay. As I have presented this particular thesis elsewhere, I will not repeat it here in detail.[17]

In the remainder of this chapter, I will explore how different concepts of democratic order inspire different approaches to democratic house cleaning; not only in the Netherlands but in other countries as well. Another country providing interesting examples of democratic house cleaning is the United Kingdom. In Box 2.1, I will look at two particular instances: the rejection of Alternative Voting (AV) as a potential replacement of traditional First-Past-the-Post voting by referendum in 2011; and the historical termination of EU-membership by referendum in 2016. First, however, I will further specify my Douglas-inspired take on democratic reform as cleaning, polishing, tidying, keeping things in order—some cherished order.

Box 2.1: The AV and Brexit referendums as 'house cleaning'

In 2011, a large majority of over two-thirds of Britons (67.9 per cent) voted against replacing First Past The Post (FPTP) elections with Alternative Voting (AV). In the—historic—2016 Brexit referendum a tight but clear majority of Britons (51.9 per cent) voted in favour of leaving the EU. Interpreting these two occurrences in terms of the institutional feedback mechanisms discussed in this chapter and depicted in Figure 1.1—admittedly just one of many ways of interpretating such cases—reveals a common pattern. In both cases, more consensual democratic arrangements (AV, EU) were rejected in a majoritarian democratic system (Westminster-style pendulum democracy), applying *ad hoc* instruments of voter democracy (politically-initiated referendums), triggering the bifurcation of campaigns (Leave vs. Remain, Yes vs. No), refraining from methods for public deliberation in a more integrative fashion.[a]

The referendum on Alternative Voting (AV) resulted from an uncommon coalition agreement reached between Conservatives and Liberal Democrats in May 2010.

---

[17] Hendriks, F., Democratic Reform between the Extreme Makeover and the Reinvention of Tradition: The Case of the Netherlands, *Democratization*, 2009, 12, 2, pp. 243–68.

The latter were (and are) in favour of various counter-majoritarian democratic reforms. While preferring a stronger version of Proportional Representation (PR), Alternative Voting (AV) was at this point the maximum achievable reform option, which would give parties beyond the traditional Labour vs. Conservatives dichotomy, *inter alia* the Liberal Democrats, a bigger chance of winning seats in the various electoral districts. Even this relatively small step towards a less dichotomous political system was strongly opposed, not only by politicians with a vested interest in FPTP voting, but also by a vast majority of the general electorate.[b] In the Vote No campaign, majoritarian sentiments were effectively played at. One particular video showed a 100-meter run that ended in the trophy not being handed to the clear winner but to the number three in the race; the imagery made it abundantly clear that this is not how it should be in a 'proper' race.[c] In PR-systems in the European Rhineland, in contrast, it is not at all uncommon that a party that comes third in an electoral race, or even further down, gets rewarded with power and positions in a governing coalition.

In Lijphart's *Patterns of Democracy*, the institutions of the EU are categorized as strongly inclining to consensus democracy, and strongly contrasting with majoritarian democracy Westminster-style. Responding to growing Euroscepticism in his own Conservative party, and in the political and public realm more widely, erstwhile PM David Cameron, called a 'once and for all, in or out' referendum on EU membership. Like the AV-referendum earlier, the Brexit-referendum was an *ad hoc*, politically-triggered, top-down referendum, formally advisory befitting the sovereignty of the Westminster Parliament.[d] Notwithstanding the formal-advisory character, the end result of the Brexit-referendum (51.9 per cent voting for an exit) was politically interpreted in the most majoritarian and decisive terms—in that sense a very British referendum. Cameron's 'once and for all, in or out' framing was continued by his successor as PM, Theresa May, who kept repeating 'Brexit means Brexit'. Interestingly, the sovereignty of Westminster politics, which leaving the EU was supposed to restore, was *de facto* bracketed on this particular topic. Champions of the Leave campaign called the referendum of 23 June 2016 'a victory for real people' (Boris Johnson) and even 'our independence day' (Nigel Farage), cultivating a narrative of a citizenry 'taking back control' *vis-à-vis* a political elite and a supranational, communitarian project that in this narrative, had gone astray.

As indicated, the referendum does not sit well with consensus democracy in supranational projects like the EU and countries like the Netherlands. The friction may be smaller between the referendum instrument and pendulum democracy Westminster-style—accustomed as it is to majoritarian, winner-take-all voting—but it is not absent. The Brexit-referendum was only the third UK-wide referendum—the first was the 1975 referendum that confirmed EU membership; the second the AV-referendum—and all three were politically-initiated, *ad hoc* referendums. There is no legislation that allows citizens with enough signatures to initiate a national referendum and enforce a formally-decisive direct vote. That a formally-advisory, *ad hoc* referendum—firmly in the hands of the majority leadership when it comes to its triggering and framing—can also backfire to its political initiator was dramatically illustrated by the case of the 'once-and-for-all' Brexit referendum called by PM David Cameron.

[a] Ultimately, after the fact, an experimental Citizens' Assembly on Brexit was organized. See Box 2.2 for more about this.

[b] On the AV referendum: Qvortrup, M., Voting on Electoral Reform: A Comparative Perspective on the Alternative Vote Referendum in the United Kingdom, *The Political Quarterly*, January–March 2012, 83, 1, pp. 108–16; Curtice, J., Politicians, Voters and Democracy: The 2011 UK Referendum on the Alternative Vote, *Electoral Studies*, June 2013, 32, 2, pp. 215–23; Renwick, A., *The Alternative Vote: A Briefing Paper*, Political Studies Association, 2011; Lundberg, T.C. and M. Steven, Framing Electoral Reform in the 2011 UK Alternative Vote Referendum Campaign, *Australian Journal of Political Science*, 2013, 48, 1, pp. 15–27.

[c] For the video, see: Conservatives, AV Sports Day [Video], Youtube, <https://www.youtube.com/watch?v=9cmvl3tikUA>, 18 April 2011. In the No Campaign AV is generally juxtaposed to FPTP as more complicated voting system with less clear and clarifying results.

[d] On the Brexit referendum: Clarke, H.D., M. Goodwin, and P. Whiteley, *Brexit: Why Britain Voted to Leave the EU*, Cambridge, Cambridge University Press, 2017; Hobolt, S., T. Leeper, and J. Tilley, Divided by the vote: Affective Polarization in the Wake of the Brexit Referendum, *British Journal of Political Science*, 2021, 51, 4, pp. 1476–93; Bennet, S., 'Crisis' as a Discursive Strategy in Brexit Referendum Campaigns, *Critical Discourse Studies*, 2019, 16, 4, pp. 449–64; Vasilopoudou, S., UK Euroscepticism and the Brexit Referendum, *The Political Quarterly*, April–June 2016, 87, 2, pp. 219–27; Freeden, M., After the Brexit Referendum: Revisiting Populism as an Ideology, *Journal of Political Ideologies*, 2017, 22, 1, pp. 1–11; Marshall, H. and A. Drieschova, Post-Truth Politics in the UK's Brexit Referendum, *New Perspectives*, 26, 3, pp. 89–105.

Four ways of cleaning democracy

My understanding of democratic reform as an encompassing phenomenon begins with distinguishing four democratic 'beauty ideals', which imply different notions of proper versus improper democracy and which inspire different attempts at polishing up or brushing away particular democratic institutions. Table 2.1 juxtaposes two distinctions that are often used in democratic theory but not regularly in combination.[18] The first distinction, between direct and indirect democracy, I alluded to in the introductory section of this chapter when discussing conflicting approaches to the referendum (as an expression of 'pure' democracy, or an 'impure' anomaly).

[18] Hendriks, F., *Vital Democracy: A Theory of Democracy in Action*, Oxford, Oxford University Press, 2010.

Table 2.1 Models of democracy.[a]

	Aggregative (Majoritarian)	Integrative (Counter-majoritarian)
Indirect (Representation)	Pendulum democracy	Consensus democracy
Direct (Self-determination)	Voter democracy	Participatory democracy

[a] Hendriks, F., *Vital Democracy: A Theory of Democracy in Action*, Oxford, Oxford University Press, 2010.

The underlying conflict here concerns the fundamental question who should take public decisions in a proper democracy: the citizens themselves, through self-determination (direct democracy), or caretakers, delegates, or trustees, through representation (indirect democracy).

The second distinction, between aggregative and integrative democracy, concerns the question how democratic decisions should be taken in a proper democracy: in a 'counting heads' process of aggregation, in which a simple majority vote is decisive; or in an integrative process of conferring, seeking the widest possible consensus, voting down minorities as little as possible. In essence, the aggregative vs integrative distinction that I propose runs parallel to Lijphart's well-known majoritarian vs counter-majoritarian distinction,[19] but other than Lijphart whose analysis focuses on national and formal models of representative democracy, I suggest taking this distinction also to the understanding of subnational and nonformal democratic institutions, both in representative (indirect) democracy and non-delegative (direct) democracy.

Combining the direct–indirect and the aggregative–integrative distinctions produces four democratic ideal types: pendulum democracy, consensus democracy, voter democracy, and participatory democracy (see Table 2.1). As divergent democratic 'beauty ideals' they inspire divergent plans, proposals, and instruments for democratic reform (Table 2.2 presents an overview).[20]

Pendulum democracy is in its general logic akin to Lijphart's concept of majoritarian or Westminster democracy, although I suggest also looking beyond the British sphere of influence and beyond 'Westminster' as a symbol and centre of the national state. Hence the alternative metaphor of the pendulum, referring to the general democratic logic which makes political

[19] Lijphart, A., *Patterns of Democracy: Government Forms and Performance in Thirty-Six Countries*, New Haven, Yale University Press, 1999.
[20] Following this approach, a typology narrowed-down to political and administrative reforms, has been proposed. See Zieman, K., *Democratic Reforms and Legitimacy in Established Western Democracies*, PhD Thesis, Leiden University, 2014, p. 84.

power alternate between two competing political protagonists or parties. Power follows the movements of the pendulum, and the pendulum follows the movements of general elections or polls. Pendulum democracy is fundamentally indirect and representative in nature: citizens periodically cast their votes and hand over decision-making powers to their elected representatives. Decision-making is largely majoritarian and aggregative. In constituencies, owing to the first-past-the-post electoral system, the winner takes all, and the majority party forms the government, even if its majority is minimal.[21]

Democratic reform following the logic of pendulum democracy would typically polish up elements of indirectly aggregative democracy while brushing away traces of direct and integrative democracy as much as possible. The former would be 'in order', the latter would be 'matter out of place' to use Douglasian terms. As Table 2.2 shows, darlings of democratic reform include winner-take-all voting, strong (quasi-) presidentialism, competitively elected (non-appointed) mayors and other political figureheads, strong centres of executive power, backed by clear electoral mandates. Items mentioned include elements that Lijphart listed as fitting a majoritarian democratic state, and more—that is, also items that advance the spirit of pendulum democracy in subnational and nonformal democracy. For instance, the spirit of strong leadership competition for which democratic reformers often find inspiration in the USA with its highly competitive, win-or-lose selection and deselection processes.[22] Table 2.2 lists some other transformations that theoretically appeal to proponents of pendulum democracy; a crucial feature here is the preference for lean-and-mean democratic institutions, supporting loud-and-clear voter signals and accountability mechanisms, vigorously felt in politics and administration. A party losing elections, for instance, should not get executive power; this is 'not done' in the pendulum system, unlike in consensus-based systems.

Consensus democracy is in its general logic similar to Lijphart's counter-majoritarian variant of democracy, as the quest for consensus, through political accommodation and pacification, is crucial in this model of indirect and integrative democracy. Its influence is strongly felt in today's European Union institutions and the countries of the European Rhineland, but it is not confined to this period or region. Representatives of groups and sections of society—partly elected, partly appointed—are the delegated, prime decision-makers in consensus democracy. They habitually go about their business

---

[21] French democracy indisputably contains many elements of pendulum democracy (even though associations with 'Westminster' would be disputed for other reasons).

[22] See Hendriks, F., Democratic Reform between the Extreme Makeover and the Reinvention of Tradition: The Case of the Netherlands, *Democratization*, 2009, 12, 2, pp. 243–68; Michels, A.M.B., Debating Democracy: The Dutch Case, *Acta Politica*, 2008, 43, 4, pp. 472–92.

in an integrative, consensus-seeking way, usually in conference-room or round-table types of settings. The majority preferably does not brusquely overrule substantial minorities by simply counting heads: this is 'not done' and to be avoided as much as possible. Public policy is preferably built on a broad-based platform of support, both socially and politically.

Democratic reform in the spirit of consensus democracy would typically polish up elements of indirectly integrative democracy while polishing away as much as possible traces of its antithesis: direct and majoritarian democracy. Table 2.2 lists items that proponents of consensus democracy would regard as 'in order' and not 'to be avoided': electoral reform geared at proportional representation, advancing coalition politics and collegial decision-making, political decentralization, (quasi) federalization, and—in general—the dispersal, sharing and balancing of power in democratic politics and administration. For instance, to redress what they saw as 'excessive' centralization and concentration of power in the UK's Westminster system, leading parts of the Labour Party and the Liberal Democrats championed devolution and regionalization throughout the system and flirted with co-government, co-production, coalition politics, and social partnerships with the 'third sector'—such practices are commonly associated with consensus democracy and its conceptual relatives consociationalism and neo-corporatism.[23] Again, items mentioned in Table 2.2 include elements that Lijphart listed as fitting his consensus democracy, and more: for example interventions advancing the spirit of consensualism beyond the formal and the national institutions of the state.

In his research for *Patterns of Democracy*, Lijphart focused on the national-level institutions of thirty-six democratic states. At this elevated level, the indirect models of democracy—either majoritarian or consensual—tend to dominate. When digging deeper into the systems, and certainly when investigating democratic reforms, expressions of more direct democracy promoting civic self-determination also get into the picture, and into the mix of models that reality tends to present. This means that we also need to understand voter democracy and participatory democracy as beauty ideals inspiring democratic reform.

Voter democracy combines direct, unmediated citizen governance with aggregative, majoritarian decision-making. For instance, in a straightforward decision-making referendum or initiative, a common majority of 50%+1 (or more) can swing decisions for either option A or option B. A more

---

[23] Flinders, M., *Delegated Governance and the British State: Walking without Order*, Oxford, Oxford University Press, 2008; Hendriks, F. and A. Michels, Democracy Transformed? Reforms in Britain and the Netherlands (1990–2010), *International Journal of Public Administration*, 2011, 34, 5, pp. 307–17.

moderate and smaller-scale example is the Swiss-style voter assembly, the *Landsgemeinde*, to be found in two of its cantons and most of its municipalities, in which assembled citizens fairly efficiently take majority decisions by a show of hands and a count of ayes and nays.[24] Following the logic of voter democracy, public decision-making should be propelled by self-governing communities of individuals who as voters make choices between binary options in referendums, raise hands on matters in town meetings, tick preference boxes in user questionnaires, opinion polls, etc. (a wide range of direct, issue-focused polls extending far beyond the general elections for candidates and parties that are organized every four or five years in pendulum or consensus democracy). Many variants of the smaller-scale voter assembly and the larger-scale voter initiative or referendum have been designed and attempted.

Democratic reform following the logic of voter democracy would typically remove traces of what in this logic is seen as paternalism (the perceived risk of representative democracy) and viscosity (the perceived risk of integrative democracy). Instead, it would rather shore up individual voters' means to get their opinions and interests aggregated and heard, loudly and clearly, in a way that is also easily accessible and user-friendly. A critical mass of preference indicators should be enough to compel attention and force decisive action. In this vein, the progressive movement in the USA has supported reforms to bring in the initiative, the referendum, and the recall.[25] In a small number of other countries formalized voter democracy 'progressed' so far, even though in many other countries groups and individuals pressed for similar reforms. Regulated forms of direct voting, like the formal referendum or initiative, are increasingly surrounded by weakly or non-regulated plebiscites in the shape of consumer surveys, public polls, digital petitions and the like, which lend themselves to easy numerical aggregation. The latter is characteristic for a developing 'new plebiscitary democracy' that is reinventing and often radicalizing the received practices of an older plebiscitary democracy (more about this in Chapter 4). It is fascinating to see how such developments are welcomed as democratic innovation by some, and brushed away as democratic dirt by others.

Participatory democracy, finally, combines a preference for direct self-governance and self-determination with a focus on integrative—preferably

---

[24] Lucardie, P., *Democratic Extremism in Theory and Practice*, Routledge, 2014, pp. 48–50; Mansbridge, J., *Beyond Adversary Democracy*, New York, Basic Books, 1980; Reinisch, C. and J. Parkinson, *Swiss Landsgemeinden: A Deliberative Democratic Evaluation of Two Outdoor Parliaments*, Helsinki, ECPR Joint Sessions, 2007.

[25] Cronin, T.E., *Direct Democracy: The Politics of Initiative, Referendum, and Recall*, Cambridge, MA, Harvard University Press, 1989.

highly interactive and deliberative—ways of dealing with public issues. Communion and communication—getting together and tying the roots—are important democratic goods here.[26] The deep and extensive participation of individual citizens and civic associations is considered desirable in its own right (exceeding thinly instrumental participation in mass elections). Including minority and fringe voices in bottom-up processes of decision-making is also expected to produce better and more legitimate decisions. In participatory democracy, 'the other' or 'the alternative' should in one way or another be included, not excluded. In participatory democracy, numerical minorities are not easily overruled by numerical majorities; 50%+1 democracy is flimsy democracy here. Counting heads, if done at all, takes place in the final stages of decision-making, to confirm a shared view rather than to forge one. The general logic of participatory democracy has been translated in different ways, most prominently in recent decades in the specific version of deliberative democracy (more about this in Chapter 3).

Democratic reform in the spirit of participatory democracy would as much as possible polish up elements of directly integrative democracy, while swiping away elements of indirect democracy (too distant, high-and-mighty) and aggregative democracy (too flimsy, quick-and-dirty). Darlings of democratic reform include more action-oriented variants (do-it-yourself democracy, communal self-government, and the like) as well as more deliberation-oriented variants (mini-publics, common future forums, planning cells, citizen conferences, and other reflective meetings of minds)—again listed in Table 2.2. Mass opinion polling, which is fully 'in order' in the context of voter democracy, is approached with suspicion from the viewpoint of participatory democracy and only becomes acceptable as a possible innovation if it mutates into something like deliberative polling: an extensive procedure for transforming so-called 'raw' public opinion to 'refined' public opinion.[27] Consensus-seeking, tying the roots, in bottom-up get-togethers of commoners is the preferred option; delegation of consensual decision-making to political trustees and selected experts, as in consensus democracy, is to be avoided. Empowered participation, Participatory Budgeting, and the like will be shored up as democratic reform to the extent that it involves, connects, and preferably transforms citizens in a bottom-up way.

---

[26] See Habermas, J., *Theorie des kommunikativen Handelns*, Frankfurt, Suhrkamp Verlag, 1981; Pateman, C. *Participation and Democratic Theory*, Cambridge, Cambridge University Press, 1970; Foucault, M., *Archeology of Knowledge*, London, Routledge, 1969.

[27] Fishkin, J., *Democracy and Deliberation: New Directions for Democratic Reform*, New Haven, Yale University Press, 1991.

Table 2.2 Darlings of democratic form and reform.

Pendulum democracy	*Consensus democracy*
In order	*In order*
Indirect (representative), aggregative (majoritarian) democracy	Indirect (representative), integrative (counter-majoritarian) democracy
Out of place	*Out of place*
Direct (self-determining), integrative (non-majoritarian) democracy	Direct (self-determining), aggregative (majoritarian) democracy
Darlings of democratic reform	*Darlings of democratic reform*
Strong, undivided centres of executive power, backed by clear, unequivocal electoral mandates	Broad-based, multi-party coalitions, furthering social partnership and power-sharing
Competitive leadership selection and deselection; popualry-elected (vs. appointed) mayors, regional governors, prime-minister selected by voters (vs. coalition parties); strong (quasi-)presidentialism	Consensus-building consultations, elite and expert summits, round tables
Winner-take-all, first-past-the post, plurality voting, competitive, district-based elections, 'may the best party or person win'	Proportional voting, lowering electoral thresholds, 'may all relevant voices be represented'
Unification, amalgamation, simplification, streamlining of democratic institutions	Federalization, decentralization, deconcentration, devolution of power
Democratic accountability, clarification, transparency, clear chains of command	Intensive multi-level, intergovernmental cooperation, connecting umbrella organizations
	Constitutional review, independent central banks and other counter-majoritarian authorities, checks and balances

Voter democracy	*Participatory democracy*
In order	*In order*
direct (self-determining), aggregative (majoritarian) democracy	direct (self-determining), integrative (counter-majoritarian) democracy
Out of place	*Out of place*
indirect (representative), integrative (counter-majoritarian) democracy	indirect (representative), aggregative (majoritarian) democracy
Darlings of democratic reform	*Darlings of democratic reform*
Large-scale initiatives, referendums, not only consultative and local, but also decisive and national plebiscites	Communicative/strong/deep/deliberative democracy, civic round-tables, random mini-publics (ad hoc, permanent)
Small-community voting, citizen assemblies, directly-aggregative plebiscites, by show of hands, Swiss-style voter assemblies, New England-style town hall plebiscites	Citizens' Assemblies, consensus conferences, citizens' juries, deliberative polls, Citizens' Initiative Reviews, planning cells
Agenda-setting citizens' initiatives, (e-)petitions, counting signatures (or clicks) for or against	Do-ocracy, do-it-yourself democracy, communal self-governance, collective-action committees, supporting hands-on 'everyday makers'
Permanent user and consumer research, internet panels and public opinion polls, aggregating (digital) demand and choice signals	Co-steering citizen committees, neighbourhood budgets, participatory budgeting, empowered participation and other types of civic coproduction

Cultural biases and elective affinities

After *Purity and Danger*, which assumed a universal block against matter out of place, Douglas began to pluralize her concept of cultural bias and pollution reduction. As *Purity and danger* had focused on very strong and tight classification systems 'the obvious next stage would be to differentiate between weak and strong classification systems.'[28] This ultimately led to the seminal grid-group typology, which differentiates between weak and strong classification systems along two dimensions, grid and group, producing four ideal-typical cultural biases: hierarchy (high-grid and high-group), individualism (low-grid and low-group), egalitarianism (high-group and low-grid), and atomism (high-grid and low-group).[29] The four cultural biases are ideal types, theoretical constructs. They relate to real-life cultural manifestations as primary colours do to real-world coloured varieties. In the reality of culture, mixing and mingling is the rule. Nevertheless, in real-life mixtures one particular type of culture may be more pronounced than another. Egalitarianism, for instance, may be the dominant flavour in the cultural cocktail of a particular social group, or hierarchy in the cultural mix of a certain political party.

Underlying systems of classification, ordering, and organizing are understood along two theoretical dimensions. The 'group' dimension refers to the degree in which people's thoughts and actions are driven by their engagement in a social group. In the ideal-typical 'high-group' culture or 'we-culture' people are defined by the group with which they share strong feelings of solidarity and commitment. In the ideal-typical 'low-group' culture or 'me-culture' the individual operates as an autonomous being in its own right. The 'grid' dimension refers to the degree to which people's thoughts and actions are regulated by detailed role prescriptions, specifying how people are expected to act in particular positions. The ideal-typical 'high-grid' culture is one of 'roles ascribed': roles are to a large extent determined from the outside and are strongly specifying and guiding for people in particular positions. The ideal-typical 'low-grid' culture is one of 'roles achieved': people enjoy wide margins to decide about the scripts they play out and are free and equal in doing so. Put these together and you get, in the words of Mary

---

[28] Douglas, M., *A history of grid and group cultural theory*, <https://fliphtml5.com/lxsr/vpej/basic>, 2006, p. 2.

[29] The following are also used as shorthand: outlooks on life, ways of life, world views, cultural biases, solidarities. See Thompson, M., R. Ellis, and A. Wildavsky, *Cultural Theory*, Boulder, Westview Press, 1990; Hood, C., *The Art of the State: Culture, Rhetoric, and Public Management*, Oxford, Oxford University Press, 1998; Wildavsky, A., Democracy as a Coalition of Cultures, *Society*, 1993, 31, pp. 80–3; M. Thompson, G. Grendstad, and P. Selle (eds), *Cultural Theory as Political Science*, London, Routledge, 1999; Verweij, M. and M. Thompson (eds), *Clumsy Solutions for a Complex World: Governance, Politics and Plural Perceptions*, Basingstoke, Palgrave Macmillan, 2006.

Douglas: 'four opposed and incompatible types of social control, and plenty of scope for mixing, modifying, or shifting in between the extremes'.[30]

The cultural biases summarized in Table 2.3 display elective affinity—or *Wahlverwandtschaft* in Weber's terms[31]—with the democratic beauty ideals presented earlier. Logically and theoretically one can expect a magnet and a horseshoe to attract each other; likewise, sociologically, and cultural-theoretically one can expect egalitarianism and participatory institutions and instruments to attract each other in the field of democracy. The attraction is mutual: the former is a favourable 'sociotope' for the latter, and the latter is favourable to this sociotope in turn. This does not mean that an empirical-causal connection between the two is inevitable—elective affinity is about theoretical connectedness. To what degree and in which way this plays out in real life is always codetermined by intervening factors; there are always laws, practical drawbacks, and other factors that work on cultural-sociological *Wahlverwandtschaft*.

Egalitarianism—in the realm of democracy, there is elective affinity between egalitarianism and participatory democracy as both champion people to get together, to reach out and touch, and voluntarily associate. In tune with participatory discourse, egalitarianism holds that human beings thrive in an inclusive community (high-group rather than low-group), that decision-making in such a community must be widely shared (consensual rather than competitive), and that minority interests should be integrated as much as possible (integrative rather than aggregative). In addition, egalitarianism also cherishes the idea that positions and roles should be stratified and discriminatory as little as possible (low-grid, 'roles achieved' rather than high-grid, 'roles ascribed'), that everyone should be allowed to take part in basically everything, irrespective of age, status, or expertise (power equality rather than power distance), and that all should be able to speak

Table 2.3 Types of culture.

	Low-group (Me-culture)	High-group (We-culture)
High-grid (Roles ascribed)	Atomism (Isolate culture)	Hierarchy (Positional culture)
Low-grid (Roles achieved)	Individualism (Market culture)	Egalitarianism (Enclave culture)

[30] Douglas, M., *A history of grid and group cultural theory*, <https://fliphtml5.com/lxsr/vpej/basic>, 2006, p. 3.
[31] Weber, M., *Economy and Society: An Outline of Interpretive Sociology*, New York, Bedminster Press, 1968 (originally 1922).

for themselves (direct speech and action rather than representation and delegation).

Individualism has in common with egalitarianism that it favours a social structure that leaves people free and equal; the major difference is that individualism speaks the language of 'me' whereas egalitarianism speaks the language of 'us'.[32] Regarding the proper form of democracy, there is elective affinity between individualism and voter democracy. Individualism assumes that individual determination comes before group ties (low-group rather than high-group), that the individual should be able to choose between rival alternatives that compete for support (contest rather than convergence), and that public choice should be sensitive to citizen demand (aggregative mechanisms rather than integrative systems). In addition, individualism cherishes the principle that people may think and do as they please (low-grid rather than high-grid), that citizens can make their own choices independently of officials or experts (power equality rather than power distance), and that self-steering is always better than being guided or patronized by others (self-determination rather than representative institutions).

Hierarchy—when it comes to democracy, there is an elective affinity between hierarchy and consensus democracy. Contrary to what some believe, hierarchy need not be the onset of authoritarianism; hierarchy and democracy may well go together, as they do in consensus democracy.[33] Hierarchy cherishes the idea that each member of the community is embedded in comprehensive umbrella units (high-group rather than low-group), that the collective is kept together by communality and willingness to accommodate (convergence rather than contest), and that in decision-making the parts should be incorporated into the whole as much as possible (integrative rather than aggregative procedures). In addition, hierarchy holds that different roles go with different positions (high-grid rather than low-grid), that everyone, each according to merit and expertise, has their own responsibilities within the wider system (each to their niche rather than all the same), and that the structured division of labour decides who is to represent and who is to be represented (expertise and representation rather than self-rule).

---

[32] An author like Barber believes we should have more of the one (the language of 'we') and less of the other (the language of 'me'). See Barber, B.R., *Strong Democracy: Participatory Politics for a New Age*, Berkeley, University of California Press, 2004 (originally 1984).

[33] The link between hierarchy and consensus democracy is also made by Wildavsky, A, Democracy as a Coalition of Cultures, *Society*, 1993, 31, p. 82. To be able to see this link properly, we need to let go of a common negative bias in the approach to hierarchy. See Douglas, M., Being Fair to Hierarchists, *University of Pennsylvania Law Review*, 2003, 151, pp. 1349–70.

Atomism—in the realm of democracy, there is mutual attraction between atomism and pendulum democracy.[34] Atomism is founded on the idea that individuals are singular units in fields of other discrete individuals (low-group rather than high-group), that each individual must fend for him- or herself and not appeal to others (hardball rather than melting together), that in decision-making it must be the biggest who carries away the spoils—the winner takes all—the others drawing the short straw until they themselves gain enough mass to win the game (aggregative and majoritarian rather than integrative and counter-majoritarian, not to speak of minoritarian). In addition, atomism is based on the principle that responsibilities differ according to position, weight, strength, and ability (high-grid rather than low-grid), that not everyone can take part or be involved in everything (each to their niche rather than all count equally), and that some have the role and the position to govern while others do not (representative rather than direct rule). This is all considered proper and normal in this context, just as hierarchical, individualistic, or egalitarian institutions are considered appropriate in other cultural settings.

Competing reforms: Dynamics and potential virtues

Next to pluralizing her concept of cultural bias, Douglas also dynamized the understanding of cultural bias. 'What had started as a static mapping of cultures upon organisations was thereby transformed into a dynamic theoretical system.'[35] Each culture defines itself by contrast with the others. Each culture tries to institutionalize and polish up fitting elements, while de-institutionalizing and brushing away incongruous elements. Michael Thompson, Perri 6, and others using grid-group theory have reformulated the dynamic interplay between the different cultural biases (or 'solidarities') in terms of positive and negative feedback mechanisms, terms inspired by complex systems theory.[36] In contemporary cultural analysis, developed in the

---

[34] In order to undo the concept from unwanted connotations as much as possible, 'atomism' is preferred to 'fatalism' here. In essence, the concept does not imply anything beyond a culture of both weak group integration and strong person-oriented regulation.

[35] Douglas, M., *A history of grid and group cultural theory*, <https://fliphtml5.com/lxsr/vpej/basic>, 2006, p. 8.

[36] See Thompson, M., Man and Nature as a Single but Complex System, in T. Munn (ed), *Encyclopedia of Global Environmental Change*, Chichester, John Wiley, 2002, 5, pp. 384–93; Thompson, M., *Organising and Disorganising: A Dynamic and Non-Linear Theory of Institutional Emergence and its Implications*, Devon, Triarcy Press, 2008; Perri 6, Institutional Viability: A Neo-Durkheimian Theory, *Innovation: The European Journal of Social Science Research,* 2003, 16, pp. 395–415.

wake of Douglas, the positive feedback mechanism is described as the in-built tendency to affirm and reinforce what is considered appropriate or 'in place', while the negative feedback mechanism refers to the in-built tendency to undercut and disorganize what is alien or 'out of place'.

Returning to the four models of democracy and related cleaning cultures, one can say that each model has the tendency to provide negative feedback to democratic institutions that are assumed to be 'out of place' and give positive feedback to democratic institutions that are held to be 'in order'. Staunch proponents of participatory democracy, for example, are likely to condemn traces of indirect and aggregative democracy, which signify 'matter out of place' in their conception of proper democracy. The latter, in their view, is directly-integrative democracy, and any reform plan, proposal, or instrument tending that way may bank on their support. Similar feedback mechanisms—negative and positive—are theoretically connected to the other models of democracy. What differs is what the diverging models hold as 'in order' and 'out of place', which explains a great deal of the competitive interplay that we find in the real world of democratic reform.

Positive and negative feedback mechanisms—depicted schematically in Figure 2.1—are discernable and played out in real life. For instance, fierce

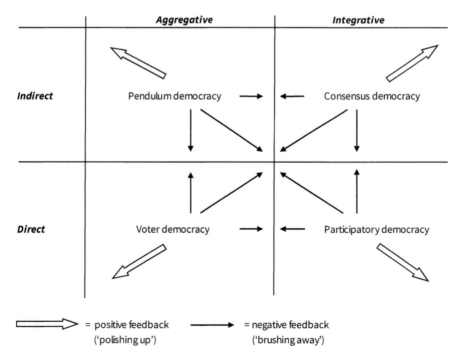

Figure 2.1 Positive and negative feedback in democracy and reform

supporters of consensus democracy are often among the strongest opponents of furthering instruments of voter democracy such as the referendum. Vocal advocates of the referendum, on the other hand, are often among the fiercest critics of democratic reform through neo-corporatist, 'meeting room' methods. Champions of participatory democracy agitate against proposals to fortify political leadership and streamline decision-making processes; while proponents of pendulum democracy, supporting the latter, tend to oppose the lengthy deliberative procedures that participatory democratic reform holds in store.

Blending reforms: Exploring the scope and limits

Positive and negative feedback mechanisms can help to keep democracy in shape, as long as one way of cleaning is kept in check by other ways of cleaning. An excess of positive feedback emanating from one domineering model of democracy may lead to institutional lock-in; the model's inherent weaknesses would not be kept in check. An overkill of negative feedback may lead to democracy resembling still water; the endogenous would get bogged down, and the exogenous would not get the chance to shake up the all-too familiar with out-of-the-box ingredients.

Positive and negative feedback mechanisms are vital for democracy but arguably they need to be plural—inspired by different, competing, possibly complementary ways of approaching democracy. 'Though one culture may be dominant, it must avoid excluding the other three from the public forum. A dominant culture should not drive the others underground or reduce any of them to silence'.[37] This is what Douglas wrote about cultural biases in general, but it goes for democratic models reflecting cultural biases just as well, or even more so if one takes the view that organizing pluriformity and interaction is at the very heart of democracy.

This book takes such a view. It proposes to explore the scope for democratic hybridity and to keep the cultural block against impurity (mixophobia) in check. Looking at democratic reform from a Douglasian perspective, the quest for purity runs the risk of vulnerability while hybridity increases the chances of democratic vitality. On the drawing board, reform plans for pure—clean and tidy—democracy may seem attractive. In the real world, however, resilient democracies cannot afford to indulge too much

---

[37] Douglas, M., *A history of grid and group cultural theory*, <https://fliphtml5.com/lxsr/vpej/basic>, 2006, p. 10.

in intellectual or ideological purity; they necessarily encompass a certain dilution, a certain blend of models.

The question is which blends come to the fore, and how fitting are they in view of real-life challenges and requirements. In the following chapters I will take up this question in successive steps, generally moving from less to more blended views of democratic betterment.

3

Democratic innovation beyond deliberative reflection

Without losing sight of the wider and longer-standing discourse on democratic reform, this chapter takes a closer look at the more recent and presently most conspicuous democratic-innovations discourse, which since the 1990s has been strongly coloured by variants of deliberative democracy. While they are perceptive about some ills of and cures for democracy, deliberative democracy models are also biased in particular ways. For good measure, this chapter sets out to broaden the focus on current variations in ways that include instruments for deliberative reflection (relevant as they are) but also looks beyond these to new plebiscitary and action-oriented (in addition to deliberative and talk-oriented) models of change. A case is made for paying more attention to concretization (getting things done) in addition to reflection (getting opinions refined) in the public domain. Three cases of innovation beyond deliberative reflection are discussed.

Innovation beyond deliberation

Since the early 1990s, the literature on democratic innovations has been strongly focused on deliberative democratic innovations. Although these continue to offer important and relevant focus points of research, there are more interpretations and versions of democratic innovation that warrant serious research. This chapter offers an extended conceptual framework that serves to recognize and understand a wide range of democratic innovations that includes non-deliberative as well as deliberative models and methods. More empirically, this chapter offers a closer look at three exemplary cases that diverge from the predominantly reflective and transformative definition of democratic innovation inspired by deliberative-democracy theory.

Graham Smith, widely acknowledged as a democratic-innovations expert, observed in 2016: 'Deliberative democracy has established an almost hegemonic hold on democratic theory and the analysis of participatory governance'. He asked: 'does the dominance of deliberative democracy skew the

Rethinking Democratic Innovation. Frank Hendriks, Oxford University Press. © Frank Hendriks (2023).
DOI: 10.1093/oso/9780192848291.003.0003

way we conceptualise and analyze democratic innovations, and the democratic system more generally?'[1] With regard to democratic innovations, the focus of this chapter, I arrive at an affirmative, though qualified answer. When research on democratic innovations took its abundantly documented 'deliberative turn', roughly since the early 1990s, non-deliberative innovations were significantly less centralized. 'Deliberative' democratic innovations were clearly *en vogue* in the academic field surrounding the subject. However, while being backgrounded, non-deliberative democratic innovations, focusing more on direct action and grassroots participation for instance, did continue to attract some attention, as Carole Pateman and others rightly observed.[2] We can build on this when developing a balanced and wider framework of democratic innovation. Also, the 'systemic turn' in deliberative theory acknowledges non-deliberative practices as part of deliberative systems, more than earlier deliberative theory did.[3]

This chapter has two purposes. The first purpose is to contribute to a balanced conceptual perspective on democratic innovations, by rendering heightened attention to plebiscitary and action-oriented democratic innovations that are not primarily focused on deliberative reflection. The result is an extended framework of democratic options, and values to consider when developing or assessing such options. The second purpose is to take a closer, case-sensitive look at variants that seek democratic innovation beyond deliberative reflection. This results in three case studies illuminating respectively: the rebound of aggregative democracy through the (quasi-) referendum, the advent of collaborative democratic governance through concerted action, and do-it-ourselves democracy through pragmatic activism.[4]

---

[1] Smith, G., Introduction to the panel 'beyond deliberative hegemony ', ECPR general conference, Prague, 2016.

[2] Pateman, C., Participatory Democracy Revisited, *Perspectives on Politics*, 2012, 10, 1, pp. 7–19, particularly draws attention to Participatory Budgeting, 'an example also claimed by some deliberative democrats', but distinctive in giving all citizens a right to participate; she also notes the difference between deliberative democracy of the 1990s and participatory democracy of the 1960s, the spirit of protest and social movements, which to some extent still lives on. See also Mutz, D.C., Hearing the Other Side: Deliberative Versus Participatory Democracy, Cambridge, Cambridge University Press, 2006; Baiocchi, G. & E. Ganuza, *Popular Democracy: The Paradox of Participation*, Stanford, Stanford University Press, 2016.

[3] Mansbridge, J., J. Bohman, S. Chambers, T. Christiano, A. Fung, J. Parkinson, D.F. Thompson, and M.E. Warren, A Systemic Approach to Deliberative Democracy, in J. Parkinson, and J. Mansbridge (eds), *Deliberative Systems: Deliberative Democracy at the Large Scale*, Cambridge, Cambridge University Press, 2012, pp. 1–26; Warren, M.E., A Problem-Based Approach to Democratic Theory, *American Political Science Review*, 2017, 111, 1, pp. 39–53.

[4] Pateman, C., Participatory Democracy Revisited, *Perspectives on Politics*, 2012, 10, 1, pp. 7–19; Elstub, S. and O. Escobar (eds), *Handbook of Democratic Innovation and Governance*, Cheltenham, Edward Elgar, 2019. This handbook is also sensitive to democratic innovations beyond deliberative reflection, including innovations in referendums and initiatives, and in collaborative governance; do-it-ourselves democracy through pragmatic activism is more or less subsumed under collaborative governance; not separately treated.

In this chapter, I engage with the literature on democratic innovations in a critical though constructive way. In this spirit, I take on but also extend Smith's definition of democratic innovations, focusing on institutions that have been specifically designed to increase and deepen societal participation in public policy-making—broadening the somewhat narrower focus on citizen participation in political decision-making, mentioned in Smith's original definition.[5] This slightly adapted definition is compatible with a perspective on democratic governance that recognizes the importance of collective action beyond the formulation of political decisions, and the role therein of societal stakeholders besides citizens.[6] Put differently, this definition connects an approach to democratic innovations more common in Political Science (focusing on political decision-making and citizen participation therein) to one more common in Public Administration (focusing on policy-making and governance beyond government and politics, with the involvement of a plethora of actors, organizations, and associations).

The turn to deliberation: Core themes and focus points

A detailed review of the literature on deliberative democracy is not a central objective here, but an account of dominant features is in order. In this account, the focus is on common themes in deliberative-democracy discourse.[7] The deliberative mini-public may currently be the most prominent model of democratic innovation (the attention-grabbing centrepiece of the reform cake, as I argued in Chapter 1) but around and beneath it are kindred expressions of intensified deliberation. Although deliberation has been defined in different ways, there is an underlying 'bedrock agreement' in deliberative democracy-discourse 'that democratic process should involve communication about, rather than merely aggregation of (fixed) preferences.'[8]

---

[5] Smith, G., *Democratic Innovation: Designing Institutions for Citizen Participation*, Cambridge, Cambridge University Press, 2009, p. 2. His definition connects democratic innovations to institutions that have been specifically designed to increase and deepen citizen participation in political decision-making.

[6] Parkinson, J., Why Deliberate? The Encounter Between Deliberation and New Public Managers, *Public Administration*, 2004, 82, 2, pp. 377–95; Brugué, Q. and R. Gallego, A Democratic Public Administration?, *Public Management Review*, 2010, 5, 3, pp. 425–47.

[7] Acknowledging that different authors vary in their adherence to common themes in deliberative-democracy discourse. See Bächtiger, A., S. Niemeyer, M. Neblo, M.R. Steenbergen, and J. Steiner, Disentangling Diversity in Deliberative Democracy: Competing Theories, Their Empirical Blind-spots, and Complementarities, *Journal of Political Philosophy*, 2010, 18, 1, pp. 32–63.

[8] Bächtiger, A., S. Niemeyer, M. Neblo, M.R. Steenbergen, and J. Steiner, Disentangling Diversity in Deliberative Democracy: Competing Theories, Their Empirical Blind-spots, and Complementarities, *Journal of Political Philosophy*, 2010, 18, 1, p. 35.

Conventional wisdom has it that deliberative democracy gained momentum in the 1990s, continuing its influence in the new millennium.[9] According to the Deliberative Democracy Consortium, the virtual community behind the *Deliberative Democracy Handbook* edited by Gastil and Levine: 'deliberative democracy strengthens citizen voices in governance by including people of all races, classes, ages, and geographies in deliberations that directly affect public decisions'.[10] Elsewhere, Gastil underscored the privileging of 'reason, argument, respect, and dialogue' in deliberative democracy, which would reject not only thin forms of aggregation in representative democracy but also non-reflective modes of mass mobilization in participatory democracy.[11]

The most influential theory that inspired the deliberative turn in the 1990s, according to Elster, was Habermas's theory of communicative action.[12] Ideally, such action would be:[13]

- *inclusive*, hearing all voices, in an unbiased way;
- *open*, genuinely communicative, non-manipulative;
- *power free*, accepting the 'unforced force of the better argument', abstaining from powerplay;
- *argumentative*, based on an extensive exchange of views, rather than a mere addition or barter of preferences and interests;
- *transformative*, changing initial 'raw opinions' into a more refined, enriched collective understanding.

The deliberative turn implied a counter-majoritarian turn towards a rather specific interpretation of integrative democracy, in particular participatory democracy (as introduced in Chapter 2). In addition to authors rooted in the highly egalitarian Habermasian approach to communicative rationality, authors with a broader interest in deliberative democracy came forward.

---

[9] Elster, J., Introduction, in J. Elster (ed.), *Deliberative Democracy*, Cambridge, Cambridge University Press, 1998, p. 1; Goodin, R., *Innovating Democracy: Democratic Theory and Practice after the Deliberative Turn*, Oxford, Oxford University Press, 2010, pp. 1–3.

[10] Gastil, J. and P. Levine (eds), *The Deliberative Democracy Handbook*, San Francisco, Jossey-Bass, 2005.

[11] Gastil, J., Preface, *Democracy in Small Groups: Participation, Decision Making, and Communication*, State College, PA, Efficacy Press, 2nd Edition, 2014 (originally 1993); Gutmann, A. and D. Thompson. *Why Deliberative Democracy?*, Princeton, Princeton University Press, 2003; Mutz, D.C., *Hearing the Other Side: Deliberative Versus Participatory Democracy*, Cambridge, Cambridge University Press, 2006; Chambers, S., Rhetoric and the Public Sphere: Has Deliberative Democracy Abandoned Mass Democracy?, *Political Theory*, 2009, 2, 3, pp. 323–50; Baiocchi, G. and E. Ganuza, *Popular Democracy: The Paradox of Participation*, Stanford, Stanford University Press, 2016.

[12] Elster, J., Introduction, in J. Elster (ed.), *Deliberative Democracy*, Cambridge, Cambridge University Press, 1998, pp. 1–18; Habermas, J., *Theorie des kommunikativen Handelns*, Frankfurt, Suhrkamp Verlag, 1981.

[13] Hendriks, F., *Vital Democracy: A Theory of Democracy in Action*, Oxford, Oxford University Press, 2010, p. 116; Chappel, Z., *Deliberative Democracy: A Critical Introduction*, Basingstoke, Palgrave, 2012, p. 7–10.

Bächtiger et al. refer to the former as 'Type I' and to the latter as 'Type II' deliberation. 'Type II deliberation does not directly repudiate the Type I agenda', the authors stress, 'so much as shift emphasis from an ideal conception of the political to the phenomenological'.[14]

In 2007, John Dryzek wrote: 'deliberative democracy now constitutes the most active area of political theory in its entirety (not just democratic theory)'.[15] The explosive growth of peer-reviewed scholarship on deliberative democracy has been further documented by Gastil.[16] After the first 'conceptual' wave, a second 'empirical' wave of studies followed.[17] A number of cases is repeatedly described (the Citizens' Assembly in British Columbia, the Listening to the Town process in New York, Deliberative Polling in Texas, and the Chinese township Zegua), but much more lies beneath the prominently exposed tip of the iceberg.[18]

Deliberative-democracy innovations are varied, as subsequent analysis will show. Mobilized deliberation (with non-randomized, selective participation) can be distinguished from microscopic deliberation (with randomized, a-selective participation); deliberative mini-publics can range from really small-scale (10–25) to relatively larger-scale (500–1000); they can be delineated in restrictive, intermediate, and expansive ways.[19]

Bringing democratic action and aggregation back in

To avoid misunderstandings, I do not question the occurrence of deliberative innovations in parts of democratic practice, nor do I question that particular

---

[14] Bächtiger, A., S. Niemeyer, M. Neblo, M.R. Steenbergen, and J. Steiner, Disentangling Diversity in Deliberative Democracy: Competing Theories, Their Empirical Blind-spots, and Complementarities, *Journal of Political Philosophy*, 2010, 18, 1, p. 42.

[15] Dryzek, J.S., Theory, Evidence and the Task of Deliberation, in S.W. Rosenberg (ed.), *Deliberation, Participation and Democracy: Can the People Govern?*, New York, Palgrave Macmillan, 2007.

[16] Gastil, J., *Democracy in Small Groups: Participation, Decision Making, and Communication*, State College, PA: Efficacy Press, 2nd Edition, 2014 (originally 1993), Figure 3.

[17] Owen, D. and G. Smith, Survey Article: Deliberation, Democracy, and the Systemic Turn, *Journal of Political Philosophy*, 2015, 23, 2, pp. 213–34.

[18] Smith, G., *Democratic Innovation: Designing Institutions for Citizen Participation*, Cambridge, Cambridge University Press, 2009; Chappel, Z., *Deliberative Democracy: A Critical Introduction*, Basingstoke, Palgrave, 2012; Geissel, B. and K. Newton (eds), *Evaluating Democratic Innovations: Curing the Democratic Malaise?*, Abingdon, Routledge, 2012, Chwalisz, C., *The Populist Signal: Why Politics and Democracy Need to Change*, London, Rowman & Littlefield, 2015; Escobar, O., Scripting Deliberative Policy-Making: Dramaturgic Policy Analysis and Engagement Know-How, *Journal of Comparative Policy Analysis: Research and Practice*, 2015, 17, 3, pp. 269–85.

[19] Fishkin, J., *When the People Speak: Deliberative Democracy and Public Consultation*, Oxford, Oxford University Press, 2009; Bächtiger, A., S. Niemeyer, M. Neblo, M.R. Steenbergen, and J. Steiner, Disentangling Diversity in Deliberative Democracy: Competing Theories, Their Empirical Blind-spots, and Complementarities, *Journal of Political Philosophy*, 2010, 18, 1, pp. 32–63; Ryan, M. and G. Smith, Defining Mini-Publics, in K. Grönlund, A. Bächtiger, and M. Setälä (eds), *Deliberative Mini-Publics*, London, ECPR Press, 2014, pp. 9–26.

versions of deliberation may have beneficial effects.[20] I do, however, question the inclination to equate, a priori, democratic innovations with deliberative models. There is more to be seen in the field of democratic innovation, and there is plenty of reason to call for heightened attention to non-deliberative variants of democratic innovation.[21]

In this chapter, preparing for later chapters, I take a closer look at the rebound of plebiscitary democracy of an aggregative rather than transformative type, and the push for cooperative democracy of an action-oriented rather than reflection-oriented type. Plebiscitary and cooperative democracy encompass distinctive developments that can be subdivided into various subcurrents, but what they generally have in common, and what distinguishes them from most deliberative methods, is a move away from a reflection-oriented account of democratic innovation in which the quantity and quality of political conversation and, as a result the achieved transformation of public opinion, have become standards for the accomplishments of democracy.[22] Plebiscitary democracy is, in essence, a majoritarian, vote-counting type of democracy, without highly communicative or transformative ambitions.[23] Cooperative democracy is, in essence, an action-oriented, selectively inclusive type of democracy; it does not come with highly deliberative or all-inclusive ambitions. Cooperative democracy may come with more cross-cutting communicative action than plebiscitary democracy, but other than in most deliberative models of innovation this is not a goal in and of itself; cross-cutting communication is an instrument to be used for what is deemed more important in cooperative democracy: getting things done, assembling vital resources for collective action.[24]

---

[20] Young, I., *Inclusion and Democracy*, Oxford, Oxford University Press, 2000; Fung, A., *Empowered Participation: Reinventing Urban Democracy*, Princeton, Princeton University Press, 2004; Lodge, M., The Public Management of Risk: The Case for Deliberating among Worldviews, *Review of Policy Research*, 2009, 26, 4, pp. 395–408; Ney, S. and M. Verweij, Exploring the Contributions of Cultural Theory for Improving Public Deliberation about Complex Policy Problems, *The Policy Studies Journal*, 2014, 42, 4, pp. 620–43.

[21] Pateman, C., Participatory Democracy Revisited, *Perspectives on Politics*, 2012, 10, 1, pp. 7–19; Elstub, S. and O. Escobar (eds), *Handbook of Democratic Innovation and Governance*, Cheltenham, Edward Elgar, 2019.

[22] Shapiro, I., Enough of Deliberation: Politics is about Interests and Power, in S. Macedo (ed.), *Deliberative Politics*, Oxford, Oxford University Press, 1999, pp. 28–38; Mutz, D.C., *Hearing the Other Side: Deliberative Versus Participatory Democracy*, Cambridge, Cambridge University Press, 2006.

[23] Cain, B.E., R.J. Dalton, and S.E. Scarrow, *Democracy Transformed: Expanding Political Opportunities in Advanced Industrial Democracies*, Oxford, Oxford University Press, 2003; Green, J.E., *The Eyes of the People: Democracy in an Age of Spectatorship*, Oxford, Oxford University Press, 2010; Green, J.E., Analysing Legislative Performance: a Plebeian Perspective, *Democratization*, 2013, 20, 3, pp. 417–37.

[24] Stone, C.N., *Regime Politics: Governing Atlanta 1946–1988*, Lawrence, University Press of Kansas, 1989; Ansell, C. and A. Gash, Collaborative Governance in Theory and Practice, *Journal of Public Administration Research and Theory*, 2008, 18, 4, pp. 543–71.

Paying closer attention to expressions of plebiscitary and cooperative democracy is imperative as they have become empirically more prominent as a result of technological and social change in recent decades. The 1990s saw not only the advent of the deliberative turn in academic writing, but it was also the period in which the internet and web-based technology took off. The massive uptake of broadband internet in the early 2000s and mobile technology in the last decade facilitated the expansion of online, digital voting with a markedly plebiscitary logic (more about this in Chapter 4); it also facilitated new forms of cooperative democracy, which Noveck has tried to capture with the image of 'wiki governance', highlighting the co-production of dispersed, but emphatically selective actors (more about this in Chapter 5).[25] I will further introduce and illustrate these developments, both theoretically (in the next section), and empirically (in the section thereafter).

Looking beyond deliberative models

When it comes to putting deliberative-democracy innovations in a wider perspective, Fishkin provides a practical stepping stone. Although he eventually advocates a specific subtype, Deliberative Polling, he also describes other deliberative models, as well as non-deliberative expressions of democracy. Combining various sources, Fishkin sketches a trilemma of democratic values—(political) equality, (massive) participation, and (meaningful) deliberation—which he presents as equally crucial to democracy, but very difficult to acquire at the same time. Attempts to achieve any two of these values will undermine the realization of the third.[26]

The forte of mass democracy, for instance, is mass participation (large numbers turn out at election day) combined with political equality (one man one vote); but meaningful deliberation among all these voters is very hard to achieve (see the pluses and minuses, derived from Fishkin, in Table 3.1). The opposite of mass democracy is microscopic deliberation as operationalized in deliberative polls, citizen juries, deliberative panels, consensus conferences, and the like. These invest strongly in deliberation

---

[25] Hill, S., *Digital Revolutions: Activism in the Internet Age*, Oxford, New Internationalist Publications, 2013; Noveck, B., *Wiki Government: How Technology Can Make Government Better, Democracy Stronger, and Citizens More Powerful*, Washington, DC., Brookings Institution Press, 2009.

[26] Fishkin, J., *When the People Speak: Deliberative Democracy and Public Consultation*, Oxford, Oxford University Press, 2009. Considering a larger set of 'democratic goods', Smith also recognizes the fundamental difficulty of acquiring different desirables at the same time; which in his study are more specifically connected to innovations geared at citizen participation. See Smith, G., *Democratic Innovation: Designing Institutions for Citizen Participation*, Cambridge, Cambridge University Press, 2009.

Table 3.1 Fishkin's equality–participation–deliberation trilemma.[a]

	Equality	Participation	Deliberation
1. Mass democracy (general suffrage)	+	+	−
2. Mobilized deliberation (non-randomized selection)	−	+	+
3. Microscopic deliberation (randomized sampling)	+	−	+

[a] Fishkin, J., *When the People Speak: Deliberative Democracy and Public Consultation*, Oxford, Oxford University Press, 2009.

through various communicative methods, as well as in political equality through (more or less) representative sampling.[27] The ambition is to equalize the odds of getting included in a sample that is expected to be a reflection of the wider population. The big trade-off, however, is with participation. Numbers of participants are by definition small—'microscopic'—in relation to the wider population.

Positioned between mass democracy and microscopic deliberation is the option of mobilized deliberation: actively inviting people to participate in deliberative events, for instance the National Issues Forums in the USA. Such events invest in participation combined with deliberation, although some authors would argue that the increased focus on participation leads to a decreased quality of deliberation.[28] The crucial trade-off, however, is with the value of political equality. Processes of self-selection tend to amount to a participating group of like-minded people, often with similar backgrounds. In the extreme, self-selected deliberation could become what Sunstein calls 'enclave deliberation'—not 'hearing-the-other-side' and 'cross-cutting' but 'self-confirming' and 'staying-within-one's-bubble' deliberation.[29]

Compared to the strictest norms of communicative action—Type I norms according to Bächtiger et al.[30]—mobilized deliberation seems to be the 'weaker' version, and microscopic deliberation the 'stronger', more principled

[27] Full randomization is one way of doing this. Regularly some sort of stratified sampling is used, to guarantee some underrepresented groups at least a place in the sample.
[28] Atlee, T., *Empowering Public Wisdom: A Practical Vision of Citizen-led Politics*, Berkely, North Atlantic Books, 2012.
[29] Sunstein, C., The Law of Group Polarization, *Journal of Political Philosophy*, 2002, 10, 2, pp. 175–95; Mutz, D.C., *Hearing the Other Side: Deliberative Versus Participatory Democracy*, Cambridge, Cambridge University Press, 2006.
[30] Bächtiger, A., S. Niemeyer, M. Neblo, M.R. Steenbergen, and J. Steiner, Disentangling Diversity in Deliberative Democracy: Competing Theories, Their Empirical Blind-spots, and Complementarities, *Journal of Political Philosophy*, 2010, 18, 1, p. 36.

version. As such, the latter also comes with a stronger bias, however, as discussed in the following section.

Towards an extended framework of democratic innovations

The equality–participation–deliberation trilemma (Table 3.1) serves as a practical stepping stone to an adapted framework (Table 3.2), which helps to reflect on the points that receive strong and weak emphasis in deliberative models of democratic innovation. A central bias, producing selective attention, concerns the focus on the democratic process as a reflective and transformative process that should ultimately lead to more refined public views on public matters.[31]

There are different variants of this theme in deliberative democracy. The specific variant propagated by Fishkin—Deliberative Polling—is explicitly designed to transform 'raw public opinion', which would arise from standard opinion polling, to more 'refined public opinion' through deliberative discussions in mini-publics. These mini-publics should do their transformative work in the period between pre-deliberation polling and post-deliberation polling. As already mentioned, levelling the odds of getting included in the mini-public is expected to contribute to political equality, to more levelled, less elite-dominated politics. At the same time, the random-sampling procedure is expected to produce a diversified sample of citizens—the mini-public—which is expected to be representative of the wider population, for which it could 'therefore' speak.[32]

In the same vein, smaller-scale deliberative meetings-of-minds (citizens' juries, consensus conferences, planning cells, citizen deliberative councils)

[31] Parkinson, J., Legitimacy Problems in Deliberative Democracy, *Political Studies*, 2003, 51, 1, pp. 180–96; Mutz, D.C., *Hearing the Other Side: Deliberative Versus Participatory Democracy*, Cambridge, Cambridge University Press, 2006; Chambers, S., Rhetoric and the Public Sphere: Has Deliberative Democracy Abandoned Mass Democracy?, *Political Theory*, 2009, 2, 3, pp. 323–50; Bächtiger, A., S. Niemeyer, M. Neblo, M.R. Steenbergen, and J. Steiner, Disentangling Diversity in Deliberative Democracy: Competing Theories, Their Empirical Blind-spots, and Complementarities, *Journal of Political Philosophy*, 2010, 18, 1, pp. 32–63.

[32] Fishkin, J., *When the People Speak: Deliberative Democracy and Public Consultation*, Oxford, Oxford University Press, 2009; Sintomer, Y., Random Selection, Republican Self-Government, and Deliberative Democracy, *Constellations*, 2010, 17, 3, pp. 472–87; Goodin, R., *Innovating Democracy: Democratic Theory and Practice after the Deliberative Turn*, Oxford, Oxford University Press, 2010; Setälä, M., K. Grönlund, and K. Herne, Citizen Deliberation on Nuclear Power: A Comparison of Two Decision-Making Methods, *Political Studies*, 2010, 58, 4, pp. 688–714; Ryan, M. and G. Smith, Defining Mini-Publics, in K. Grönlund, A. Bächtiger, and M. Setälä (eds), *Deliberative Mini-Publics*, London, ECPR Press, 2014, pp. 9–26; Olsen, E.D.H. and H.J. Trenz, From Citizens' Deliberation to Popular Will Formation? Generating Democratic Legitimacy in Transnational Deliberative Polling, *Political Studies*, 2014, 62, 1, pp. 117–33; Elstub, S., Mini-Publics: Issues and Cases, in S. Elstub and P. MacLaverty (eds), *Deliberative Democracy: Issues and Cases*, Edinburgh University Press, 2014, pp. 166–88.

attempt to enrich and transform public opinion, which in some cases is presented as a *People's Verdict*,[33] and in other cases as the public's advice, proposition, or request.[34] Larger-scale citizens' assemblies based on random-ized invitations or weighted sampling (for example, the national G1000-assembly for Belgium and the local G1000 meetings in various Dutch towns) tend to find closure in memoranda of 'enriched' national priorities or local desirabilities.[35] Such methods of deliberative democracy attempt to tease out what groups of citizens would think about public issues if they had the oppor-tunity to properly reflect on the issues.[36] This would make these methods superior to plebiscitary methods such as referendums, which would only aggregate what the people think when they have not been allowed or facil-itated to think properly. The result of deliberatively democratic processes would be better, more validated and substantiated, public views on public matters.

Democracy, however, is more than a procedure for distilling 'better argu-ments' from and instilling 'better views' among the public. As a form of public governance, it is also concerned with practically getting things done for the people, to some extent with the people. As Elster aptly noted on the essence of democracy: 'A better analogy might be engineering rather than science: the aim is to find an approximation that works rather than the truth.'[37] In his view, the early deliberative-democracy discourse was too much concerned with transforming and clarifying public opinion (collective knowing), and too little with engineering workable interventions in the real world (prag-matic bricolage). In the same vein, Shapiro among many others criticized deliberative-democracy theory for ignoring the reality that politics is not

[33] The People's Verdict was the way in which the Maclean's Forum, an experiment with deliberative democracy in Canada, was named and framed. See Chwalisz, C., *The People's Verdict: Adding Informed Citizen Voice to Public Decision-Making*, London, Rowman & Littlefield, 2017.

[34] Atlee, T., *Empowering Public Wisdom: A Practical Vision of Citizen-led Politics*, Berkely, North Atlantic Books, 2012, pp. 217–32; Goodin, R., *Innovating Democracy: Democratic Theory and Practice after the Deliberative Turn*, Oxford, Oxford University Press, 2010, pp. 16–18; Smith, G., *Democratic Innovation: Designing Institutions for Citizen Participation*, Cambridge, Cambridge University Press, 2009, pp. 72–110; Gastil, J. and P. Levine (eds), *The Deliberative Democracy Handbook*, San Francisco, Jossey-Bass, 2005, pp. 80–138.

[35] Caluwaerts, D. and M. Reuchamps, Strengthening Democracy through Bottom-up Deliberation: An Assessment of the Internal Legitimacy of the G1000 Project, *Acta Politica*, 2015, 50, 2, pp. 151–70; Lucardie, P., *Democratic Extremism in Theory and Practice*, London, Routledge, 2014, pp. 114–53; Rey-brouck, D. van, *Against Elections: The Case for Democracy*, London, Penguin Random House, 2013, p. 106; Smith, G., *Democratic Innovation: Designing Institutions for Citizen Participation*, Cambridge, Cam-bridge University Press, 2009, pp. 144–6; Meijer, A., R. van der Veer, A. Faber, and J. Penning de Vries, Political Innovation as Ideal and Strategy: the Case of Aleatoric Democracy in the City of Utrecht, *Public Management Review*, 2017, 19, 1, pp. 20–36.

[36] Reybrouck, D. van, *Against Elections: The Case for Democracy*, London, Penguin Random House, 2013; Fishkin, J., *Democracy When the People are Thinking*, Oxford, Oxford University Press, 2018.

[37] Elster, J., Introduction, in J. Elster (eds), *Deliberative Democracy*, Cambridge, Cambridge University Press, 1998, p. 9.

about the furthering of 'understanding' and 'the better argument' but about the mobilization of interest, power, and governing capacity.[38]

Following this line of reasoning, we need to add a crucial dimension of democratic quality, which is missing in Table 3.1, namely practical concretization. In line with a common dictionary definition of concretization— 'make (an idea or concept) real'[39]—a pragmatic working definition of concretization in democratic innovation would be: developing democratic practices that serve to accomplish practical, down-to-earth interventions and improvements in the public domain. Or indeed, going back to Elster, finding approximations that work in practice, rather than forging public statements or decisions that are more or less 'true' to the enlightened public will. It is consequentiality in a hands-on, action-oriented sense.[40] Stating that something is collectively willed or decided does not automatically entail that it is practically done (see Box 3.1.).

Box 3.1:   The deliberative wave and the issue of practical impact

In 2020, the OECD published a study that looked into evidence on 282 cases representing a so-called 'deliberative wave' in OECD member countries. Selected processes were presented as 'deliberative' and 'representative' (in the sense that assembled citizens were selected via random sampling), and also geared to having 'impact'.[a] The latter was to exclude processes merely geared at bringing people together to improve public relations. To gauge the impact of deliberative processes on public policy the commissioned researchers looked at: (a) process outputs such as tangible reports, documents, etc., (b) face-to-face responses by authorities to recommendations (c) implementation of recommendations, and (d) monitoring and evaluation.

A seasoned policy scientist would respond to this list by pointing out that having policy advice written down (a), getting face-to-face responses (b), and getting *ex post* reports in hand (d) does not say all that much about the real-world impact

---

[38] Shapiro, I., Enough of Deliberation: Politics is about Interests and Power, in S. Macedo (ed.), *Deliberative Politics*, Oxford, Oxford University Press, 1999, pp. 28–38; Hibbing, J.R. and E. Theiss-Morse, *Stealth Democracy: Americans' Beliefs about how Government Should Work*, Cambridge, Cambridge University Press, 2002; Helms, L., Democracy and Innovation: From Institutions to Agency and Leadership, *Democratization*, 2015, 23, 3, pp. 459–77; Ringen, S., *Nation of Devils: Democratic Leadership and the Problem of Obedience*, New Haven, Yale University Press, 2013.

[39] *Oxford Dictionary*, concretize, <https://www.lexico.com/definition/concretize>, n.d.

[40] Dryzek has called for the 'consequentiality' of deliberation, putting the matter more abstractly, granting that 'impact need not be direct'. See Dryzek, J.S., Democratization as Deliberative Capacity Building, *Comparative Political Studies*, 2009, 42, 11, p. 1382. In a sense, concretization is a practice- and action-oriented version of what Smith called for: popular control. See Smith, G., Review of 'When the People Speak', *Perspectives on Politics*, 2010, 8, 3, pp. 908–09.

of recommended policy interventions.[b] With regard to the implementation of recommendations (c), the commissioned researchers acknowledged how elusive to measurement this is. They reported available data on 'implementation' in 55 of the 282 cases, that is 19 per cent of cases that were selected on being geared to impact. They asserted that in 36 per cent of these 55 cases all recommendations and in 76 per cent over half of the recommendations had been implemented; in just 16 per cent of these cases none or only some of the recommendations were implemented.[c]

These amount to astonishing success rates that should make us alert as to what is exactly being counted here. The researchers themselves conceded that for making more robust claims further research and analysis are needed 'about which proposals are accepted and whether there is a general tendency to "cherrypick".[d] Other research suggests that there is plenty of room for this in such processes.[e] It is often easy and opportune to applaud and embrace policy papers developed by temporary citizens' assemblies, knowing that such assemblies will not be around for too long, and that in walking the talk of policy recommendations there is plenty of room for manoeuvre.

The OECD-study drew attention to practical impact and went much further in this than most multiple-case studies in this field, which is commendable. Yet, it also revealed the worrying fact that in more than 80 per cent of cases specifically selected on being geared to real-life impact data on implementation was missing. Attention to other aspects—the integrity of random selection, the communicative richness of the process, the transformation of public opinion, attitudes, and learning in participants—is much more visible in the evidence.

[a] OECD, *Innovative Citizen Participation and New Democratic Institutions: Catching the Deliberative Wave*, Paris, OECD Publishing, 2020, p. 13.

[b] See e.g. Figure 3.8 (p. 73) in the OECD-report, used to substantiate that 'representative deliberative processes have been most popular in addressing issues that have a direct impact on a community's life'. Urban planning gets the biggest bar in the bar graph. This only means, however, that the largest number of deliberative processes (43 of the total of 282) pertained to urban planning. One cannot conclude from this that achieved policy effects are the biggest in the real world of urban planning, which remains to be assessed in empirical research.

[c] OECD, *Innovative Citizen Participation and New Democratic Institutions: Catching the Deliberative Wave*, Paris, OECD Publishing, 2020, p.105–6.

[d] OECD, *Innovative Citizen Participation and New Democratic Institutions: Catching the Deliberative Wave*, Paris, OECD Publishing, 2020, p. 105, 165.

[e] Font J., S. Pasadas del Amo, and G. Smith, Tracing the Impact of Proposals from Participatory Processes: Methodological Challenges and Substantive Lessons, *Journal of Public Deliberation*, 2016, 12, 1. Michels. A. and H. Binnema, Assessing the Impact of Deliberative Democratic Initiatives at the Local Level: A Framework for Analysis, *Administration & Society*, 2019, 51, 5, pp. 749–69; Jacquet, V. and R. van der Does, Deliberation and Policy-Making: Three Ways to Think about Minipublics' Consequences, *Administration & Society*, 2021, 53, 3, pp. 468–87; Vrydagh, J., Measuring the Impact of Consultative Citizen Participation: Reviewing the Congruency Approaches for Assessing the Uptake of Citizen Ideas, *Policy Sciences*, 2022, 55, 1, 65–88.

Some democratic formats are more geared toward practical intervention than others: random appointment to practical public offices, for instance, is more geared toward practical intervention than is a random selection to citizens' assemblies; Participatory-Budgeting processes more than general elections. Hereafter, I will look at such options and such implications more closely, using Table 3.2 as an extended framework.

Two more recent and still evolving theoretical approaches also propagate a wider view of democratic innovations. The first is the 'systemic approach' to deliberative democracy, which suggests widening the scope to practices that may appear non-deliberative in isolation but may well contribute to deliberation at a systemic level.[41] The prime focus of this approach remains deliberation, now elevated to the system level. The second theoretical approach is the 'problem-based approach' to democratic theory pioneered by Warren, one of the authors behind the systemic turn who, in this new approach, suggests taking a next step to link the locus of systems to a spotlight on functions, with 'deliberative contributions to collective will formation as just one of the functions necessary'.[42] Warren's problem-based approach is focused on general democratic systems and their functions; not so much on specific models of democratic innovation. Nevertheless, the attention given to non-deliberative besides deliberative practices is consonant with the approach propagated here.[43]

Table 3.2 presents the general framework of democratic innovation that appears when pragmatic concretization is added as a democratic value and when democratic innovations that are not primarily focused on reflection and transformation are also fully recognized; the three main options distinguished earlier by Fishkin (Table 3.1) are expanded and refined

[41] Mansbridge, J., J. Bohman, S. Chambers, T. Christiano, A. Fung, J. Parkinson, D.F. Thompson, and M.E. Warren, A Systemic Approach to Deliberative Democracy, in J. Parkinson and J. Mansbridge (eds), *Deliberative Systems: Deliberative Democracy at the Large Scale*, Cambridge, Cambridge University Press, 2012, pp. 1–26. The recent turn to 'deliberative systems' implies a partial move away from some of the preoccupations developed during previous waves of deliberative democracy. However, as Hendriks points out, the deliberative systems approach 'remains a work in progress, and the concept is by no means settled'. See Hendriks, C.M., Coupling Citizens and Elites in Deliberative Systems, *European Journal of Political Research*, 2016, 55, p. 43. The implications of a general-systemic approach for the more specific debate on democratic innovations still need to be specified. See Warren, M.E., A Problem-Based Approach to Democratic Theory, *American Political Science Review*, 2017, 111, 1, p. 51. Also Felicetti, A., Learning from Democratic Practices: New Perspectives on Institutional Design, *The Journal of Politics*, 2021 83, 4, pp. 1589–601.
[42] Warren, M.E., A Problem-Based Approach to Democratic Theory, *American Political Science Review*, 2017, 111, 1, p. 41. Warren distinguishes 'seven generic practices' (of which deliberation is just one, besides voting, representing, recognizing, resisting, joining, exiting) that may serve three general functions in democratic systems (empowered inclusion; collective agenda and will formation; collective decision-making). Hands-on democratic action is not explicitly mentioned.
[43] As Warren observes the original 'deliberation vs non-deliberation' frame, while productive in some ways, has organized other issues out of the picture. See Warren, M.E., A Problem-Based Approach to Democratic Theory, *American Political Science Review*, 2017, 111, 1, p. 4.

Table 3.2 Fishkin's democratic options and values extended.

	Political equality	Massive participation	Thoughtful deliberation	Practical concretization
1. General elections and plebiscites				
1a. General elections	+	+	−	−
1b. General assembly voting	+	+	−/+	−/+
1c. Plebiscites, petitions, polls	+	+	−	−
1d. Quasi-referendums, digital votes	−	−/+	−	−
2. Mobilized deliberation and cooperation				
2a. Mobilized deliberative assemblies	−	+	−/+	−
2b. Empowered participation	−	−	+	+
2c. Do-it ourselves democracy	−	−	−/+	+
2d. Collaborative democratic governance	−	−	−/+	+
3. Randomized deliberation and appointment				
3a. Random citizens' panels (#10–25)	+	−	+	−
3b. Random citizens' assemblies (#100–1000)	+	−	+/−	−
3c. Deliberative polls (#500–1000+)	+	−	+	−
3d. Lottery appointments	+	−	−	+

Note: + and − indicate comparatively strong and weak emphasis.

accordingly in Table 3.2. I will elaborate on the refined, expanded categories in the following.

Randomized deliberation and appointment—Taking a wider view of democratic innovations allows us, among other things, to rediscover the classic option of the randomly appointed public official (Category 3d in Table 3.2). Compared to the currently more popular formats of random sampling—smaller-scale citizens' panels (3a), larger-scale assemblies (3b), deliberative polls (3c)—lottery appointments for concrete tasks (3d) are focused more on concretization than on deliberation.

Randomly rotating offices were institutionalized in ancient Athens, where yearly about 700 citizens selected by lot would handle practical matters in particular fields of public life.[44] Randomly selected officials mostly just performed a public duty for a year or so, without a lot of deliberative reflection: controlling garbage disposal, maintenance of temples, wharfs, grain shelters, etc. They worked alongside the Athenian males who were selected for public duty in courts and assemblies, which were partly randomized and partly mobilized deliberative institutions. While courts and assemblies were decision-making bodies, rotating offices were primarily action-oriented institutions.

Although the Athenian practice of randomly rotating offices may not match well with modern culture, it is at least remarkable that more modest versions of it—say, rotating the monitoring of road maintenance or non-specialized care for the elderly—have hardly been considered in the literature—especially when there is research showing that many citizens would rather do something together on a practical level than deliberate with randomly assembled others on a more abstract and potentially sensitive level.[45] Weaker mechanisms for concretization, such as randomized appointments to representative bodies or advisory boards, have received somewhat more attention in recent deliberative-democracy discourse.[46]

Mobilized deliberation and cooperation—There is more between mass democracy and microscopic deliberation than 'mobilized deliberation' as Fishkin denotes his middle category. Mobilized deliberation occurs in large-scale meetings such as National Issues Forums or Occupy-type general assemblies (examples of category 2a), which prioritize the mobilization of droves of participants over the random-equalization of entry chances. The other three options in category 2 also mobilize participants on special characteristics, but in different ways.

As defined by Fung, empowered participation (2b) mobilizes citizens affected by and interested in particular fields of public service—in Fung's seminal research: policing and education in Chicago—to deliberate and

---

[44] Hornblower, S., Creation and Development of Democratic Institutions in Ancient Greece, in J. Dunn (ed.), *Democracy: the Unfinished Journey 508 BC to AD 1993*, Oxford, Oxford University Press, 1992.

[45] Wijdeven, T. van de and F. Hendriks, A Little Less Conversation, a Little More Action: Real-Life Expressions of Vital Citizenship, in J.W. Duyvendak, F. Hendriks, and M. van Niekerk (eds), *City in Sight*, Amsterdam, Amsterdam University Press, 2009, pp. 121–41; Lee, C.W., *Do-It-Yourself Democracy: The Rise of the Public Engagement Industry*, Oxford, Oxford University Press, 2015; Mutz, D.C., *Hearing the Other Side: Deliberative Versus Participatory Democracy*, Cambridge, Cambridge University Press, 2006.

[46] Chwalisz, C., *The Populist Signal: Why Politics and Democracy Need to Change*, London, Rowman & Littlefield, 2015. The OECD distinguishes a budding new category of permanent deliberative councils based on lot. See OECD, *Innovative Citizen Participation and New Democratic Institutions: Catching the Deliberative Wave*, Paris, OECD Publishing, 2020. Landemore, H., *Open Democracy: Reinventing Popular Rule for the Twenty-First Century*, Princeton, Princeton University Press, 2020 takes sortitioned representative bodies seriously, but does not elaborate on lottery appointments. Such appointments are more invested in—to use Aristotelian terms—practical wisdom (phronesis) and operational action (techné); less in the sphere of epistemic wisdom (episteme).

cooperate with professional policymakers.[47] To be sure, there is deliberation involved in empowered participation, but this deliberation stays close
to concrete action, focusing on the pooling of vital resources needed for
practical interventions, steering clear of self-selected or enclave deliberation by those-who-already-agree. Compared to self-selected deliberative
platforms (e.g. Occupy-type general assemblies), participants tend to be
fewer, in addition to being more practice-oriented, in cases of empowered
participation.

Do-it-ourselves democracy (2c) and collaborative democratic governance
(2d) deserve special attention;[48] we will take a closer, case-sensitive look
at them in the next section. Generally speaking, do-it-ourselves democracy
involves concrete action by groups of people who agree that something needs
to be done—not necessarily discussed again—about something. This may
involve a recognized problem ('let's keep this community centre open'), or an
emerging opportunity ('let's use our WhatsApp-group to coordinate safety-
enhancing walks through the neighborhood'). The groups involved operate
as if inspired by Elvis Presley's 'a little less conversation, a little more action'.
Cross-cutting, transformative deliberation is not their forte, and participating communities tend to be smaller than those who turn up for deliberations
of the Occupy Wall Street type.[49]

In the sphere of collaborative democratic governance (2d) many transformations are unfolding. These are not conventionally connected to deliberative democracy, notwithstanding some shared precedents.[50] Experiences
with elite deliberation in the Federalist tradition in the USA, and the consociational and neo-corporatist traditions in Europe, constituted a bedrock on

---

[47] Fung, A., *Empowered Participation: Reinventing Urban Democracy*, Princeton, Princeton University Press, 2004.
[48] Open democracy as presented by Landemore, H., *Open Democracy: Reinventing Popular Rule for the Twenty-First Century*, Princeton, Princeton University Press, 2020 is essentially open to various demo-cratic options, but the ones mentioned here are largely missing in her depiction of open democracy. What options 2c and 2d have in common is a focus on pragmatic bricolage and strategic coupling; they are less focused on epistemic wisdom generation.
[49] Wijdeven, T. van de and F. Hendriks, A Little Less Conversation, a Little More Action: Real-Life Expressions of Vital Citizenship, in J.W. Duyvendak, F. Hendriks, and M. van Niekerk (eds), *City in Sight*, Amsterdam, Amsterdam University Press, 2009, pp. 121–41. See also Hulst, M.J. van, L. de Graaf, and G. van den Brink, The Work of Exemplary Practitioners in Neighborhood Governance, *Critical Policy Studies*, 2012, 6, 4, pp. 433–50.
[50] In an overview article, Ansell and Gash display the wide scope of collaborative governance. It is remarkable, and illustrative of the separation of research fields, that they hardly refer to democracy (searching on 'democra' gets only one hit in the main text); on the other hand, they highlight issues not prioritized in the innovations literature focusing on deliberative reflection (issues such as public–private networks, pooling of resources, negotiations, leadership). See Ansell, C. and A. Gash, Collaborative Gov-ernance in Theory and Practice, *Journal of Public Administration Research and Theory*, 2008, 18, 4, pp. 543–71.

which new types of collaborative democratic governance could grow.[51] In the next section, I will discuss the exemplary case of Brainport-Eindhoven, a metropolitan cooperative that brings together elites that represent various governments, companies, and higher-education providers on a highly pragmatic agenda. Collaborative-governance practices like these have one thing in common: a firm choice for a highly practical type of deliberation—the preferred terms are 'co-production' and 'co-creation'—often at the expense of wide and equal participation from the general public.[52]

General elections and plebiscites—Thirdly, we may take a wider perspective at the 'weapons of mass democracy' (see Box 3.2 for additional, specific observations). Regarding trade-offs between core values, general elections and directly democratic plebiscites such as referendums could be grouped together. In one sense this is correct: they give electorates in their entirety equalized opportunities to participate in ballots.[53] Even so-called 'low turn-outs' at the ballot box involve a lot more participants than the other options discussed here. We should, however, also see the differences between general elections, formal plebiscites, and other modes of aggregative voting.

General elections (1a) hardly need specification. As central to representative democracy, they legitimate the parties and candidates that win executive offices or seats in representative bodies that are expected to do the political work for the people, based on an electoral mandate by the people. General assembly voting (1b), essentially a local phenomenon, prevails when the entire citizenry is invited to participate in direct voting. The Swiss *Landesgemeinde* is a case in point, as is the New England Town Meeting.[54] These meetings are primarily focused on voting, and discussion time per voting item is relatively scarce. Yet, there is to some extent room for deliberation,

---

[51] On elite deliberation in the Federalist tradition, see Fishkin, J., *When the People Speak: Deliberative Democracy and Public Consultation*, Oxford, Oxford University Press, 2009. On elite consensualism and consociationalism, see Lijphart, A., The Evolution of Consociational Theory and Consociational Practices, 1965–2000, *Acta Politica*, Spring/Summer 2002, 37, pp. 7–140; Steiner, J. and T. Ertman, Consociationalism and Corporatism in Western Europe: Still the Politics of Accomodation?, *Acta Politica*, Spring/Summer 2002, 37, pp. 7–140.

[52] Noveck, B., *Wiki Government: How Technology Can Make Government Better, Democracy Stronger, and Citizens More Powerful*, Washington, DC, Brookings Institution Press, 2009, pp. 170–2. Cf. K. Emerson and T. Nabatchi, *Collaborative Governance Regimes*, Washington: Georgetown University Press, 2015.

[53] Cain, B.E., R.J. Dalton, and S.E. Scarrow, *Democracy Transformed: Expanding Political Opportunities in Advanced Industrial Democracies*, Oxford, Oxford University Press, 2003, pp. 23–58; Smith, G., *Democratic Innovation: Designing Institutions for Citizen Participation*, Cambridge, Cambridge University Press, 2009, pp. 111–41.

[54] Mansbridge, J., *Beyond Adversary Democracy*, New York, Basic Books, 1980; Zimmerman, J.F., *The New England Town Meeting: Democracy in Action*, Westport, Praeger, 1999; Reinisch, C. and J. Parkinson, *Swiss Landsgemeinden: a Deliberative Democratic Evaluation of Two Outdoor Parliaments*, Helsinki, ECPR Joint Sessions, 2007.

giving different sides in the discussion opportunities to speak up before an often straight majority vote is taken. The small-scale, down-to-earth nature of the meetings brings a level of sensitivity to hands-on, concrete action, albeit weaker than what we saw in category 2. Electoral systems and assembly-voting models are templates and outcomes of institutional change, but once established they are often prey to institutional fixation.

Recent developments in the techno-cultural context of democracy prompt a closer look at plebiscites, polls, and petitions (1c), and the burgeoning, but ill-understood, range of quasi-referendums and digital votes (1d) that aggregate individual preferences via new, often electronic mechanisms—sometimes called 'clicktivism', activism geared at amassing electronic signs of public (dis)approval.[55] The first exemplary case in the next section will illustrate how formal and quasi-referendums tend to be increasingly entangled. Deliberative-democracy discourse before the systemic turn has been mainly aversive of such advances in plebiscitary democracy.[56] The plebiscitary focus on public emotions combined with aggregative, often adversarial methods with little attention to deliberative conversation, has fuelled the disinclination. Deliberative designs that take plebiscitary voting as a starting point, such as the Citizen Initiative Review, are scarce.[57]

Box 3.2: Specific extensions and combinations of variants

Table 3.2 inevitably abstracts from specific extensions and combinations of variants. A few extensions from the first category—which has taken a back seat in democratic-innovations discourse under the deliberative turn—are worth mentioning here.[a]

General elections have been extended with the primary and the recall—first and foremost in the USA—as methods for preselecting candidates for political office (primary), and deselecting them when in office (recall). Preselection methods used in the primary process vary from general elections (1a), to voting in general assemblies or conventions of political parties (2b), to specific party 'referendums' (2c), and digital votes (2d). The recall is often put in the direct-voting category together with referendums and initiatives (1c)—being an instrument for which petitioners need to collect enough signatures, and through which a bare majority can effectuate a direct veto—but it should be recognized that the recall also extends electoral

---

[55] Halupka, M., Clicktivism: A Systematic Heuristic, *Policy & Internet*, 2014, 6, 2, pp. 115–32.

[56] Chambers, S., Rhetoric and the Public Sphere: Has Deliberative Democracy Abandoned Mass Democracy?, *Political Theory*, 2009, 2, 3, p. 331; Green, J.E., *The Eyes of the People: Democracy in an Age of Spectatorship*, Oxford, Oxford University Press, 2010.

[57] Gastil, J. and R. Richards, Making Direct Democracy Deliberative through Random Assemblies, *Politics & Society*, 2013, 41, 2, pp. 253–81. I will delve into mixed models such as the Citizen Initiative Review in Chapters 7 and 8. See Box 3.2 for a look ahead.

democracy with an extra, earlier, opportunity to deselect office-holders per general election (1a).

Issue-focused plebiscites, petitions, and polls have branched out in many ways. The specialized literature distinguishes mandatory (constitutional) referendums from top-down (politically initiated) referendums, and bottom-up (petitioned) voter initiatives to veto or propose legislation (1c). A petition stage has become standard practice in bottom-up referendums and initiatives, but as an instrument for amassing written signatures for or against an issue, the petition or (citizens' request) has a much longer history preceding general elections (1a) as well as formal plebiscites (1c). Public polling has become entangled with voting in general elections and issue-focused plebiscites (1a, 1c), using random sampling for statistical representativeness or non-random 'straw polling' for convenience purposes. The latter is still quite common in web-based internet polls (1d).

Hybrid models that emphatically combine different varieties will be discussed in later chapters. There, I will delve into hybrids that combine, for instance, the initiative (1c) and the random citizens' panel (3a), as in the Oregon-style Citizens' Initiative Review; or the referendum (1c) and the random citizens' assembly (3b), as in the Irish process that led to new legislation on abortion; or digital voting (1d), empowered participation (2b), and do-it-ourselves democracy (2c), as in Participatory Budgeting-new style developed in Antwerp.[b]

[a] On extensions from the first category see Cain, B.E., R.J. Dalton, and S.E. Scarrow (eds), *Democracy Transformed: Expanding Political Opportunities in Advanced Industrial Democracies*, Oxford, Oxford University Press, 2003 (Part I); Cronin, T. E., *Direct Democracy: The Politics of Initiative, Referendum and Recall*, Cambridge, MA, Harvard University Press, 1989; Sandri, G. and A. Seddone (eds), *Party Primaries in Comparative Perspective*, Routledge, 2016; van Vos, L. Heerma (ed.), *Petitions in Social History*, Cambridge, Cambridge University Press, 2002; Smith, T.W., The First Straw A Study of the Origins of Election Polls, *Public Opinion Quarterly*, 1990, 54, 1, pp. 21–33; Holtz-Bacha, C. and J. Strömbäck, *Opinion Polls and the Media*, New York, Palgrave, 2012.
[b] The Oregon-style CIR returns are discussed in Chapters 4, 6, and 7; the Irish deliberative referendum is the central case of Chapter 7; and Antwerp's model of PB-new style is the central case of Chapter 8. Variations on the theme of the statewide hybrid and the local-level hybrid are discussed in Chapters 7–8.

Beyond deliberative reflection: Taking a closer look

It is not my aim to empirically delve into all the democratic options that were compared in conceptual terms in the previous section. As argued, many variants of deliberative reflection are widely covered in the literature already (2a, 2b, 3a, 3b, 3c), as are the general voting models from which deliberative democracy-discourse has turned away since the 1990s (1a, 1b). For good measure, this section zooms in on three contemporary versions of

democratic innovation that are particularly in need of heightened attention: the rebound of plebiscitary democracy through the (quasi-)referendum,
the advent of do-it-ourselves democracy through pragmatic activism, and
of collaborative democratic governance through concerted action. To bring
the point home that these are salient developments that deserve heightened
attention in scholarly discourse on democratic innovations, three exemplary
cases derived from democratic practice in the Netherlands will be discussed
in this chapter:[58]

- aggregative campaigning against the Ukraine-EU Treaty;
- tripartite concerted action in Brainport-Eindhoven;
- hands-on residence cooperation in Biest-Houtakker.

In terms of Table 3.2, the first case exemplifies the advent of the non-
formal quasi-referendum (1d), linked with the language and logic of the formal referendum (1c). The second and third cases exemplify do-it-ourselves
democracy (2c) and collaborative democratic governance (2d).[59] With three
nested cases that share the same national context, one can hold general
context-characteristics constant, and focus attention on what makes them
particular. In addition to efficiency considerations, focusing on this central
country case brings the benefits of a 'least-likely' case study strategy into
view.[60] The Netherlands is generally viewed as a fertile breeding ground for
deliberative democracy of the reflective, widely inclusive type.[61] It may be
regarded as significant that democratic innovations diverging from these
characteristics should also take root on this breeding ground. 'If they can
make it there, then they can make it anywhere'.[62]

---

[58] In subsequent Chapters, 4 and 5, but also 7 and 8, more cases will follow.

[59] Although lottery appointment for concrete tasks (category 3d in Table 3.2) fits the profile of an action-
oriented option for democratic innovation, underconceptualized in the democratic-innovations literature
(in contrast to the widely covered variants of randomized deliberation: 3a, 3b, 3c in Table 3.2), it fails on
the criterium of being empirically salient in the central country case of the Netherlands (or other country
cases for that matter) to be detailed as a within-case study in this section.

[60] George, A.L. and A. Bennett, *Case Studies and Theory Development in the Social Sciences*, Cambridge,
MIT Press, 2005; Flyvbjerg, B., *Making Social Science Matter*, Cambridge, Cambridge University Press,
2001, pp. 77–81; Peters, B.G., *Strategies for Comparative Research in Political Science*, London, Palgrave
Macmillan, 2013, p. 68.

[61] Vree, W. van, *Meetings, Manners and Civilization*, Leicester, Leicester University Press, 1999;
Lijphart, A., The Evolution of Consociational Theory and Consociational Practices, 1965–2000, *Acta
Politica*, Spring/Summer, 2002, 37, pp. 7–140; Hendriks, F., Democratic Reform between the Extreme
Makeover and the Reinvention of Tradition: The Case of the Netherlands, *Democratization*, 2009, 12, 2,
pp. 243–68; Heijstek-Ziemann, K., Exploring the Impact of Mass Cultural Changes on the Patterns of
Democratic Reform, *Democratization*, 2014, 21, 5, pp. 888–911.

[62] Guy Peters uses this theme from New York-New York to demonstrate the logic of a so-called least-
likely case study strategy. Peters, B.G., *Strategies for Comparative Research in Political Science*, London,

Reinventing the referendum: Aggregative campaigning against the Ukraine–EU Treaty

Stock-taking exercises demonstrate that the Dutch referendum on the Ukraine–EU Treaty, held on 6 April 2016, joins a growing category within plebiscitary democracy. Using data from the Centre for Direct Democracy, *The Economist* signals a rise in Europe of an average of three (national) referendums in the 1970s to eight in recent years.[63] This does not include Switzerland and Liechtenstein, nor the growing number of local and regional referendums.[64] And this also does not include the explosive growth of quasi-referendums that bring the aggregative logic to the public domain with new mechanisms—often the count of electronic 'clicks', such as Facebook-likes, e-signatures, and other electronic thumbs-up or thumbs-down (Chapter 4 delves deeper into this).[65]

Formal referendums and quasi-referendums tend to gain traction when sharing the same issue frame. The aggregative logic and language of formal referendums is easily transposed to quasi-referendums—also focusing on numbers, percentages, majority and minority shares—which in turn can support the build-up to a formal referendum. The Dutch referendum on the EU trade agreement with Ukraine is a case in point of referendums and quasi-referendums sharing the same issue frame in a mutually supportive way. (Another is the Brexit case. The build-up to the Brexit referendum, also held in 2016, was accompanied by a plethora of predictive surveys and (electronic) polls; as was the aftermath, including an e-petition demanding a second referendum and post-Brexit polls showing majorities for the opposite.)[66]

The final vote in the 'Ukraine referendum'—61 per cent of Dutch voters turned down the trade agreement—was the culmination of an intensive, aggregative process that included multiple steps. A significant role in this was played by the website *GeenPeil.nl* (translation: NoLevel.nl), a spin-off from the shock-blog *GeenStijl.nl* (translation: NoStyle.nl). A tipping point

Palgrave Macmillan, 2013, p. 68. 'Least-likely' is generally interpreted as among the least likely, not exactly the least likely of all.

[63] The Economist, Referendumania: Plebiscites in Europe, <https://www.economist.com/europe/2016/05/19/referendumania>, 21 May 2016; Qvortrup, M. (ed.), *Referendums Around the World: The Continued Growth of Direct Democracy*, Houndmills, Palgrave Macmillan, 2017; Matsusaka, J., *Let the People Rule: How Direct Democracy Can Meet the Populist Challenge*, Princeton, Princeton University Press, 2020.

[64] Qvortrup, M., Referendums in Western Europe, in M. Qvortrup (ed.), *Referendums around the World*, Houndmills, Palgrave Macmillan, 2017, pp. 19–45; Holtkamp, L. (ed.), *Direktdemokratische Hochburgen in Deutschland*, Wiesbaden, Springer, 2016.

[65] Hill, S., *Digital Revolutions: Activism in the Internet Age*, Oxford, New Internationalist Publications, 2013; Halupka, M., Clicktivism: A Systematic Heuristic, *Policy & Internet*, 2014, 6, 2, pp. 115–32.

[66] More on the Brexit referendum in Box 2.1.

was reached when GeenStijl sent out this message: 'Hurray. We have done it. It is now possible to sign the GeenPeil referendum online'.[67] Helped by volunteer software developers, who designed a purpose-built app, the effort from this point on was turned into a massive open online petition with the flavour of a plebiscite. Sympathizers could sign the e-petition-for-referendum on their PC, tablet, or smartphone, and the app would do the rest: fold a PDF, print it, and submit it. The official institution overseeing electoral processes in the Netherlands had accepted the online bypass after some hesitation.

Interestingly, this expression of 'clicktivism' was already presented as a 'referendum' when the official referendum was yet to be triggered. To do this, 300,000 signatures still needed to be collected. When the 300,000 mark was ultimately reached, just in time, other pollsters became increasingly active. Their question was not only 'will the nay-sayers outnumber the yes-voters?', it was also 'will the turn-out reach the necessary 30% of the eligible voters?' On the day of the official referendum the answer to both questions turned out to be affirmative—61 per cent said no, and 32.3 per cent turned out. At that point, the latter was the most remarkable fact as previous (web) polls—mimicking the vote-counting logic of the referendum—had indicated that those inclining to vote yes would probably not win more votes, but could defeat the other side by staying at home. The no-camp—increasingly motivated by the added suspension due to pre-referendum polling—turned out in numbers large enough to ultimately win the day. Looking back on their referendum campaign, the driving actors behind GeenPeil later clarified that, notwithstanding a growing anti-EU sentiment to work with, their campaign would not have survived the necessary signature-collection stage without the aggregative potential of modern information technology and internet jockeys capable of unleashing that potential.[68]

The intertwining of official referendums and quasi-referendums (such as the 'Geen-Peil referendum online' and similar practices mimicking the plebiscitary logic of referendums) warrants more attention, both analytical and critical, in democratic innovation research. Pioneering research into new forms of aggregative democracy by Cain et al. has not been updated or widened to include the new quasi-referendums of the internet age.[69] Specialized literature reports on the institutionalization of formal but

[67] Hendriks, F., K. van der Krieken, and C. Wagenaar, *Democratische zegen of vloek?Aantekeningen bij het referendum*, Amsterdam University Press, 2017, pp. 19–53.

[68] Based on interviews with insiders: Dongen, M. van, Het success can GeenPeil in 12 lessen, <https://www.volkskrant.nl/nieuws-achtergrond/het-succes-van-geenpeil-in-12-lessen~b25cfda5/>, 31 March 2016.

[69] Cain, B.E., R.J. Dalton, and S.E. Scarrow (eds), *Democracy Transformed: Expanding Political Opportunities in Advanced Industrial Democracies*, Oxford, Oxford University Press, 2003.

not quasi-referendums,[70] which are also understudied in the democratic-innovations literature. In Chapter 4, therefore, I will elaborate more extensively on the quasi-referendum and associated development.

Rediscovering collaborative governance: Concerted action in Brainport-Eindhoven

In the Dutch city of Eindhoven—the breeding ground of the established electronics giant Philips as well as the new microelectronics world leader ASML—a special case of collaborative governance has been developed that fuses and adapts elements described in American urban politics literature under the heading of 'urban regimes' together with Rhinelandic neo-corporatism and consensualism.[71]

In Stone's classic analysis of the urban regime that governed Atlanta for decades, a black political elite and a white business elite pooled vital resources in a stable long-term coalition that turned Atlanta into a 'city too busy to hate'.[72] The collaborative-governance system of Brainport-Eindhoven also connects urban elites on a joint agenda—in this case: boosting the metropolitan knowledge-intensive economy—but does so in a more inclusive and encompassing way. The basic model is tripartite, bringing together top-level representatives of subnational governments (such as the city of Eindhoven), major knowledge-intensive businesses (such as Philips), and central knowledge institutions (such as the universities of Eindhoven and Tilburg). It is said that each of them has the mobile numbers of all the others at hand.[73]

The tripartite Brainport model is not fully open, but it is much less closed than the Atlanta regime that Stone revealed. At certain times, the network opens up and invites a wider circle of spokespersons from various social domains. On other occasions, the network narrows down to a subset that is deemed necessary for the task at hand. Rob van Gijzel, the former social-democratic mayor of Eindhoven, recalls how within days after the collapse of

---

[70] Altman, D., *Direct Democracy Worldwide*, Cambridge, Cambridge University Press, 2011; Qvortrup, M., Referendums in Western Europe, M. Qvortrup (ed.), *Referendums around the World*, Houndmills, Palgrave Macmillan, 2017, pp. 19–45.

[71] Stone, C.N., *Regime Politics: Governing Atlanta 1946–1988*, Lawrence, University Press of Kansas, 1989; Steiner, J. and T. Ertman, Consociationalism and Corporatism in Western Europe: Still the Politics of Accomodation?, *Acta Politica*, Spring/Summer, 2002, 37, pp. 7–140.

[72] Stone, C.N., *Regime Politics: Governing Atlanta 1946–1988*, Lawrence, University Press of Kansas, 1989, p. 11.

[73] Schaap, L. and J. van Ostaaijen, Good Multi-Level Governance: Brainport-Eindhoven, in L. van den Dool, F. Hendriks, A. Gianoli, and L. Schaap (eds), *The Quest for Good Urban Governance*, Wiesbaden, Springer VS, 2015, pp.147–64.

Lehman Brothers, he could assemble business leaders in the region to discuss the best way to deal with the expected loss of jobs in the Brainport region: 'The solidarity, really unbelievable what we achieved together: the knowledge worker arrangement, the parttime unemployment benefits; after that we really only had economic growth in the region.'[74] In 2011, Brainport-Eindhoven was declared 'the smartest region in the world' by the Intelligent Community Forum.

The type of democratic legitimacy claimed by the Brainport model is output-legitimacy rather than input-legitimacy, although the latter has not been fully neglected. In 2016, an ad hoc mini-public was organized, a so-called G1000, designed to widen representation descriptively (based on background characteristics). Alternatively, the model of Brainport-Eindhoven has been continually aimed at furthering representation organically (based on different stakes and perspectives). Political and social representatives come together and share resources in a tripartite model, geared at mutual accommodation. Their connected power is not so much 'power over' as it is 'power to'—the joint capacity to get things done.[75] It involves deliberation, to some extent and in some form, quite different from the microscopic take on deliberation that has become centralized in the democratic innovations literature.

Reviving do-it-ourselves democracy: Residents' Cooperation Biest-Houtakker

If we zoom in even further on Dutch democracy, we can find many instances of do-it-ourselves democracy, or in Dutch '*sociaal doe-het-zelven*'. Discussing the latter, Hilhorst and Van der Lans distinguished no less than four subcurrents of this phenomenon, which they illustrate with numerous examples.[76] Here, we look at just one encompassing case to highlight the contrast with models of deliberative reflection. In the small village of Biest-Houtakker, Van de Wijdeven closely followed a citizens' initiative that at the height of its

---

[74] Based on an interview with Eindhoven's mayor at the time, Rob van Gijzel, see: Graaf, P. de, Eindhoven leent zich voor experimenten, <https://www.volkskrant.nl/nieuws-achtergrond/eindhoven-leent-zich-voor-experimenten~b1a668cd/ >, 1 June 2016.

[75] Stoker, G., Regime Theory and Urban Politics, in D. Judge, G. Stoker, and H. Wolman (eds), *Theories of Urban Politics*, London, Sage, 1995; Stone, C.N., *Regime Politics: Governing Atlanta 1946–1988*, Lawrence, University Press of Kansas, 1989.

[76] Lans, J. van der and P. Hilhorst, *Sociaal doe-het-zelven*, Amsterdam, Atlas Contact, 2013; Lee, C.W., *Do-It-Yourself Democracy: The Rise of the Public Engagement Industry*, Oxford, Oxford University Press, 2015. Lee's focus on 'yourself', instead of 'ourselves', does not quite capture the phenomenon described here.

existence turned into a building society, involved in the construction of a new multifunctional accommodation in the village's centre. The Residents' Cooperation Biest-Houtakker, established in 2012, enabled local residents to shape their meeting space in this venue and to be in charge of its running as of March 2014, when the centre opened its doors.[77]

For the opening ceremony, the Cooperation's website extended this telling invitation: 'did you help with: serving coffee, sweeping floors, hammering, cleaning, congregating, moving out, moving in, choice-making, circulating letters, arranging electrics, purging, etc.—be warmly invited!' Congregation and communication were evidently part of the process, but not in the way that some deliberative theorists would prescribe—as developing a more enlightened public opinion while and 'when the people are thinking'.[78] Collective communication was mainly action-oriented. At the height of the reconstruction period around 70 to 80 residents would participate in working groups named after themes such as 'building', 'funding', 'exploitation', 'decoration', 'outside area', 'care', 'name giving', 'communication'. The chairs of these working groups would sit together once a month, again highly action-oriented. At one point, for instance, it transpired that a regional bank was willing to donate its office furniture to the Resident's Association—if only they could collect it at short notice. The Association almost automatically thought about a neighbour called Rina, one of the active citizens known to be 'very good in assembling people, and in energizing them to contribute'.[79]

Such collective action and selective invitation characterize self-governance in this case. The accompanying conviction, often uttered, was 'everyone can do something—if you are handy in moving stuff with a group of people, you can do this, and if you are well-versed at making minutes of meetings, you can do that. The logic of do-it-ourselves democracy is in this sense closer to the action-oriented version of participatory democracy than to the reflection-oriented version of deliberative democracy.[80] It is, however, not strongly inspired by ideological thinking associated with new social

[77] Wijdeven, T. van de, Bewonerscoöperatie Biest-Houtakker: 'Iedereen kan iets', T. van de Wijdeven and L. de Graaf (eds), *Kernkracht: over doe-democratie in het landelijk gebied*, Tilburg, Tilburg University Reports, 2014. This case study is part of 'The Rural Alliances Project', facilitated by Interreg IVB North West Europe. See: Rural Alliance, Skills Plotting Tool Version 4, <http://www.rural-alliances.eu/downloads/Skills-Plotting-Tool-Version-4-(Nov-13)-(NL)-final.pdf>, n.d., retrieved 1 April 2019.
[78] Fishkin, J., *Democracy When the People are Thinking*, Oxford, Oxford University Press, 2018.
[79] Wijdeven, T. van de, Bewonerscoöperatie Biest-Houtakker: 'Iedereen kan iets', T. van de Wijdeven and L. de Graaf (eds), *Kernkracht: over doe-democratie in het landelijk gebied*, Tilburg, Tilburg University Reports, 2014, pp. 54–5.
[80] Mutz, D.C., *Hearing the Other Side: Deliberative Versus Participatory Democracy*, Cambridge, Cambridge University Press, 2006.

or political movements.[81] Participants get their energy not so much from elevated social thought, but rather from down-to-earth social practice— from the other pioneers involved, the joint actions, and the emerging results.[82]

Do-it-ourselves democracy is different from the face-to-face assembly democracy that Mansbridge analysed many years ago.[83] It has its own amalgam of small-community problems that needs further theorizing. Although Van de Wijdeven's study connects to a European project looking at do-it-ourselves democracy in six North-European countries, theory development is still in its infancy.

Beyond deliberation: Innovation in the modern mixed regime

Table 3.3 summarizes the key elements of the aforementioned cases and their connections to the core values specified in Table 3.2. Together, the cases illustrate how a democratic system known for its sensitivity to deliberative reflection can also, and at the same time, be home to democratic shifts of a different—aggregative and action-oriented—variety.[84]

At first glance, the case of the Ukraine referendum and its accompanying quasi-referendums confirms what is said about plebiscitary democracy in general: participation is comparatively large, while deliberation is not its prime concern. However, it also prompts two qualifications. First, although participation in a formal referendum is comparatively wide-ranging and open to all, this is less true for the quasi-referendums that may accompany a referendum like this. These tend to use selective samples that are neither wide-ranging nor open to all.[85] Second, while deliberation may not be the hallmark of a binary, vote-counting referendum, in the case of the Dutch Ukraine referendum it was evidently an external effect. Public debate on EU

[81] Tormey, S., *The End of Representative Politics*, Cambridge, Polity Press, 2015, pp. 105–25.
[82] Wijdeven, T. van de, Bewonerscoöperatie Biest-Houtakker: 'Iedereen kan iets', T. van de Wijdeven and L. de Graaf (eds), *Kernkracht: over doe-democratie in het landelijk gebied*, Tilburg, Tilburg University Reports, 2014, pp. 88–90.
[83] Mansbridge, J., *Beyond Adversary Democracy*, New York, Basic Books, 1980; Zimmerman, J.F., *The New England Town Meeting: Democracy in Action*, Westport, Praeger, 1999; Reinisch, C. and J. Parkinson, *Swiss Landsgemeinden: a Deliberative Democratic Evaluation of Two Outdoor Parliaments*, Helsinki, ECPR Joint Sessions, 2007.
[84] Hendriks, F., Democratic Reform *between* the Extreme Makeover and the Reinvention of Tradition: The Case of the Netherlands, *Democratization*, 2009, 12, 2, pp. 243–68; Heijstek-Ziemann, K., Exploring the Impact of Mass Cultural Changes on the Patterns of Democratic Reform, *Democratization*, 2014, 21, 5, pp. 888–911.
[85] More about the peculiarities of quasi-referendums and related expressions of the new plebiscitary democracy in Chapter 4.

Table 3.3 Three cases compared on core values and key elements.

	Ukraine referendum	Brainport-Eindhoven	Biest-Houtakker
Key elements			
Mode of concretization	Conclusive answer without implementation strategy	Tripartite collaboration on strategic (economic) agenda	Practical cooperation on 'real world' action points
Mix of deliberation and aggregation	Mainly aggregative process with large impact on public debate	Horizontal communication among pluriform though not all-inclusive elites	Coordination through deliberation or voting secondary to coordination-in-action
Claim to democratic fame	Rule by the people; giving the electoral majority a loud and clear voice	Rule for the people; organic representation as alternative to statistical representativeness	Rule of the people; self-government by those concerned; 'no-diploma-needed democracy'
Relative strengths	Everyone can choose to vote (or not); Non-fuzzy outcome: bold statement	Inclusion of those with vital resources; Synchronized agenda's facilitate concerted action	'Action speaks louder than words'; Non-fuzzy outcome: visible results
Relative weaknesses	Polarization of the public will; uncertainty after will-formation	Link with economic growth plausible but indirect and hard to prove	Small steps per project; Like-minded action groups: not cross-cutting
Core values			
Equality	+	–	–
Participation	+/–	–	–/+
Deliberation	–/+	+	–/+
Concretization	–	+	+

politics had never been so wide-ranging and lively before. It was surely more intensive than public debate resulting from the last national experiment with a deliberative mini-public in the Netherlands.[86]

Of the three exemplary cases reviewed, Brainport-Eindhoven comes closest to some version of deliberation—albeit of a rather utilitarian and selective type, which characterizes collaborative governance in general.[87] Participation is diverse but not open to all. The claim to democratic fame is not primarily rule 'by the people', as in a directly aggregative referendum, but rather rule 'for the people' through concerted action. By contrast, 'rule of by people' is the claim to fame of do-it-ourselves democracy as evidenced in the Biest-Houtakker case. They may share this claim with deliberative democrats, but do-it-ourselves democrats translate it in a distinctive way—not prioritizing joint visioning, but joint action.

All in all, the three cases represent substantially different and viable alternatives to deliberative models of reflection and transformation, but they are not without their specific problems. Democratic innovation of the Biest-Houtakker type tends to be confined to smaller social interventions; sometimes, however, the public good requires bigger interventions in terms of budgets and other resources to be pooled. Innovations of the Brainport-Eindhoven type claim to be good at doing exactly this, but compared to do-it-ourselves-democracy the links between meeting-room interactions and results on the ground tend to be less directly visible in such collaborative governance models. The flipside of coming to a seemingly clear conclusion at the end of an aggregative process, like the one leading to the Ukraine referendum, is not only the polarization in two camps, of which one camp remains defeated, but also the difficulty of implementing a unilateral 'no' in a fundamentally multilateral context.

At the micro-level of a lab or survey experiment, a particular democratic innovation may be singled out. At the meso- and macro-level of real-existing democratic systems, different innovations often share the same space, as indicated and exemplified in this chapter. A modern democracy can be home to and a meeting ground for models of deliberative reflection, in addition to plebiscitary and action-oriented models of democratic innovation. The result may resemble what Rosanvallon called a 'modern mixed regime', a blend of democratic models that partly overlap and supplement each other.[88] A

[86] Kolk, H. van der, *Kiezen voor een nieuw kiessstelsel*, Enschede, Universiteit Twente, 2008, p. 47.
[87] Ansell, C. and A. Gash, Collaborative Governance in Theory and Practice, *Journal of Public Administration Research and Theory*, 2008, 18, 4, pp. 543–71; Noveck, B., *Wiki Government: How Technology Can Make Government Better, Democracy Stronger, and Citizens More Powerful*, Washington, DC, Brookings Institution Press, 2009.
[88] Rosanvallon, P., *Counter-Democracy: Politics in an Age of Distrust*, Cambridge, Cambridge University Press, 2008, p. 314. Cf. Saward, M., Making Democratic Connections: Political Equality, Deliberation

challenge for twenty-first century democratic innovation is to get a deeper understanding of the tensions and variations in such modern mixed regimes, and to explore the potential and limits of mixing and mingling, as I set out to do in this book.

Before proceeding to more mixed and mingled arrangements of democratic innovation, I will first delve into another significant and strongly biased field of democratic innovation—the new plebiscitary democracy, resulting from an immensive reinvention of directly aggregative technologies, in many ways contradictory to the deliberative turn. This is an urgent and necessary step for a deeper understanding of the variations and oppositions in democratic-innovations discourse, the objective of Part I—as well as a stepping stone to Part II, advancing and exploring democratic innovations beyond mixophobia.

and Direct Democracy, *Acta Politica*, 2001, 36, pp. 361–79; Hendriks, F., *Vital Democracy: A Theory of Democracy in Action*, Oxford, Oxford University Press, 2010; Mansbridge, J., *Beyond Adversary Democracy*, New York, Basic Books, 1980; Warren, M.E., A Problem-Based Approach to Democratic Theory, *American Political Science Review*, 2017, 111, 1, pp. 39–53.

4
Exploring the new plebiscitary democracy

In an explorative way, Chapter 3 called attention to the rebound of plebiscitary democracy. This chapter sets out to further unravel the emerging, hitherto underconceptualized new plebiscitary democracy, which reinvents and radicalizes longer-existing plebiscitary methods (initiative, referendum, recall, primary, petition, poll) with new tools and applications (mostly digital). Behind it is a comparatively thin conception of democracy, which invokes the bare notion of a *demos* whose aggregated will is to steer actors and issues in public governance in a straight majoritarian way. As systematic research into the various guises, drivers, and implications of the new plebiscitary democracy is largely missing, and much less advanced than research into the deliberative turn, a gap-filling research agenda is being teased out.

Vox populi redux

In May 2018, the Spanish left-wing political party Podemos organized a digital party referendum, as they called it, on its leadership. What had happened? Pablo Iglesias, the party's outspoken leader, and his life partner Irene Montero, the party's parliamentary spokeswoman, had purchased a relatively luxurious €600,000 home with a swimming pool and a guest house. According to many within and outside the party this was a hypocritical act, running counter to earlier public statements about perverse mechanisms on the housing market. To re-establish its credibility, the leadership supported an unplanned vote of confidence, organized via the party's website, saying 'if they say we have to resign, then we will resign.'[1] Although the words 'party referendum' were being used, the procedure could just as well be likened to a recall: a voting procedure to accept or decline a leader already in the saddle.[2]

---

[1] Marcos, J., Podemos' Pablo Iglesias Calls Leadership Vote in Response to Country House Scandal, *El País*, <https://elpais.com/elpais/2018/05/21/inenglish/1526892734_555474.html>, 21 May 2019.
[2] See Box 3.2 about the recall, and its associations with representative and direct democracy. Therein also a few preliminary remarks on digital plebiscites of the type illustrated here.

Rethinking Democratic Innovation. Frank Hendriks, Oxford University Press. © Frank Hendriks (2023).
DOI: 10.1093/oso/9780192848291.003.0004

The couple ultimately survived the vote, on 28 May 2018, after winning 68.4 per cent of nearly 190,000 votes cast.

In March 2016, the Natural Environment Research Council (NERC) in the UK organized an online poll, as they called it, to involve the wider public in the naming of a new research vessel—publicly funded, then why not publicly named, the reasoning went. The NERC suggested some names—Endeavour, Falcon, Henry Worsley, David Attenborough—on which people could cast an online vote. The public was asked to suggest additional names, which could then also compete for support. The hashtag on social media became #NameOurShip. More than 3000 additional names were suggested. Former radio presenter James Hand jokingly suggested 'Boaty McBoatface', which became an instant hit. This name ultimately won the online vote, with more than 124,000 declarations of support (four times more than the name in second place: 'Poppy-Mai'). The public's favourite did, however, not become the name of the ship, but only of one of the submersibles aboard. Jo Johnson, then minister for universities and science, decided to go along with the more traditional name RSS Sir David Attenborough.[3] The formal line was that the online poll, although open to public input, was never meant to be a binding referendum.

These are just two illustrations, common practices rather than best practices, which take public voting on political actors and public governance issues well beyond the realm of traditional voting for politicians and their programmes. This is emblematic for the new twenty-first-century plebiscitary democracy that is reinventing long-existing methods (initiative, referendum, recall, primary, petition, poll) with new tools and applications (mostly and prominently online, occasionally also offline). The new plebiscitary democracy is a sprawling phenomenon that needs more all-encompassing scholarly research, as it comes in a great range of guises, with various possibilities and problems, and many critical questions still to answer. Hence, this chapter includes a research agenda—necessarily open ended—based on an explorative review of new plebiscitary formats, developing on a substratum of older plebiscitary formats, which have the following characteristics in common:

- a focus on the swift aggregation of individually expressed choices—including electronic clicks, checks, likes and other signs of support—into a collective signal believed to be the voice of the demos or the vox populi, which tends to be revered (*'vox populi, vox dei'*);

- a concentration of such citizen-input, aggregative processes on political actors and issues in public governance tending to result in binary public verdicts ('yes/no', 'for/against');
- a belief in direct voting of a highly competitive and majoritarian sort ('you vote, you decide'), centralizing mass and quantity, a bigger-the-better logic, a 'democracy of numbers'.[4]

The new plebiscitary democracy reinvents and radicalizes methods of aggregative, in particular voter democracy (as introduced in Chapter 2). It comes with a comparatively thin conceptualization of democracy, invoking the bare notion of a demos whose aggregated, amassed will is to steer actors and issues in public governance in a straight majoritarian way.[5]

Unlike deliberative democracy (and more like, for instance, stealth democracy[6]), there is no sophisticated normative political theory in place from which plebiscitary practices are deduced and legitimated. Democratic claims develop in and around new plebiscitary practice. Such claims cannot be taken for granted, but neither can they be dismissed a priori. How and to what extent democratic claims are actually realized is to be determined by the type of research proposed in the following pages.

The adjective used in plebiscitary democracy—the new incarnation as well as the older—refers to the more or less democratic uses of plebiscites or direct votes beyond merely the ballot box of general elections.[7] Direct votes or plebiscites can be either bottom-up or top-down, issue-oriented or elite-oriented (more on this in the next section). The leader-dominated variant is one of the possibilities of plebiscitary democracy, not its one and only option.[8]

---

[4] Lepore, J., *These Truths: A History of the United States*, New York, W.W. Norton, 2018.

[5] Lijphart, A., *Patterns of Democracy: Government Forms and Performance in Thirty-Six Countries*, New Haven, Yale University Press, 1999and Powell, G.B., *Elections as Instruments of Democracy: Majoritarian and Proportional Visions*, Cambridge, MA, Harvard University Press, 2000 focus on the majoritarian principle in representative electoral democracy and juxtapose it to the consensual principle. Additionally, Hendriks, F., *Vital Democracy: A Theory of Democracy in Action*, Oxford, Oxford University Press, 2010and Della Porta, D., *Can Democracy Be Saved? Participation, Deliberation and Social Movements*, Cambridge, Polity Press, 2013 focus on majoritarian versus consensual/deliberative patterns in direct and participatory democracy.

[6] Hibbing, J.R. and E. Theiss-Morse, *Stealth Democracy: Americans' Beliefs About How Government Should Work*, Cambridge, Cambridge University Press, 2002.

[7] An alternative, less common term for a direct voting procedure, borrowed from Switzerland, is 'votation', denoting '(t)he act of voting, especially when not to elect a government or head of state': Wikipedia, *Votation*, <https://en.wiktionary.org/wiki/votation>, 28 October 2019. Cheneval, F. and A. el-Wakil, The Institutional Design of Referendums: Bottom-Up and Binding, *Swiss Political Science Review*, 2018, 24, 3, pp. 294–304, reflecting on Swiss direct voting practice, use the related concept 'popular vote processes' for referendum and initiative voting in the widest sense.

[8] Green, J.E., *The Eyes of the People: Democracy in an Age of Spectatorship*, Oxford, Oxford University Press, 2010, p.5; Qvortrup, M., B. O'Leary, and R. Wintrobe, Explaining the Paradox of Plebiscites,

'May we have your votes now?'

In present-day, twenty-first-century democracy, the request 'May we have your votes now?' entails more than it used to. Not only has the 'we' taking and aggregating votes been enlarged, but so has the 'votes' that are being taken and aggregated. Citizens may still cast their votes in ballot boxes on election day, as citizens have done for decades. But nowadays they can also see them aggregated as digital signatures, checks, likes, and various sorts of electronic declarations of support in the periods between election days. The actors initiating such votes can be other citizens, non-political and non-governmental actors, but they can also be political or governmental actors with an institutionalized stake in the political system *à la* David Easton.[9] The votes may be directed at political leaders and authorities that operate within the political system or at issues or topics in the public domain. They are not confined to formal democratic decision-making.

While conceptual stretching of the concept of voting is not uncommon—'voting with your feet', popularizing some areas more than others, 'voting with your purse', supporting some brands more than others—the exploration here is primarily focused on practices that can be viewed as variants of 'voting with your hands' on public and political issues. This means that the focus is on contemporary—often device-clicking[10]—extensions of the longer-existing hand-raising, box-ticking, and button-pressing activities of individuals that amount to a collective signal with regard to political leaders or issues of public governance. (Therefore, I consider the naming of a publicly funded 'flagship' within the boundaries of the exploration but not, for example, the digital vote for 'best book of the year'). Such a constrained stretch of the public vote concept is both justifiable and urgent. New voting formats are spreading, changing democratic discourse and relations in ways not yet well understood.

We should differentiate the new plebiscitary democracy, which assumes human agency, including democratic action and discourse, from the strictly 'instrumentarian' surveillance systems that Shoshana Zuboff describes as deeply anti-democratic,[11] working towards a data-driven, behaviourist

Government and Opposition, (ahead of print) 2018, pp. 1–18; Felicetti, A. Casting a New Light on the Democratic Spectator, Democratization, 2022.

[9] Easton, D., *A Systems Analysis of Political Life*, New York, Wiley, 1965.

[10] Hill, S., *Digital Revolutions: Activism in the Internet Age*, Oxford, New Internationalist Publications, 2013; Halupka, M., Clicktivism: A Systematic Heuristic, *Policy & Internet*, 2014, 6, 2, pp. 115–32; Jeffares, S., *Interpreting Hashtag Politics: Policy Ideas in an Era of Social Media*, London, Palgrave, 2014.

[11] Zuboff, S., *The Age of Surveillance Capitalism: The Fight for a Human Future at the New Frontier of Power*, London, Profile Books, 2019, p. 20.

society model in which 'the algorithms know best'[12] and in which political action is to be avoided. Harari uses the term 'dataism' to denote the belief that refined algorithms can render democratic action and discourse obsolete in the not-too-distant future.[13] The rival idea—'techno-activism'—assumes that technology extends human agency and collective action.[14] The formats of the new plebiscitary democracy that are explored here largely follow a techno-activist approach to democracy, albeit with a particular, plebiscitary leaning. In exploring these formats, I do not negate the scope for technical applications with non-democratic ambitions in dire need of investigation too; the examination of these, however, falls outside the scope of this book.

New plebiscitary, deliberative, and established electoral democracy

This chapter focuses on the sprawling new plebiscitary democracy. Emerging twenty-first-century plebiscitary practices (the highlighted circle on the left in Figure 4.1) are viewed in addition to established electoral democracy (the rectangle in Figure 4.1), next to communicative practices associated with the deliberative turn at the end of the twentieth century (the circle on the right in Figure 4.1). As indicated in Chapter 3, deliberative additions include random mini-publics, juries, citizens' assemblies, consensus conferences, planning cells, and the like; they are geared at thoughtful, reflective, and transformative processes of public opinion formation.[15] Such formats have thus far received far more encompassing attention in the democratic-innovations literature than the sprawling and nascent formats of the new plebiscitary democracy.

The new plebiscitary formats are comparatively underconceptualized, notwithstanding the existence of important alerts of related developments.[16] The subfield of the new 'digital-age' democracy is covered by many studies

[12] Zuboff, S., *The Age of Surveillance Capitalism: The Fight for a Human Future at the New Frontier of Power*, London, Profile Books, 2019, p. 433.

[13] Harari, Y.N., *Homo Deus: A Brief History of Tomorrow*, London, Vintage, 2017, pp. 428–62.

[14] The term 'techno-activism' is preferred to Harari's term 'techno-humanism' that may prompt much wider meanings of 'humanistic' (people's better qualities), which are not automatically included in techno-activism. See Harari, Y.N., *Homo Deus: A Brief History of Tomorrow*, London, Vintage, 2017, pp. 409–27.

[15] See Dryzek, J.S., *Deliberative Democracy and beyond: Liberals, Critics, Contestations*, Oxford, Oxford University Press, 2000; Gastil, J. and P. Levine (eds), *The Deliberative Democracy Handbook*, San Francisco, Jossey-Bass, 2005; Bächtiger, A., S. Niemeyer, M. Neblo, M.R. Steenbergen, and J. Steiner, Disentangling Diversity in Deliberative Democracy: Competing Theories, Their Empirical Blind-spots, and Complementarities, *Journal of Political Philosophy*, 2010, 18, 1, pp. 32–63.

[16] Cain, B.E., R.J. Dalton, and S.E. Scarrow (eds), *Democracy Transformed: Expanding Political Opportunities in Advanced Industrial Democracies*, Oxford, Oxford University Press, 2003; Rowe, G. and L.J. Frewer, A Typology of Public Engagement Mechanisms, *Science, Technology & Human Values*, 2005, 30, 2, pp. 251–90; Rosanvallon, P., *Counter-Demcoracy: Politics in an Age of Distrust*, Cambridge, Cambridge University Press, 2008; Keane, J., *The Life and Death of Democracy*, London, Simon & Schuster, 2009;

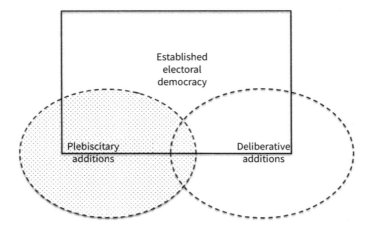

Figure 4.1 New plebiscitary, deliberative, and electoral democracy

that often focus on versions with a deliberative or collaborative setup: digital town meetings, online discussion forums, Wiki-style law-making, hackathons, collaborative editing, and similar formats for interactive co-creation.[17] More voting-oriented, plebiscitary versions have attracted some attention,[18] but in terms of systematic theorizing and comparative analysis much ground is still uncovered. Therefore, the central objective of this chapter is to take a next step in exploring and mapping the diversity of twenty-first-century plebiscitary democracy, and to formulate a much-needed research agenda with regard to it.

Green, J.E., *The Eyes of the People: Democracy in an Age of Spectatorship*, Oxford, Oxford University Press, 2010.

[17] Noveck, B., *Wiki Government: How Technology Can Make Government Better, Democracy Stronger, and Citizens More Powerful*, Washington, DC, Brookings Institution Press, 2009; Noveck, B., *Smart Citizens, Smarter State: The Technologies of Expertise and the Future of Governing*, Cambridge, MA, Harvard University Press, 2015; Mulgan, G., *Big Mind: How Collective Intelligence Can Change our World*, Princeton, Princeton University Press, 2018; Bernholz, L., H. Landemore, and R. Reich (eds), *Digital Technology and Democratic Theory*, Chicago, Chicago University Press, 2021.

[18] Susskind, J., *Future Politics: Living Together in a World Transformed by Tech*, Oxford, Oxford University Press, 2018, p. 239–43 distinguishes five roads that future digital democracy can take: the one that he calls 'direct democracy' is akin to the plebiscitary additions to electoral democracy that I discuss in the next section; a particular part of what I discuss there also comes close to what Susskind calls 'data democracy'. His other three roads lead to 'AI democracy' (using artificial intelligence systems to perform specific tasks), 'wiki democracy' (digital co-production in Wikipedia-style) and 'deliberative democracy' (reflective discussion by digital means) are not plebiscitary by design. In Susskind's terms, the latter reflect the 'talkers' and not the 'counters' in democratic innovation debate. See Susskind, J., *Future Politics: Living Together in a World Transformed by Tech*, Oxford, Oxford University Press, 2018, pp. 224–5. A lot of energy, according to Susskind, has been invested in 'new ways of doing old things', electronically enhanced but not radically new: working together on projects, organizing campaigns, action, and protest. See Susskind, J., *Future Politics: Living Together in a World Transformed by Tech*, Oxford, Oxford University Press, 2018, pp. 219–21.

Established electoral democracy, the rectangle in Figure 4.1, is far from underconceptualized.[19] Here, the distinction between plurality/majority systems versus systems of proportional representation, indicative of pendulum versus consensus democracy, is most useful and relevant (see Chapter 2). Although winner-takes-all systems of plurality/majority voting at face value seem fertile breeding grounds for new plebiscitary practices, we do not yet know whether the emerging formats of plebiscitary democracy are taking root any less in electoral systems of proportional representation. This is actually one of the questions that requires more systematic research, the basic lines of which will be drawn in the concluding section. There the relationship between deliberative and plebiscitary additions to electoral democracy will also be interrogated.

The new plebiscitary democracy: Emerging formats

In the following, I propose a tentative typology of the new plebiscitary democracy, distinguishing between four types of emerging plebiscitary formats. The new formats regenerate longer-existing methods (initiative, referendum, recall, primary, petition, poll) with new tools and applications. The Podemos and NERC votes mentioned as opening examples illustrate, in specific ways, two of these general types: Type-I plebiscitary voting that operates 'inside-out'—pushed by parties or institutions that make up the political system—and is primarily 'leader-focused' (the Podemos example); and Type-II plebiscitary voting that also operates 'inside-out' but is basically 'issue-focused' (the NERC example).[20]

There are also new types of votes emerging that work from the outside in—pushed by actors or groups beyond the set of parties and institutions that are commonly understood as the political system. Ideal-typically, they can focus their vote-collecting activities on political elites and leaders—Type III plebiscitary voting—or on particular public issues—Type IV plebiscitary voting. The resulting matrix of ideal-typical options is depicted in Table 4.1. In democratic practice, we may see combinations or clusters of such ideal types developing, but to understand these properly we first need to see the underlying mechanisms and diversity of formats.

---

[19] Sartori, G., *Parties and Party Systems: A Framework for Analysis*, Cambridge, Cambridge University Press, 2016 (originally 1976); Lijphart, A., *Patterns of Democracy: Government Forms and Performance in Thirty-Six Countries*, New Haven, Yale University Press, 1999; Diamond, L. and M.F. Plattner (eds), *Electoral Systems and Democracy*, Baltimore, The Johns Hopkins University Press, 2006.

[20] The 'party referendum' organized by Podemos was targeted at its political leadership. The online poll/design contest organized by the NERC was focused on the proper naming of a publicly funded research vessel: arguably an issue of public governance.

Table 4.1 The new plebiscitary democracy: mapping emerging formats.

	Focus: political leaders (elite-oriented)	Focus: public issues (content-oriented)
Initiative: inside-out ('top-down')	*TYPE I* *Emerging formats* Leadership-challenging clicksultation (e.g. Podemos e-referendum/recall on party leadership) Elite-forging digital primaries (e.g. European Green Party OpenOnline Primary) Leadership-monitoring internet polls (e.g. party-commissioned popularity polls made public) Elite-monitoring social media/data analytics (e.g. government-commissioned sentiment ratings made public) *Underlying formats* Party-organized primaries and recalls, elite-monitoring polls (pre-internet)	*TYPE II* *Emerging formats* Ideas contest with audience voting (e.g. NERC NameOurShip; Rotterdam City Initiative contest) Ad hoc consultative plebiscites (e.g. European daylight saving survey; Australian gay marriage plebiscite) Party-organized clicksultation on political issues and ideas (e.g. Five Star Movement e-referendums) Politically directed social media rallies on 'hot topics' (e.g. Trump social media framing of 'migrant caravan') *Underlying formats* Top-down referendums and plebiscites, issue-oriented polls (pre-internet)
Initiative: outside-in ('bottom-up')	*TYPE III* *Emerging formats* Elite-rating vox polls/online surveys (e.g. media-commissioned online popularity contests) Leadership-challenging clicktivism (e.g. Zutphen mayor's challenge, #NotMyPresident) Leader-supporting clicktivism (e.g. #ImWithHer, #StudentsForTrump) Elite-monitoring social media/data analytics (e.g. watchdog-exposed sentiment ratings of elites) *Underlying formats* Voter-imposed recalls, elite-focused petitions and polls (pre-internet)	*TYPE IV* *Emerging formats* Idea-challenging/supporting e-petitions (e.g. e-petition for second Brexit referendum) Issue-focused clicktivism platforms (e.g. Decide-Madrid, #YouthForClimate) Unofficial quasi-referendums (e.g. ANWB quasi-referendum on road pricing) Divisive content pushing/hot-topic trolling (e.g. foreign actors campaigning for anti-Islam clicks in the USA) *Underlying formats* Voter-imposed initiatives, bottom-up referendums, issue-oriented petitions and polls (pre-internet)

Emerging formats: Inside-out

Type-I and Type-II plebiscitary votes share a top-down or more precisely an inside-out logic of mobilizing choice signals and interpreting them as an aggregated public choice. They reinvent, with new formats, longer-existing mechanisms such as party primaries, party recalls, and top-down (i.e. government-initiated) referendums and (pre-internet) opinion polling steered by political actors and public authorities.[21] When these initiatives involve the aggregation of electronic clicks, the term 'clicksultation' is used as a contraction of clicks and consultation.[22] Clicksultation operates top-down or more precisely inside-out, and should be distinguished from clicktivism,[23] which combines clicks with activism, operating bottom-up or rather outside-in.[24] At this point we should recall that we are looking here at formats that numerically aggregate individual signals into a collective signal or *vox populi*, not just any form of online engagement. Two people sharing a political post may be an expression of online engagement but not so much an expression of twenty-first-century plebiscitary democracy as, say, a crowd of two million liking such a post.[25]

Type I, inside-out and elite-focused—Besides Podemos, various other political parties have also taken steps into the realm of Type-I voting. The European Green Party, for instance, organized an 'open online primary', as they called it, to select top candidates (*Spitzenkandidaten*) for the European parliamentary elections of 2014. Such a digital primary has an elite-forging logic to it, but leadership-challenging digital consultations can also be organized quite easily, as the earlier Podemos example testifies. As we saw, this worked practically as a party-initiated recall, organized through the Podemos website, even

[21] Cain, B.E., R.J. Dalton, and S.E. Scarrow (eds), *Democracy Transformed: Expanding Political Opportunities in Advanced Industrial Democracies*, Oxford, Oxford University Press, 2003; Altman, D., The Potential of Direct Democracy: A Global Measure (1900–2014), *Social Indicators Research*, 2017, 133, 3, pp. 1207–27; Hollander, S., *The Politics of Referendum Use in European Democracies*, London, Palgrave, 2019.

[22] Conventionally a plebiscite is called 'consultative' when political actors heed the voice of the people in a top-down fashion without formally binding consequences. This was the case here (although the Podemos vote was taken seriously, the compliance by the leadership was voluntary) and is usually also the case in similar forms of digital voting.

[23] Halupka, M., Clicktivism: A Systematic Heuristic, *Policy & Internet*, 2014, 6, 2, pp. 115–32; Lindgren, S., The Work of Audiences in the Age of Clicktivism; On the Ins and Outs of Distributed Participation, *Media Fields Journal*, 2015, 10, pp. 1–6.

[24] Although 'top-down' versus 'bottom-up' are often used as (slightly imprecise) shorthand for similar patterns, I take 'inside-out' versus 'outside-in' as the preferred analytical distinction, as it highlights the difference between direct votes that are initiated from positions within the political system *à la* Easton versus direct votes that are initiated from positions external or peripheral to the political system. See Easton, D., *A Systems Analysis of Political Life*, New York, Wiley, 1965.

[25] Jeffares, S., *Interpreting Hashtag Politics: Policy Ideas in an Era of Social Media*, London, Palgrave, 2014.

though it was called a 'party referendum' in line with more publicly resonant language.

Party- and government-initiated polls to legitimize and serve political and executive leadership have become easier and less expensive to organize on a frequent basis with present-day technology. Under pre-internet circumstances, specialized organizations were often hired for designing and conducting large-scale public polls, while nowadays virtually all of this can be done in-house. That the quality of public polling often falls back to straw-polling practices—straying from the scientific approach to representative sampling and proper authentication—is often taken for granted in these practices.[26] I include such practices here to the extent that their results are expressed as representative claims in democratic discourse,[27] regarding, in this subcategory, the selection or deselection of political leadership. (Party- or government-initiated popularity polls that are used only internally to monitor the approval rates of politicians are excluded from this overview of the new plebiscitary democracy.)

A next step on this path (inside-out, elite-focused) is the deployment of social media and big data analytics to reveal which politician, party, or authority is developing positive or negative sentiment among the public. The promise of data analytics is that vital information, when it comes to political preferences, can be distilled from social media choices already collected in various places. Only when the aggregated choices are publicly revealed and made part of democratic discourse—which is not very often thus far—do the underlying practices fit the previous definition of the new plebiscitary democracy.[28] Until now, the results of social media and big data analytics in the political realm have tended to stay within campaign teams, using the information for covert political micro-targeting: knowing who to focus on with variable political messages from a political party or candidate in order to get better results on election day.[29]

Type II, inside-out and issue-focused—The Type-II illustration that figured at the start of this chapter was the NERC-initiated digital consultation of the

---

[26] Bishop, G., *The Illusion of Public Opinion*, New York, Rowman & Littlefield, 2005.

[27] Saward, M., *The Representative Claim*, Oxford, Oxford University Press, 2010.

[28] In these cases plebiscitary democracy overlaps with what Susskind describes as data democracy. See Susskind, J., *Future Politics: Living Together in a World Transformed by Tech*, Oxford, Oxford University Press, 2018, pp. 246–50. More on the instrumental version of data democracy in Dunleavy, P., H. Margetts, S. Bastow, and J. Tinkler, New Public Management is Dead: Long Live Digital-Era Governance, *Journal of Public Administration Research and Theory*, 2005, 16, 3, pp. 467–94; Giest, S., Big Data for Policymaking: Fad or Fasttrack?, *Policy Sciences*, 2017, 50, 3, pp. 367–82.

[29] Zuiderveen Borgesius, F.J., J. Möller, S. Kruikjemeier, R. Fathaigh, K. Irion, T. Dobber, B. Bodo, and C. de Vreese, Online Political Microtargeting: Promises and Threats for Democracy, *Utrecht Law Review*, 2018, 14, 1, pp. 82–96.

general public that resulted in 'Boaty-McBoatface' being pushed forward as the name for the publicly financed flagship in question. Here, the aggregated voice of the people, backed by 124,000 declarations of support, was ultimately not followed by the public authorities that had sought it. It this sense, the new plebiscitary democracy is not so different from older and other expressions of democracy, in which the public voice is also not always or automatically followed.

There are various instances reported, however, where clicksultation did in fact lead to government action. For instance, like so many other cities, Rotterdam experimented with a so-called design competition for city-enhancing ideas. Social entrepreneurs could propose ideas, the general public could express their support digitally, and the winning idea would be implemented.[30] Practices like these mobilize support digitally, through clicks of various sorts, and are often set up in a competitive fashion: ideas competing with each other for support in a win-or-lose format. In popular television language of the day: 'you vote, you decide'.[31]

If two options are specifically compared (yes or no to an idea or proposal, to a plan A or a plan B), the language of referendums is never far away, even when a referendum is formally speaking not on the roll. When Australia, between 12 September and 7 November 2017, organized a non-formal citizen survey on same-sex marriage, *The Economist* described it plainly as 'a plebiscite by another name'.[32] The Australian coalition government of the day had pledged to allow a private member's bill and a conscience vote in parliament on same-sex marriage if the informal plebiscite returned a majority 'yes', which it did (with 61.6 per cent). This opened the road to parliamentary debate and ultimately an approved Marriage Amendment. The Australian informal plebiscite was a special exhibit of present-day plebiscitary democracy using non-digital infrastructure—technically it was a non-formal postal survey.[33] When in 2018 the European Commission organized a citizen survey

---

[30] In subsequent years the winning ideas were a pedestrian air-passage, a skating rink, and an urban surf arena.

[31] The slogan made popular by the *Idols* song contest, which travelled from the UK to the USA, and then to a great many other countries. See Ross, S.M., *Beyond the Box: Television and the Internet*, Oxford, Blackwell, 2008. *American Idol* introduced text-message voting in 2003 and online voting in 2011.

[32] The Economist, *Almost there—Australian voters approve gay marriage*, <https://www.economist.com/asia/2017/11/15/australian-voters-approve-gay-marriage>, 16 November 2017. The qualification 'plebiscite by another name' is consonant with e.g., Altman's classification, which distinguishes top-down, government-initiated, facultative plebiscites (the Australian example checks all these boxes) from bottom-up, signature-triggered referendums and initiatives. See Altman, D., The Potential of Direct Democracy: A Global Measure (1900–2014), *Social Indicators Research*, 2017, 133, 3, pp. 1207–27.

[33] Another rare example would be a majoritarian 'hat-on hat-off' voting procedure, referring to popular TV formats ('you vote, you decide!') in public meetings that previously averted direct voting. Non-digital, low-tech, but significant in cultural terms.

on the issue of daylight saving, however, it complied again with the default of the new plebiscitary democracy and organized it as an online survey.

Digital consultations such as the recurring internet votes on specific issues triggered by the populist Five Star Movement in Italy are supposed to establish a direct connection between politicians and voters on an issue-by-issue basis.[34] Here, plebiscitary votes are closely associated with a populist vision of direct democracy, in opposition to the established elites and institutions of representative democracy.[35] Looking into the Five Star Movement as well as Podemos, Paolo Gerbaudo detects a dominant top-down and quantitative 'plebiscitarian' logic in their digital voting practices, overshadowing the bottom-up, qualitative, more or less deliberative digital innovations that have also been attempted.[36]

A next step in this category—a step that goes too far, according to many—is the strategic mobilization of online and social media 'rallies' on hot topics, organized by political actors interested in showing mass traction on such topics. An illustration is the framing of the 'migrant caravan' by the Trump presidency in 2018.[37] Social media traction was used as vindication of presidential policy: your worries steer my policy on this issue. Consent for (re)using digital footprints in such a way is often taken for granted, while proper authentication (is the aggregation based on a verified one-person-one-signal basis or the product of bots and fake accounts?) is often lacking.

The issue of voting inflation—The previous illustration prompts an issue that affects all four categories. The core idea of democracy assumes a *demos* consisting of free (non-coerced) and equal citizens ('one person, one vote'). Theoretically, it cannot consist of (ro)bots steered to push numbers of electronic votes (likes, retweets, and so on) or fake accounts suggesting individual citizens. The problem is, however, that it is not so clear when this is happening, which may result in artificially inflated claims dressed up as the public voice being pumped around.[38] Proper mechanisms for authentication are

[34] Other political parties experimenting with digital voter feedback include the German Pirates, Podemos in Spain, and Jeremy Corbyn's Labour Party that organized internet polls on issues such as military action against IS. In the USA, Capitol Bells is a voter app that allows constituents to informally vote on bills in the US House of Representative.

[35] Franzosi, P., F. Marone, E. Salvati, Populism and Euroscepticism in the Italian Five Star Movement, *The International Spectator*, 2015, 50, 2, pp. 109–24.

[36] Gerbaudo P., Are Digital Parties more Democratic than Traditional Parties? Evaluating Podemos and Movimento 5 Stelle's Online Decision-Making Platforms, *Party Politics*, 2021, 27, 4, p. 731.

[37] Ahmed, A., K. Rogers, and J. Ernst, How the Mighty Caravan Became a Trump Election Strategy, *New York Times*, <www.nytimes.com/2018/10/24/world/americas/migrant-caravan-trump.html>, 24 October 2018; Dreyfuss, E., Alert: Don't Believe Everything You Read About the Migrant Caravan, *Wired*, <www.wired.com/story/mexico-migrant-caravan-misinformation-alert>, 23 October 2018.

[38] Tanasoca, A., Against Bot Democracy: The Dangers of Epistemic Double-Counting, *Perspectives on Politics*, 2019, pp. 1–15.

needed but not always present. Experiment first and improve later is quite typical of how the new plebiscitary democracy is being designed.

Another issue, also related to voting inflation, is the mobilization of click baits to give traction to 'leading' politicians and 'trending' topics in pumped-up numbers. New tech is clearly interfering here, although voting cascades and crazes are not new to democratic life.[39]

Emerging formats: Outside-in

Type-III and Type-IV plebiscitary votes share a bottom-up or, more precisely, an outside-in logic of collecting and aggregating choice-signals via regenerated plebiscitary formats. This means that the initiative lies predominantly with societal and private actors that approach the political system and its dealings from an external vantage point, attempting to force their messages into the political system, and onto it (as opposed to being consulted by system actors, which is the realm of Type-I and Type-II). The organizers of Type-III and Type-IV votes emulate, in new ways, existing formats like the voter-imposed recall, the voter-imposed initiative, the bottom-up referendum, the signature-based petition, and—again—the opinion poll (here the bottom-up version of it, commissioned by actors external to the political system).

Type III, outside-in and elite-focused—In 1824, the *Harrisburg Pennsylvanian* organized one of the first political polls, asking a convenience sample about their preferred candidate in the Jackson–Adams presidential race.[40] It was a typical straw poll based on a non-random sample, which in new guises can be found as 'vox polls' on the websites of numerous media and other public organizations nowadays.[41] Such instances of digital polling, using electronic convenience samples to gauge the vox populi quickly, have become virtually countless since the massive uptake of broadband internet in the early 2000s. If digital readers and website visitors are asked to rate political leaders, parties, or authorities, we have an instance of a Type-III vox poll. (If they

---

[39] Some would say that creating a 'buzz' via old-school, podium-to-podium, and door-to-door political canvassing was in essence a similar, although offline, process.

[40] According to Smith this was the first contested presidential election that would be largely decided by popular vote. See Smith, T.W., The First Straw A Study of the Origins of Election Polls, *Public Opinion Quarterly*, 1990, 54, 1, p. 23. According to Lepore, the Jackson–Adams race, won by Jackson, marked the birth of American populism, and the ascendency of 'King Numbers'. See Lepore, J., *These Truths: A History of the United States*, New York, W.W. Norton, 2018, pp. 180–8. 'The rule of numbers had begun' Lepore, J., *These Truths: A History of the United States*, New York, W.W. Norton, 2018, p. 188.

[41] Bishop, G., *The Illusion of Public Opinion*, New York, Rowman & Littlefield, 2005; Holtz-Bacha, C. and J. Strömbäck, *Opinion Polls and the Media: Reflecting and Shaping Public Opinion*, New York, Palgrave, 2012.

are asked to say 'yes' or 'no' to particular issues, we get the attributes of the Type-IV version that will be discussed next.)

A modern case of outside-in clicktivism (bottom-up activism using digital clicks) to challenge political leadership was played out in the Dutch city of Zutphen. In 2015, the politically selected candidate for the office of mayor (*ad interim*) in this town was attacked by an internet poll organized by a regional newspaper and by an e-petition organized by a worried citizen. Both were highly negative about the candidate: 95 per cent of the participants in the internet poll agreed with the statement that this candidate 'should stay away'; the e-petition against this candidate immediately received 2,326 signatures. Even though neither had any formal status within the nomination procedure they effectively forced the withdrawal of the candidate, who before these bouts of clicktivism had been very close to nomination.[42]

An example of political leader-supporting clicktivism pushed by non-system actors was the hashtag action #ImWithHer, a digital campaign that was meant to show massive support for Hillary Clinton as candidate for the US presidential elections of 2016. The hashtag was actively pushed by celebrities such as Jennifer Lopez, Alicia Keys, Rihanna, and others.[43] #ImWithHer was not invented or hosted by the relatively centralized official Clinton campaign, which nevertheless jumped on the bandwagon quite happily, albeit not with the desired result. The 2016 Trump campaign organization showed a different, more decentralized, way of combining its own activities with external clicktivism. The combined effect in terms of aggregated supportive social media traction was significantly larger for Trump as a candidate and ultimately president-elect.[44]

Distilling from social media choices how people react to political leaders—who's trending, who's not?—is an important playing field for (new) media and (big) data and knowledge centres. When such elite-monitoring analyses are pushed outside-in by knowledge centres or media on their own initiative or commissioned by civil society organizations, they can be viewed as expressions of Type-III formats. The precondition for acknowledging these as formats of new plebiscitary democracy is, again, that the aggregated public

---

[42] The candidate mayor (*ad interim*) was the liberal-conservative politician Loek Hermans of the People's Party for Freedom and Democracy (VVD), who was nominated for this office by Clemens Cornielje, the Queen's Commissioner of the same political party responsible for pre-selection.

[43] Leow, A., Celebrities Take to Social Media to say #ImWithHer or Just Get out the Vote, *Straits Times*, <www.straitstimes.com/world/united-states/celebrities-take-to-social-media-to-say-imwithher-or-just-get-out-the-vote>, 20 November 2016.

[44] Loon, A. van, Social Media Predicted Trump's Win, *We Are Social*, <https://wearesocial.com/blog/2016/11/social-media-predicted-trumps-win.>, 26 November 2016; Pettigrew, E., How Facebook Saw Trump Coming When No One Else Did, *Medium*, https://medium.com/@erinpettigrew/how-facebook-saw-trump-coming-when-no-one-else-did-84cd6b4e0d8e, 9 November 2016.

voice must be publicly revealed and made part of democratic discourse. The difference with the elite-rating internet polls described previously is that in such polls people are explicitly asked to evaluate politicians, whereas in social media analytics evaluative questions are asked after data collection, which means that consent to use clicks for evaluative purposes is assumed rather than explicitly given.[45] The common denominator here is the aggregative construction of a public verdict based on individually expressed evaluations, combined with and driven by an interest in mass and quantity ('King Numbers' in Lepore's terms). The more positive digital traffic there is, the more support a politician is supposed to have.

Type IV, outside-in and issue-focused—Type-IV voting practices share this interest in mass and quantity, working from the outside in, but are primarily focused on support for public issues. On top of the longer-existing offline version of the petition—basically an aggregated declaration of support—the phenomenon of the e-petition has spread widely. Some portals for e-petitions are privately hosted, some are publicly hosted, but as a rule e-petitions are an outside-in phenomenon. For instance, the UK government may host www.petition.parliament.uk but it does not initiate the e-petitions that appear on this site, nor does it canvass support for it. When an e-petition receives more than 10,000 signatures the UK government promises to respond to the public request voiced in it, and above 100,000 signatures a debate in parliament is considered.[46] Shortly after the Brexit-referendum, more than 4.15 million people supported an e-petition posted on this website calling for a second EU referendum. The government rejected the 'representative claim' of the initiators, arguing that the original referendum had produced a clear and legitimate majority, which did not silence the popular call for a second referendum.[47]

Beyond purpose-built e-petition websites, various other electronic platforms serve to collect and amass electronic signs of public (dis)approval. First, these may be websites built for other purposes besides signature collection that, however, also facilitate the count of likes, checks, thumbs-up,

---

[45] Craglia, M. and L. Shanley, Data Democracy: Increased Supply of Geospatial Information and Expanded Participatory Processes in the Production of Data, *International Journal of Digital Earth*, 2015, 8, 9, pp. 679–93.

[46] Many countries have similar e-petition websites and procedures. In the USA it is aptly named 'We the People'. For a critical analysis, see Noveck, B., *Smart Citizens, Smarter State: The Technologies of Expertise and the Future of Governing*, Cambridge, MA, Harvard University Press, 2015.

[47] A more successful example from the UK is the website 38Degrees which hosted an e-petition to help stop England's publicly owned forests and woodland from being privatized. In 2011, half a million people put their name to its petition which forced the environment secretary to reverse her policy. See Howard, E., How 'Clicktivism' Has Changed the Face of Political Campaigns, *The Guardian*, <www.theguardian.com/society/2014/sep/24/clicktivism-changed-political-campaigns-38-degrees-change>, 24 September 2014.

or equivalent signs of support. Illustrations include the websites of *Decide-Madrid* and *Frankfurt Fragt Mich*, which among other things track the support for different urban initiatives in quantitative terms.[48] Secondly, these may be social media platforms like Facebook, WhatsApp, Twitter, and Instagram, which, in addition to many other things, facilitate the bottom-up aggregation of support for issues. This works to a large extent numerically and competitively.[49] How many Facebook likes did some claim by an ideational group get? How many (re)tweets were voiced and counted on Twitter in support of some political message? How many digital photos were shared under a particular hashtag? Prominent hashtag actions for an issue are #YouthForClimate, #JeSuisCharlie, #Blacklivesmatter.[50] As usual in the new plebiscitary democracy 'size matters': the more declarations of public support aggregated, the stronger the initiators' political claim—in this category regarding an issue of public concern—is assumed to be.[51]

In 2010, the automobile club of the Netherlands, the ANWB, asked their numerous members to respond to a poll on their website related to government plans to introduce a version of road pricing. It also worked as an unofficial bottom-up referendum because it was presented as such by the car-friendly national newspaper *De Telegraaf*. For several days in a row it ran headlines like 'For or against?', 'Numbers go through the roof', 'Crushing no, more than 89% against road pricing'. The government withdrew its plans, with reference to the 'apparent' opposition in society.

A next step in this category—arguably onto a slippery slope, and not to be ignored in a candid group portrait of new plebiscitary practices—is the mobilization of clicks on hot topics by political outsiders (sometimes foreign) with the intention of aggregating and amplifying political opinions that are favourable, materially or immaterially, to these actors. An example is a group working from former Yugoslavia, trying to get as many lucrative clicks from American Trump supporters, feeding them with anti-Islam

---

[48] See <https://decide.madrid.es/condiciones-de-uso> and < https://www.ffm.de/frankfurt/de/home>, n.d. Such websites are places where people can start an urban initiative. In addition, they do what electronic formats do well: quantifying numbers of comments and declarations of support.

[49] Sunstein, C., *#Republic: Divided Democracy in the Age of Social Media*, Princeton, Princeton University Press, 2017; Nagle, A., *Kill All Normies: Online Culture Wars from 4chan and Tumblr to Trump and the Alt-Right*, London, Zero Books, 2017.

[50] A more ironic, but no less iconic, example is the hashtag action/petition #JusticeForHarambe, commemorating the shot Cininnati Zoo gorilla called Harambe, 'demanding' the authorities to hold the child's parents responsible. See Nagle, A., *Kill All Normies: Online Culture Wars from 4chan and Tumblr to Trump and the Alt-Right*, London, Zero Books, 2017.

[51] Although uncontested definitions of the political versus the apolitical are hard to find, it is widely accepted that #Blacklivesmatter is deeply political, focused on an issue of public concern, other than, for instance, a hashtag action in support of some sports team—clearly not the focus of the exploration here.

content such as: 'MOB of angry muslims ravage through US neighborhood threatening to rape women'.[52] While getting their clicks, and perhaps kicks, such disrupters create public sentiments, revealed in numbers, around public issues. Again: not an entirely new challenge to democracy, but technically facilitated in ways hitherto unseen.

Central points and caveats

The claim here, it needs to be emphasized, is not that new plebiscitary formats are successful all round. The point is that new formats of plebiscitary democracy are widely emerging and, as an interrelated complex of practices, changing democratic discourse and relations in many significant ways that are as yet under-researched and under-conceptualized. Hence, the call to develop a systematic research agenda and the attempt to understand emerging formats as interrelated empirical phenomena. The four types previously outlined can help to map the variety of forms as well as the evolving hybrids involving present-day plebiscitary formats (see Table 4.1).

Table 4.1 maps new territory in four general directions, sketching the currently most relevant variety without pretending to be complete or exhaustive. This would indicate a grave misunderstanding of the situation. Plebiscitary democracy is a sprawling phenomenon that is still very much in development. The contemporary formats mentioned are in different stages of institutionalization. The e-petition and the internet poll, for instance, are more institutionalized than the digital primary and the electronic design contest. Some formats, such as the Rotterdam City Initiative contest, were discontinued after a few years of practice and have been exchanged for other experiments. Compared to the new plebiscitary formats, the older underlying formats—initiative, referendum, recall, primary, petition, public poll (pre-internet)—are clearly further regularized and codified in textbook varieties.[53] The developing formats of the new plebiscitary democracy are not yet

[52] Real Truth Exposed, *Muslims ravage through US neighborhood*, <https://www.facebook.com/1121413461303246/posts/muslims-ravage-through-us-neighborhoodreal-truth-exposed-againheadlines-mob-of-2/1126824964095429/>, 30 January 2017. Or: Schenk, M., *Muslim figure: 'We must have pork-free menus or we will leave US' What's your response?*, <https://leadstories.com/hoax-alert/2019/03/fake-news-muslim-figure-we-must-have-pork-free-menus-or-we-will-leave-us-how-would-you-respond-this.html>, 10 March 2019.

[53] Cronin, T. E., *Direct Democracy: The Politics of Referendum, Initiative, and Recall*, Cambridge, MA, Harvard University Press, 1989; Altman, D., *Direct Democracy Worldwide*, Cambridge, Cambridge University Press, 2011; Altman, D., *The Potential of Direct Democracy: A Global Measure (1900–2014)*, Social Indicators Research, 2017, 133, 3, pp. 1207–27.

in that stage of institutionalization and codification. The emergent, varied, and sprawling nature of the phenomenon will complicate but should not stop the exploration and documentation of the phenomenon.

It is clear that the developing plebiscitary democracy comes in many shapes and forms. Yet, under the many expressions common traits can be detected, most prominently the centralization of individual choice signals, which in one way or another are aggregated into a collective vote or public voice. The related message, always implicit, sometimes explicit, is that everyone can effectively rate things and people in the public realm—Andrew Keen called this 'The Cult of the Amateur'[54]—and that the resulting aggregated ratings should be taken seriously in the formation and translation of public opinion.[55] The classic expression 'vox populi, vox dei', rendering the voice of the people sacrosanct, is refurbished and writ large in the new plebiscitary democracy.[56]

New plebiscitary mechanisms are often electronically enhanced, which makes this a prominent instrumental feature.[57] More central to its character, however, is the fact that the new plebiscitary voting practices tend to boil down to binary public verdicts (for/against, yes/no) wherein a bigger-the-better logic prevails. Claims with many clicks, likes, and checks behind them are assumed to be the more legitimate claims than those with less, and presumably strong enough to compete with the representative claims of political parties and ideational groups. Numbers of followers make the difference in a democratic ethos that is fiercely majoritarian and competitive. Jill Lepore argues that a 'democracy of numbers', as she calls it, is deeply American,[58]

---

[54] Keen, A., *The Cult of the Amateur*, New York, Doubleday, 2007.

[55] Harari, Y.N., *Homo Deus: A Brief History of Tomorrow*, London, Vintage, 2017, p. 271; Susskind, J., *Future Politics: Living Together in a World Transformed by Tech*, Oxford, Oxford University Press, 2018, p. 139.

[56] The classic expression was literally quoted by Elon Musk in a tweet announcing the return of Donald Trump on Twitter after a digital plebiscite, 20 November 2022: 'The people have spoken. Trump will be reinstated. Vox Populi, Vox Dei'—a rather primitive variant of a Type-III (elite-oriented/outside-in initiated) digital plebiscite. In a wink, more than 15m Twitter votes were cast, with 51.8 per cent in favour of reinstating Trump on Twitter. During the poll, Elon Musk acknowledged that the vote numbers were being affected by automated bots, and indicated there was a need to clean up Twitter polls from being influenced by 'bot and troll armies'. *The Guardian* <https://amp.theguardian.com/us-news/2022/nov/20/twitter-lifts-donald-trump-ban-after-elon-musks-poll> 20 November 2022.

[57] Yet we must resist the temptation to equate 'plebiscitary democracy' automatically with 'digital democracy', even when the double meaning of digital (electronic and dichotomous) nicely captures a large part of the new plebiscitary democracy. There are, however, also non-electronic expressions of plebiscitary democracy to consider, as well as non-binary votes. Moreover, digital democracy also comprises formats (for instance platforms used for networked deliberation) that are not plebiscitary in the sense of the advanced argument.

[58] Lepore, J., *These Truths: A History of the United States*, New York, W.W. Norton, 2018.

but as we have seen a new democracy of numbers is coming to the fore in other places as well.[59]

New plebiscitary practices tend to expand or radicalize longer-existing formats with new means. The centuries-old petition, for instance, is being echoed and blown up in numerous present-day expressions of clicktivism. In addition, new ways of voting are often likened to or presented as a 'referendum', even when technically speaking a party recall (see the Podemos example) or an internet survey (see the ANWB example) would be a more accurate frame of reference. The use of referendum language far beyond its formal niche is a remarkable by-product of the new plebiscitary democracy. When the US Congressional elections of 2018 are dubbed a 'referendum' on the Trump presidency, or when the European Parliament elections of 2019 are framed as a 'referendum' on the borderless Europe of the elites versus the Europe of the people, we see plebiscitary discourse hooking onto the realm of electoral democracy.

As Figure 4.1 suggests, the new plebiscitary democracy develops to some extent connected with, and to some extent detached from, established electoral democracy. Clicktivism of the #JeSuisCharlie type, for instance, has a clear political message and meaning but does not primarily appeal to representative politics. To a considerable extent, however, plebiscitary democracy is also entangled with the realm of established electoral democracy.[60] Take the digital votes that are used to (de)select political leaders, or to select a winning 'city initiative' to be funded by a municipality. Or look at some of the other aforementioned exhibits: the Australian postal survey that opened the door to a private member's bill on gay marriage, and the unofficial 'referendum' organized by the Dutch automobile club that directly affected government decision-making.

What we have here is more refined than a simple zero-sum game. What plebiscitary democracy wins is not necessarily lost by electoral democracy, or vice versa. To better understand such interactions, we need to delve deeper into them. In the next section, I demarcate the relevant interactions to be investigated more deeply. In addition, I discuss the relationship between

---

[59] See Susskind, J., *Future Politics: Living Together in a World Transformed by Tech*, Oxford, Oxford University Press, 2018, pp.61–9 where the 'increasingly quantified society' is discussed, and Davies, W., *Nervous States: Democracy and the Decline of Reason*, London, Norton, 2018, when pondering on 'the new era of crowds'.

[60] The focus here is on new plebiscitary practices in established democracies, but we should note that hybrid regimes and authoritarian ones are not excluded from some of the formats described. See e.g., #WhiteWednesdays used in Iran to protest against the compulsory hijab. Thanks to Ammar Maleki for pointing this out.

present-day plebiscitary and deliberative democracy—in essence competing views on how democracy should be extended. The aggregative, majoritarian, and competitive spirit that inspires plebiscitary democracy runs counter in many ways to the integrative, consensual, and transformative spirit that infuses deliberative democracy.[61]

Towards a research agenda

The argument advanced in this chapter is that we need to understand the new plebiscitary democracy better than we presently do, not only its inherent dynamics but also its relation to the established systems of electoral democracy and the prominent alternative of deliberative democracy. Compared to the ever-expanding universe of deliberative-democracy investigation, research into the various guises, drivers, and implications of the new plebiscitary democracy is far less advanced. For this reason, Figure 4.1 is transformed into an analytical scheme—Figure 4.2—with elements and relationships to be prioritized in empirical research of the new plebiscitary democracy (marked A, B, and C).[62]

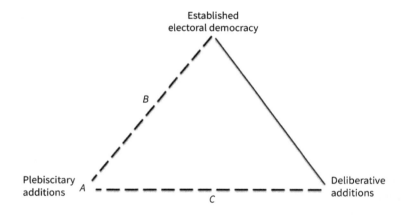

Figure 4.2 Tackling the new plebiscitary democracy: priority research areas

[61] Hendriks, F., Democratic Innovation Beyond Deliberative Reflection, *Democratisation*, 2019, 26, 3, p. 453; Gerbaudo, P., Are Digital Parties more Democratic than Traditional Parties? Evaluating Podemos and Movimento 5 Stelle's Online Decision-Making Platforms, *Party Politics*, 2021, 27, 4, p. 732.
[62] I readily admit that concentrating on empirical issues related to the new plebiscitary democracy as a political phenomenon is a choice. I do not deny that there are wider-ranging normative and societal questions to ask, which deserve separate treatment.

Plebiscitary additions: Expressions, drivers, implications

The analytical triangle of Figure 4.2 has three corners pointing to, first, established electoral democracy; second, deliberative additions that have been promoted and investigated widely since the 1990s; and third, comparatively uncharted plebiscitary additions that have accelerated strongly in the 2010s. The bottom-left corner of the picture is thus far less well documented by empirical research. This may be understandable from a historical perspective, but in view of twenty-first-century developments this urgently needs to be changed. The exploration of plebiscitary democracy developments in previous sections prompt a number of follow-up questions, of which the following take precedence.

- What are the enduring expressions of twenty-first-century plebiscitary democracy? (A1)
- What are the main drivers behind these expressions? (A2)
- What are the implications for citizen participation and civic culture? (A3)

Expressions—First, we need to track and trace which of the developing formats of twenty-first-century plebiscitary democracy, summarized in Table 4.1, develop into more or less durable expressions. Of the many new formats that are tried and tested at some point in time, a smaller set of formats is expected to become institutionalized and passed on. Some of these formats may develop within the confines of the four ideal-typical categories distinguished in Table 4.1; a strong candidate is, for instance, the issue-supporting e-petition, mobilizing outside-in digital support for particular causes. Some other formats may cross boundaries: we could think of the new-style political party website that is used for leadership votes as well as issue-related vox polls. When the deliberative turn was proclaimed in the 1990s. it took years of extensive research to reach a significant level of consensus on the main empirical formats of deliberative democracy.[63] A similar trajectory could be expected for the new plebiscitary democracy. To incite future research, it is postulated that inside-out formats developed by governments and political actors will increasingly be designed to arrest or placate outside-in pressures for direct voting, which will in turn trigger alternative outside-in formats.

[63] Gastil, J. and P. Levine (eds), *The Deliberative Democracy Handbook*, San Francisco, Jossey-Bass, 2005; Bächtiger, A., S. Niemeyer, M. Neblo, M.R. Steenbergen, and J. Steiner, Disentangling Diversity in Deliberative Democracy: Competing Theories, Their Empirical Blind-spots, and Complementarities, *Journal of Political Philosophy*, 2010, 18, 1, pp. 32–63.

Additionally, it is postulated that plebiscitary formats with staying power will be leader-focused as well as issue-focused, as both reflect more general tendencies of information-age societies to rate people as well as things.[64]

Drivers—Second, we should understand the driving (f)actors behind the new formats of voting better than we presently do. In addition to technological drivers there are cultural and related political drivers to consider. The turn to deliberative democracy in the late twentieth century was seen to be related to the coming of age of a new social and political culture, which had pushed the values of active participation, open communication, and self-expression since the late 1960s.[65] Likewise, it seems that the new plebiscitary democracy is pushed by the more recent rise of populism—favouring more 'hardball', aggregative, and majoritarian practices.[66] If populism is about 'who' should govern,[67] then the new plebiscitary democracy seems to fill in 'how' this can be done: with renewed and radicalized variants of plebiscites. Relatedly, it seems quite plausible that new plebiscitary instruments are turned and appealed to as a response to a real or perceived crisis of established parties and electoral politics.[68] The technological push behind the new plebiscitary democracy is evident, but at the same time insufficiently understood. New digital and social media applications, connecting user-friendly smart devices to broadband internet, seem to push competitive, vote-counting practices.[69] But what are the underlying mechanisms and connections, and who are the actors and organizations that actually forge the technological push?

Implications—Focusing on the empirical-political consequences of the new plebiscitary democracy, as we do here, the consequences for civic culture and democratic citizenship are highly urgent.[70] One of the obvious questions here

[64] Keen, A., *The Cult of the Amateur*, New York, Doubleday, 2007; Hill, S., *Digital Revolutions: Activism in the Internet Age*, Oxford, New Internationalist Publications, 2013; Nagle, A., *Kill All Normies: Online Culture Wars from 4chan and Tumblr to Trump and the Alt-Right*, London, Zero Books, 2017; Susskind, J., *Future Politics: Living Together in a World Transformed by Tech*, Oxford, Oxford University Press, 2018.

[65] Inglehart, R., *Culture Shift in Advanced Industrial Society*, Princeton, Princeton University Press, 1990; Dryzek, J.S., *Deliberative Democracy and beyond: Liberals, Critics, Contestations*, Oxford, Oxford University Press, 2000.

[66] Mudde, C., The Populist Zeitgeist, *Government and Opposition*, 2004, 39, 3, pp. 541–63; Kriesi, H., The Populist Challenge, *West European Politics*, 2014, 37, 2, pp. 361–78; Mounk, Y., *The People Vs Democracy: Why Our Freedom is in Danger and How to Save it*, Cambridge, MA, Harvard University Press, 2018; Müller, J.W., *What is Populism?*, Philadelphia, University of Pennsylvania Press, 2016.

[67] Norris, P. and R. Inglehart, *Cultural Backlash: Trump, Brexit and Authoritarian Populism*, Cambridge, Cambridge University Press, 2019, p. 248.

[68] Biezen, I. van, P. Mair, and T. Poguntke, Going, Going … Gone? The Decline of Party Membership in Contemporary Europe, *European Journal of Political Research*, 2012, 51, 1, pp. 24–56; Bardi, L., S. Bartolini, and A. Trechsel, Party Adaptation and Change and the Crisis of Democracy, *Party Politics*, 2014, 20, 2, pp. 151–9.

[69] Halupka, M., Clicktivism: A Systematic Heuristic, *Policy & Internet*, 2014, 6, 2, pp. 115–32; Harari, Y.N., *Homo Deus: A Brief History of Tomorrow*, London, Vintage, 2017, p. 394 and p. 435 et seq.

[70] Implications for institutions of the established electoral system are dealt with under cluster B and implications in terms of democratic merits under cluster C.

is how and to what extent new plebiscitary practices help or hinder different types and groups of citizens in a political sense. Studies of political clicktivism suggest that its participants display a rather different profile than participants in deliberative-democracy practices: on average they are less highly educated, less interested in detailed policy-oriented meetings, and more adept in quick messaging via mass media.[71] While this may be true for particular expressions, there is reason to believe that this does not work in exactly the same way for all expressions of plebiscitary democracy. For instance, the initiators of and the participants in the e-petition demanding a second referendum on Brexit, another previous example, displayed a rather different profile from the ones behind the #LockHerUp Twitter rally.[72] A more refined picture of what plebiscitary democracy in its various guises does with citizens and participation is thus needed. Another obvious question here is how and to what extent new plebiscitary practices push a shift from pluralism to populism (the reverse of what is asked under question A2).

Plebiscitary additions and established electoral democracy

While the interplay between deliberative democracy and established electoral democracy (the continuous line in Figure 4.2) has been problematized and investigated for many years,[73] a lot of catching up needs to be done for the connection between the new plebiscitary democracy and established electoral democracy. As plebiscitary practices are basically more majoritarian in their set-up, it would be pertinent to compare their uptake in majoritarian (winner-take-all) versus proportionally representative (PR) electoral systems, besides looking at how they impact on electoral democracy's central institutions and political culture:

- To what extent and in which way does the uptake of twenty-first-century plebiscitary formats differ in majoritarian versus PR electoral systems— indicative of pendulum versus consensus democracy? (B1)

---

[71] Halupka, M., Clicktivism: A Systematic Heuristic, *Policy & Internet*, 2014, 6, 2, pp. 115–32; Sunstein, C., *#Republic: Divided Democracy in the Age of Social Media*, Princeton, Princeton University Press, 2017; Nagle, A., *Kill All Normies: Online Culture Wars from 4chan and Tumblr to Trump and the Alt-Right*, London, Zero Books, 2017.

[72] Or compare the participants in other earlier examples: the digital rally for Boaty-McBoatface vs the EU online survey on daylight saving—different publics, different dynamics.

[73] Dryzek, J.S., *Deliberative Democracy and beyond: Liberals, Critics, Contestations*, Oxford, Oxford University Press, 2000; Gastil, J. and P. Levine (eds), *The Deliberative Democracy Handbook*, San Francisco, Jossey-Bass, 2005; Setälä, M., Connecting Deliberative Mini-Publics to Representative Decision Making, *European Journal of Political Research*, 2017, 56, 4, pp.846–63.

- What are its implications for electoral democracy's central institutions? (B2)
- What are its implications for political discourse and governing style? (B3)

Uptake—It might be argued that winner-take-all (district-based majority or plurality) systems present a more fertile breeding ground and more conducive political opportunity structure for twenty-first-century plebiscitary formats than PR electoral systems. A rival hypothesis would be that PR electoral systems, because of their diluted compromises between multiparty elites, trigger plebiscitary reactions that follow extra-institutional pathways.[74] If we look at the underlying, longer-existing formats of plebiscitary democracy, we do not see one clear pattern for all formats. Primaries and recalls have spread most prominently in the US two-party system. Public polling (of both political personae and issues) also developed earlier and stronger in this context—but not uniquely there. Referendum practices have developed strongly under PR circumstances in Switzerland, Italy, and more recently subnational Germany, while the majoritarian electoral systems of France and the UK have also seen referendums—albeit of different kinds.[75] By the same token, we should expect the emerging formats of the new plebiscitary democracy to follow not one but various institutional pathways. More specifically, we should expect majoritarian and PR systems to both trigger elite-focused and issue-focused votes, outside-in as well as inside-out—following different paths of action and reaction, yet to be understood.

Impact on central institutions—New political tools and applications potentially impact positions and resources of central institutions in electoral democracy such as executive offices, representative bodies, and political parties. Institutional and network analyses should reveal whether and how this is the case, first and foremost for the countervailing powers of executive and representative institutions. Both sides can organize inside-out votes, and both can be the target of outside-in votes, but differences are likely to exist. The expectation is that representative bodies (parliaments, regional, and local councils) have more leeway to direct or redirect the vox populi towards the executive (governing boards and office-holders) than the other way around. The executive branch seems more challenged, potentially disrupted, by direct votes targeting specific issues and politicians, further reducing governing

---

[74] Caramani, D. and Y. Mény (eds), *Challenges to Consensual Politics: Democracy, Identity, and Populist Protest in the Alpine Region*, New York, Peter Lang, 2005.
[75] Altman, D., *Direct Democracy Worldwide*, Cambridge, Cambridge University Press, 2011; Qvortrup, M., *Referendums Around the World*, Houndmills, Palgrave Macmillan, 2017.

discretion. It is particularly interesting to trace how new populist politicians position themselves in the matrix of plebiscitary pressures and possibilities (typologically explored in Table 4.1) when taking up executive responsibilities, and how this differs from more traditional governing elites. Not only in executive office, but in the political realm in general, the strategic positioning of populist parties is worth following. It could be argued that the new plebiscitary democracy gives them a strategic advantage vis-à-vis establishment parties as this 'medium' seems closest to their 'message'.[76] History, however, teaches us to not rule out surprises. Catholic conservatives in nineteenth-century Switzerland, for instance, were originally far removed from the referendum instrument, but nevertheless discovered and captured its strategic use.[77]

Political discourse and style—An important question is how political debate (including claim-making and rhetoric) and governing style (including manner of communication and interaction) change in connection with new plebiscitary practices. Do we see the discourse surrounding plebiscitary voting—with its strong focus on mass, traction, and numbers—echoed or reframed in the political (speech) acts that emanate from the benches in parliaments and local and regional councils? Do we see governments develop new ways of dealing with the general public—proactively or reactively tackling the public voice that is constructed around issues or people? Cultural and more specific discourse analyses should reveal whether and how this is the case. It was already asked if and how plebiscitary practices spread differently in majoritarian (winner-take-all) versus countermajoritarian (consensual) democracies (question B1). A logical follow-up question is: do they touch these systems differently on a cultural level? The proposition—sharp on purpose—is that cultural disturbance following the emergence of new plebiscitary practices are more intense in consensus democracies than in majoritarian systems. The clash with consensus democracy's focus on integrative elite deliberation and its fear for mass politics by the numbers is comparatively more intensive, and could be expected to inspire rejective discourse and aversive action sooner and more strongly.[78]

---

[76] Mudde, C., The Populist Zeitgeist, *Government and Opposition*, 2004, 39, 3, pp. 541–63; Müller, J.W., *What is Populism?*, Philadelphia, University of Pennsylvania Press, 2016.

[77] Kriesi, H. and A.H. Trechsel, *The Politics of Switzerland*, Cambridge, Cambridge University Press, 2008.

[78] In Chapter 2, I go back to Mary Douglas's classic idea from *Purity and Danger*—'dirt is matter out of place'—to discuss processes of 'pollution reduction' in democratic discourse and practice; Douglas, M., *Purity and Danger*, London, Routledge & Kegan Paul, 1966.

Deliberative and plebiscitary additions

The various formats of deliberative democracy—from mini-publics to consensus conferences and everything in between—have been extensively described; this also pertains to how deliberation may clash with and how it can contribute to established electoral democracy.[79] The relationship between deliberative democracy and twenty-first-century plebiscitary democracy, however, still needs to be defined properly.[80] The two can be viewed as rival democratic innovations, but also as formats that to some extent may be combined to contribute to the democratic process. This prompts two types of questions:

- What are the comparative merits—advantages and disadvantages—of new plebiscitary versus deliberative formats? (C1)
- What is the feasible space for combinations—for connecting new plebiscitary and deliberative formats? (C2)

Comparative merits—Comparative (dis)advantages need to be analysed, first of all, at the level of internal qualities. What is it that new plebiscitary formats, because of their design characteristics, do better or worse than deliberative formats? As they involve different technologies and organizational models, they should be expected to have different sorts of leverage for different purposes. In Chapter 3, I tentatively compared the merits of (new) forms of voting with (randomized or mobilized) forms of deliberation, connecting them to four general criteria (equality, participation, deliberation and concretization). Empirically, I explored new aggregative tools deployed in the context of the Dutch Ukraine referendum, but clearly more empirical work should be done on the various tools of the new plebiscitary democracy (quasi-referendum, e-petition, ideas contest, digital primary, etc., outlined

[79] Dryzek, J.S., *Deliberative Democracy and beyond: Liberals, Critics, Contestations*, Oxford, Oxford University Press, 2000; Setälä, M., Connecting Deliberative Mini-Publics to Representative Decision Making, *European Journal of Political Research*, 2017, 56, 4, pp.846–63; Beauvais, E. and M.E. Warren, What Can Deliberative Mini-Publics Contribute to Democratic Systems? *European Journal of Political Research*, 2019, 58, 3, pp. 893–914; Hendriks, C. and A. Kay, From 'Opening Up' to Democratic Renewal: Deepening Public Engagement in Legislative Committees, *Government and Opposition*, 2019, 54, 1, pp. 25–51.

[80] Notwithstanding calls for more attention to the relation between deliberative and (new) plebiscitary formats in some works: Knight, J. and J. Johnson, Aggregation and Deliberation: On the Possibility of Democratic Legitimacy, *Political Theory*, 1994, 22, 2, pp. 277–96; Saward, M., Making Democratic Connections: Political Equality, Deliberation and Direct Democracy, *Acta Politica*, 2001, 36, pp. 361–79; McKay, S., Building a Better Referendum: Linking Mini-Publics and Mass Publics in Popular Votes, *Journal of Public Deliberation*, 2019, 15, 1; Susskind, J., *Future Politics: Living Together in a World Transformed by Tech*, Oxford, Oxford University Press, 2018, p. 212; Landemore, H., *Open Democracy: Reinventing Popular Rule for the Twenty-First Century*, Princeton, Princeton University Press, 2020, p. 140.

in Figure 4.2). In addition to internal qualities, external effects of different formats in relation to established electoral democracy requires attention. Not unlike deliberative formats, plebiscitary formats often depart from a critical diagnosis of electoral democracy, which might get less 'thin' or 'detached' by adding deliberative, or plebiscitary, ingredients. Whereas deliberative formats promise added value in terms of deeper and richer collective reflection,[81] plebiscitary formats claim increased sensitivity to feelings and perceptions in society. In a comparative analysis of merits, the question should not only be 'Is it true?' (can they actually deliver the qualities that they claim), but also 'Does it matter?' (to what extent and how are they able to change courses of action, politics, and policies in the real world).

Space for combinations—New plebiscitary and deliberative formats display different democratic logics, which are in many ways at odds with each other. The 'counters' and the 'talkers', as Susskind aptly calls them,[82] can often not see eye to eye. Does this mean the twain shall never meet? Not necessarily, as some promising trials of deliberative-plebiscitary mixing show. The Irish Citizens' Assembly on abortion was primarily a deliberative and integrative affair, but it also involved moments of aggregation and counting, most prominently in the final referendum that confirmed the advice that the randomized mini-public had produced.[83] The Citizen Initiative Review or CIR renders another hybrid, in which a deliberative mini-public is asked to look into and advise on the voting options put forward by citizen initiative, prior to massive, dichotomous voting.[84] Various new combinations of digital voting and electronic deliberation have come to the fore.[85] For future empirical research, the relevant questions are where, when, how, and to what effect such hybrid forms appear. In general, it may be expected that keeping deliberative and plebiscitary formats apart is the default position and that mixing them requires special circumstances. To put it differently, 'mixophobia' (fear of pollution) is the primary pattern to be

---

[81] Bächtiger, A., S. Niemeyer, M. Neblo, M.R. Steenbergen, and J. Steiner, Disentangling Diversity in Deliberative Democracy: Competing Theories, Their Empirical Blind-Spots, and Complementarities, *Journal of Political Philosophy*, 2010, 18, 1, pp. 32–63.

[82] Susskind, J., *Future Politics: Living Together in a World Transformed by Tech*, Oxford, Oxford University Press, 2018, pp. 224–5. More about the tension between counters and talkers in Chapter 5.

[83] Farrell, D.M., J. Suiter, and C. Harris, 'Systematizing' Constitutional Deliberation: The 2016–18 Citizens' Assembly in Ireland, *Irish Political Studies*, 2019, 34, 1, pp. 113–23. More about this case in Chapter 7.

[84] Gastil, J., G.F. Johnson, S. Han, and J. Rountree, *Assessment of the 2016 Oregon Citizens' Initiative Review on Measure 97*, State College, Pennsylvania State University, 2017. See also Chapters 6–7.

[85] Susskind, J., *Future Politics: Living Together in a World Transformed by Tech*, Oxford, Oxford University Press, 2018, pp. 212–13; Noveck, B., *Smart Citizens, Smarter State: The Technologies of Expertise and the Future of Governing*, Cambridge, MA, Harvard University Press, 2015; Bernholz, L., H. Landemore, and R. Reich (eds), *Digital Technology and Democratic Theory*, Chicago, Chicago University Press, 2021.

expected in the relation between new plebiscitary and deliberative practices, while 'heterophilia' (love for the different) is the exception requiring special triggers, which need to be pinpointed. Alternatively, one might think that democratic innovators, notwithstanding various inhibitions, are ultimately forced to respond to the heterogeneous needs of users and fields of practice. Later in this book, I will further elaborate on mixed innovation models (Chapter 7–9).

Taking the new plebiscitary democracy on

The upshot of the foregoing is quite simply that a new plebiscitary democracy is developing, with various new formats building and varying on longer-existing formats, and that this presents an urgent development that warrants more systematic attention than is presently available. For this purpose, I developed a sensitizing framework of central expressions of the new plebiscitary democracy (Table 4.1), and demarcated priority areas for research into the phenomenon itself and its relationship with established electoral democracy and deliberative democracy as an alternative source of democratic transformation (Figure 4.2).

Plebiscitary transformations partly overlap with deliberative ones and with established electoral democracy. The Venn diagram with three overlapping spheres (Figure 4.1) can be compared to the one used by Dalton, Cain, and Scarrow to summarize their seminal study of democratic transformations in eighteen OECD countries between 1960 and 2000.[86] In the Venn diagram suggested by Dalton et al. 'direct democracy' and 'advocacy democracy' are the main alternatives to established electoral democracy. While the latter roughly maintained their importance in the last four decades of the twentieth century, the alternative spheres of direct and advocacy democracy grew significantly, the authors suggested.[87]

In the present study, considering twenty-first-century developments in democratic discourse and practice, the main competing alternatives to electoral democracy are partially reframed as plebiscitary democracy and deliberative democracy. As the turn to the latter has been documented extensively

---

[86] Dalton, R.J., B.E. Cain, and S.E. Scarrow, Democratic Publics and Democratic Institution, in B.E. Cain, R.J. Dalton, and S.E. Scarrow (eds), *Democracy Transformed*, Oxford, Oxford University Press, 2003, pp. 252–6. See Chapter 1 about this work.

[87] Dalton, R.J., B.E. Cain, and S.E. Scarrow, Democratic Publics and Democratic Institution, in B.E. Cain, R.J. Dalton, and S.E. Scarrow (eds), *Democracy Transformed*, Oxford, Oxford University Press, 2003, p. 255.

elsewhere,[88] this chapter set out to explore contemporary developments in the sphere of plebiscitary democracy, inspired by and often radicalizing the formal expressions of what Dalton et al. classified as direct democracy (referendum, initiative, recall, and the like). A multitude of new twenty-first-century plebiscitary practices are emerging on a substratum of such older plebiscitary formats.

Echoing the words of Dalton et al.,[89] it is possible to sketch only in 'imprecise terms' the growing significance of the circle of plebiscitary additions. At present, the available evidence is mainly qualitative. But as quantitative monitors for the prevalence of formal referendums have been built over time,[90] such monitors might also be developed for the (often digital) quasi-referendums of the new plebiscitary democracy, although this will need time and a good deal of creativity.[91] The very nature of the new plebiscitary democracy—varied and variable, often working under the official radar—is inherently more difficult to capture in statistics.

Some objections to this account can be envisioned. The first and potentially most damaging objection would be that there is no such thing as a new plebiscitary democracy. It is a deep truth that in the world of democracy almost nothing is unrelated to something old. As argued, new plebiscitary formats reinvent and radicalize longer-existing formats. They do so in a period of revolutionary technological change—a massive uptake of broadband internet, an explosion of smart devices and interactive social media—which takes plebiscitary formats to a next stage and level. While technological innovations make new ways of direct voting increasingly possible, related shifts in popular culture make them increasingly popular. Since the turn of the century interactive television with popular televoting formats has strongly converged with internet and social networking.[92] Countless new and old media have followed suit, which has contributed to the uptake and popularity of practices such as the ones described here.[93]

---

[88] Dryzek, J.S., *Deliberative Democracy and beyond: Liberals, Critics, Contestations*, Oxford, Oxford University Press, 2000; Bächtiger, A., S. Niemeyer, M. Neblo, M.R. Steenbergen, and J. Steiner, Disentangling Diversity in Deliberative Democracy: Competing Theories, Their Empirical Blind-Spots, and Complementarities, *Journal of Political Philosophy*, 2010, 18, 1, pp. 32–63. See Chapter 3.

[89] Dalton, R.J., B.E. Cain, and S.E. Scarrow, Democratic Publics and Democratic Institution, B.E. Cain, R.J. Dalton, and S.E. Scarrow (eds), *Democracy Transformed*, Oxford, Oxford University Press, 2003, p. 255.

[90] Altman, D., *Direct Democracy Worldwide*, Cambridge, Cambridge University Press, 2011; Qvortrup, M., *Referendums Around the World*, Houndmills, Palgrave Macmillan, 2017.

[91] See C2D—Centre for Research on Direct Democracy, *About this project*, <www.c2d.ch>, 2018 and Direct Democracy Navigator, *Welcome to the navigator to direct democracy*, <https://www.direct-democracy-navigator.org/>, 2022 for alternative ways of mapping the territory of formal direct democracy, particularly referendums and initiatives.

[92] Bignell, J., *An Introduction to Television Studies*, London, Routledge, 2012, pp. 283–93.

[93] Ross, S.M., *Beyond the Box: Television and the Internet*, Oxford, Blackwell, 2008.

At this point, a small thought experiment is suggested: take the matrix of new plebiscitary options in mind (Table 4.1), follow the political news for a month or so, and then ask yourself whether the new plebiscitary democracy is any less real in an empirical sense than the turn to deliberative democracy which was proclaimed earlier.

A second objection would be to say that new plebiscitary practices may be coming to the fore, but should not be taken seriously, accredited with academic research, compared with consciously designed democratic innovations backed up by refined political theory like deliberative-democracy theory. Are new practices of voting not often ill-designed, flimsy, quick-and-dirty, and potentially dangerous? New plebiscitary votes may be popular, but does this not make them vulnerable to populism, to democratic illiberalism?

Even if we assumed that previous questions could already be answered with an unequivocal yes for all new plebiscitary practices, then the case for doing more research into the phenomenon would be fortified, not weakened. Even though there are dubious practices that need to be exposed, not all the new plebiscitary voting practices can be dismissed so easily. Guilty by association is not fair grounds for sentencing, and could be challenged with reason. If new political parties or social movements are experimenting with digital plebiscites, then the relation with democratic values needs to be investigated properly, not a priori assumed to be negative.[94]

A third objection would be to argue that the new plebiscitary democracy is indeed real and to be investigated seriously, but not described with enough detail in this chapter. Surely, specific exhibits of the new plebiscitary democracy (the Podemos digital referendum, for instance, or the EU online survey) could be developed into more detailed individual case studies. However, the specification of depth and singularity has been deliberately sacrificed here, revealing empirical breadth and typological variety of the phenomenon. More fundamental than the details of individual cases are the regularities of the new plebiscitary formats emerging on a substratum of longer-existing methods.

---

[94] Gerbaudo, P., Are Digital Parties more Democratic than Traditional Parties? Evaluating Podemos and Movimento 5 Stelle's Online Decision-Making Platforms, *Party Politics*, 2021, 27, 4, pp. 730–42 gives a good example of such an investigation, although he does not focus on democratic values specifically.

5

Between counters and talkers

Grasping the full matrix

In Chapter 3, I discussed the dominant position of deliberative-democracy models, particularly the deliberative mini-public, in contemporary democratic-innovations discourse. For good measure, I called attention to variants and options diverging from reflection-oriented deliberation. In Chapter 4, I concentrated on new plebiscitary models of change, which theoretically present the starkest contrast with models of change put forward in the wake of the deliberative turn. While Chapters 3 and 4 thus focused on current contrasts in democratic innovations, this chapter will take such contrasts back to the broader theoretical perspective set out in Chapter 2. In the next section, I will first revisit the plebiscitary-deliberative opposition from the angle of democratic-cum-cultural theory. Then, from this theoretical angle, I will look at what is budding, often experimentally, in the area between the two poles, and what can be seen by way of (non)reform on the side of representative democracy. Finally, I will reflect on taking the step from understanding variation (Part I) to advancing innovation (Part II).

Contrasting moves: The deliberative vs plebiscitary (re)turn

In theoretical terms, going back to the framework set out in Chapter 2, the moves to deliberative and plebiscitary democracy present a stark contrast. The turn to deliberation and the plebiscitary return draw on different sides of Table 2.1 (models of democracy), Table 2.2 (darlings of democratic reform), and Table 2.3 (types of culture). Figure 5.1 visualizes the contrasting moves.

Rethinking Democratic Innovation. Frank Hendriks, Oxford University Press. © Frank Hendriks (2023). DOI: 10.1093/oso/9780192848291.003.0005

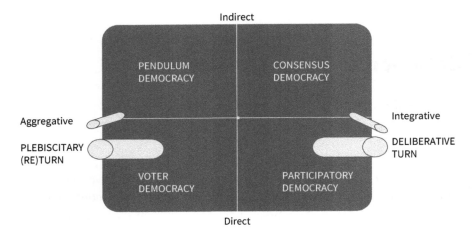

Figure 5.1   Contrasting moves in democratic innovation

Deliberative talk, thorough integration, and the spirit of communion

Deliberative models of democratic innovation turn to an integrative, talk-oriented approach to democracy, radicalizing elements of participatory democracy (we the people can do it better, coming together in a bottom-up fashion), while tapping also, to a more limited extent, into consensus democracy (we need to sit down, take our time, and patiently talk things through). At the core, deliberative models turn away from thinly aggregative and agonistic interpretations of democracy, both the directly democratic and representative expressions of divisive voting.

In cultural-theory terms, innovations such as the deliberative mini-public turn to high-group, we-focused, communitarian ways of associating, and steer clear of low-group, me-focused, competitive ways of approaching the democratic process. The democratic process ideally transforms and transcends the individualism and atomism that lurks in modern society.[1] The egalitarian ethos, stressing the equal right to participation, dominates the institutional set up. Hierarchy is mostly avoided, short of a preference for communitarian convergence over agonistic divergence, and a belief in a unified body politic from which equally unified samples can be drawn

[1] Gutmann, A. and D. Thompson, *Why Deliberative Democracy?*, Princeton University Press, 2003; Fishkin, J., *When the People Speak: Deliberative Democracy and Public Consultation*, Oxford, Oxford University Press, 2009; Goodin, R., *Innovating Democracy: Democratic Theory and Practice after the Deliberative Turn*, Oxford, Oxford University Press, 2010.

with confidence. Hierarchy in the sense of a markedly vertical, high-grid, stratification of mandates, however, runs counter to the dominant logic of the randomized mini-public. Giving special, overarching roles, to discrete individuals is easily mistrusted.

A telling example is presented by the French Convention on Climate Change (CCC), as described by Landemore.[2] The so-called *Convention Citoyenne pour le Climat* assembled 150 randomly selected citizens to deliberate about the energy transition in France. President Macron had installed the CCC in 2019, pressured by angry Yellow Vest protests against higher fuel taxes earlier, and influenced by deliberative-democracy thinkers recommending the reflection-oriented mini-public as a possible way out of the energy and climate controversy.

How might this be a way out? By way of design, a deliberative 'mini-France' would make the acting group smaller and more regulated—as opposed to massive and unruly—and the discussion arguably more rational and responsible—as opposed to emotional and populist, as the energy debate was perceived to be. CCC-members were assigned to five working groups by way of stratified randomization. All working groups, and all participants, were supposed to be equal. A problem arose, however, when a sixth working group was formed, mainly on the basis of self-selection, which in practice brought most of the 'natural leaders' of the CCC together, and the problem deepened when this special working group called 'the squad' was tasked with centralizing the common reflections of the Convention.

Landemore, who closely followed the CCC, describes how a spokesperson of the non-squad members of the CCC vocalized the resistance to a special squad standing apart and above the rest of the group, not even being authorized by the wider CCC: 'He insisted that the 150 needed to work on these question all together and "the social contract" had been "broken" between the squad and the rest of the 150'.[3] Votes were never taken about the issue, so it is not clear what all 150 members thought about the issue. In deliberative institutions, votes are preferably exhibiting achieved convergence, as opposed to highlighting divergence. Nevertheless, the squad was dissolved on account of being an alien element to the egalitarian cultural logic designed-into the CCC.

---

[2] Landemore, H., *Open Democracy: Reinventing Popular Rule for the Twenty-First Century*, Princeton, Princeton University Press, 2020, pp. 212–14.
[3] Landemore, H., *Open Democracy: Reinventing Popular Rule for the Twenty-First Century*, Princeton, Princeton University Press, 2020, p. 212.

Plebiscitary voting, efficient aggregation, and the spirit of competition

A cultural block against potentially divisive votes is, conversely, not a characteristic of the new plebiscitary democracy, which is unashamedly majoritarian, radicalizing elements of voter democracy (the voter is always right), besides, to some extent and in a particular way, pendulum democracy (the biggest vote wins).[4] Efficient aggregation and agonistic competition tend to be much preferred to lengthy deliberations in communalist get-togethers.

In cultural-theory terms, the ethos behind many of the contemporary expressions of plebiscitary democracy is low-group (individualistic, me-focused), rather than high-group (communitarian, we-focused). The individual voter is to make up his or her own mind in choosing A or B in plebiscites of various sorts. A shared, transformative process to make up the collective mind, to find out what the people think when they think together, is not required, and is to some extent distrusted. Seen from a low-group cultural perspective, deliberative democracy has something of 'a schoolmarmish, eat-your-spinach air about it', to quote Surowiecki who rather views independent choice and competition as essential to a healthy democracy.[5]

Although some of the new plebiscitary formats are elite-focused or top-down initiated, they mostly refrain from giving elected leaders a free rein or mandate in between general elections, as in the ideal-typical pendulum democracy. More often, the new voting formats amount to stronger public pressure on political personae as well as public issues. While the new plebiscitary formats to some extent cultivate the adversarial, pugnacious, 'kick-and-rush' style of political action associated with pendulum democracy, the overriding culture is maybe best described as market-like, casting the citizen as a voting consumer of public goods and action.

The platform *Frankfurt Fragt Mich* (FFM), which we encountered in Chapter 4, nicely illustrates the consumerist logic. FFM is a platform on which individual citizens can push individual demands, and collect

---

[4] See Chapter 4. Also Harari, Y.N., *Homo Deus: A Brief History of Tomorrow*, London, Vintage, 2017., pp. 271–3.

[5] Surowiecki, J., *The Wisdom of Crowds: Why the Many are Smarter than the Few*, New York, Doubleday, 2004, p. 2016. Sunstein is also critical of deliberative democracy, pointing to serious flaws. See Sunstein, C., *Infotopia: How Many Minds Produce Knowledge*, Oxford, Oxford University Press, 2008, 11, pp. 220–1 summarizes common criticisms. However, he also mentions open source projects in the context of 'eureka' type problems where deliberation may work well. See Sunstein, C., *Infotopia: How Many Minds Produce Knowledge*, Oxford, Oxford University Press, 2008, p. 195.

supportive votes in favour of it. A short video on YouTube shows how this may work: a father and a young child walk the streets of Frankfurt, when they are almost run over by a car, the father grabs his smartphone, opens the app of FFM, fills in 'Ich will . . . I want . . . more zebra stripes', and after a (virtual) tally has counted more than 200 votes of support, we see the zebra path already appear in front of them (virtually). The mayor of Frankfurt, a guardian of FFM, gives an accompanying explanation on the internet: 'You have an idea, and if it gets more than 200 supporters, it will become our assignment'.[6] The citizen demands, the government supplies—it is virtually an ad for voter democracy. In terms of democratic citizenship, two realities coexist here. On the one hand, it is true that the new plebiscitary formats are widely available at a relatively low cost to those who want to be active—citizens who like to initiate action and make waves in the public domain. On the other hand, it is also unmistakable that for large groups the new plebiscitary formats culti-vate a relatively detached and passive type of citizenship—remotely checking boxes designed by others, waiting to see the results on-screen, as spectators in the public stand.

Surely, not all expressions of the deliberative turn nor the plebiscitary return are similar. Case histories reveal various idiosyncrasies. Yet, contrasts between models of deliberative reflection and plebiscitary aggregation are often paramount. It is quite clear that the pragmatic-consumerist ethos of the aforementioned *Frankfurt Fragt Mich* format is a far cry from the radical-deliberative ethos expressed by for instance 'Occupy Frankfurt', manifesting briefly in the same city in the fall of 2011.

Underlying tensions: From referendum voting to participatory budgeting

Figure 5.1 reminds us that behind contemporary calls for democratic innovations—more plebiscitary or more deliberative in appearance—we can find older and earlier concepts for (re)arranging the democratic process. (Earlier, and in a purely metaphorical way, Figure 5.1 underscored the layered quality of democratic innovation.)

Behind the new plebiscitary formats we can discern longer-existing aggregative formats: referendum, initiative, petition, recall, and more.[7] As noted, the language of referendums in particular reappears in various new

---

[6] Stadt Frankfurt am Main, *Bürgerbeteiligung leicht gemacht*, <https://www.ffm.de/frankfurt/de/home>
[7] See Chapter 4, Table 4.1 in particular.

guises, often calling something a referendum that in fact would be better described as a thematic poll or digital recall. In the meantime, the formal referendum format is also still there and spreading its wings. In terms of usage, various authors and groups report growing numbers.[8] And that does not even say everything; the UK counted just one national referendum in 2016, but this single referendum triggered a massive institutional change.

Besides and behind present-day versions of the deliberative mini-public—the most avidly recommended expression of participatory democracy at present[9]—older formats of participatory planning and budgeting are also still present and developing: from Chicago-style empowered participation to Porto Alegre-style participatory budgeting and many variants in between.[10] Modes of participant selection and modes of interaction differ, but participatory formats that have been in existence for longer share with the deliberative mini-public a clear interest in citizen involvement of a highly integrative sort—tying the roots, bottom-up, turning away from thinly majoritarian as well as elite-oriented approaches to democracy. The big difference is the reliance, in deliberative mini-publics, on emphatically small groups of participants—randomly selected and statistically representative (at least theoretically), which adds a taste of representative democracy to the deliberative mini-public.

Whereas referendums and newer plebiscitary tools facilitate 'thinking fast'—quickly translating individual inclinations to collective signals—schemes for participation planning and budgeting, as well as newer forms of deliberative reflection, are rather inclined to 'thinking slow', patiently tying the roots.[11]

---

[8] Matsusaka, J., *Let the People Rule: How Direct Democracy Can Meet the Populist Challenge*, Princeton University Press, 2020; Qvortrup, M. (ed.), *Referendums Around the World: The Continued Growth of Direct Democracy*, Houndmills, Palgrave Macmillan, 2017; The Economist, Referendumania: Plebiscites in Europe, <https://www.economist.com/europe/2016/05/19/referendumania>, 21 May 2016. See also C2D—Centre for Research on Direct Democracy, About this project, <www.c2d.ch>, 2018 and Direct Democracy Navigator, Welcome to the navigator to direct democracy, <https://www.direct-democracy-navigator.org/>, 2022 for alternative ways of mapping the territory of formal direct democracy, particularly referendums and initiatives.

[9] An OECD study in 2020 codifies no less than twelve contemporary variants in four main categories. See OECD, *Innovative Citizen Participation and New Democratic Institutions: Catching the Deliberative Wave*, Paris, OECD Publishing, 2020; see also Chapter 3 and Box 3.1.

[10] See Chapter 3; Fung, A., Varieties of Participation in Complex Governance, *Public Administration Review*, 2006, 66, 1, pp. 66–75; Smith, G., *Democratic Innovation: Designing Institutions for Citizen Participation*, Cambridge, Cambridge University Press, 2009; Elstub, S. and O. Escobar (eds), *Handbook of Democratic Innovation and Governance*, Cheltenham, Edward Elgar, 2019.

[11] Referring to the well-known distinction advanced by Kahneman between model 1 and model 2 thinking: thinking fast, reflexively, versus thinking slow, reflectively. Kahneman, D., *Thinking Fast, Thinking Slow*, New York, Farrar, Straus & Giroux, 2011.

Budding in midfield: Varieties of pooled democracy

The previous discussion focused on the contrast between highly aggregative and plebiscitary formats versus highly integrative and deliberative formats of democratic innovation. Although the extremes are salient—referendum versus mini-public, ideas contest versus consensus conference, straw poll versus deliberative poll—we should not overlook the fact that there is also movement in the middle.

For want of a better term, I propose 'pooled democracy' as a container concept for various initiatives budding in the middle ground between new plebiscitary and deliberative democracy—acknowledging that alternative concepts circulate: 'co-creative', 'co-productive', 'collaborative' democracy,[12] 'wiki', 'smart', 'crowd-ocracy';[13] 'big mind', 'epistemic', 'open' democracy.[14] Such notions are incorporated in the following subsections, which distinguish between three basic approaches to pooled democracy:

- The approach of cooperative do-ocracy and collaborative governance— pooling resources (including operative authority and capacity) for concerted action (for instance: Biest-Houtakker resident cooperative);[15] comparatively *high-touch, low-tech, smaller-group.*
- The approach of the 'counters'—pooling dispersed signals (including crowd estimates and dispersed bets) for epistemically right answers (for

[12] Emerson, K., T. Nabatchi, and S. Balogh, An Integrative Framework for Collaborative Governance, *Journal of Public Administration Research and Theory*, 2012, 22, 1, pp. 1–29; Hartley, J., E. Sørensen, and J. Torfing, Collaborative Innovation: A Viable Alternative to Market Competition and Organizational Entrepreneurship, *Public Administration Review*, 2013, 73, 6, pp. 821–30; Voorberg, W.H., V.J.J.M. Bekkers, and L.G. Tummers, A Systematic Review of Co-Creation and Co-Production: Embarking on the Social Innovation Journey, *Public Management Review*, 2014, 17, 9, pp. 1333–57; Nabatchi, T., A. Sancino, and M. Sicilia, Varieties of Participation in Public Services: The Who, When, and What of Coproduction, *Public Administration Review*, 2017, 77, 5, pp. 766–76.

[13] Noveck, B., *Smart Citizens, Smarter State: The Technologies of Expertise and the Future of Governing*, Cambridge, MA, Harvard University Press, 2015; Noveck, B., *Wiki Government: How Technology Can Make Government Better, Democracy Stronger, and Citizens More Powerful*, Washington, DC, Brookings Institution Press, 2009; Watkins, A. and I. Straitens, *Crowdocracy: The End of Politics*, Rochester, Urbane Publications, 2016; Susskind, J., *Future Politics: Living Together in a World Transformed by Tech*, Oxford, Oxford University Press, 2018.

[14] Atlee, T., *Empowering Public Wisdom: A Practical Vision of Citizen-led Politics*, Berkeley, North Atlantic Books, 2012; Landemore, H., Collective Wisdom: Old and New, in Elster, J. and H. Landemore (eds), *Collective Wisdom: Principles and Mechanisms*, Cambridge, Cambridge University Press, 2012, pp. 1–20; Landemore, H., *Democratic Reason: Politics, Collective Intelligence, and the Rule of the Many*, Princeton University Press, 2017; Landemore, H., *Open Democracy: Reinventing Popular Rule for the Twenty-First Century*, Princeton, Princeton University Press, 2020; Mulgan, G., *Big Mind: How Collective Intelligence Can Change our World*, Princeton, Princeton University Press, 2018.

[15] Wijdeven, T. van de, Bewonerscoöperatie Biest-Houtakker: 'Iedereen kan iets', in T. van de Wijdeven and L. de Graaf (eds), *Kernkracht: over doe-democratie in het landelijk gebied*, Tilburg, Tilburg University Reports, 2014.

instance: Iowa Electronic Market); comparatively *low-touch, high-tech, larger-group.*

- The approach of the 'talkers'—pooling complementary responses (including crowd comments and dispersed edits) for smart solutions (for instance: Wiki-planning platform); comparatively *low-touch, high-tech, larger group.*

Cooperative do-ocracy and collaborative governance

Two cases of pooling resources for concerted action—both remarkably high touch, but fairly low tech, and smaller-group—were discussed in Chapter 3. First, the case of the resident cooperative Biest-Houtakker served to illustrate the highly pragmatic, action-oriented version of pooled democracy that can also be found in, for instance, local energy cooperatives or resident initiatives based on the Right to Challenge. (This is the right to take over a public task that can be done better or more cheaply by a cooperative following a competitive bid.) Compared to the participatory activism of the 1960s, contemporary do-ocracy is less ideologically and more pragmatically geared to collective participation, direct action, and social change.[16] Nevertheless, interpersonal relations are also fairly egalitarian—focused on doing things together in a close-knit and horizontal way.

Second, the case of Brainport-Eindhoven served to illustrate collaborative governance regimes as can be found in many urban regions today: public institutions collaborating with a selection of societal institutions in particular fields of public action—in the case of Brainport-Eindhoven the development of a knowledge-intensive regional economy. Societal participation is channelled by civil society and private organizations and their delegates. Thus, in Figure 5.2 a somewhat higher position on the vertical axis is assigned to collaborative governance regimes (more indirect representation, less direct self-determination) compared to a somewhat lower position for expressions of do-ocracy (less indirect representation, more direct self-determination). Both, however, are geared to pooling resources in a pragmatic, results-oriented way—less focused on aggregative voting or deliberative transformation of public opinion.

[16] See Wijdeven, T. van de, Bewonerscoöperatie Biest-Houtakker: 'Iedereen kan iets', in T. van de Wijdeven and L. de Graaf (eds), *Kernkracht: over doe-democratie in het landelijk gebied*, Tilburg, Tilburg University Reports, 2014. Compare, for instance, the cooperative action in Biest-Houtakker with collective action of the Provo movement, the self-styled 'provocations', played out in Amsterdam in the 1960s. For close-ups from the UK, see Parker, S., *Taking Power Back: Putting People in Charge of Politics*, Policy Press, 2015, p. 123 on 'communism', 'do-it-yourself social action', see Parker, S., *Taking Power Back: Putting People in Charge of Politics*, Policy Press, 2015, p. 68 and a 'democracy of doing' Parker, S., *Taking Power Back: Putting People in charge of Politics*, Policy Press, 2015, p. 83.

In these two examples, the digital technologies used and social networks involved are relatively modest compared to some of the pooled-democracy formats that have developed together with fast internet, smart devices, and widely accessible platforms since the late 1990s and particularly the early 2000s. What these newer formats have in common is the claim that 'smarter solutions' to problems—smarter laws, policies, decisions—can result from pooling dispersed group and crowd knowledge. With a focus on knowledge pooling, some theorists prefer to use terms like epistemic democracy, collective wisdom, or collective intelligence,[17] while others prefer adjectives and concepts in the co-category: co-creation, co-production, coordination, cooperation.[18] The ways in which and the extent to which the shared claim is actualized differ significantly.

Behind those who expect dispersed group knowledge to render 'epistemic' benefits or 'smarter solutions', Jamie Susskind detects the variable influence of two types of theorists—the 'counters' and the 'talkers'.[19] Introducing an edited volume titled *Collective Wisdom*, Landemore also distinguishes two types of mechanisms that may advance collective wisdom: 'deliberative practices on the one hand, and aggregation procedures that do not require actual communication or an exchange of views among the participants'.[20] Susskind's and Landemore's distinctions resonate with the contrast between deliberative versus plebiscitary practices, and with the pooled-democracy formats that I will discuss in the following, which are often pushed by either aggregative or integrative mechanisms. There are, however, distinctive elements that prompt me to give them variable positions in the midfield depicted in Figure 5.2, roving between the plebiscitary and deliberative wings of the field.

The counters in the midfield rely on votes (and similar tokens of individual choice), yet they combine this with very specific expectations regarding healthy (knowledge) aggregation that are not common to all plebiscitary practices. The talkers rely on comments (and similar contributions to verbal exchange) combined with a focused 'solutions-first-deliberations-second' approach, which is not characteristic of all champions of a deliberative turn.

[17] Elster, J. and H. Landemore (eds), *Collective Wisdom: Principles and Mechanisms*, Cambridge, Cambridge University Press, 2012; Atlee, T., *Empowering Public Wisdom: A Practical Vision of Citizen-led Politics*, Berkeley, North Atlantic Books, 2012.
[18] Emerson, K., T. Nabatchi, and S. Balogh, An Integrative Framework for Collaborative Governance, *Journal of Public Administration Research and Theory*, 2012, 22, 1, pp. 1–29; Noveck, B., *Smart Citizens, Smarter State: The Technologies of Expertise and the Future of Governing*, Cambridge, Harvard University Press, 2015; Nabatchi, T., A. Sancino, and M. Sicilia, Varieties of Participation in Public Services: The Who, When, and What of Coproduction, *Public Administration Review*, 2017, 77, 5, pp. 766–76.
[19] Susskind, J., *Future Politics: Living Together in a World Transformed by Tech*, Oxford, Oxford University Press, 2018, pp. 223–225.
[20] Landemore, H., Collective Wisdom: Old and New, in Elster, J. and H. Landemore (eds), *Collective Wisdom: Principles and Mechanisms*, Cambridge, Cambridge University Press, 2012, pp. 1–20.

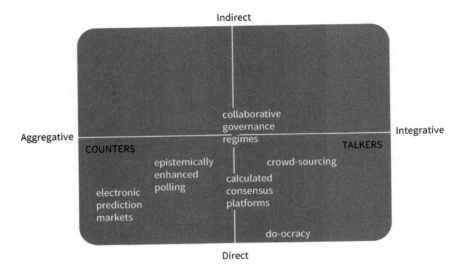

Figure 5.2 Varieties of pooled democracy

The counters and the aggregative push for pooled democracy

In the realm of pooled democracy, the counters (Susskind's predicate is very apt here) lean on aggregative mechanisms with the promise of rendering better, more intelligent, answers to questions. Aggregation of votes and other tokens of individual choice is not just a practical way of taking collective decisions, exerting popular pressure, making public views known, or comparing propositions competitively—as in the old-school or new-style plebiscites that we discussed previously. The promise is 'healthy aggregation',[21] aggregation towards more truthful, knowledgeable, cognitively sound answers to questions. In some situations, more truthful answers can be distinguished—like the closest estimate of the location of something (a missing submarine), or a correct prediction of who will win a competitive election (or a prize like an Academy Award). Collective choice is approached here as a cognitive challenge to be met, with good choices being the epistemically superior choices. By way of comparison, in most of the new plebiscitary formats explored in Chapter 4 (and summarized in Table 4.1) the aggregation of votes is serving various purposes deemed useful by the champions of these formats, but not necessarily epistemically superior.

---

[21] Sunstein, C., *Infotopia: How Many Minds Produce Knowledge*, Oxford, Oxford University Press, 2008, p. 8.

Aggregation towards numerical majorities and averages can, under very specific conditions, produce the healthy aggregation that adds up to cognitively sound answers.[22] The mathematician Marquis de Condorcet proved, in his famous Jury Theorem, that if a large group votes on a yes-or-no question, the majority is virtually certain to track the 'truth' when: (a) voters are better than random at choosing true propositions, (b) voters vote independently of each other, and (c) voters vote sincerely or truthfully, not strategically. The statistician Francis Galton observed the 'miracle of aggregation' at the country fair in Plymouth, where the average estimate of some 800 participants in a weight-estimation game came very close to the actual weight of an exhibited ox; many similar observations are reported in the literature.[23]

It is critical that the combination of the participating group and the question asked is such that a sizeable part of the group can give an answer to the question asked that is better than a random guess; if the answers of all others display a random or symmetrical distribution of error, then statistical aggregation will have the effect that error ('noise') is cancelled out so that relevant information ('signal') will stand out. If necessary conditions are not met then the 'miracle of aggregation' does not work so well, or can even lead to answers that are way off.

The complex-systems thinker Scott Page has explained why and how sizeable groups can come to accurate predictions, pointing at the negative correlations among people's predictive models, which will lower the collective error and will make the group at large smarter.[24] The key is group diversity—people pooling their different perspectives on the matter at hand.[25] Landemore considers the puzzle of deciding about who of two

---

[22] This is not the place to elaborate on all the technical details and often mathematical reasoning involved. There is an established literature that already does a splendid job in this respect. See Surowiecki, J., *The Wisdom of Crowds: Why the Many are Smarter than the Few*, New York, Doubleday, 2004; Page, S.E., *The Difference: How the Power of Diversity Creates Better Groups, Firms, Schools, and Societies*, Princeton University Press, 2007; Sunstein, C., *Infotopia: How Many Minds Produce Knowledge*, Oxford, Oxford University Press, 2008; Landemore, H., Collective Wisdom: Old and New, in Elster, J. and H. Landemore (eds), *Collective Wisdom: Principles and Mechanisms*, Cambridge, Cambridge University Press, 2012, pp. 1–20. For a critical view on this literature, see Brennan, J., *Against Democracy*, Princeton University Press, 2016.
[23] Surowiecki, J., *The Wisdom of Crowds: Why the Many are Smarter than the Few*, New York, Doubleday, 2004; Page, S.E., *The Difference: How the Power of Diversity Creates Better Groups, Firms, Schools, and Societies*, Princeton University Press, 2007; Sunstein, C., *Infotopia: How Many Minds Produce Knowledge*, Oxford, Oxford University Press, 2008.
[24] Page, S.E., *The Difference: How the Power of Diversity Creates Better Groups, Firms, Schools, and Societies*, Princeton University Press, 2007.
[25] Diverse groups with different cognitive perspectives perform better than homogenous groups as well as expert groups with less diverse perspectives on the matter at hand. This is formalized in a Diversity Trumps Homogeneity Theorem and a Diversity Trumps Ability Theorem by Page, S.E., *The Difference: How the Power of Diversity Creates Better Groups, Firms, Schools, and Societies*, Princeton University Press, 2007.

candidates is most competent for a political office.[26] A cognitively diverse group will look at different dimensions of the same quality (in this example competence for office), which on the aggregate level would lead to the most competent candidate being singled out—'where one voter makes a mistake, another is more likely to get it right and vice versa. In the aggregate . . . mistakes cancel each other not randomly but systematically'.[27]

An ingenious instrument for capitalizing on dispersed bits of information is the electronic prediction market. Page recommends exploring its potential further.[28] The electronic prediction market or 'decision market' is an aggregative mechanism on steroids, so to speak, connected as it is to the 'marvel' of pricing à la Hayek—starkly contrasted with deliberation à la Habermas.[29] A classic example in the political realm is the Iowa Electronic Market (IEM), which has allowed people since 1988 to bet on the outcome of presidential elections. The IEM has generally outperformed professional polls that are based on simply asking people what they expect to vote. The IEM asks participants in the electronic prediction market whom they expect to win, and also, importantly, to put their money where their mouth is—that is: to add a certain weight or amount of money to their guesses (see Box 5.1 for another and newer way of adding weight to choice: Quadratic Voting).

Box 5.1: Quadratic Voting (QV) as a new foundational paradigm?

A novel concept in the counters' realm is Quadratic Voting (QV), advanced by Eric Posner and Glen Weyl in their book *Radical Markets*.[a] To some extent, QV is akin to the methods of 'healthy aggregation' developed earlier but it also exceeds these in scope and ambition. QV is geared to aggregate dispersed knowledge as well as preference in more measured and healthier ways—in referendums, public polling, and social rating of all sorts of issues; but potentially also in candidate selection and political

---

[26] Landemore, H., Democratic Reason: The Mechanisms of Collective Intelligence in Politics, in Elster, J. and H. Landemore (eds), *Collective Wisdom: Principles and Mechanisms*, Cambridge, Cambridge University Press, 2012, pp. 251–89. See also on the Hong–Page theorem Landemore, H., *Open Democracy: Reinventing Popular Rule for the Twenty-First Century*, Princeton, Princeton University Press, 2020, p. 42. See Brennan, J., *Against Democracy*, Princeton University Press, 2016 for a number of fatal flaws, in his analysis, of the Hong–Page theorem.
[27] Landemore, H., Democratic Reason: The Mechanisms of Collective Intelligence in Politics, in Elster, J. and H. Landemore (eds), *Collective Wisdom: Principles and Mechanisms*, Cambridge, Cambridge University Press, 2012, p. 269.
[28] Page, S.E., *The Difference: How the Power of Diversity Creates Better Groups, Firms, Schools, and Societies*, Princeton University Press, 2007, p. 348. See also Surowiecki, J., *The Wisdom of Crowds: Why the Many are Smarter than the Few*, New York, Doubleday, 2004; Sunstein, C., *Infotopia: How Many Minds Produce Knowledge*, Oxford, Oxford University Press, 2008.
[29] Sunstein, C., *Infotopia: How Many Minds Produce Knowledge*, Oxford, Oxford University Press, 2008, pp. 11–16.

voting in representative systems. In terms of ambitions, it is in a class of its own. The authors suggest that QV, like one-person-one-vote, is no more and no less than a new foundational paradigm for collective decision-making, to be used in a variety of ways.

Like the Iowa electronic decision market, but operationalized quite differently, QV induces those who vote for (or click on) particular choice options to add a certain weight or price to their choices, in order to make all individual signals and hence the collective signal more refined. Based on microeconomic reasoning, the authors argue that voting must be squared in the sense that casting one vote would cost one 'voice credit' (to be bought out of their budget of voice credits) while casting two votes would cost four credits (i.e. two squared), casting three would cost nine credits (i.e. three squared), and so on. The quadratic rule would be the only one that induces rational individuals to spend votes in proportion to how much they know and care about an issue or candidate. Instead of putting increasingly expensive voice credits on their number-one choice, voters would be nudged to cast some relatively cheap votes for second- or third-choice options that they to some extent also appreciate. QV would encourage moderation by giving people an incentive to express, but not overstate, the intensity of their beliefs.

The moderating effects of QV are party hypothetical. It is conjectured that in 2016 a moderate Republican candidate would have been most likely to win the nomination, not Donald Trump, had QV been used; and that under QV the Brexit-referendum of the same year would have been a different ball game with arguably different results. Empirical proofs of concept are in the development stage. Empirical research confirmed that public polling based on QV may indeed produce more refined results than conventional polling that tends to W-shaped results on a Likert scale (with most participants clustering toward the extremes, some expressing indifference and a few in between). QV-based internet polling is further commercialized and battle-tested by a company created by the authors. In a political context, QV has been used in a few places, for instance by the city council of Gramado in Brazil to decide on next year's priorities and to find consensus on tax amendments. It is a way to go beyond 'the simplicity of yes or no', the council's president remarked.[b]

---

[a] This box is based on E.A. Posner and G.W. Weyl, *Radical Markets: Uprooting Capitalism and Democracy for a Just Society*, Princeton University Press, 2018, particularly Chapter 2; *The Economist*, The Mathematical Method that Could Offer a Fairer Way to Vote, <https://www.economist.com/christmas-specials/2021/12/18/the-mathematical-method-that-could-offer-a-fairer-way-to-vote>, 18 December 2021.

[b] Quoted in *The Economist*, The Mathematical Method that Could Offer a Fairer Way to Vote, 18 December 2021; there also the other hypothetical and empirical examples mentioned, as in E.A. Posner and G.W. Weyl, *Radical Markets: Uprooting Capitalism and Democracy for a Just Society*, Princeton University Press, 2018, pp. 111–22.

All electronic prediction or decision markets add this element one way or another, and this is of consequence. As the pay-off depends on the accuracy of participants' estimates, they have a strong incentive to neither overestimate nor underestimate. Companies like Hewlett-Packard and Google have used internal decision markets to predict in this way things such as printer sales and the number of active Gmail users for the coming months. Public institutions are more hesitant. A so-called Policy Analysis Market focusing on the Middle East was discontinued, as betting on potential catastrophes was widely seen as offensive and morally wrong.[30] Yet, on a less controversial plane, electronic markets might be helpful in predicting, for instance, the usage of a new public transport line or recreational facility, the cost of and willingness to pay for energy-saving home improvements as required by public policy.

Another format following the counters' line of reasoning is the epistemically enhanced public poll or vote. Sunstein suggests that, under the right conditions for healthy aggregation, even the often-ridiculed opinion poll can be revalued as a sensible tool.[31] While regular opinion polls aggregate how people feel about a matter at hand, knowledge or estimation polls aggregate what people know about something or what they deem likely to happen based on their experience. All polls work with statistical groups, with calculated averages and majorities, and miss the price mechanism that helps to sharpen collective predictions in the electronic market previously described. Nevertheless, under the right circumstances statistical groups are said to outperform deliberating groups that rely on less diversity in aggregating distributed knowledge.[32]

There are, however, as already mentioned, key conditions for healthy knowledge aggregation to be met. This is not easy. Especially independent and non-strategic choices are hard to get in a highly connected world, with all sorts of media, networks, and platforms in place that almost incessantly confront people with the views of peers and others in various bubbles. Diversity

---

[30] Surowiecki, J., *The Wisdom of Crowds: Why the Many are Smarter than the Few*, New York, Doubleday, 2004, p. 81.

[31] Sunstein, C., *Infotopia: How Many Minds Produce Knowledge*, Oxford, Oxford University Press, 2008, p. 27. See also Page, B.I. and R.Y. Shapiro, *The Rational Public: Fifty Years of Trends in Americans' Policy Preferences*, University of Chicago Press, 1992. Not taking into account the key conditions, however, the aggregation of public sentiment may easily turn sour, as also underscored by Sunstein, C., *Infotopia: How Many Minds Produce Knowledge*, Oxford, Oxford University Press, 2008, p. 28 et seqq.

[32] See Sunstein, C., *Infotopia: How Many Minds Produce Knowledge*, Oxford, Oxford University Press, 2008, pp. 45–102. Selection bias is hard to overcome in deliberating groups; even when the initial invitation is sent out randomly, self-selection is bound to make the deliberative mini-public less diverse than theoretically expected. The presence of different age groups, genders, and ethnicities can obscure the fact that very particular cognitive perspectives are drawn to the deliberative mini-public more than others.

seems easier to achieve in times of social fragmentation until one looks at the specific diversity requirements for 'healthy' aggregation previously mentioned: each person is more likely to be correct than not (not always likely); random or symmetrical distribution of error (not always likely). Page adds that for healthy aggregation cognitive (perspectivistic) diversity is more important than social (demographic) diversity.[33] This will be difficult to uphold in everyday democracy—would it mean only including actors with different perspectives and excluding those with similar ones?

The very focus on epistemic wisdom as the ability to arrive at knowledgeable collective conclusions brings its own limitations. As Mulgan writes: 'crowds can estimate stock prices, the number of beans in a jar or the weight of a cow'. But as he rightfully argues we should not set our hopes too high for 'tasks that require much higher bandwidth and iterative, mutual communication'.[34] Consider the coordinated interplay of the Biest-Houtakker resident cooperative, or the concerted action developed in the collaborative governance regime of Brainport-Eindhoven as discussed in Chapter 3. We could imagine an enhanced public poll or vote to enrich, but not to supplant, the sequential and iterative pooling of resources in such a regime or cooperative.

There are very few examples of statistical groups that come anywhere close to this bandwith of practical interaction. One approximation that I can think of is rather old. In 1999, a 'World Team' played a prolonged game of chess against then world champion Garry Kasparov. The World Team's decisions were aggregated by way of majority or plurality vote, in response to suggested moves by four young chess players. Kasparov ultimately won, but it was a remarkably close game, considering that almost none of the players in the World Team was anywhere near Kasparov's level.[35] On the one hand, this illustrates that a group that aggregates individual signals into collective choices can indeed develop and sustain a strategic string of moves. On the other hand, chess is a highly cognitive game with characteristics that mirror democratic governance to only a limited extent—characteristics that explain why we have very good chess computers, while we do not

---

[33] Page, S.E., *The Difference: How the Power of Diversity Creates Better Groups, Firms, Schools, and Societies*, Princeton University Press, 2007. A socially diverse crowd can be less diverse in perspectives on a matter at hand than a group that at face value seems less diverse in terms of background characteristics but in fact brings in a wider diversity of cognitive perspectives.

[34] Mulgan, G., *Big Mind: How Collective Intelligence Can Change our World*, Princeton, Princeton University Press, 2018, p. 114.

[35] Sunstein, C., *Infotopia: How Many Minds Produce Knowledge*, Oxford, Oxford University Press, 2008, p. 28.

have very good computers that successfully play the 'game' of democratic governance.[36]

The 'talkers' and the integrative push for pooled democracy

There are also formats that lean less on aggregative 'counting' and more on integrative 'talking' (still following Susskind's distinction) in the quest for better, smarter, solutions. Such formats are not literally confined to talking; they are in fact geared at a much wider communicative repertoire that includes corresponding, commenting, and editing in groups or crowds towards some practical aim.

Various authors mention Wikipedia as an inspirational idea for the use of wikis and similar pooled formats for problem solving in the public domain—as in 'wiki government'[37] and 'wiki democracy'.[38] The corporate world was ahead in developing 'wikinomics' and offered many examples of how crowd-sourcing platforms, collaborative editing tools, hackatons, meshatons, and the like could be used to develop 'smart solutions'. The multinational IBM, for instance, organized electronic 'world jams' to engage creative people in the search for new (business) solutions. The pharmaceutical company Eli Lilli shared difficult questions with an electronic network of 160,000 'problem solvers'. The operating system Linux was the result of the collaborative coding of a dispersed crowd of programmers, iteratively improving the operating system while working on it at a distance from each other.[39]

In pooled problem-solving of this type, the focus is primarily on getting the most resourceful and creative set of people involved, neither necessarily a large crowd, nor a random group of citizens in order to achieve representativeness. Getting smarter output—as in more effective solutions—is the first priority in such practices. A means towards this goal is pooling diverse input—as in diverse and useful input.

---

[36] Or rather, only very specific aspects of it.

[37] Noveck, B., *Wiki Government: How Technology Can Make Government Better, Democracy Stronger, and Citizens More Powerful*, Washington, DC, Brookings Institution Press, 2009.

[38] Susskind, J., *Future Politics: Living Together in a World Transformed by Tech*, Oxford, Oxford University Press, 2018.

[39] This is crowd-sourcing with the crowd interactively coordinating itself, disciplined by the architecture of the platform, to be distinguished from crowd-sourcing used by a central actor that uses the crowd input for its own process. In public governance, more specifically, we need to distinguish at least two types of crowd-sourcing. First, governments developing crowd-sourcing as brainstorming 2.0, supplementary to other sources of input. Second, governance-beyond-government platforms developing crowd-sourcing as the primary process, with government input as merely one type of input. See Hilgers, D. and C. Ihl, Citizensourcing: Applying the Concept of Open Innovation to the Public Sector, *International Journal of Public Participation*, 2010, 4, 1, pp. 67–88.

In the public domain, an early experiment with 'wiki planning', developed in the Australian city of Melbourne 2008—2009, used collaborative editing software to engage a wider group of actors, with various perspectives and fields of expertise, in the development of a new ten-year plan for the city. In 2015, France's Cap Collective engaged 21,000 people in drafting a digital law.[40] In Finland, the Ministry of the Environment and the Parliamentary Committee for the Future experimented with crowd-sourced law reform for better regulation of off-road traffic; this resulted in 500 ideas and 4,000 comments from more than 700 users of the online platform.[41] The pooling of diverse resources—whether we call it crowd-sourcing or wiki-something— may result in a new plan, law, or regulation, but it can also result in the smarter coordination of capacities and activities (for instance people pooling measurements of flora and fauna, of air and water quality). Noveck describes the whole gamut: the crowd-sourcing of ideas, opinions, data, funds, and tasks, which under the right circumstances would engage 'smart citizens' in a 'smarter state'.[42]

Noveck highlights the contrast with much of deliberative-democracy thinking, focused on transforming public opinion on public issues of representative groups of citizens, as well as a lot of participatory practice, geared at egalitarian and inclusive participation as a goal in itself.[43] In her approach to smart solutions, equal and inclusive participation is a possibility, not a normative imperative. Sometimes, a smart solution needs broad-based participation, sometimes it requires the involvement of a particular network from which the necessary pieces of information, resources, or competencies can be pooled.[44] The Wikipedia model, a seminal model of inspiration here, is clearly egalitarian and bottom-up in comparison to the model of the traditional encyclopedia. But it is also targeted and specific in its operations; not

[40] Mulgan, G., *Big Mind: How Collective Intelligence Can Change our World*, Princeton, Princeton University Press, 2018.

[41] Aitamurto, T., H. Landemore, and J. Saldivar Galli, Unmasking the Crowd: Participants' Motivation Factors, Expectations, and Profile in a Crowdsourced Law Reform, *Information, Communication & Society*, 2017, 20, 8, pp. 1239–60.

[42] See Noveck, B., *Smart Citizens, Smarter State: The Technologies of Expertise and the Future of Governing*, Cambridge, MA, Harvard University Press, 2015. See also Hilgers, D. and C. Ihl, Citizensourcing: Applying the Concept of Open Innovation to the Public Sector, *International Journal of Public Participation*, 2010, 4, 1, pp. 67–88.

[43] Noveck, B., *Smart Citizens, Smarter State: The Technologies of Expertise and the Future of Governing*, Cambridge, MA, Harvard University Press, 2015.

[44] Noveck, B., *Wiki Government: How Technology Can Make Government Better, Democracy Stronger, and Citizens More Powerful*, Washington, DC, Brookings Institution Press, 2009; Noveck, B., *Smart Citizens, Smarter State: The Technologies of Expertise and the Future of Governing*, Cambridge, MA, Harvard University Press, 2015.

everyone can or should work on each wiki or lemma, for it to become use-ful. Pooling the most resourceful inputs comes first; deliberation on an equal footing comes second or still later.

That being said, compared to the previous formats of aggregation toward intelligent solutions (the electronic prediction market, the epistemically enhanced public poll or vote), wikis and other crowdsourcing platforms are evidently more inclined to extensive 'talking' and communicating, and clearly less to efficient 'counting' and voting.[45] Many of said platforms are open to deliberation, albeit not as the ultimate aim of the platform. If one were to apply an elaborate checklist of deliberative quality some boxes would be checked but certainly not all.[46]

There are no thick walls separating different formats in the pooled-democracy midfield. Some formats display 'talkers' besides 'counters' ele-ments and just slightly veer to one side or the other. We can see this in platforms such as Pol.is that facilitate efficient voting on statements, used in primarily consensus-seeking processes on targeted issues. As explained on Participedia (itself a collaborative 'wiki') Pol.is works as a survey platform where users can enter statements, on which other users can express their positions clicking either 'agree', 'disagree', or 'pass'.[47] Using artificial intelli-gence and real-time machine learning that has been possible since the early 2010s, Pol.is helps to cluster users who voted similarly in opinion groups, visually defining them and identifying the points of consensus. The 'graphic interface shows how opinion clusters emerge, divide, and recombine; this is possible because pol.is develops and analyses a matrix that comprises what each person thinks about every comment', defining minority opinions along with majority opinions.[48]

---

[45] Hilgers, D. and C. Ihl, Citizensourcing: Applying the Concept of Open Innovation to the Public Sec-tor, *International Journal of Public Participation*, 2010, 4, 1, pp. 67–88; Noveck, B., *Smart Citizens, Smarter State: The Technologies of Expertise and the Future of Governing*, Cambridge, MA, Harvard University Press, 2015.

[46] See e.g., Bächtiger, A., S. Shikano, S. Pedrini, and M. Ryser, Measuring Deliberation 2.0: Standards, Discourse Types, and Sequenzialization. Paper presented at ECPR General Conference, Potsdam, 5–12 September 2009.

[47] Participedia, Method, <https://participedia.net/method/4682>, n.d.; see also Colin Megill, founder of Pol.is, explaining the platform, Pol.is, Pol.is Explainer and Demo [Video], Youtube, <https://www.youtube.com/watch?v=FrIin_omVn4>, 9 September 2016; Pol.is, Input Crowd, Output Meaning, <https://pol.is/home>, 2022; Roamresearch, Pol.is method, <https://roamresearch.com/#/app/polis-methods/page/EK79EAAcB>, n.d. ; Public Voice, Polis, <https://www.publicvoice.co.nz/online-engagement-tools/entry/194/>, 3 October 2016.

[48] Barry, L., vTaiwan: Public Participation Methods on the Cyberpunk Frontier of Democracy, Civic Hall, Civicist, <https://civichall.org/civicist/vtaiwan-democracy-frontier/,> 11, August 2016; Miller, C., Taiwan is Making Democracy Work again. It's Time We Paid Attention, Wired, <https://www.wired.co.uk/article/taiwan-democracy-social-media>, 26 November 2019; Pol.is, Mission and Values, <https://pol.is/company>, 17 July 2014. See also Participedia, Method, <https://participedia.net/method/4682, n.d.

In 2016, Pol.is was integrated into vTaiwan, a sophisticated platform for deciding about matters such as opinions toward Uber-taxis, self-driving vehicles, and a range of other cases. Audrey Tang, the first digital minister of Taiwan, contends that in all cases the graphic interface ultimately shows a particular picture. In a presentation posted on the internet, Tang displays it with emphasis: in the end, there will not be two or three competing clusters, even though this is how it may all start, but ultimately the graphic interface will show one dominant cluster of dots around what Tang calls a rough consensus. The key take-away from the presentation is to regulate the rough consensus first and to continue from there. 'Most people agree with most of their neighbours about most of the things most of the time', Tang argues.[49]

vTaiwan was triggered by civil unrest, an assault on national parliament, following a divisive referendum in 2014 about Taiwan's relation to mainland China. Motivated to make a change, the Taiwanese government engaged civic hackers to work on what would become vTaiwan (integrating the Pol.is platform). The intention was to do better than traditional politics. Nevertheless, representative institutions and expert authorities were not cancelled out. According to its website, vTaiwan 'brings together government ministries, elected representatives, scholars, experts, business leaders, civil society organisations and citizens'.[50]

With consensus-seeking technology, the addition of mini-hackatons and other collaborative tools, vTaiwan inclines to the more integrative—'talkers'—side of pooled democracy. Yet, it is clearly distinguished from more pronounced deliberative formats of democratic innovation. vTaiwan includes swift voting on the agree–disagree spectrum, which adds an aggregative element. It stays away, however, from more hard-ball plebiscitary voting, as in Taiwan's divisive referendum of 2014 that triggered the wish to handle tensions in different and more innovative ways. In a way, vTaiwan favours hybrid democratic innovation (which will be explored more extensively in Chapters 7 and 8 using two more advanced cases of hybridization).

Box 5.2: Restoring or bringing down the Golden Wall?

In *The Discovery of Heaven* by Harry Mulish, a seasoned politician and son of a former prime minister explains how an impressive wall, which he calls the Golden Wall, used to separate the powerful from the powerless in politics.[a] For a long time, the

---

[49] TEDx Talk, Digital Social Innovation to Empower Democracy| Audrey Tang| TEDxVitoriaGasteinz [Video], YouTube, <https://www.youtube.com/watch?v=LscTx6DHh9I>, 8 May 2019.
[50] Pol.is, Input Crowd, Output Meaning, <https://pol.is/home>, 2022.

world of power behind the Golden Wall was believed to work in mysterious ways: 'contained, reliable, clearly structured like a chessboard'. In actual fact, as this politician explains, the world behind the wall was just as messy and haphazard as the world before it, only this was not so evident because of the very existence of the wall and the associated suggestions and beliefs. In recent times, all sorts of cracks in the Golden Wall would have allowed people to peek inside, to see how things really work, which would have made those spectators lose the necessary faith. The only way to recapture faith, according to this politician, would be to restore the Golden Wall and together with it the separation of those with and without political power.

This relates to a work of fiction, but some politicians in established democracies have in fact responded in quite similar—that is defensive and protective—ways to repeated calls to 'open up' representative democracy and let people peek and get inside the corridors of power. Their response is, in essence, that not the distribution of political power should change, but calls to open-up representative democracy need to be toned down. Converted to the matrix used in this book, this response says: defend and restore the upper half, keep the lower half in check, and maintain a clear separation between the two.

To be sure, not all politicians and parties active in representative democracy are so allergic to opening up the system. Some have even developed far-reaching reform plans, resonating with societal calls for change. Between plans and implementation, however, many barriers exist. In the upper half of the matrix, the realm of representative democracy and its established institutions, the barriers are commonly higher and more tenacious than in the lower half of the matrix. They are related to hard-to-change constitutional rules and traditions. And attempts to change these depend on the support of the very political parties and actors that rely for their position and authority on these rules and traditions.

[a] The original Dutch version was published in 1992, the English translation four years later: Mulish, H., *The Discovery of Heaven*, London, Penguin Books, 1996. A movie with the same title came out in 1992.

Meanwhile on the other side: Rigid representative systems?

The previously discussed movements are predominantly located in the lower half of the matrix that I use to understand democratic innovations (see Chapter 2). This is the realm where experimentation abounds, where new ways of doing democracy are tried out, often with high ambitions for bottom-up democracy and civic self-determination. But what about the upper half of the matrix, the realm of representative democracy, where political leaders and political parties have their base camp? (the other side of the Golden Wall as Mulish would have it, see Box 5.2). It is commonly assumed that much less is really changing and little is achieved in terms of democratic reform or innovation in this realm. This is not without grounds, considering the realities of electoral and party systems. Electoral systems are often codified in more or less rigid constitutional legislation; changes therein often require qualified or even double majorities, giving veto powers to entrenched minority parties or minority blocks.[51]

Party systems are less 'frozen' than earlier literature suggested.[52] In fact, many established democracies have experienced remarkable shifts in their party landscapes, wherein new cleavages have appeared. Yet, it is also evident that such changes remain influenced and constrained by constitutionally defined conditions. The majoritarian electoral models of the UK and the USA continue to favour bipolar political systems; just like the PR models of the Netherlands and Belgium continue to suppress the establishment of a duopoly in electoral and political relations. Consequently, change agents in these countries are led to think that Washington, London, The Hague, and Brussels are hopeless places for real democratic change to take root, and that representative democracy is to be worked around if a significant change is desired. The situation in other entrenched representative systems—whether more inclined to pendulum or consensus democracy—is no different in this respect. Some suggest we could better pin our hopes for real change on post-representative democracy.[53] It is not difficult to understand those who disparage representative democracy as a realm of democratic betterment. But looking away and turning away from this realm is ill-advised.

Even though representative democracy is a realm where democratic change is often stalled or blocked, this realm cannot be ignored in serious studies of democratic reform and innovation. To begin with, almost all new methods discussed in this book can neither be understood nor

---

[51] Renwick, A., *The Politics of Electoral Reform: Changing the Rules of Democracy*, Cambridge, Cambridge University Press, 2010; Scharpf, F, The Joint-Decision Trap Revisited, *Journal of Common Market Studies*, 44, 4, pp. 845–64; Rahat, G. and R.Y. Hazan, The Barriers to Electoral System Reform: A Synthesis of Alternative Approaches, *West European Politics*, 2011, 34, 3, pp. 478–94.

[52] Lipset, M. and S. Rokkan (eds), *Party Systems and Voter Alignments: Cross-National Perspectives*, New York, The Free Press, 1967.

[53] Tormey, S., *The End of Representative Politics*, Cambridge, Polity Press, 2015; Reybrouck, D. van, *Against Elections: The Case for Democracy*, London, Penguin Random House, 2013.

deployed well in isolation from representative democracy, which continues to hold considerable sway as an authorizing environment, retaining often crucial decision and veto powers.[54] Figure 4.1 underscored the fundamental interdependency of innovations that attempt to make some turn in the foreground—whether more deliberative or more plebiscitary in character—and the representative system that in the background continues to be the predominant operating system (a bit like the OS of a PC that needs to be worked with for a new application to become durably functional).

Furthermore, the representative realm itself is not without relevant reform experience. In Chapter 1, the metaphor of the reform cake was used to clarify that there are at least three layers of relevant discourse: (a) present-day discourse on the deliberative mini-public and other citizen-oriented democratic innovations; (b) longer-standing reform debates on petitions, consultations, neighborhood councils, and the like, which also focus on citizen involvement; and (c) at the base of the reform cake, longer-standing reform discourse targeting the central institutions of representative democracy. I attached a number of reform concepts (electoral reform, party reform, primaries, recall, etc.) to this layer in an illustrative, non-exhaustive way. In Chapter 2, I approached reform concepts in representative democracy more analytically (besides reform concepts in direct democracy), distinguishing between darlings of reform consonant with pendulum democracy versus consensus democracy (see Table 2.2 for a summary).

Ank Michels and I used this distinction between pendulum-democracy and consensus-democracy reforms as a starting point for comparing reform experiences in the UK and the Netherlands between 1990 and 2010.[55] It is instructive to reflect on the reform experiences in these two countries, which traditionally boast rather different democratic systems. They are commonly seen as exemplary for pendulum democracy (Westminster style) and consensus democracy (Rhineland style), all the more so when viewed beyond the formal-constitutional institutions, as we did. We analysed reforms in representative democracy in two steps.

First, we analysed democratic reforms in statewide and formal terms, following Lijphart's executive–parties and federal–unitary dimensions. On the executives–parties dimension, notwithstanding some cosmetic and rhetorical reforms, both systems displayed little real change. On the

[54] Moore, M., *Creating Public Value: Strategic Management in Government*, Cambridge, MA, Harvard University Press, 1997; Tsebelis, G., *Veto Players: How Political Institutions Work*, Princeton University Press, 2002.
[55] Hendriks, F. and A. Michels, Democracy Transformed? Reforms in Britain and the Netherlands (1990–2010), *International Journal of Public Administration*, 2011, 34, 5, pp. 307–17.

federal–unitary dimension, the Dutch system displayed no formal reform, whereas in the UK—interestingly—some consensual ingredients were added, namely: devolution of power to the Scottish and Welsh areas of the UK and Central Bank independence (which in Lijphart's classification is one indicator of consensus democracy). We concurred with Flinders that by the end of the first decade of the twenty-first century the UK displayed 'democratic drift' and 'majoritarian modification' rather than any fundamental 'shift' away from the Westminster model in statewide formal terms.[56]

In the second decade of the twenty-first century, the contrast between British majoritarianism and Dutch consensualism continued to predominate, at least in statewide and formal terms. Conservatives and Liberal-Democrats governed between 2010–2015 on a coalition agreement, which allowed a referendum (held in 2011) on a potentially less majoritarian electoral system (AV). However, the referendum returned a solid 'no' to replacing Winner-Take-All elections, and single-party majority cabinets have confirmed the norm again since 2015. With Brexit, the UK broke away from the EU institutional framework, a paragon of consensus democracy according to Lijphart, and in many ways returned to the fold of Westminster (see Box 2.1 on the AV and Brexit referendums). In the Netherlands, a Citizens' Assembly looked into possible changes to PR-voting in 2016, recommending rather limited changes to the system, which were still ignored by government and parliament. Other formal reforms in the Lijphartian sense were not realized in the Dutch system, despite decades of debate about reform in Dutch democracy.[57]

Second, we extended the Lijphartian majoritarian vs consensual divide by analysing reforms geared at the subnational or nonformal expressions of representative democracy. Here, the picture was more varied. Reforms in this category partly strengthened the position of pendulum democracy in the UK and consensus democracy in the Netherlands—as could be expected— but interestingly also added consensual elements to UK democracy and majoritarian elements to Dutch democracy. Representative democracy in both countries became to some extent 'mixed-up' with ingredients associated

---

[56] Flinders, M., *Delegated Governance and the British State: Walking without Order*, Oxford, Oxford University Press, 2008.

[57] Michels, A., Debating Democracy: The Dutch Case, *Acta Politica*, 2008, 43, 4, pp. 472–92; Hendriks, F., Democratic Reform between the Extreme Makeover and the Reinvention of Tradition: The Case of the Netherlands, *Democratization*, 2009, 12, 2, pp. 243–68; Geurtz, C., *Immune to Reform? Understanding Democratic Reform in Three Consensus Democracies: The Netherlands Compared with Germany and Austria*, PhD dissertation, Tilburg University, 2012. Referendum legislation does not figure in the Lijphartian framework. I can also be short about it: legislation regulating corrective referendums was in force for a few years (2014–2018) before being repealed by government and Parliament; two national corrective referendums had been organized under the auspices of this legislation.

with the other country. Unexpected reforms, against-the-grain, came paired with expected reforms, consonant with the traditionally dominant models of representative democracy in the two countries.

In the UK, the Local Government Act adopted in 2000 facilitated the installation of majoritarian local cabinets ('mini-Westminster' systems) and a competitively elected mayor (winner-take-all style) in London and a series of other locations. Conversely, the Regional Assemblies Act of 2003 created regional assemblies in the English part of the UK, potentially invoking a less dual and centralized polity, and a somewhat more decentralized multi-level governance system with hints to the Rhinelandic-European pattern.[58] We also observed scattered experiments with coalition government at the sub-national level in the UK. In the Netherlands, a reform called 'dualization' intended to separate executive and council roles in provinces and munici-palities, true to the spirit of consensus democracy. In the same spirit, new practices of reaching state–society accords were advanced, attaching fancy neologisms like 'triple helix' to deeply ingrained traditions. Conversely, we noted that top-down induced amalgamations were taking the Dutch local-government system closer to a Westminster pattern of large-scale, unified, in itself centralized local units.

Scattered experiments with so-called 'mayoral referendums' in Dutch local government were in fact experiments with the competitively elected mayor as a local political leader with a clear and independent mandate, quite dif-ferent from the traditionally appointed mayor as guardian of local consensus democracy. The strongest push to more adversarial politics and new forms of polarization amidst traditional pacification, however, was not the result of new legislation or experimentation by design. The advent of the self-styled majoritarian Pim Fortuyn in 2001 and his assassination in 2002 sparked a series of actions and reactions that resulted in a waxed populist fringe and a waned core of middle parties, the traditional backbone of Dutch con-sensualism.[59] Dutch consensus democracy has not disappeared through all this—it is institutionally still conserved in many ways—but it has become mixed up with a few conspicuous elements of pendulum democracy.[60] At

[58] For more about such patterns in local and regional democracy, see Loughlin, J., F. Hendriks, and A. Lidström (eds), *The Oxford Handbook of Local and Regional Democracy in Europe*, Oxford University Press, 2010.
[59] Hendriks, F. and M. Bovens, Pacificatie en polarisatie: Kentering en continuïteit in politiek en bestuur in Nederland post 2002, *Bestuurskunde*, 2008, 17, 3, pp. 56–63; Pellikaan, H., S. De Lange, and T. van der Meer, The Centre Does Not Hold: Coalition Politics and Party System Change in the Netherlands, 2002–12, *Government and Opposition*, 2018, 53, 2, pp. 231–55.
[60] Pennings, P. and H. Keman, The Changing Landscape of Dutch Politics since the 1970s, *Acta Polit-ica*, 2008, 43, 2–3, pp. 154–79; Hendriks, F., Democratic Reform between the Extreme Makeover and the Reinvention of Tradition: The Case of the Netherlands, *Democratization*, 2009, 12, 2, pp. 243–68.

the same time, in the UK, and mainly subnationally, a few striking elements of consensus democracy have been added to democratic governance, even though majoritarian patterns still prevail in statewide formal and constitutional terms. Had we looked at just the latter, the first step in our analysis, and had we not added a second step, we would have missed relevant reforms in representative democracy.[61]

All in all, there is indeed a lot of institutional persistence, even outright resistance to institutional change, but there is also some actual democratic reform going on in long-standing democracies like the British and the Dutch. Countries such as New Zealand and Belgium, furthermore, demonstrate that large-scale reform is at times actually implemented and maintained in entrenched representative systems. For New Zealand, the adoption and retention of Proportional Representation (PR) from 1996 onwards has meant a major shift away from the majoritarian Westminster model, of which it had been an almost perfect example up to 1996.[62] A Royal Commission on the Electoral System had effectively recommended this shift towards PR, a big leap to consensualism on Lijphart's executive–parties dimension, as well as a path towards public endorsement by referendum (organized twice: in 1992 and 1993). In Belgium, it was particularly on Lijphart's federal–unitary dimension that marked reforms were pushed through in a series of so-called state reforms. Powers and responsibilities were strongly dispersed from the centre of the former unitary state to the regions and communities of now federalized Belgium.[63] While consensus democracy already dominated the politics–executives dimension, it now also dominated the federal–unitary dimension.

The point that I want to make here is not that reform of representative democracy is in any way superior or more worthy than the innovations in bottom-up oriented democracy previously discussed. The point is that reform of representative democracy is still relevant and at times even real,[64] which should not be overlooked by those who truly want to understand

---

[61] We actually added a third step, looking into reforms beyond the realm of representative democracy, reforms positioned in the lower half of Figure 2.2. Both the UK and the Netherlands appeared to experiment with innovations in direct democracy, fortifying the image of hybrid democracy, to which I will return in Chapter 7.

[62] Lijphart, A., *Patterns of Democracy: Government Forms and Performance in Thirty-Six Countries*, New Haven, Yale University Press, 1999.

[63] Deschouwer, K., From Consociation to Federation: How the Belgian Parties Won, in K.R. Luther and K. Deschouwer (eds), *Party Elites in Divided Societies*, London, Routledge, 1999, 74–100.

[64] See also Vatter, A., M. Flinders, and J. Bernauer, A Global Trend Toward Democratic Convergence? A Lijphartian Analysis of Advanced Democracies, *Comparative Political Studies*, 2014, 47, 6, pp.903–29. The authors detect important shifts in a Lijphart-inspired matrix of democratic models.

the changing landscape of democracy, nor by those who effectively want to revitalize this landscape with bottom-up innovations.

The added value of representative-democracy reform can and should be discussed critically. It is not often a resounding success. Compared to the vast institutional continuities in representative democracy, changes therein are often of relative weight. Let us not forget that the same is true for previously discussed turns to citizen-oriented innovations, some of which are even advanced as microscopic. Champions of such innovations often invoke a social-science version of the butterfly thesis positing that small changes can trigger large effects. If this has relevance for innovations in citizens-oriented democracy, it also has relevance for innovations in representative democracy, especially considering that one tends to impact the other.

Among the institutional continuities and stalemates, moreover, there are some that are simply so questionable and controversial that democratic-reform pressure needs to be kept up even when successful short-term change is not very likely. In the context of American democracy, many would put the infamous filibuster, gerrymandering, and party-finance reform high on the list. Looking away from such hard-to-change issues is tempting for change agents who want to make a difference in the shorter term but, with an eye on future generations, this would seem ill-advised. History teaches us that investments in the long shot, repeated and mounting reform pressure, may still pay off many years later. Democratic-reform research—monitoring the existing barriers and the proposed openings, the slight and the somewhat more promising—has an important role to play here.

From understanding to advancing democratic innovation

In this chapter—the last in Part I, focused on understanding variation—I revisited the contrast between deliberative and plebiscitary formats from the angle of democratic-cum-cultural theory discussed in Chapter 2. From this theoretical angle, I continued to look at what is budding, often experimentally, in the area between the two poles. As in the more radical plebiscitary and deliberative innovations, much of this seems to be confined to the lower half of the theoretical matrix (Figures 5.1 and 5.2). This is where bottom-up formats of aggregative voting and counting coexist with bottom-up formats of integrative reflection and joint action. On closer inspection, however,

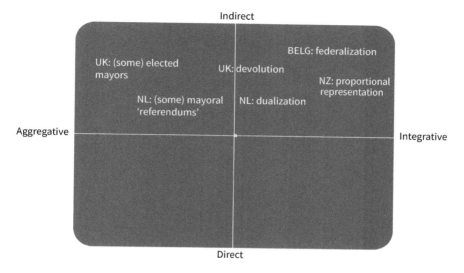

Figure 5.3 Specimens of reform in representative systems

there is more to this. Concepts of democratic innovation that favour the citizen, the demos, and the crowd in a bottom-up fashion always compete with and sometimes connect to visions championing power distance in democracy—political representation, delegation, mandate, and leadership. We need the full matrix to understand the interplay, which is also likely to help in advancing democratic innovations.

Understanding and advancing democratic innovations both require taking the logic and dynamics of representative democracy into account, the pervasive continuities and rigidities as well as the occasional institutional changes, however modest or restrained they may be (Figure 5.3 presents a few salient examples of reform in the upper half of the matrix). In Part II of the book—focusing on advancing innovation—I will continue to view democratic innovations within the full matrix of varieties explored in this part of the book. Besides connecting democratic innovations to representative systems as just mentioned, I will look into possible and actual links between different formats: such as a Citizens' Assembly linked to a referendum, or Participatory Budgeting extended with new forms of voting, embedded in representative systems (Chapters 7–8). Approached in this way, democratic innovations are not singular instruments, singular dots on the conceptual map, but varied and dynamic combinations or hybrids (Chapter 9). The crucial question of which values or goods are to serve as guiding lights for such practices is central to the next chapter.

PART II
ADVANCING INNOVATION

6

Key values for democratic-governance innovation

Recognizing the good and the better

This chapter marks the beginning of Part II, which will take the book's argumentation more specifically to the realm of design thinking and evaluation focused on democratic-governance innovations. Such innovations are commonly justified as attempts to improve democratic governance for the 'better'—to do 'good' and add 'value' to democratic governance.[1] But how can we recognize the value, the good, and the better when we see it? This question is not easily answered. The problem is not a lack of available answers, but rather a confounding abundance of answers coming from various directions.[2]

In this Chapter, I will try to clarify the key values for democratic-governance innovation by integrating into one values framework two important discourses with different strengths and focus points, thus capitalizing on their mutually reinforcing potential. On the one hand, I will go back to Dahl's seminal approach to democratic values and the follow-up debate about 'democratic goods' which should arguably inform the design, evaluation, and

---

[1] Fung, A., Varieties of Participation in Complex Governance, *Public Administration Review*, 2006, 66, 1, pp. 66–75; Ansell, C. and A. Gash, Collaborative Governance in Theory and Practice, *Journal of Public Administration Research and Theory*, 2008, 18, 4, p. 543–71; Smith, G., *Democratic Innovation: Designing Institutions for Citizen Participation*, Cambridge, Cambridge University Press, 2009; Geissel, B. and K. Newton (eds), *Evaluating Democratic Innovations: Curing the Democratic Malaise?*, Abingdon, Routledge, 2012; Elstub, S. and O. Escobar (eds), *Handbook of Democratic Innovation and Governance*, Cheltenham, Edward Elgar, 2019.

[2] Andrews, M., Good Government Means Different Things in Different Countries, *Governance*, 2010, 23, 1, pp. 7–35; Bühlmann, M. and H. Kriesi, Models for Democracy, in H. Kriesi, S. Lavenex, F. Esser, J. Matthes, M. Bühlmann, and D. Bochsler (eds), *Democracy in the Age of Globalization and Mediatization*, Basingstoke, Palgrave Macmillan, 2013, pp. 44–69; Beetham, D., Evaluating New vs Old Forms of Citizen Engagement and Participation, in B. Geissel and K. Newton (eds), *Evaluating Democratic Innovations: Curing the Democratic Malaise?*, London, Routledge, 2012, pp. 56–67; Bryson, J.M., K.S. Quick, C. Schively Slotterbak, and B.C. Crosby, Designing Public Participation Processes, *Public Administration Review*, 2012, 73, 1, pp. 23–34; Lucardie, P., *Democratic Extremism in Theory and Practice*, London, Routledge, 2014; Rosanvallon, P., *Good Government: Democracy Beyond Elections*, Cambridge, MA, Harvard University Press, 2015; Hendriks, F., Democratic Innovation Beyond Deliberative Reflection, *Democratization*, 2019, 26, 3, pp. 444–64; O'Flynn, I., Democratic Innovations and Theories of Democracy, in S. Elstub and O. Escobar (eds), *Democratic Innovation and Governance*, Cheltenham: Edward Elgar, 2019, pp. 32–44.

Rethinking Democratic Innovation. Frank Hendriks, Oxford University Press. © Frank Hendriks (2023).
DOI: 10.1093/oso/9780192848291.003.0006

calibration of democratic innovations.[3] On the other hand, I will return to Hood's equally seminal approach to values in public administration, and the subsequent debate about shifts in governance and their pertaining values.[4] The two strands of literature suggest varying approaches to valuing democratic governance—with varying sensitivities and focus points—which can be fortified through integration.

That different approaches can in fact learn from each other and work better together in a mutually reinforcing way is one important motivation for developing an integrative values framework and exploring its scope. The other, overriding, motivation is that citizens and *demoi* are confronted with democratic-governance innovations as comprehensive, multi-faceted interventions. Scholars may usefully concentrate on one facet, say the effect of a particular innovation on the value of inclusiveness.[5] But for citizens and *demoi* at large, democratic-governance innovations are not confined to one facet; plural *demoi* are interested in inclusive and effective democratic governance, in procedural appropriateness and systemic counterbalance, to refer to just two value pairs that are brought together in the integrative values framework. From a civic and societal perspective, the development of a comprehensive values framework is thus essential (in addition to research focused on particular values) to keep sight of the bigger picture and the wider set of values relevant to democratic-governance innovation.

This chapter proceeds as follows. First, it reconstructs dominant thinking about key values for democratic-governance innovation in discourses focusing on the 'democratic' element and the 'governance' element respectively. The focus is on seminal definitions and widely used formulations

---

[3] I explored this line of reasoning in Chapter 3. Here, I will further elaborate on democratic-innovations discourse, and synthesize it with governance-innovations discourse. For more on 'democratic goods', see: Dahl, R.A., *On Democracy*, New Haven, Yale University Press, 2000; Smith, G., *Democratic Innovation: Designing Institutions for Citizen Participation*, Cambridge, Cambridge University Press, 2009; Fishkin, J., *When the People Speak: Deliberative Democracy and Public Consultation*, Oxford, Oxford University Press, 2009; Michels, A.M.B., Innovations in Democratic Governance: How Does Citizen Participation Contribute to a Better Democracy, *International Review of Administrative Sciences*, 2011, 77, 2, pp. 275–93; Geissel, B. and K. Newton (eds), *Evaluating Democratic Innovations: Curing the Democratic Malaise?*, Abingdon, Routledge, 2012.

[4] Hood, C., A Public Management for All Seasons?, *Public Administration*, 1991, 69, 1, pp. 267–82; Toonen, Th.A.J., Networks, Management and Institutions: Public Administration as 'Normal Science', *Public Administration*, 1998, 76, 2, pp. 229–52; Rothstein, B. and J. Teorell, What is Quality of Government? A Theory of Impartial Government Institutions, *Governance*, 2008, 21, 2, pp. 165–90; Nabatchi, T., Public Values Frames in Administration and Governance, *Perspectives on Public Management and Governance*, 2017, 1, 1, pp. 59–72; Chandra, Y. and R.M. Walker, How Does a Seminal Article in Public Administration Diffuse and Influence the Field? Bibliometric Methods and the Case of Hood's 'A Public Management For All Seasons?', *International Public Management Journal*, 2019, 22, 5, pp. 712–42.

[5] Wojciechowska, M., Towards Intersectional Democratic Innovations, *Political Studies*, 2019, 67, 4, pp. 895–911; Ansell, C., C. Doberstein, H. Henderson, S. Siddiki, and P. 't Hart, Understanding Inclusion in Collaborative Governance: A Mixed-Methods Approach, *Policy and Society*, 2020, 39, 4, pp. 570–91.

of key values, discussing relevant variations in the two strands of literature. Next, the chapter takes a synthesizing step toward an integrative values framework, reviewing this framework internally (how the component parts work together) as well as externally (how the framework could be used). Throughout this chapter, the term innovation—which has become the prominent signifier in contemporary discourse about improvements in both democracy and governance[6]—will be used in a broad sense, taking on board longer-standing discourse on improvements in democratic governance under the heading of reform.[7] This is entirely consistent with the combined view of democratic reform and innovation presented earlier (specifically in Chapter 1).

Democratic-innovations discourse and values

An obvious place to start this quest is the literature which sets out to authoritatively formulate the values or 'goods' upon which democratic innovations are to be grafted. Various formulations can be found, but the hard core of virtually all of them is that the people (*demos*) are the driving force and touchstone of public governance (*kratos*), and that citizens constituting the demos are equally accredited in this sense.[8] In a democracy, according to Saward, 'citizens themselves have an equal effective input into the making of binding collective decisions.'[9] Dahl underscores the elementary normative principle, 'that all the members are to be treated as if they were equally qualified to participate in the process of making decisions about the policies the association will pursue.'[10]

From this normative principle, Dahl derived five core values: inclusion of adults; equality in voting; effective participation (effective in terms of making citizen views known); enlightened understanding; control of the agenda (so

[6] Goodin, R., *Innovating Democracy: Democratic Theory and Practice after the Deliberative Turn*, Oxford, Oxford University Press, 2010; Torfing, J. and P. Triantafillou (eds), *Enhancing Public Innovation by Transforming Public Governance*, Cambridge, Cambridge University Press, 2016; Elstub, S. and O. Escobar (eds), *Democratic Innovation and Governance*, Cheltenham, Edward Elgar, 2019.

[7] Fishkin, J., *Democracy and Deliberation: New Directions for Democratic Reform*, New Haven, Yale University Press, 1991; Toonen, Th.A.J., Administrative Reform: Analytics, in B.G. Peters and J. Pierre (eds), *Handbook of Public Administration*, New York, Sage, 2003, pp. 467–76; Hendriks, F., Democratic Reform Between the Extreme Makeover and the Reinvention of Tradition, *Democratization*, 2009, 16, 2, pp. 243–68; Renwick, A., *The Politics of Electoral Reform: Changing the Rules of Democracy*, Cambridge, Cambridge University Press, 2010; Jacobs, K. and M. Leyenaar, A Conceptual Framework for Major, Minor and Technical Electoral Reform, *West European Politics*, 2011, 34, 3, pp. 495–513.

[8] Beetham, D., Key Principles and Indices for a Democratic Audit, in D. Beetham (ed.), *Defining and Measuring Democracy*, London, Sage, 1994, pp. 25–43.

[9] Saward, M., *The Terms of Democracy*, Cambridge, Polity Press, 1998, p. 15.

[10] Dahl, R.A., *On Democracy*, New Haven, Yale University Press, 2000, p. 37.

that policies of the association are always open to change by the members).[11] Influential authors in the democratic-innovations literature resort to similar normative standards, sometimes a tad narrower defined, sometimes somewhat broader. The listed standards are typically at the same level of generality as Dahl's core values of democratic process; as opposed to the more specific requirements for state-level representative democracy that Dahl specified in line with his core principles.[12]

Beetham uses three normative criteria for evaluating democratic practices: participatory range (inclusiveness and numbers of participants); deliberative mode; and impact on participants, public debate, and policy outcomes.[13] Fishkin proceeds from what he calls 'the root notions of inclusion and thoughtfulness' and ultimately arrives at a triplet of democratic values: participation, equality, deliberation.[14] Because he sees two legitimate roads to democratic inclusion, this notion bifurcates in his view in the standards of mass participation (involvement in large numbers) and political equality (equal chances of being heard or represented). The third value in his triplet is deliberation, or thoughtfulness (enlightened understanding in Dahl's earlier formulation).[15]

Smith slightly adapted and widened Dahl's shortlist. His six 'goods' for guiding and evaluating democratic innovations also encompass inclusiveness, considered judgement, and popular control, with the latter somewhat broadening Dahl's agenda control. In Smith's thinking, the people ideally control all the stages of problem definition, option analysis, option selection, and implementation thereof. Moreover, Smith adds transparency (for both participants and the wider public) and completes his list with two criteria that are responsive to critical voices contending that democratic innovations are too often impractical and constrained to specific contexts: efficiency (regarding the burdens for participants and the public purse) and transferability (regarding the extent to which innovations can be applied elsewhere).[16]

[11] Dahl, R.A., *On Democracy*, New Haven, Yale University Press, 2000, p. 37–8.

[12] Dahl, R.A., *On Democracy*, New Haven, Yale University Press, 2000, p. 85.

[13] Beetham, D., Evaluating New vs Old Forms of Citizen Engagement and Participation, in B. Geissel and K. Newton (eds), *Evaluating Democratic Innovations: Curing the Democratic Malaise?*, London, Routledge, 2012, p. 59.

[14] Fishkin, J., *When the People Speak: Deliberative Democracy and Public Consultation*, Oxford, Oxford University Press, 2009.

[15] Fishkin's work was already mentioned in Chapter 3 as an important steppingstone to understanding democratic governance innovation and pertaining values; here I build further on his distinctions, combined with those of others.

[16] Smith, G., *Democratic Innovation: Designing Institutions for Citizen Participation*, Cambridge, Cambridge University Press, 2009.

In Dahl's take and related debate on democratic legitimacy, values, or goods, a fundamental tension is being assumed between democratic participation and governance effectiveness, or more specifically between achieving citizen input in public governance on the one hand and achieving policy outputs on the other.[17] They may not be incompatible per se, but it is underscored that the two are not easily achieved at the same time. Special care is needed to assure that sensitivity to input-legitimacy—the typical starting point for democratic-innovations discourse[18]—does not preclude attention to output-legitimacy.

As pointed out elsewhere, democratic governance 'by the people' is just one side of the coin; effective governance 'for the people' is the other side, increasingly important for achieving and maintaining legitimacy.[19] Further refining the sequence, other authors use the distinction of input-, throughput- and output-values—deemed crucial for achieving input-, throughput-, and output-legitimacy.[20] Throughput-values are associated by these authors with procedural and interactional qualities that should come to the fore, in some way or another, in the transmission of inputs into outputs.

Taking the input–throughput–output sequence as a frame of reference, we can say that democratic-innovations discourse tends to proceed from the input-side, where the strongest emphasis is traditionally located (inclusion and equal input; popular control and participation), followed by a specific interest in throughput-qualities (transparency, deliberation, and enlightened understanding).[21] Moving towards the output-side, the emphasis in

---

[17] Dahl, R.A., A Democratic Dilemma: System Effectiveness versus Citizen Participation, *Political Science Quarterly*, 1994, 109, 1, pp. 3–34; Dahl, R.A., *On Democracy*, New Haven, Yale University Press, 2000; Putnam, R.D., *Making Democracy Work: Civic Traditions in Modern Italy*, Princeton, Princeton University Press, 1993, p. 62; Lijphart, A., *Patterns of Democracy: Government Forms and Performance in Thirty-Six Countries*, New Haven, Yale University Press, 1999; Scharpf, F.W., *Governing in Europe: Effective and Democratic?*, Oxford, Oxford University Press, 1999.

[18] Pogrebinschi, T. and M. Ryan, Moving Beyond Input Legitimacy: When Do Democratic Innovations Affect Policy Making, *European Journal of Political Research*, 2017, 57, 1, pp. 135–52; Smith, G., *Democratic Innovation: Designing Institutions for Citizen Participation*, Cambridge, Cambridge University Press, 2009, p. 577.

[19] Scharpf, F.W., *Governing in Europe: Effective and Democratic?*, Oxford, Oxford University Press, 1999; Hibbing, J.R. and E. Theiss-Morse, *Stealth Democracy: Americans' Beliefs about how Government Should Work*, Cambridge, Cambridge University Press, 2002; Strebel, M.A., D. Kübler, and F. Marcinkowski, The Importance of Input and Output Legitimacy in Democratic Governance, *European Journal of Political Research*, 2019, 58, pp. 488–513.

[20] Heinelt, H., D. Sweeting, and P. Gemitis (eds), *Legitimacy and Urban Governance*, London, Routledge, 2006; Papadopoulos, Y. and P. Warin, Are Innovative, Participatory and Deliberative Procedures in Policy Making Democratic and Effective?, *European Journal of Political Research*, 2007, 46, 4, pp. 445–72; Geissel, B. and K. Newton (eds), *Evaluating Democratic Innovations: Curing the Democratic Malaise?*, Abingdon, Routledge, 2012; Schmidt, V.A., Democracy and Legitimacy in the European Union Revisited: Input, Output and 'Throughput', *Political Studies*, 2013, 61, 1, pp. 2–22.

[21] A good example is Landemore, H., *Open Democracy: Reinventing Popular Rule for the Twenty-First Century*, Princeton, Princeton University Press, 2020, p. 12 who highlights five institutional principles: participation rights; deliberation; majoritarian principle; democratic representation; transparency—all

democratic-innovations discourse becomes weaker, although Smith's short-list of democratic goods is particularly sensitive to related considerations. Popular control in his view should also extend to the stage of implementing the will of the people.[22] Others have argued that public participation and deliberation should be 'consequential', taken to practice.[23] It needs to be noted that this is not automatically the same as effectively solving public problems or creating public value, which Smith recognizes.

Acknowledging that democratic innovations are often criticized for being impractical exercises in public participation, Smith added efficiency and transferability as items five and six on his list of desirables[24]—not because they are expected core qualities of democratic innovations, but because they are traditional vulnerabilities. In a recent reflection[25] on democratic-innovations discourse, Smith is again mindful of the criticism that too much attention has focused on the 'input' side of the political process.[26]

On the whole, the input–throughput–output sequence is a sensible and practical way of distinguishing values relevant to democratic innovations at the application level. It is undoubtedly one of the conceptual threads to be woven into an integrative values framework. More recently, however, democratic-innovations discourse has revalued and reformulated another relevant thread to be taken to such a framework. Authors behind the so-called 'systemic turn' argued that democratic-innovations research has focused too much on individual instances of democratic innovation and not enough on the interdependence of individual applications within larger systems.[27] These authors are particularly concerned about furthering deliberative democracy,

input and process qualities—and see Landemore, H., *Open Democracy: Reinventing Popular Rule for the Twenty-First Century*, Princeton, Princeton University Press, 2020, pp. 82 & 87 who brings to the centre the 'principle of inclusiveness and equality among citizens' in her notion of 'democraticity'—an evidently input-side principle.

[22] Smith, G., *Democratic Innovation: Designing Institutions for Citizen Participation*, Cambridge, Cambridge University Press, 2009.

[23] Dryzek, J.S., Democratization as Deliberative Capacity Building, *Comparative Political Studies*, 2009, 42, 11, p. 1379–402.

[24] Smith, G., *Democratic Innovation: Designing Institutions for Citizen Participation*, Cambridge, Cambridge University Press, 2009.

[25] Smith, G., Reflections on the Theory and Practice of Democratic Innovations, in S. Elstub and O. Escobar (eds), *Democratic Innovation and Governance*, Cheltenham, Edward Elgar, 2019, p. 577.

[26] Pogrebinschi, T. and M. Ryan, Moving Beyond Input Legitimacy: When Do Democratic Innovations Affect Policy Making, *European Journal of Political Research*, 2017, 57, 1, pp. 135–52; O'Flynn, I., Democratic Innovations and Theories of Democracy, in S. Elstub and O. Escobar (eds), *Democratic Innovation and Governance*, Cheltenham: Edward Elgar, 2019, p. 36.

[27] Mansbridge, J., J. Bohman, S. Chambers, T. Christiano, A. Fung, J. Parkinson, D.F. Thompson, and M.E. Warren, A Systemic Approach to Deliberative Democracy, in J. Parkinson and J. Mansbridge (eds), *Deliberative Systems: Deliberative Democracy at the Large Scale*, Cambridge, Cambridge University Press, 2012, p. 1; Elstub, S., S.A. Ercan, and R.F. Mendonça (eds), *Deliberative Systems in Theory and Practice*, London, Routledge, 2018; Parkinson, J., Deliberative Systems, in A. Bächtiger, J. Dryzek, J. Mansbridge, and M.E. Warren (eds), *The Oxford Handbook of Deliberative Democracy*, Oxford, Oxford University Press, 2018, pp. 432–46.

and argue that application-level deliberation may be good to have, but that system-level deliberation should instead be the larger good to strive for. In his writings about democracy as a regime, Rosanvallon takes an even wider angle.[28] According to this French theorist, improving democracy systematically requires not only the 'positive' forces of deliberation and reflection but also the 'negative' power and challenge of counter-democracy.[29] Making democracy more complex and mixed would improve the democratic system at large, while nourishing the varied repertoires needed for legitimacy at the level of interactions within systems.[30]

The notion of system-level values—beyond the more specific input–throughput–output sequence—need to be recognized in any sensible synthesis of values for democratic-governance innovation.

Governance-innovations discourse and values

When exploring values relevant to democratic-governance innovation, a second obvious place to look is the literature geared at governance innovations. We can safely say that this literature is more strongly rooted in Public Administration, while research focusing on democratic innovations is more strongly rooted in Political Science.[31]

The previously discussed tension between 'democracy' and 'effectiveness' is also a recurring theme in the literature about governance networks[32]—albeit approached the other way around, starting from the angle of effectiveness. In the conventional view, governance networks are first and foremost functional

---

[28] Rosanvallon, P., *Counter-Democracy: Politics in an Age of Distrust*, Cambridge, Cambridge University Press, 2008; Rosanvallon, P., *Good Government: Democracy Beyond Elections*, Cambridge, MA: Harvard University Press, 2015.

[29] Rosanvallon, P., *Counter-Democracy: Politics in an Age of Distrust*, Cambridge, Cambridge University Press, 2008, p. 314.

[30] Rosanvallon suggests that electoral democracy alone may degenerate into electoral aristocracy, that without entrenchment deliberative-reflective democracy may dissolve in abstractions, and without mitigation counter-democracy may radicalize in antipolitical and populist excesses. Together, however, extremes can be controlled and strengths pooled. See Rosanvallon, P., *Counter-Democracy: Politics in an Age of Distrust*, Cambridge, Cambridge University Press, 2008, p. 314.

[31] Raadschelders, J., *Public Administration: The Interdisciplinary Study of Government*, Oxford, Oxford University Press, 2011; Nabatchi, T., Public Values Frames in Administration and Governance, *Perspectives on Public Management and Governance*, 2017, 1, 1, pp. 59–72; Talpin, J., Qualitative Approaches to Democratic Innovations, in S. Elstub and O. Escobar (eds), *Democratic Innovation and Governance*, Cheltenham, Edward Elgar, 2019, p. 495.

[32] Rhodes, R.A.W., *Understanding Governance: Policy Networks, Governance, Reflexivity and Accountability*, London, Open University Press, 1997; Klijn, E.H. and C. Skelcher, Democracy and Governance Networks: Compatible or Not?, *Public Administration*, 2007, 85, 3, pp. 587–608; Sørensen, E. and J. Torfing, Making Governance Networks Effective and Democratic Through Metagovernance, *Public Administration*, 2009, 87, 2, pp. 234–58; Bevir, M., *Democratic Governance*, Princeton, Princeton University Press, 2010.

alternatives to markets and hierarchies (and some would add clans) for effectively getting things done. Arrangements for network collaboration, co-creation and co-production are primarily sought and improved with the objective of achieving policy solutions and public value.[33] The quest for effectiveness comes first, but, as underscored by Sørensen and Torfing,[34] democratic values and democratic anchorage will and should be brought into view as soon as possible, at least in the democratized countries of the world.

In order to take a more refined look at the values relevant to public governance and associated public management, a useful starting point is still the Sigma-Theta-Lambda value framework proposed by Hood.[35] Sigma-type values are typically relevant to what E. Ostrom called operational choice,[36] while Theta-type and Lambda-type values are more pertinent to what she called, respectively, collective choice and constitutional choice.[37] In Hood's original formulation, Sigma-type values are geared to 'keep it lean and purposeful'.

[33] Stoker, G., Governance as Theory: Five Propositions, *International Social Science Journal*, 1998, 68, 2, pp. 15–24; Bovaird, T. and E. Löffler, Evaluating the Quality of Public Governance: Indicators, Models and Methodologies, *International Review of Administrative Sciences*, 2003, 69, pp. 313–28; Hartley, J., E. Sørensen, and J. Torfing, Collaborative Innovation: A Viable Alternative to Market Competition and Organizational Entrepreneurship, *Public Administration Review*, 2013, 73, 6, pp. 821–30; Voorberg, W.H., V.J.J.M. Bekkers, and L.G. Tummers, A Systematic Review of Co-Creation and Co-Production: Embarking on the Social Innovation Journey, *Public Management Review*, 2014, 17, 9, pp. 1333–57.

[34] Sørensen, E. and J. Torfing, Making Governance Networks Effective and Democratic through Metagovernance, *Public Administration*, 2009, 87, 2, pp. 234–58. See also Pierre, J., Reinventing Governance, Reinventing Democracy?, *Policy & Politics*, 2009, 37, 4, pp. 591–609.

[35] Hood, C., A Public Management for All Seasons?, *Public Administration*, 1991, 69, 1, pp. 267–82. See also Hood, C. and M. Jackson, *Administrative Argument*, Aldershot, Dartmouth, 1991. Hood focused initially on New Public Management discourse, but his three value types have also proven to be of heuristic value in follow-up discourse about the New Public Governance. See Chandra, Y. and R.M. Walker, How Does a Seminal Article in Public Administration Diffuse and Influence the Field? Bibliometric Methods and the Case of Hood's 'A Public Management For All Seasons?', *International Public Management Journal*, 2019, 22, 5, p. 723; Pyun, H.O. and C. Edey Gamassou, Looking for Public Administration Theories?, *Public Organiz Rev*, 2018, 18, pp. 245–61.

[36] Ostrom, E. (ed.), *Strategies of Political Inquiry*, Beverly Hills, CA: Sage, 1982; Ostrom, E., *Governing the Commons*, Cambridge, Cambridge University Press, 1990. In the realm of operational choice, a desirable innovation would be one that helped the effective management of common pool resources (CPRs) such as collectively owned grounds, waters, etc.), which could otherwise fall prey to the tragedy of the commons (deterioration). In this realm, the value of effective management would take precedence over achieving deliberative quality, which may be centralized in the realms of collective and constitutional choice.

[37] Toonen, Th.A.J., Networks, Management and Institutions: Public Administration as 'Normal Science', *Public Administration*, 1998, 76, 2, pp. 229–52; Toonen, Th.A.J., Resilience in Public Administration: The Work of Elinor and Vincent Ostrom from a Public Administration Perspective, *Public Administration Review*, 2010, 70, 2, pp. 193–202. Chan and Gao add 'Delta-type' values to the Sigma-Theta-Lambda trio, based on a case study of Chinese performance measurement. Delta-type values are introduced to include 'unified politics-administration regimes'. As guiding lights for *democratic*-governance innovation, which is the central concern here, Delta-type values are less suitable, and to the extent that they might be relevant (reliability, continituity) overlapping with Lambda-type system values. See Chan, H.S. and J. Gao, Can the Same Key Open Different Locks?, *Public Administration*, 2012, 91, 2, pp. 366–380.

The instrumental trinity of economy, efficiency, and effectiveness (EEE) is clearly Sigma-type—related to the matching of resources to tasks.[38] Witnessing the surge of New Public Management (NPM), Hood noted a strong preoccupation with cost-efficiency and economy (leanness).[39] In later years, under the influence of New Public Governance (NPG) and its focus on co-creation and co-production in networks, effectiveness came to the fore as a central Sigma-type value, with economy and efficiency as still relevant co-values.[40]

Theta-type values stress 'keep it honest and fair' in the process of governance. This opens up a wider range of processual and interactive norms such as due process, fair play, neutrality, impartiality, integrity, and procedural justice.[41] Lambda-type values are geared to 'keep it robust and resilient' at the system level of governance, and would include security and survival values such as adaptive self-regulation and robustness.[42] Growing criticism of NPM-thinking, with its strong Sigma-type bias, coincided with a growing sensitivity to Theta-type and Lambda-type values.

Other than in the previously discussed democratic-innovations literature, democratic input values are not the starting point of reasoning in the literature on innovations in public governance and associated management. Input values are not absent in this literature, but approached differently. Comparatively speaking, the focus is less on the equal input of individual citizens, and more on mobilizing and connecting the diverse resources, interests, insights, and perspectives necessary for getting things done in more productive and creative ways. We can find this focus on the requisite variety of useful

[38] Hood, C. and M. Jackson, *Administrative Argument*, Aldershot, Dartmouth, 1991, p. 13.

[39] Hood, C., A Public Management for All Seasons?, *Public Administration*, 1991, 69, 1, pp. 267–82.

[40] Toonen, Th.A.J., Networks, Management and Institutions: Public Administration as 'Normal Science', *Public Administration*, 1998, 76, 2, pp. 229–52; Toonen, Th.A.J., Administrative Reform: Analytics, in B.G. Peters and J. Pierre (eds), *Handbook of Public Administration*, New York, Sage, 2003, pp. 467–76; Hood, C. and G. Peters, The Middle Aging of New Public Management: Into the Age of Paradox?, *Journal of Public Administration Research and Theory*, 2004, 14, 3, pp. 267–82; Pierre, J., Reinventing Governance, Reinventing Democracy?, *Policy & Politics*, 2009, 37, 4, pp. 591–609.

[41] Tyler, T.R., Governing amid Diversity: The Effect of Fair Decisionmaking Procedures on the Legitimacy of Government, *Law and Society Review*, 1994, 28, 4, pp. 809–32; Tyler, T. and Y.J. Huo, *Trust in the Law: Encouraging Public Cooperation with the Police and Courts*, New York, Russell Sage Foundation, 2002; Rothstein, B. and J. Teorell, What is Quality of Government? A Theory of Impartial Government Institutions, *Governance*, 2008, 21, 2, pp. 165–90.

[42] Hood, C., A Public Management for All Seasons?, *Public Administration*, 1991, 69, 1, pp. 267–82; Toonen, Th.A.J., Networks, Management and Institutions: Public Administration as 'Normal Science', *Public Administration*, 1998, 76, 2, pp. 229–52; Toonen, Th.A.J., Administrative Reform: Analytics, in B.G. Peters and J. Pierre (eds), *Handbook of Public Administration*, New York, Sage, 2003, pp. 467–76; Chan, H.S. and J. Gao, Can the Same Key Open Different Locks?, *Public Administration*, 2012, 91, 2, pp. 366–80; Gaus, G., What Might Democratic Self-Governance in a Complex Social World Look Like?, *San Diego Law Review*, 2019, 56, 967.

inputs in various subliteratures ranging from urban coalitions and regimes,[43] to collaborative and 'triple helix' partnerships,[44] social innovation and copro-duction,[45] pluri-rational, co-creative, and 'clumsy' solutions.[46] The requisite variety of useful inputs is so closely linked to the achievement of desired out-puts (social innovation, co-creation, and co-production are presented as ways of connecting and ways of producing at the same time) that it is often difficult to distinguish the two elements.

Theta-type values in governance-innovations discourse are akin, but not identical, to the previously discussed throughput values evident in democratic-innovations discourse. The latter (throughput values) stress proper political process—emphasizing the deliberative exchange of view-points and the rendering of account to democratic forums. The for-mer (Theta-type values) centralize due administrative process—proceeding in lawful, fair, impartial, incorruptible, and accountable ways. Procedu-ral fairness and impartiality have become central notions in an increas-ingly influential strand of the 'good governance' literature, which reinvents administrative-law values from a wider social-science perspective.[47]

A more traditional, but still indispensable, strand of the good gover-nance literature emphasizes proper relations at the system level—the proper distribution of rights and responsibilities, the separation of powers and coun-tervailing forces to the effect that structural checks and balances appear, and systemic malfunctioning is being suppressed. The value of checks and

---

[43] Stone, C.N., *Regime Politics: Governing Atlanta 1946–1988*, Lawrence, University Press of Kansas, 1989; Stoker, G., Regime Theory and Urban Politics, in D. Judge, G. Stoker, and H. Wolman (eds), *Theories of Urban Politics*, London, Sage, 1995.

[44] Lowndes, V. and C. Skelcher, The Dynamics of Multi-Organizational Partnerships: An Analysis of Changing Modes of Governance, *Public Administration*, 1998, 76, 2, pp. 313–33; Leydesdorff, L. and H. Etzkowitz, The Triple Helix as a Model for Innovation Studies, *Science and Public Policy*, 1998, 25, 3, pp. 195–203; Noveck, B., *Wiki Government: How Technology Can Make Government Better, Democracy Stronger, and Citizens More Powerful*, Washington, DC, Brookings Institution Press, 2009; Emerson, K., T. Nabatchi, and S. Balogh, An Integrative Framework for Collaborative Governance, *Journal of Public Administration Research and Theory*, 2012, 22, 1, pp. 1–29; Ansell, C., C. Doberstein, H. Henderson, S. Sid-diki, and P. 't Hart, Understanding Inclusion in Collaborative Governance: A Mixed-Methods Approach, *Policy and Society*, 2020, 39, 4, p. 570–91.

[45] Nabatchi, T., A. Sancino, and M. Sicilia, Varieties of Participation in Public Services: The Who, When, and What of Coproduction, *Public Administration Review*, 2017, 77, 5, pp. 766–76; Hartley, J., E. Sørensen, and J. Torfing, Collaborative Innovation: A Viable Alternative to Market Competition and Organizational Entrepreneurship, *Public Administration Review*, 2013, 73, 6, pp. 821–30.

[46] Verweij, M., M. Douglas, R. Ellis, C. Engel, F. Hendriks, S. Lohman, S. Ney, S. Rayner, and M. Thomp-son, Clumsy Solutions for a Complex World: The Case of Climate Change, *Public Administration*, 2006, 84, 4, pp. 817–43; Sunstein, C., *Infotopia: How Many Minds Produce Knowledge*, Oxford, Oxford University Press, 2008; Mulgan, G., *Big Mind: How Collective Intelligence Can Change our World*, Princeton, Princeton University Press, 2018.

[47] Tyler, T. and Y.J. Huo, *Trust in the Law: Encouraging Public Cooperation with the Police and Courts*, New York, Russell Sage Foundation, 2002; Rothstein, B. and J. Teorell, What is Quality of Government? A Theory of Impartial Government Institutions, *Governance*, 2008, 21, 2, pp. 165–90.

balances has long been recognized in constitutional thinking and rule of law theory,[48] adding from this angle to the system-level values.

Lambda-type values, together with Theta- and Sigma-type also need to be recognized in any sensible synthesis of values for democratic-governance innovation, and are thus also taken to the next section.

An integrative values framework

Now I am ready to take the next step, formulating an integrative values framework based on a synthesis of the democratic-innovations and governance-innovations literatures previously discussed. As an additional stepping stone towards this aim, I adapt a values catalogue developed in research into innovations at the urban level, which, along two dimensions, distinguished five core values: responsiveness, effectiveness, procedural justice, resilience, and counterbalance.[49] With due amendments and useful insights derived from the previous discussion, the values catalogue can be redesigned and transformed into a more robust general framework for democratic-governance innovation.

The integrative values framework—summarized in Table 6.3—distinguishes on the one hand between the application-level and the system-level (as discussed in previous sections), and on the other hand between constructive and constrained democratic governance as the focus of attention.[50] The latter was hinted at but not explicitly defined in the original values catalogue.[51] Here, I consciously draw on Rosanvallon's opposition of positive (constructive) and negative (constraining) power invested in

[48] Ostrom, V., A Forgotten Tradition: The Constitutional Level of Analysis, in J.A. Gillespie and D.A. Zinnes (eds), *Missing Elements in Political Inquiry*, New York, Sage, 1982, pp. 237–52; Alexander, L., *Constitutionalism: Philosophical Foundations*, Cambridge, Cambridge University Press, 2001.

[49] Hendriks, F., Understanding Good Urban Governance: Essentials, Shifts, and Values, *Urban Affairs Review*, 2014, 50, 4, pp. 553–76; Dool, L. van den, F. Hendriks, A. Gianoli, and L. Schaap (eds), *The Quest for Good Urban Governance: Theoretical Reflection and International Practices*, Wiesbaden, Springer, 2015; Hendriks, F. and G. Drosterij (eds), De Zucht naar Goed Bestuur in de Stad, The Hague, Boom/Lemma, 2012.

[50] The system/application-level distinction has already been made in previous sections and is largely in tune with the earlier formulation of the mentioned values catalogue, which separates system values (resilience, counterbalance) from values pertaining to more specific governance arrangements (responsiveness, effectiveness, procedural justice). See Hendriks, F., Understanding Good Urban Governance: Essentials, Shifts, and Values, *Urban Affairs Review*, 2014, 50, 4, p. 565; Dool, L. van den, F. Hendriks, A. Gianoli, and L. Schaap (eds), *The Quest for Good Urban Governance: Theoretical Reflection and International Practices*, Wiesbaden, Springer, 2015. The constructive/constrained democratic-governance distinction is uncovered and reformulated here.

[51] Hendriks, F., Understanding Good Urban Governance: Essentials, Shifts, and Values, *Urban Affairs Review*, 2014, 50, 4, p. 565.

democracy and counter-democracy;[52] an opposition that also reverberates in discourse on governance as a model of coproduction (constructive power) and of mutual restraint (constraining power).[53]

Democratic-governance innovations differ in the way they work on the constructive versus constraining side of democratic governance. The Oregon Citizen Initiative Review (CIR), to take a specific example, is partly a constructive mechanism (it brings a sample of citizens together to learn jointly about an initiative on the ballot and co-produce a collective statement about it), partly a constraining mechanism (it ties deliberation to process rules and potentially checks the initiative process in Oregon).[54] This is meant to be valuable at the application level (facilitating an inclusive, appropriate process of co-production) as well as the system level (contributing to critical self-rule, checking citizen initiative by public review). How and to what extent such goods are actually delivered is a question for empirical evaluation research. Here, the Oregon CIR is just used to illustrate the dimensions of Table 6.3.

The values integrated under the five core categories of Table 6.3 are derived from democratic-innovations discourse and governance-innovations discourse as discussed in previous sections. Two preceding tables exhibit how central value concepts and preoccupations in the two discourses can be mapped onto the general framework: Table 6.1 for democratic-innovations

Table 6.1 Values derived from democratic-innovations discourse.

Level Focus	Application		System
Democracy as constructive popular rule	Input values - Inclusion, equal input - Popular control, effective participation	Output values - Efficiency, implementation	System values - Systemic deliberation - Counter-democracy
Democracy as constructive popular rule	Throughput values - Deliberation, enlightened understanding - Transparency, openness		

[52] Rosanvallon, P., *Counter-Democracy: Politics in an Age of Distrust*, Cambridge, Cambridge University Press, 2008.

[53] Pierre, J. (ed.), *Debating Governance: Authority, Steering and Democracy*, Oxford, Oxford University Press, 2000; Kjaer, A.M., *Governance*, Cambridge, Polity, 2004; Dean, R.J., Counter-Governance: Citizen Participation Beyond Collaboration, *Politics and Governance*, 2018, 6, 1, pp. 180–8.

[54] Gastil, J., R.C. Richards, and K.R. Knobloch, Vicarious Deliberation: How the Oregon Citizens' Initiative Review Influenced Deliberation in Mass Elections, *International Journal of Communication*, 2014, 8, pp. 62–89; Gastil, J., K.R. Knobloch, J. Reedy, M. Henkels, and K. Cramer, Assessing the Electoral Impact of the 2010 Oregon Citizens' Initiative Review, *American Politics Research*, 2017, 46, 3, pp. 534–63. There are further remarks about the CIR in Chapters 3, 4, and 7 (Box 7.1).

discourse, and Table 6.2 for governance-innovations discourse. One previously discussed value has been omitted: 'transferability', defined by Smith as the extent to which an innovation can be transferred to other contexts. High transferability is primarily a quality from the perspective of a particular design (or designer) of an instrument, not the perspective of the involved public(s) from which I take my cue here. If a specific instrument does not achieve more central values in a satisfactory manner, then high transferability is not desirable, and low transferability is not a problem.[55]

Together, Tables 6.1, 6.2, and 6.3 allow for an integrative view of the value diversity, which can also be disaggregated when needed; the contributions of the divergent value perspectives and literatures remain recognizable and available. In Table 6.3, the received 'goods' of democratic innovation and governance innovation are integrated into the general values framework and matched with the five core categories of this framework. The names of the core categories are slightly adapted: efficaciousness is preferred to effectiveness as the somewhat wider and more encompassing concept; for the same reason appropriateness is preferred to procedural justice, and inclusiveness to responsiveness.[56] Resilience and counterbalance are retained as signifiers, completing the set of five core values.

Table 6.2 Values derived from governance-innovations discourse.

Level Focus	Application	System
Governance		Sigma-type values	Lambda-type values
as constructive steering	- Plural, vital input	- Effectiveness, efficiency, economy - Co-production, co-creation	- Adaptivity, robustness, resilience - Integration, consolidation
Governance	Theta-type values		
as constructive steering	- Due justification, impartial treatment - Integrity, incorruptibility		- Countervailing powers, checks and balances

[55] See Smith, G., *Democratic Innovation: Designing Institutions for Citizen Participation*, Cambridge, Cambridge University Press, 2009. As indicated, Smith recognized the peculiar, additional character of 'transferability' as a democratic good. His other additional democratic good—efficiency—is integrated here together with other Sigma-type values. On Smith's democratic goods, also see O'Flynn, I., Democratic Innovations and Theories of Democracy, in S. Elstub and O. Escobar (eds), *Democratic Innovation and Governance*, Cheltenham, Edward Elgar, 2019, pp. 34–6.

[56] Although the term 'effectiveness' is also used to denote output-legitimacy and is mentioned as central to Sigma-type arguments, the term as such may limit thinking to producing effects, whereas considerations of efficiency, economy, parsimony, delivery, etc. also belong to this category of justification. Although 'procedural justice' is close to what is meant here, the term(s) may limit thinking to justifiability of formal procedure, whereas the relevant democratic-governance processes involve more than procedure. Although

Table 6.3 Values for democratic-governance innovations: an integrative framework.

Level Focus	Application		System
Constructive democratic governance	**Inclusiveness** - Inclusion, equal input - Popular control, effective participation - Plural, vital input	**Efficaciousness** -Efficiency, implementation - Effectiveness, efficiency, economy - Co-production, co creation	**Resilience** - Adaptivity, robustness, resilience - Systemic deliberation
Constrained Democratic governance	**Appropriateness** - Deliberation, enlightened understanding - Transparency, openness - Due justification, impartial treatment - Integrity, incorruptibility		**Counterbalance** - Countervailing powers, checks and balances - Counter-democracy

Complementarities and tensions

The core values in the integrative framework are complementary but not without tensions. Most prominent are between-category tensions, but there are also more subtle within-category frictions to be mindful of. Figure 6.1 gives a schematic overview of the fields of tension—five spheres and ten dyads—discussed in the following two subsections.

Within-category complementarities and tensions

In the field of efficaciousness, output- and Sigma-type values largely hang together, but there is some tension between, on the one hand, efficiency and economy ('keep it lean', in Hood's formulation) and, on the other hand, effectiveness and productiveness ('keep it purposeful'). Surely, it can be argued that public management theory and practice is all about finding better ways of connecting the two—getting the most out of scarce bucks—but this only further illustrates that raising efficaciousness is something of a balancing act in itself.

In the inclusiveness category, input values stressed in the different literatures largely point in the same direction: good input as a key to good

---

'responsiveness' is also understood as being sensitive to stakes and stakeholders, it can become a concept that conflates all good things that decision-makers may do with inputs and outputs; as an umbrella concept, inclusiveness is more clearly connected to the input side of democratic governance.

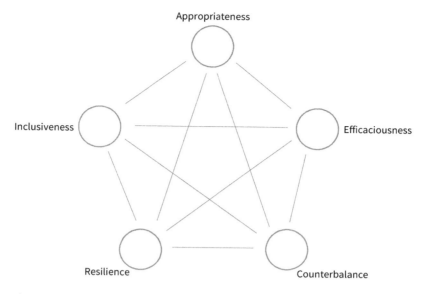

Figure 6.1 Fields of complementarities and tensions

democratic governance. Yet, the notion of equal citizens' input that is prominent in democratic-innovations discourse is at least partially challenged
by the notion of requisite social input that is prominent in governance-
innovations discourse (see the sections above titled 'Democratic-innovations
discourse and values' and 'Governance-innovations discourse and values').
It may be argued that proper innovations ascertain that both types of inputs
are recognized and received, but this will not take away the subtle difference
between attempting to listen to all citizens equally and focusing on bringing
together the perspectives and interests deemed vital for a task.[57]

Acknowledging such differences of interpretation, and bringing them up
for discussion is to serve democratic-governance innovation better than
glossing them over or assuming one singular meaning of inclusiveness or
efficaciousness.

Within-category tensions are less prominent in the appropriateness category. Throughput values stressed in democratic-innovations discourse and
Theta-type values flagged in calls to fortify good governance as due process complement each other without much friction. Processual openness
and administrative incorruptibility fortify each other. The same goes for

---

[57] Noveck, B., *Wiki Government: How Technology Can Make Government Better, Democracy Stronger, and Citizens More Powerful*, Washington, DC, Brookings Institution Press, 2009; Landemore, H., *Open Democracy: Reinventing Popular Rule for the Twenty-First Century*, Princeton, Princeton University Press, 2020.

deliberative-democracy values stressing reflective proceedings and due motivation ('the forceless force of the better argument'), and good-governance values emphasizing procedural correctness, argumentative accuracy, equal and proportional treatment ('treating equals equally').

Within-category tensions are also less prominent in the resilience and counterbalance categories. The democratic-innovations and the governance-innovations take on systemic resilience are somewhat different but largely compatible, with the former mainly focused on systemic deliberation as a key to learning systems, and the latter focused on even broader diversity and complexity as central features of robustly adaptive systems.[58] In the counterbalance category, notions of counter-democracy and constitutional checks are highly compatible, notwithstanding their appearance in different literatures.

Between-category complementarities and tensions

Tensions get more prominent when setting the system-level values of resilience and counterbalance side by side. The resilience category contains the systemic capacity for adaptive self-regulation, joint deliberation, and learning in democratic governance. Conversely, the counterbalance category comprises the systemic mobilization of dissent, opposition, and negative power. In the governance-innovations literature the two are viewed separately, even when complementary qualities are recognized. Lambda-type values as defined by Hood are about getting and keeping the system's act together through dynamic stabilization and adaptivity ('keep it robust and resilient').[59] The opposite is defined in terms of risk, breakdown, and collapse.[60] In the constitutional, rule of law perspective on good governance, division, veto, stalemate, and non-decision making are to a certain extent accepted consequences of constituting negative, constraining, power. Preferably, constraining and constructive powers are complementary, and different ways of balancing are being proposed. The modern mixed regime as proposed

[58] Teisman, G.R. and E.H. Klijn, Complexity Theory and Public Management: an Introduction, *Public Management Review*, 2008, 10, 3, pp. 287–97; Toonen, Th.A.J. Resilience in Public Administration: The Work of Elinor and Vincent Ostrom from a Public Administration Perspective, *Public Administration Review*, 2010, 70, 2, pp. 193–202; Mansbridge, J., J. Bohman, S. Chambers, T. Christiano, A. Fung, J. Parkinson, D.F. Thompson, and M.E. Warren, A Systemic Approach to Deliberative Democracy, in J. Parkinson and J. Mansbridge (eds), *Deliberative Systems: Deliberative Democracy at the Large Scale*, Cambridge, Cambridge University Press, 2012, pp. 1–26.
[59] Hood, C., A Public Management for All Seasons?, *Public Administration*, 1991, 69, 1, pp. 267–82.
[60] Hood, C., A Public Management for All Seasons?, *Public Administration*, 1991, 69, 1, p. 11; Hood, C., *The Art of the State: Culture, Rhetoric, and Public Management*, Oxford, Oxford University Press, 1998, p. 23–70.

by Rosanvallon is a hybrid of both negative and positive components.[61] Deliberative systems as suggested by Mansbridge et al.[62] are more strongly inclined to constructive deliberation but—as the authors recognize—non-constructive, non-deliberative components may be part of the deliberative system's mix.

Further reviewing between-category tensions (the dyads in Figure 6.1), it transpires that efficaciousness is party to three of the more prominent ones. I already discussed the tension between efficaciousness and inclusiveness that figures prominently in both reviewed literatures (even though they proceed from different starting points). There is also friction between efficaciousness and appropriateness, with the latter demanding due process and interactional quality, and the former encapsulating the idea that it is not the beauty of the game but the result that counts (or: 'you can't make an omelet without breaking eggs'). The friction between efficaciousness and counterbalance is set in the same key, with the latter coming at it from a higher (system) level of aggregation. In motor vehicle language, the value of counterbalance draws attention to the braking system, and the value of efficaciousness to the accelerator. In political debate, this friction reverberates in controversies about constitutional viscosity working at the expense of operational decisiveness, or the other way around: constitutional guardrails overwhelmed by operational recklessness.[63]

Between-category frictions to be mindful of are also the ones between resilience and inclusiveness and between resilience and appropriateness. The traditional 'system overload' thesis pointed to the risk of too many actors and groups becoming active and being included at the same time, feeding the political system with an excess of diverse demands, which could lead to destabilization of the system. Similarly, too many expectations which are too high regarding the appropriateness and correctness of processes could lead to system overload.[64] To prevent overload and guard sustainability, the

[61] Rosanvallon, P., *Counter-Democracy: Politics in an Age of Distrust*, Cambridge, Cambridge University Press, 2008, p. 314.

[62] Mansbridge, J., J. Bohman, S. Chambers, T. Christiano, A. Fung, J. Parkinson, D.F. Thompson, and M.E. Warren, A Systemic Approach to Deliberative Democracy, in J. Parkinson and J. Mansbridge (eds), *Deliberative Systems: Deliberative Democracy at the Large Scale*, Cambridge, Cambridge University Press, 2012, pp. 1–26. See also Elstub, S., S.A. Ercan, and R.F. Mendonça (eds), Deliberative Systems in Theory and Practice, London, Routledge, 2018; Parkinson, J., Deliberative Systems, in A. Bächtiger, J. Dryzek, J. Mansbridge, and M.E. Warren (eds), *The Oxford Handbook of Deliberative Democracy*, Oxford, Oxford University Press, 2018, pp. 432–46.

[63] Olsen, M., *The Rise and Decline of Nations*, New York, Yale University Press, 1982; Levisky S. and D. Ziblatt, *How Democracies Die*, New York, Crown, 2018.

[64] Almond, G.A. and S. Verba, *The Civic Culture Revisited*, Boston, Little, Brown & Company, 1980; Hood, C., *The Art of the State: Culture, Rhetoric, and Public Management*, Oxford, Oxford University Press, 1998, p. 73–97.

traditional 'civic culture' thesis initiated by Almond and Verba called for a sensible mix of active but emphatically also passive orientations to the system.[65] Although newer approaches to adaptive systems allow for more complexity and redundancy, the concern for system solidity and stability is still very much alive, and relevant.

Between-category tensions are relatively weak for four of the dyads depicted in Figure 6.1. First, the values of counterbalance and appropriateness are complementary without significant friction points: the first instilling systemic constraints, the second procedural constraints on decision making. Next, counterbalance and inclusiveness are also largely complementary in spirit: the first mitigating potential unilateralism in decision-making with constitutional feedback, the second mitigating it with societal and citizen input. Between inclusiveness and appropriateness, value conflict is also less intense, although it is not absent. Deliberative norms may chafe with mass participation.[66] Short of that, norms of appropriateness are largely in tune with norms of inclusiveness, especially as operationalized in the democratic-innovations literature, which values a qualitatively wide variety of inputs more than a large quantity of inputs.[67] The governance-innovations take on inclusiveness values requisite variety over full variety of inputs, which may at some point rub up against norms of procedural justice and equity. Finally, while there is long-standing concern that too much inclusiveness to inputs can be detrimental to a system's stability (the traditional 'system overload' thesis), there is little concern, understandably, that too much efficaciousness will threaten the system's capacity to sustain.

The upshot of this review of the interrelated set of core values is that there are differences and frictions—to varying degrees—and that mindfulness of these is critical for understanding and handling democratic-governance innovation in a more encompassing, value-sensitive way. Tables 6.1, 6.2, and 6.3 are the main steppingstones towards this aim.

In Table 6.4, I extend the core values of democratic-governance innovation with related goods. Partially inspired by Jørgensen and Bozeman,[68] what

---

[65] Almond, G.A. and S. Verba, *The Civic Culture Revisited*, Boston, Little, Brown & Company, 1980.
[66] Mutz, D.C., *Hearing the Other Side: Deliberative Versus Participatory Democracy*, Cambridge, Cambridge University Press, 2006; Bächtiger, A., S. Shikano, S. Pedrini, and M. Ryser, Measuring Deliberation 2.0: Standards, Discourse Types, and Sequenzialization. Paper presented at ECPR General Conference, Potsdam, 5–12 September 2009; Mendonça, R.F. and E.M. Cunha, Can the Claim to Foster Broad Participation Hinder Deliberation?, *Critical Policy Studies*, 2014, 8, 1, pp. 78–100.
[67] See e.g., Rowe, G. and L.J. Frewer, Public Participation Methods: A Framework for Evaluation, *Science, Technology & Human Values*, 2000, 25, 1, pp. 3–29. In their approach, process values are input-values following from democratic innovations discourse.
[68] Jørgensen, T.B. and B. Bozeman, Public Values: An Inventory, *Administration & Society*, 2007, 39, 3, pp. 354–81.

Table 6.4 Related goods and key questions.

Core values	Input: Inclusiveness	Output: Efficaciousness	Throughput: Appropriateness	System: Resilience	System: Counterbalance
Integrated values	Inclusion, equal input Popular control, effective participation Plural, vital input	Efficiency, implementation Effectiveness, efficiency, economy Co-production, co-creation	Deliberation, enlightened understanding Transparency, openness Motivated, impartial treatment Integrity, incorruptibility	Adaptivity, robustness, resilience Integration, consolidation Systemic deliberation	Countervailing powers, checks and balances Counter-democracy
Related goods	Involvement, activation, access, voice, influence, responsiveness, sourcing, listening, interest aggregation, representation, stakeholder sensitivity	Problem-solving, public value for money, yield, delivery, speed, ingenuity parsimony, rightsizing, results-orientation	Lawfullness, procedural justice, correctness, fairness, neutrality, proportionality, reasonableness, elucidation, traceability, rendering account	Self-regulation, sustainability, stabilization, cohesion, consolidation continuity steadiness, systemic reliability	Supervision, monitoring, control, oversight, surveillance, opposition, agonism, tutelage, holding to account
Related key questions (for design thinking and evaluation)	In which way and to what extent is the application open and sensitive to diverse citizen inputs and societal signals?	In which way and to what extent is the application capable of delivering quality outputs and solutions?	In which way and to what extent is the application geared to procedural justice, to clean, fair and due process?	In which way and to what extent is the wider system's capacity for adaptive self-rule invigorated?	In which way and to what extent are the wider system's checks and balances strengthened?

they call 'neighbor values' and 'co-values' are taken together here as 'related goods'—desiderata related to the core values. I prefer 'core values', commonly used in discourse on democratic governance desiderata, to the term 'nodal values' used by Jørgensen and Bozeman for the much wider category of public values.[69] Here, the focus is on values relevant to democratic-governance innovation, which is more specific. This is reflected in the row of related goods, which all pertain to democratic-governance innovation, either at the application or the system level. Wider public-professionalism or civil-service values are outside the scope of this.[70]

In keeping with the central aim here, I have added a row to Table 6.4 with related key questions for design thinking and evaluation, following from mindfulness to the five core values. How to work with such framework is the subject of the following section.

On applying the values framework

The primary function of Figure 6.1, Tables 6.1, 6.2, 6.3, and 6.4 is to arrest sensitivity and attention to what is most important, and what is relatedly discussed as desirable, in democratic-governance innovation. Although singular frameworks facilitating the analysis of a particular value—inclusiveness, for instance—are valuable in their own right, a broader framework will bring additional advantages. Heightened sensitivity to the multifaceted reality of democratic-governance innovation can broaden design thinking and evaluation. Citizens and *demoi* are usually sensitive to more than one single value. Professionals involved in the design and evaluation of innovations in democratic governance should be mindful of this. (By way of comparison: reflections on the new design of a motor car cannot be based on visual appearance alone, but will also be connected to desiderata for aerodynamics, fuel use, etc.)

A broader integrative framework thus makes sense, but it also brings its own challenges. It is often easier to focus on one single thing, such as inclusiveness. How to apply and weigh multiple values? There is no simple answer or ready-made handbook for this. There are real challenges, yet

---

[69] For exploring this much wider category, Jørgensen and Bozeman distinguish 'neighbor values' and 'covalues' besides core values, whereas here we distinguish only 'related goods' in addition to core values. See Jørgensen, T.B. and B. Bozeman, Public Values: An Inventory, *Administration & Society*, 2007, 39, 3, pp. 354–81.

[70] Kernaghan, K., Integrating Values into Public Service, *Public Administration Review*, 2003, 63, 6, pp. 711–19; Fukumoto, E. and B. Bozeman, Public Values Theory: What is Missing?, *American Review of Public Administration*, 2019, 49, 6, pp. 635–48.

we may carve out sensible ways forward for dealing with them. Hereafter, I address some of the most pressing issues without pretending to be able to close the conversation. The conversation must in fact be open-ended—but not without conversation support as supplied here. In the following it is argued:

- that open norms fit the open society;
- that conversations about the application of democratic governance values are necessarily situated;
- that none of the core values may be overlooked a priori; but can be weighted differently after serious consideration;
- that while thinking in terms of universal quantitative yardsticks is problematic, sensible uses of situated yardsticks cannot be ruled out;
- that while situated interpretations cannot be left to an analytical tool, analysis can sensibly feed and facilitate situated conversation;
- that while discussions about 'good enough' democratic governance are bound to be complex, a well-founded integrative framework can help to ask the right questions and get the right conversation going.

Open norms, situated conversations—Although it might be feasible to operationalize the core values in a stringent and detailed way, a fundamental choice is made here for 'open norms' fitting the open society.[71] Accordingly, an integrative, sensitizing framework should facilitate—but not replace—a necessarily open and situated conversation about the way democratic governance values are to be approached, and which conclusions are to be drawn. Whereas a closed framework could become a conversation stopper, a more open—yet systematic—sensitizing framework could present an opening as well as a footing for prudent conversations.

Prudent conversations about democratic governance values are necessarily situated—time- and place-based—conversations. Efficaciousness, for instance, is a relevant value for any democratic-governance innovation, but it will need to be approached differently when designing a citizens' assembly for local road planning compared to one for, say, national health needs forecasting. Although academic guidance in operationalization could be valuable, force-feeding one stringent operationalization of efficaciousness would be lacking in prudence.[72] For the necessary loading of core values, we cannot

---

[71] Popper, K., *The Open Society and Its Enemies*, Princeton, Princeton University Press, 1945.
[72] Flyvbjerg, B., *Making Social Science Matter: Why Social Inquiry Fails and How It Can Succeed Again*, Cambridge, Cambridge University Press, 2001.

rely solely on science but need to involve the open society in its various, situated guises as well. This implies situated weighing of values and situated yardsticks.[73]

Situated weighing of values, none out of the equation—Any normative framework encompassing a range of values is sooner or later confronted with the challenging question: are all values equally important in all circumstances? To return to the previous example, for a citizens' assembly looking into local road planning, a value like efficaciousness cannot be overlooked, but how important should it be in comparison to the other core values? In line with the previous point, I would argue that this is open to situated conversation in the public domain, and that science can feed and facilitate this conversation but not have the final word.

Proper, situated conversation could legitimately lead to the conclusion that efficaciousness is the prime concern for a citizens' assembly involved in local road planning—because, for instance, a locally supported solution for traffic calming is needed most of all. For a citizens' assembly looking into long-term national health scenarios, an equally legitimate priority could be increased inclusiveness as to the different viewpoints on the matter, with efficaciousness being somewhat less emphasized—but not taken out of the equation altogether. The latter is crucial, for all core values, strongly grounded as they are in discourses on democratic and governance innovation. They may be weighted differently after serious consideration, but they may not be overlooked a priori.

Situated yardsticks, conversation-supporting analytics—The statement that none of the core values may a priori be taken out of the 'equation' is first and foremost a figurative way of putting it. However, there is room for taking 'the equation' more literally. Although I will not, for principled reasons outlined above, transform the sensitizing framework into a universal quantitative yardstick, one cannot rule out the operationalization and sensible usage of a situated yardstick in some instances (for example, one developed to evaluate citizens' assemblies working on local road planning).

Where it is useful, a situated yardstick may take the form of a radar or 'spider's web' diagram, a much-used way of operationalizing multiple values. The related challenge would be to somehow score a democratic-governance innovation in terms of its inclusiveness, efficaciousness, appropriateness, and—at the system level—its contribution to resilience and counterbalance. When

---

[73] A situated yardstick may be quantified—as in the example of the spider web diagram with numerical scores for the five core values—but can also be operationalized in a more qualitative way—producing verbal assessments of the different values and underlying desiderata. A non-situated, a priori defined universal yardstick, however, is not envisaged here.

quantification is possible, positions on the five dimensions could range from negative impact (−1), no impact (0), mildly positive impact (+1) to strongly positive impact (+2).[74] Ideally, a democratic-governance innovation would stay away from the problematic positions near the centre of the diagram and score only solid plusses on all dimensions. It would be more realistic, however, to expect a scoring pattern with bulges and dents, the interpretation of which cannot be left solely to an analytical tool. In the hypothetical case just mentioned: an aggregated score of +2 (the result of, say, −1, 0, 0, +1, +2) could open the conversation, but not end it. The underlying scores could support the necessary conversation, not replace it.

Asking the right questions, getting the right conversation—When engaging in a conversation about the quality of democratic-governance innovation—weighing pros and cons, whether translated into words or numbers—another challenging question appears: when is it 'good enough'.[75] And conversely: when is it not good enough? There are no easy, ready-made answers to these questions. There are, however, more and less difficult situations to consider. We already encountered one: an innovation that scores clear plusses or positive qualifications on all dimensions would seem at least 'good enough' to most critical observers. On the other side of the spectrum, we can imagine another unambiguous situation: if an alleged democratic-governance innovation shows no improvements or positive marks on none of the core values (it does nothing for inclusiveness, efficaciousness, appropriateness, resilience, nor counterbalance) then we can safely conclude that it does not deserve the predicate innovation.

More difficult to weigh are the mixed scoring patterns, such as the one mentioned earlier (−1, 0, 0, +1, +2, with an aggregated score of +2). A positive aggregative score seems to be the least to expect from something that is called an innovation, but it seems unwise to turn this into a general rule or automated formula ('everything above +1 must be good enough'). The underlying assessments need to be interrogated and discussed to find out whether a weak sub-assessment is simply unacceptable in its own right, or might still be acceptable in the wider scheme of things. An integrative values framework—such as the one developed here—can inspire to ask the 'right questions' and get the 'right conversation' about democratic-governance innovation going.

---

[74] In some radar or spider's-web diagrams, positions on the various dimensions are nominally defined—A to D, for instance. In other visualizations the positions range from zero to some positive score. Here, we refer to a variant with positions ranging from negative to positive scores, which seems appropriate as we cannot assume that all innovations actually deliver improvements on all relevant dimensions.

[75] Grindle, M.S., Good Enough Governance Revisited, *Development Policy Review*, 2007, 235, 5, pp. 533–74; Landemore, H., *Open Democracy: Reinventing Popular Rule for the Twenty-First Century*, Princeton, Princeton University Press, 2020, p. 107.

Guiding evaluation and design thinking

The proposed values framework extends and integrates two important, yet distinctive discourses—one on democratic innovations with a more prominent 'Political Science' lineage, another on governance innovations with a stronger 'Public Administration' pedigree—and presents an integrative overview of the core values and related normative coordinates, complementarities, and tensions. The two discourses carry different sensitivities in valuing democratic governance; the integrative values framework capitalizes on their mutually reinforcing potential and reminds scholars and practitioners alike of the fundamental value diversity surrounding this topic.

The integrative values framework arrests sensitivity and attention to what is deemed critical and what is relatedly discussed as desirable in democratic-governance innovation. As a sensitizing framework, it can guide and enrich quality assessment and design thinking in the realm of democratic-governance innovation—helping to ask the right questions and get the right conversations going. This is not only helpful to professionals involved in democratic-governance innovation. Such a broader, integrative framework is also in the citizens' interest—an interest that is essentially plural and multifaceted.

For realistically applying such a framework, relevant challenges and ways forward have been discussed. The practical application of the integrative framework should be feasible as the constituent parts of the integrative framework have been applied extensively. Applying the integrative framework involves taking sensible next steps—integrated steps—not entirely new steps. In Chapters 7 and 8, I will pursue such integrated steps when I confront the values framework with real-life democratic-governance innovations that straddle the deliberative-plebiscitary divide.

7

The deliberative referendum

Reflections on a national-level hybrid

In this chapter and the next, attention shifts to real-life attempts to connect democratic innovations across the deliberative-plebiscitary divide. The focus is on practices that are comparatively successful in advancing democratic innovation—the focus of Part II of this book—by combining contradictory formats of democratic innovation into one embedded design. In this chapter, I concentrate on national-level practices, with special attention to the Irish 'deliberative referendum' on abortion that famously sequenced the two contrasting instruments of deliberative mini-public and binary referendum. (In Chapter 8, I will descend to local-level practices, in particular the combination of diverging formats in Participatory Budgeting-new style.) Confronting the Irish case with the values framework set out in Chapter 6, and with relevant mirror cases, the Irish process is understood as a comparatively successful case of hybrid democratic innovation (HDI). The construction catered to different values and audiences and was relatively well-integrated into the established system, compared to, for instance, a similar process in Iceland.

Citizens' assembly meets referendum

The further apart the constituent elements in the combined model are from a theoretical point of view, the more challenging arguably the hybridisation is. This is certainly true for deliberative mini-publics and plebiscitary referendums. These are two instruments that, as we have seen, emanate from very different strands of democratic thought and practice, and have therefore been perceived as antithetical for long[1]—the mini-public founded on a belief in

---

[1] LeDuc, L., Referendums and Deliberative Democracy, *Electoral Studies*, 2015, 38, p. 139; El-Wakil, A., Democratic Theory: The Deliberative Potential of Facultative Referendums, *Democratic Theory*, 2017, 4, 1, p. 59; Landemore, H., Debate: Referendums are Never Merely Referendum: On the Need to Make Popular, Vote Processes More Deliberative, *Swiss Political Science Review*, 2018; Parkinson, M., The Roles of Referendums in Deliberative Systems, *Representation*, 2020, 56, 4, p. 485.

Rethinking Democratic Innovation. Frank Hendriks, Oxford University Press. © Frank Hendriks (2023).
DOI: 10.1093/oso/9780192848291.003.0007

microscopic deliberation; the referendum geared at the aggregation of mass votes. The domain of referendums and other plebiscitary formats seems to be one of 'thinking fast'—reflexively, quickly translating individual inclinations to a collective signal—the domain of citizens' assemblies and other deliberative formats one of 'thinking slow'—reflectively, patiently weaving a rug of shared meaning.[2] As LeDuc wrote: 'The twin objectives of voice and votes too often pull in opposite directions'.[3] He is among a slowly but surely growing group of scholars who explore the scope for combining concentrated deliberation with mass voting,[4] but he also succinctly points to the challenge of bringing two very different worlds together: 'Can the square peg of deliberative democratic theory be pounded into the round hole of direct democracy?'

Connecting a deliberative mini-public to a plebiscitary referendum amounts to hybridization of a significantly more advanced type than simpler forms of hybridization such as microscopic deliberation followed by a vote among the members of the same mini-public, or a referendum vote surrounded by generic, non-incentivized deliberation. Here, I am primarily interested in the more advanced type of hybridization, which is more challenging and more revealing to the extent that it appears to work against considerable odds. In this chapter, I will delve into a case of democratic innovation across the deliberative-plebiscitary divide that has received a largely appreciative response in the public media and academic literature: the case of Ireland, more specifically the hybrid construction that between 2016 and 2018 led to remarkable and profound changes in the regulation of abortion in Ireland.[5] Ireland is generally considered to be at the forefront, 'something of a trail-blazer' and 'world leader in the linking of deliberative democracy

[2] Kahneman, D., *Thinking Fast, Thinking Slow*, New York, Farrar, Straus & Giroux, 2011.

[3] LeDuc, L., Referendums and Deliberative Democracy, *Electoral Studies*, 2015, 38, p. 147.

[4] Saward, M., Making Democratic Connections: Political Equality, Deliberation and Direct Democracy, *Acta Politica*, 2001, 36, pp. 361–79; Tierney, S., Using Electoral Law to Construct a Deliberative Referendum: Moving beyond the Democratic Paradox, *Election Law Journal*, 2013, 12, 4, pp. 508–23; Levy, R., Deliberative Voting: Reforming Constitutional Referendum Democracy, *Public Law*, July 2013, pp. 555–74; LeDuc, L., Referendums and Deliberative Democracy, *Electoral Studies*, 2015, 38, pp. 139–48; Fishkin, J.S., T. Kouser, R.C. Luskin, and A. Siu, Deliberative Agenda Setting: Piloting Reform of Direct Democracy in California, *Perspectives on Politics*, 2015, 13, 4, pp. 1030–42; Setälä, M., Connecting Deliberative Mini-Publics to Representative Decision Making, *European Journal of Political Research*, 2017, 56, 4, pp. 846–63; Landemore, H., Debate: Referendums are Never Merely Referendum: On the Need to Make Popular, Vote Processes More Deliberative, *Swiss Political Science Review*, 2018, 24, 3, pp. 320–27; McKay, S., Building a Better Referendum: Linking Mini-Publics and Mass Publics in Popular Votes, *Journal of Public Deliberation*, 2019, 15, 1, pp. 1–29; Parkinson, M., The Roles of Referendums in Deliberative Systems, *Representation*, 2020, 56, 4, pp. 485–500.

[5] The Irish abortion case and the democratic process behind it are very well-researched and documented; the prime sources used are Farrell, D.M., J. Suiter, and C. Harris, 'Systematizing' Constitutional Deliberation: The 2016–18 Citizens' Assembly in Ireland, *Irish Political Studies*, 2019, 34, 1, pp. 113–23; Elkink, J.A., D.M. Farrell, S. Marien, T. Reidy, and J. Suiter, The Death of Conservative Ireland? The 2018 Abortion Referendum, *Electoral Studies*, 2020, 65, pp. 1–11; Farrell, D.M., J. Suiter, K. Cunningham, and

(mini-publics) and direct democracy (referendums)', a paragon of 'how deliberation can be inserted into the referendum process in a meaningful way'.[6] In 2022, looking back at a ten-year period of intensive democratic innovation in Ireland, David Farrell, a leading expert on the matter, continues to recognize the huge contributions of the hybrid processes that led to breakthroughs on issues like abortion and gay marriage, while being more critical of the non-hybrid processes that led to 'many, other recommendations' that have been 'ignored, rejected, or left to gather dust'.[7]

Before digging deeper into the case of the Irish Citizens' Assembly-plus-referendum on abortion, I will confront this case with some relevant precedents of state-wide Citizens' Assemblies (CAs).

CAs with and without follow-up referendums—from British Columbia to Ireland

The evolved Irish model of a deliberative mini-public followed by a binary referendum—as applied to the abortion issue (2016–2018)—differs markedly from earlier statewide cases that either featured mini-publics without a follow-up referendum (Netherlands, 2006; Belgium, 2011), or that combined mini-publics with referendums in a less fruitful way (British Columbia, Canada, 2004–2005; Iceland, 2010–2012).

In 2004, British Columbia, Canada, organized a Citizens' Assembly on Electoral Reform. This mini-public came to a proposal—the recommendation to replace the existing first-past-the-post (FPTP) system with a Single

C. Harris, When Mini-Publics and Maxi-Publics Coincide: Ireland's National Debate on Abortion, *Representation*, 2020; Suiter, J. and T. Reidy, Does Deliberation Help Deliver Informed Electorates: Evidence from Irish Referendum Votes, *Representation*, 2020, 56, 4, pp. 539–57. Of added value are publications about (hybrid) innovation in the Irish context more generally: Suiter, J., D. Farrell, and C. Harris, Ireland's Evolving Constitution, in P. Blokker (ed.), *Constitutional Acceleration within the European Union and Beyond*, London, Routledge, 2018, pp. 142–54; Elkink, J.A., D.M. Farrell, T. Reidy, and J. Suiter, Understanding the 2015 Marriage Referendum in Ireland: Context, Campaign, and Conservative Ireland, *Irish Political Studies*, 2017, 32, 3, pp. 361–81. An insightful documentary about the road to the Irish abortion referendum is *The 8th*. See Kane, A., L. Kennedy, M. O'Boyle (Directors) & A. Maher (Producer), The 8th [Film; online video], <https://the8thfilm.com/>, 28 May 2020. Supplementary media and internet sources are reported in notes. Daniël van der Lee effectively contributed to an earlier process description based on the source material, reported in Hendriks, F., K. Jacobs, and A. Michels, *Nationale burgerfora: verkenning van nationale burgerfora als democratisch gereedschap*, Den Haag, Ministerie van Binnenlandse Zaken en Koninkrijksrelaties, 2021. For valuable input on the Irish case, I am indebted to David Farrell, Theresa Reidy, Jos Elkink, and Colm Walsh.

[6] Farrell, D.M., J. Suiter, and C. Harris, Systematizing' Constitutional Deliberation: The 2016–18 Citizens' Assembly in Ireland, *Irish Political Studies*, 2019, 34, 1, p. 113 & pp. 119–20; Farrell, D.M., J. Suiter, K. Cunningham, and C. Harris, When Mini-Publics and Maxi-Publics Coincide: Ireland's National Debate on Abortion, Representation, 2020; Elkink, J.A., D.M. Farrell, S. Marien, T. Reidy, and J. Suiter, The Death of Conservative Ireland? The 2018 Abortion Referendum, *Electoral Studies*, 2020, 65, pp. 1–11.

[7] Farrell, D., We May Have Overdone it on Citizens' Assemblies, *Irish Times*, <https://www.irishtimes.com/opinion/we-may-have-overdone-it-on-citizens-assemblies-1.4803375>, 16 February 2022.

Transferable Vote (STV) system—which, according to previous agreements, was put to the general electorate of British Columbia by referendum in May 2005. Even though 77 of the 79 electoral districts turned out a majority vote for the proposal, and the overall referendum vote turned out a majority of 57.5 per cent, the required supermajority of 60 per cent was not obtained.[8] In 2006, inspired and warned by the British Columbia case, the Netherlands tasked a Citizens' Assembly to advise on electoral reform without a follow-up referendum on the proposal. The recommendation—a rather mild adaptation of Proportional Representation (PR)—was brushed aside by national politics without much ado, and without consulting the Dutch maxi-public by way of a referendum.[9]

In 2011, Belgium witnessed the organization of the first G1000, a national Citizens' Assembly aspiring to set the country's policy priorities straight, something that Belgian politicians in the eyes of the organizers failed to do, entangled as they were in a seemingly endless cabinet formation. De G1000 churned out a list of recommendations, which in following years basically evaporated.[10] In October 2012, Iceland held a national referendum on a draft for a new constitution, proposed by a Constitutional Council consisting of 25 assembled citizens, which was in turn informed by a previous National Council, as well as by various experts and the general public that could feed the process through various media. The process was said to be 'crowd-sourced'. Politicians were divorced from the process. Even though the referendum turned out the required two-thirds majority, the Icelandic national parliament could, and did, stall the bill—on which it has still not acted.

In Landemore's study *Open Democracy*, the Icelandic case is the central showcase.[11] Although this case contains some innovative elements that indeed helped to open up the process, but regrettably not close it off, it is

---

[8] Ratner, R.S., British Columbia Citizens' Assembly: The Learning Phase, *Canadian Parliamentary Review*, 2004, 27, 2, pp. 20–6; Warren, M.E. and H. Pearse, *Designing Deliberative Democracy: The British Columbia Citizens'Assembly*, New York, Cambridge University Press, 2008; Fournier, P., H. van der Kolk, R.K. Carty, A. Blais, and J. Rose, *When Citizens Decide: Lessons from Citizens'Assemblies on Electoral Reform*, Oxford, Oxford University Press, 2011; Tierney, S., Using Electoral Law to Construct a Deliberative Referendum: Moving beyond the Democratic Paradox, *Election Law Journal*, 2013, 12, 4, pp. 508–23. A Citizens' Assembly working on electoral reform in Ontario, Canada (2006-2007), followed the British Columbia precedent.

[9] Kolk, H. van der, *Kiezen Voor Een Nieuw Kiesstelsel*, <https://www.utwente.nl/en/bms/pa/staff/kolk/bf_verslag_deel_2_versie_4.pdf>, 1 February 2008; Fournier, P., H. van der Kolk, R.K. Carty, A. Blais, and J. Rose, *When Citizens Decide: Lessons from Citizens'Assemblies on Electoral Reform*, Oxford, Oxford University Press, 2011.

[10] Caluwaerts, D. and M. Reuchamps, Strengthening Democracy through bottom-up Deliberation: An Assessment of the Internal Legitimacy of the G1000 Project, *Acta Politica*, 2015, 50, 2, pp. 151–70.

[11] Landemore, H., *Open Democracy: Reinventing Popular Rule for the Twenty-First Century*, Princeton, Princeton University Press, 2020.

not the Icelandic case but rather the Irish case that will take precedence here. Reasons for doing so are elaborated in the following account of the case, in relation to democratic values as specified in Chapter 6.

The Irish CA-plus-referendum on abortion (2016–2018)

After the grave financial crisis of 2008–2009, confidence in Irish government and politics was low. The governing capacity of the state and the political class was harshly criticized, 'with many questioning whether the existing political system was fit for purpose'.[12] Many problems were left unsolved in a system that was dominated for a long time by two centre-right parties (*Fianna Fáil* and *Fine Gael*); in the 2020 election, Sinn Féin broke into the political system picking up on citizens' concerns about housing and health care, and generally creating a new dynamics.[13] Against this backdrop, a statewide mini-public was twice established to advise on national issues, in 2013 and 2016. Both prepared major breakthroughs by referendum on first-order national issues: permitting same-sex marriage and liberalizing the abortion law, in 2015 and 2018 respectively. My focus here is on the 2016 Citizens' Assembly, which integrated practices and lessons from the earlier 2013 Constitutional Convention.[14] In particular, my focus is on the process leading to a breakthrough of stalemate on the abortion issue. In this process, a deliberative assembly and a binary referendum were effectively connected to each other, as well as to the encompassing political system, in a way that is rare in a cross-national comparative perspective (see Figure 7.1).

The Irish Citizens' Assembly, assembling 99 random citizens, was established in October 2016 by the Irish Government and authorized by a Parliamentary resolution to deliberate and advise on the following topics: abortion, the challenges and opportunities of an ageing population, fixed-term parliaments, the manner in which referendums are held, and how the state can make Ireland a leader in tackling climate change.[15] The prioritization of the

---

[12] Suiter, J., D. Farrell, and C. Harris, Ireland's Evolving Constitution, in P. Blokker (ed.), *Constitutional Acceleration within the European Union and Beyond*, London, Routledge, 2018, p. 145.

[13] Müller, J.W., *Democracy Rules*, Penguin Books, 2021, pp. 83–4.

[14] On the earlier 'Constitutional Convention', see Farrell, D.M., J. Suiter, and C. Harris, The Effects of Mixed Memberships in a Deliberative Forum: The Irish Constitutional Convention of 2012–2014, *Political Studies*, 2020, 68, 1, pp. 54–73. The main difference was that in the Constitutional Convention (established 2013) 33 of the 99 members where politicians, while in the later Citizens' Assembly (established 2016) all 99 members were citizens recruited on the basis of (stratified) random selection. Relatedly, the link with the political domain differed, as described here.

[15] A basic chronology of the other themes of the 2016 Citizens' Assembly can be found in Farrell, D.M., J. Suiter, and C. Harris, Systematizing Constitutional Deliberation: The 2016–18 Citizens' Assembly in Ireland, *Irish Political Studies*, 2019, 34, 1, pp. 115–19: Ageing population: meetings 10–11 June, 8–9 July

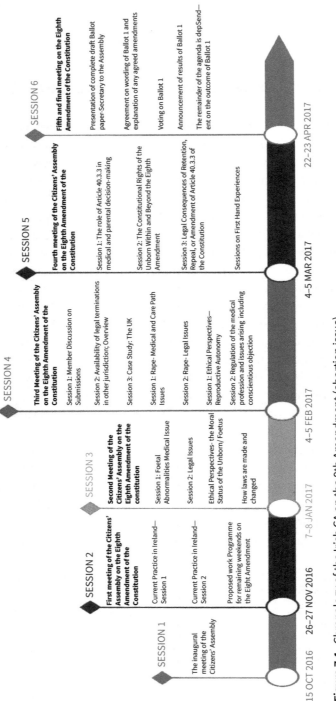

Figure 7.1 Chronology of the Irish CA on the 8th Amendment (abortion issue)

Source: The Citizens' Assembly, *First Report and Recommendations of the Citizens' Assembly, The 8th Amendment of the Constitution*, 29 June 2017.

abortion issue in the Citizens' Assembly was clear from the outset. The Irish coalition government formed in October 2016 needed the support of an independent member of Parliament, Katherina Zappone, who made this a condition for approval. Pressure to come to a settlement of this lingering and divisive issue—with, on the one hand, 'pro-life' champions eager to maintain the highly restrictive regime enshrined in the 8th Amendment of the Irish constitution; and, on the other hand, 'pro-choice' activists demanding liberalization of abortion legislation—came from within the country, but also notably from abroad. The United Nations pushed for a decisive settlement of the issue, which Irish politics seemed incapable of forging. Political parties were hopelessly divided on the issue, and politicians had more incentives to shun than to touch such an explosive issue. Opinion polls suggested growing support for extending the possibilities of legal abortion, but recent history contained evidence that actually making changes would never be easy. The pro-choice camp made its case forcefully and vocally in public debate, while the pro-life camp did no less.[16]

Abortion was the first issue on the agenda of the Citizens' Assembly. It also spent the most time on this issue: 5 weekends—more precisely 9.5 days—were dedicated to deliberating abortion.[17] After its inaugural meeting on 15 October 2018, the Citizens' Assembly as a whole came together for 11 weekends between November 2016 and April 2018; its final report was published on 21 June 2018. The inaugural meeting was held at Dublin Castle; later meetings took place at Grand Hotel Malahide in Dublin County. Meetings were usually held for most of the weekend (all day Saturday and all of Sunday morning). The Citizens' Assembly consisted of the chair, Ms Justice Mary Laffoy, and 99 citizens, randomly selected by a polling and market research agency (REDC) to represent the broader population in terms of age, gender, social

---

2017; report 8 December 2017. Organizing referendums: meeting 13–14 January 2018; report 1 June 2018. Fixed-term Parliaments: meetings 14–15 April 2018; report 18 April 2018. Tackling climate change: meetings on 30 September, 1 October, 4–5 November 2017; report 18 April 2018; for the latter theme, a special parliamentary committee has been set up.

[16] 'Pro-life': perceives abortion as murder, a crime against the unborn life; believes life-and-death choices are not up to people; wants to avoid repealing the 8th Amendment to the Irish Constitution; sends a No Road Show across Ireland (posters are put up, flyers and plastic dolls of a ten-week-old fetus are handed out to show that it is already a human in miniature form); receives support from the Roman Catholic bishops who call on their parishioners to vote no in the 2018 referendum. 'Pro-choice': considers abortion justified when the pregnant woman's well-being and life are in danger; believes that abortion should be a free choice; calls for the removal of the 8th Amendment; finds support at the European Court of Human Rights; the UN Human Rights Committee and Amnesty International also speak out in favour of women's rights.

[17] In comparison: on climate and ageing, also difficult issues, the Citizens' Assembly did not deliberate for more than 4 days each time. See Farrell, D.M., J. Suiter, and C. Harris, Systematizing' Constitutional Deliberation: The 2016–18 Citizens' Assembly in Ireland, *Irish Political Studies*, 2019, 34, 1, p. 115.

class, and place of residence.[18] Citizens' Assembly meetings were shared via live streaming and the media were allowed to attend plenary sessions under stipulated conditions. The participants had to refrain from interviews and public comment (including via social media).

The deliberation process within the Citizens' Assembly took shape through presentations, question-and-answer sessions, debates, plenary meetings, and round tables. Supported by a professional moderator and a dedicated note-taker, groups of seven to eight members deliberated with each other. Participants at the round tables rotated after each weekend to keep the process varied. Moderators were there to ensure that discussions were conducted appropriately, respectfully, and to the point. The commitment to inclusive participation and deliberation was reflected in the Assembly's core principles—openness, fairness, efficiency, equal right to speak, respect, and collegiality—leaning toward the democratic values discussed in Chapter 6 as typical input and throughput values.

During the meetings on the abortion issue, participants listened to a range of legal and medical professionals as well as penetrating stories from women as experience experts. After extensive deliberation, the Citizens' Assembly took an internal vote on the subject. Over the weekend of 22 and 23 April 2016, on the first day, participants were asked whether Article 40.3.3 of the Irish Constitution—enacted by the 8th Amendment—should be maintained unabridged or not. Subsequently, participants were asked whether the Article should be merely repealed, or repealed and replaced. A 51-to-38 majority voted in favour of replacing the Article with a constitutional provision that would give the *Oireachtas*, both houses of parliament, and president, room to enact more liberal legislation on pregnancy termination and the rights of pregnant women vis-à-vis unborn life.

On the second day, more specific recommendations for the envisaged legislation were discussed and formulated. Various cases were presented to the participants, with the question of whether and, if so, at what time (12 weeks, 22 weeks, or unlimited) abortion should or should not be possible in such cases. What is wise in the case of rape, fatal foetal abnormalities,

---

[18] There were originally 48 men and 51 women selected; 10 people aged 18–24, 29 aged 25–39, 28 aged 40–54, and 32 aged 55 and older. There were 45 participants from the ABC1 demographic group and 48 from the C2DE group. There were 6 farmers, 28 people from Dublin, 25 from the rest of Leinster, 27 from Munster, and 19 from Connacht-Ulster. See Leahy, P., Who exactly are the citizens in the Citizens' Assembly?, *The Irish Times*,<https://www.irishtimes.com/news/politics/who-exactly-are-the-citizens-in-the-citizens-assembly-1.3059708>, 24 April 2017.

serious risks to a woman's mental and physical health, and other such contingencies?[19] Discussions on these and similar cases resulted in a sequence of internal votes that clearly showed that the participants in the Citizens' Assembly recommended making legal abortion available on request (within 12 weeks, for any reason) to a greater extent than previously thought possible in Ireland.[20]

On 29 June 2017, the Citizens' Assembly's final report on abortion was published, after which a special, all-party committee of the Parliament (*Oireachtas*) took an in-depth look at the proposal, its underpinnings, and implications. This committee in many ways validated the work of the CA. It recommended a referendum on the 8th Amendment and drew up details of feasible subsequent legislation following the Assembly's lead.[21] The Irish government and parliament followed suit, and a referendum was called on 25 May 2018.[22] In this referendum 66.4 per cent of the electorate voted for repeal of the 8th Amendment, while 33.6 per cent voted against—a remarkable turnaround from the 1983 abortion referendum that had led to the 8th Amendment with a 2 to 1 ratio indicating a two-thirds conservative majority at the time.[23] The outcome of the 2018 referendum allowed for significant liberalization of the abortion legislation. To many observers it was astonishing that such liberalization was first advocated by an Irish Citizens' Assembly, then backed by political gatekeepers, and finally supported by a large majority—2 to 1—in a national referendum. This broke a longstanding stalemate in Irish politics and society.

Despite the new abortion legislation, not all of the associated problems have suddenly disappeared. Irish doctors invoked conscientious objections in droves, and even with the new legislation in place pregnant women contemplating abortion could still fall between two stools.[24] Pro-life activists and

---

[19] Following input from participants, the situations to be considered were expanded with contingencies such as: real and significant physical risks to the woman's life; real and substantial risk to a woman's life from suicide; serious risk to the woman's physical health; serious risk to the woman's mental health; pregnancy as a result of rape; foetal abnormality likely to result in death before or shortly after birth; significant foetal abnormality unlikely to result in death before or shortly after birth; socio-economic reasons; no statement of reasons.

[20] For the results of the internal votes, see: The Citizens' Assembly, *First Report and Recommendations of the Citizens' Assembly*, The 8th Amendment of the Constitution, 29 June 2017, pp. 32–7.

[21] Farrell, D.M., J. Suiter, K. Cunningham, and C. Harris, When Mini-Publics and Maxi-Publics Coincide: Ireland's National Debate on Abortion, *Representation*, 2020, pp. 1–2.

[22] More specifically, the Irish government and Parliament followed the ruling of the Irish Attorney General, who recommended replacement of the 8th Amendment if it were to be repealed by referendum—as eventually happened. See Bardon, S., Attorney General says Eight Amendment should be replaced if it is repealed, *The Irish Times*, <https://www.irishtimes.com/news/politics/attorney-general-says-Eight-amendment-should-be-replaced-if-it-is-repealed-1.3374059>, 30 January 2018.

[23] Elkink, J.A., D.M. Farrell, S. Marien, T. Reidy, and J. Suiter, The Death of Conservative Ireland? The 2018 Abortion Referendum, *Electoral Studies*, 2020, 65, p. 4.

[24] Browne, K. and S. Caulkin (eds), *After Repeal: Rethinking Abortion Politics*, London, Zed Books, 2020.

members of the opposition continue to be unhappy with the new legislation. They have criticized the Citizens' Assembly for having been biased to a pro-choice position from the outset, and have also raised doubts in relation to the high turn-over of participants in the Assembly.[25] The fact, however, that the advice of the Citizens' Assembly was supported by a large majority in the referendum makes a big difference here. A vast majority of 66.4 per cent gives a clear signal in a context coloured by Anglo-style majoritarian thinking.

Moreover, no one could say that the Irish electorate had gone to the 2018 abortion referendum totally unprepared. The preparatory Citizens' Assembly had gone through a transformation process internally, while the wider public and political realm had indirectly also experienced the process, interconnected as the process was.[26] As evidenced by the referendum, maxi-public and mini-public largely coincided in the Irish abortion case. Irish citizens turned out to be more willing to change than Irish politicians thought possible, which will have made them more comfortable with the outcome.[27]

Gradually, Irish politics seems to have developed a taste for consulting citizens by way of Citizens' Assemblies on a range of topics, followed by referendums in some cases. In 2013, the Constitutional Convention was established, followed in 2016 by the Citizens' Assembly featured here; and in 2019 a new Citizens' Assembly was set to work, this time with special attention to the issue of gender equality. The creation of multiple mini-publics deliberating on various issues in quick succession and their significant role in supporting key referendums gave Irish political scientists reason to write in terms of a successively 'systematized' form of democratic innovation.[28]

The settlement of the issues of abortion and, earlier, same-sex marriage are undeniably the best-known accomplishments to date. The same basic model—proposal by Citizens' Assembly; follow-up decision by referendum—has also been applied to the issue of blasphemy (a proposal to deconstitutionalize the ban on blasphemy was supported by a follow-up referendum) and the minimum age of presidential candidates (a proposal to lower this to 21 was declined by follow-up referendum). Other processes have

---

[25] Due to a relatively large number of replacements, eventually not 99 but a total of 152 citizens participated in the Citizens' Assembly. The more fundamental point of bias will be picked up in the next section.

[26] Elkink et al. found that voters who were aware of the deliberative innovation were more likely to support the liberal referendum option. See Elkink, J.A., D.M. Farrell, S. Marien, T. Reidy, and J. Suiter, The Death of Conservative Ireland? The 2018 Abortion Referendum, *Electoral Studies*, 2020, 65, p. 10.

[27] The Economist, Amateurs to the rescue, Politicians should take Citizens' Assembly's seriously, <https://www.economist.com/leaders/2020/09/17/politicians-should-take-citizens-assemblies-seriously>, 17 September 2020; Participedia, The Irish Citizens' Assembly, <https://participedia.net/case/5316?lang=en>, n.d.

[28] Farrell, D.M., J. Suiter, and C. Harris, Systematizing' Constitutional Deliberation: The 2016–18 Citizens' Assembly in Ireland, *Irish Political Studies*, 2019, 34, 1, pp. 113–23.

been completed less conspicuously by Citizens' Assemblies with a final report and a closing meeting.[29] Next in line is the issue of gender equality (a proposal to delete the 'woman's place is in the home' clause from the Constitution is to be voted on by referendum at a later point), and at the time of writing two new Citizens' Assemblies are deliberating, in parallel, biodiversity and a Dublin mayor.

Comparative merits of the Irish CA-plus-referendum

The hybrid format that led to the settlement of the abortion issue in Ireland has some merits that can also be found in other cases that were mentioned earlier. Previous Citizens' Assemblies in British Columbia and Iceland (with follow-up referendums), and the Netherlands and Belgium (without follow-up referendums) also paid due attention to randomized inclusiveness and deliberative appropriateness—typical input and throughput values in terms of Chapter 6.

What makes the Irish case stand out most prominently, and what the other cases missed most blatantly, is the achievement of a tangible policy breakthrough—demonstrable efficaciousness in terms of Chapter 6. Secondly, the Irish case distinguishes itself with a level of systematization—cumulating attention to system values—also not found in the other cases. Let us take a closer look at these points.

In line with expectations: Inclusiveness and appropriateness

In terms of inclusiveness and appropriateness, the Irish Citizens' Assembly that dealt with the issue of abortion functioned, by and large, as we have come to expect from a deliberative mini-public. As already noted, input and throughput values in particular were reflected in the Assembly's core principles: openness, fairness, efficiency, equal right to speak, respect, and collegiality.

In theory, a deliberative mini-public is designed to include a socially diverse, statistically representative sample of the population. In practice, the

---

[29] I already noted that Farrell continues to recognize the huge contributions of the hybrid processes that led to breakthroughs on issues like abortion and gay marriage while being more critical of the non-hybrid processes that led to 'many, other recommendations' that have been 'ignored, rejected, or left to gather dust'. See Farrell, D., We may have overdone it on citizens' assemblies, *Irish Times*, <https://www.irishtimes.com/opinion/we-may-have-overdone-it-on-citizens-assemblies-1.4803375>, 16 February 2022.

organizers came a long way but were not able to get a fully unbiased sample of Irish citizens in the Assembly—as we often find in real-life mini-publics.[30] The Irish CA on abortion had members with pro-choice, pro-life, and unde-cided starting positions on board, but the more liberal, pro-choice position was overrepresented in the mini-public as compared to polls of the wider public. Research by Farrell et al. confirmed this, but also qualifies the prob-lem, showing 'that from the outset its members were in large part in favour of the liberalisation of abortion (though a fair proportion was undecided), that over the course of its deliberations the CA as a whole moved in a more liberal direction on the issue, but that its position was largely reflected in the subsequent referendum vote by the population as a whole.'[31] In the Citi-zens' Assembly, 9 per cent of the members started from the position that the constitutional ban on abortion should be retained, compared to 23 per cent holding this position in the wider population at the time. This relatively small segment of the CA, however, also showed a relatively large transformation to a more liberal position, together with those who were undecided.[32] The final CA recommendation was firmly in favour of liberalization, which was greeted by surprise at the time but was clearly seconded by the follow-up ref-erendum in 2018 that turned out a 66 per cent vote in favour of liberalization of abortion legislation. Irish researchers concluded that the CA on abortion was in fact quite representative of the broader public, and that mini-public and maxi-public in this case effectively coincided.[33]

In the process leading up to the Irish CA recommendation, the deliberative-democracy playbook was leading and, as it appears, conscien-tiously played out. Procedures and actors were in place to ensure appropriate proceedings, based on respectful treatment of discussants as well as evi-dence. The level of satisfaction with the deliberative quality of the CA process remained high across all five weekends that the CA spent on the abortion

[30] On (self-selection) bias in mini-publics see Caluwaerts, D. and M. Reuchamps, Strengthening Democracy through bottom-up Deliberation: An Assessment of the Internal Legitimacy of the G1000 Project, *Acta Politica*, 2015, 50, 2, pp. 151–70; Curato, N. and S. Niemeyer, Reaching Out to Overcome Political Apathy: Building Participatory Capacity through Deliberative Engagement, *Politics and Policy*, 2013, 41, 3, pp. 355–83; Jacquet, V., Explaining Non-Participation in Deliberative Mini-Publics, *European Journal of Political Research*, 2017, 563, pp. 640–59; Michels, A., Participation in Citizens' Summits and Public Engagement, *International Review of Administrative Sciences*, 2019, 85, 2, pp. 211–27; O'Flynn, I. and G. Sood, What Would Dahl say? An Appraisal of the Democratic Credentials of Deliberative Polls and other Mini-Publics, in K. Grönlund, A. Bächtiger, and M. Setälä (eds), *Deliberative Mini-Publics, Involving Citizens in the Democratic Process*, Colchester, ECPR Press, 2014, pp. 41–81.
[31] Farrell, D.M., J. Suiter, K. Cunningham, and C. Harris, When Mini-Publics and Maxi-Publics Coincide: Ireland's National Debate on Abortion, *Representation*, 2020, p. 1.
[32] Farrell, D.M., J. Suiter, K. Cunningham, and C. Harris, When Mini-Publics and Maxi-Publics Coincide: Ireland's National Debate on Abortion, *Representation*, 2020, p. 8.
[33] Elkink, J.A., D.M. Farrell, S. Marien, T. Reidy, and J. Suiter, The Death of Conservative Ireland? The 2018 Abortion Referendum, *Electoral Studies*, 2020, 65, p. 10; Farrell, D.M., J. Suiter, K. Cunningham, and C. Harris, When Mini-Publics and Maxi-Publics Coincide: Ireland's National Debate on Abortion, *Representation*, 2020, p. 14.

issue.[34] There was a relatively high turn-over of CA members, but according to Farrell et al. this was more likely to reflect dissatisfaction with the lack of honoraria, combined with the length of the proceedings, than dissatisfaction with the deliberative quality of the process.[35] Members of the CA generally spoke of a procedurally just and fair process, even though matters became more tense during discussions on abortion than on the other topics.[36] In the follow-up referendum on abortion tensions built up further, as could be expected from the characteristics of this plebiscitary instrument as compared to microscopic deliberation. The procedural fairness of the referendum was, however, not seriously questioned.

A combined mini-public plus state-wide referendum as we saw in the Irish case, but also in the Canadian and Icelandic cases mentioned, renders a richer mix of publics included and listened to than a 'stand alone' mini-public, as displayed by the Dutch and Belgian Citizens' Assemblies mentioned. It was not merely a microscopic reflection of the demos that was deeply engaged, but also the wider Irish public could make itself heard—in rather different, yet complementary ways. In British Columbia and Iceland, recommendations developed by mini-publics were also submitted to referendums, but without the efficaciousness that we saw in the Irish case. Elaborating on the value of efficaciousness, next, we can see why.

Exceeding expectations: Efficaciousness

What makes the Irish case of a Citizens' Assembly-plus-referendum on abortion stand out most of all is the breakthrough it achieved for a long-standing stalemate in Irish politics and society. This was far from easy or self-evident. Abortion had 'bedeviled' politics in Ireland for a long time.[37] The 1983 national referendum on the topic was not the once-and-for-all settlement of the issue that pro-life campaigners at the time hoped it would be. Some even referred to the abortion issue as 'the second partitioning of Ireland'— repeatedly reflected in public and political debate, and in a succession of

[34] Farrell, D.M., J. Suiter, and C. Harris, Systematizing' Constitutional Deliberation: The 2016–18 Citizens' Assembly in Ireland, *Irish Political Studies*, 2019, 34, 1, p. 118.
[35] Farrell, D.M., J. Suiter, and C. Harris, Systematizing' Constitutional Deliberation: The 2016–18 Citizens' Assembly in Ireland, *Irish Political Studies*, 2019, p. 117.
[36] Farrell, D.M., J. Suiter, and C. Harris, Systematizing' Constitutional Deliberation: The 2016–18 Citizens' Assembly in Ireland, *Irish Political Studies*, 2019, p. 118–19.
[37] Elkink, J.A., D.M. Farrell, S. Marien, T. Reidy, and J. Suiter, The Death of Conservative Ireland? The 2018 Abortion Referendum, *Electoral Studies*, 2020, 65, p. 9; Suiter, J., D. Farrell, and C. Harris, Ireland's Evolving Constitution, in P. Blokker (ed.), *Constitutional Acceleration within the European Union and Beyond*, London, Routledge, 2018, pp. 142–54; Farrell, D.M., J. Suiter, and C. Harris, Systematizing' Constitutional Deliberation: The 2016–18 Citizens' Assembly in Ireland, *Irish Political Studies*, 2019, 34, 1, pp. 113–23.

divisive referendum campaigns (towards referendums in 1983, 1992, 2002, and then 2018). Growing sections of Irish society questioned the far-reaching implications of the 8th Amendment—the strict ban on abortion authorized by the 1983 referendum—the interpretation of which also shifted in practice, with Irish women travelling abroad for an abortion, and the Irish High Court ruling to allow this. Reassessment and resettlement of the legal basis under the abortion policy were widely demanded, but at the same time very hard to initiate, let alone achieve, in Irish politics. The matter was explosive and infused with post-traumatic social and political stress.[38]

The Irish combination of a preparatory Citizens' Assembly and a follow-up referendum, effectively linked to each other and to the relevant political realm changed the dynamics, and ultimately broke the stalemate. The Irish Citizens' Assembly did what regular politicians could not do in the same way: it took time to deliberate on the issue of abortion from a diversely social and deeply human perspective, helped by an agogic deliberative-democracy design geared to hear all sides and benefit from collective learning, relatively free from political pressures and dependencies; it proposed a step towards the liberalization of abortion that was deemed large and surprising. In turn, the national referendum did what only a public vote could authoritatively do: establish that the recommendation of the Irish mini-public that deliberated on abortion was in fact seconded by the Irish maxi-public that voted on the matter. In theory, mini-publics may be defined as being representative of maxi-publics, but there is always the question of whether this is true in practice. Research does confirm that this is a legitimate question to pose for all cases of mini-publics claiming to represent maxi-publics. In the Irish abortion case, the answer to the question was delivered loud and clear by the follow-up referendum, which evidently backed the line set out by the preparative Citizens' Assembly. Elkink et al. found that voters who were aware of the deliberative innovation were more likely to support the liberal referendum option.[39]

A crucial point to note is that the Irish mini-public deliberating on abortion was not a detached affair—as some mini-publics are. The transformation

---

[38] A fiercely realistic background to this is provided by the documentary movie *The 8th*. See Kane, A., L. Kennedy, and M. O'Boyle (Directors) & A. Maher (Producer), *The 8th* [Film; online video], <https://the8thfilm.com/>, 28 May 2020.

[39] Elkink, J.A., D.M. Farrell, S. Marien, T. Reidy, and J. Suiter, The Death of Conservative Ireland? The 2018 Abortion Referendum, *Electoral Studies*, 2020, 65, p. 10. The same pattern was found in the earlier marriage-equality referendum: Elkink, J.A., D.M. Farrell, T. Reidy, and J. Suiter, Understanding the 2015 Marriage Referendum in Ireland: Context, Campaign, and Conservative Ireland, *Irish Political Studies*, 2017, 32, 3, pp. 361–81.

it went through was shared with Irish society and politics in various ways: non-formally, as the public and social media were deeply involved, but also formally, as political actors and institutions were inevitably engaged. As described earlier, and as summarized in Figure 7.2, Irish politics was engaged at crucial moments in the process that went from a Citizens' Assembly to a mandatory referendum on changing the constitutional basis under abortion legislation.[40] Irish politics authorized the Citizens' Assembly, assessed its recommendations on abortion, and authorized a referendum on constitutional and legislative change that it drew up in agreement with the CA's recommendations.[41]

In this respect, there is a huge contrast with the earlier mentioned Icelandic case, where the political realm was largely detached from the process by a Constitutional Council consisting of citizens that 'refused, in a self-defeating way, to cooperate with parties and other political elites … losing the good will of the political class'.[42] The Icelandic constitutional process was stalled in Parliament, a consequential result not reached. For all its merits, according to Landemore,[43] the proposal for a new constitution for Iceland is still no more than a paper result. In British Columbia, the Citizens' Assembly recommendation did not pass the referendum's supermajority requirement, elevated to a high level by anxious politicians. The recommendations of the Citizens' Assemblies in the Netherlands (2006) and Belgium (2011) also

Figure 7.2 Citizens' Assembly plus referendum process on the 8th Amendment (abortion issue)

---

[40] Suiter, J. and T. Reidy, Does Deliberation Help Deliver Informed Electorates: Evidence from Irish Referendum Votes, *Representation*, 2020, 56, 4, p. 541.

[41] There was an explicit political commitment that the government would provide 'a response to each recommendation of the Assembly, and, if accepting the recommendation, will indicate the time-frame it envisages for the holding of any related referendum'. See Farrell, D.M., J. Suiter, and C. Harris, Systematizing' Constitutional Deliberation: The 2016–18 Citizens' Assembly in Ireland, *Irish Political Studies*, 2019, 34, 1, p. 119.

[42] Landemore, H., *Open Democracy: Reinventing Popular Rule for the Twenty-First Century*, Princeton, Princeton University Press, 2020, pp. 120 & 181; Bergsson, B.T., The Constitution as a Political Tool in Iceland, in P. Blokker (ed.), *Constitutional Acceleration within the EU and Beyond*, London, Routledge, 2018, p. 170.

[43] Landemore, H., *Open Democracy: Reinventing Popular Rule for the Twenty-First Century*, Princeton, Princeton University Press, 2020, p. 162 et seqq.

remained paper results; politicians were not obliged or committed to take it to a referendum or to Parliament other than as a low-salience discussion piece.

Participatory instruments such as the deliberative mini-public or the referendum are often criticized for throwing intractable issues at unprepared people. In the case that we consider here, a Citizens' Assembly-plus-referendum, topped-up by political involvement, was applied to the issue of abortion. This seems to have helped the model to achieve its efficaciousness. In the Irish context, abortion is a highly salient moral issue, but it is also a focused and demarcated issue of deeply human concern. No one is a stranger to women who can get pregnant, give birth to a child, or not. It is humanly possible to understand the issue space, to come to a focused recommendation, which can then also be actualized.

In terms of issue characteristics, the abortion problem is different from, for instance, the climate issue, which was taken up as another subtheme by the same Citizens' Assembly—and by similar assemblies in other countries. Climate is a complex system, fanning out to a broad array of policy fields, with complicated interactions, trade-offs, costs and benefits, actions and reactions. What does a higher environmental tax—just one measure in the policy toolbox—mean for economic competitiveness, unemployment, tax pressure, budgetary deficits, etc.? Climate policy involves long strings of technical interventions and logistical operations that need to be planned in time: what to do how, and where, in the short term, towards 2030, towards 2050? Consequently, recommendations for climate policy issued by Citizens' Assemblies tend to be extensive packages of diverse policy measures—difficult to take to the people in a referendum, and prone to political cherry-picking.[44]

In contrast, the output of the CA on abortion was, in the description of Farrell et al. '1 key recommendation (in various parts)'.[45] The key advice was to repeal the 8th Amendment and to make room for liberalized abortion legislation.[46] This has received public and political support, and the breakthrough of the long-time stalemate is now a fact. As opposed to the climate issue, the abortion issue is more akin to the same-sex marriage issue, which was previously settled by mini-public recommendation, referendum backing,

---

[44] In Ireland, the CA recommendations on climate policy were not taken to a referendum. In France, the recommendations of the Citizens' Convention for Climate, a randomized mini-public that deliberated on the matter from October 2019 to June 2020, have not been taken to a referendum either, although the French president spoke about two possible follow-up referendums. More on climate assemblies: Boswell, J., R. Dean, and G. Smith, Integrating Citizen Deliberation into Climate Governance: Lessons on Robust Design from Six Climate Assemblies. *Public Administration*, 2022, pp. 1–19, online first.

[45] Farrell, D.M., J. Suiter, and C. Harris, Systematizing' Constitutional Deliberation: The 2016–18 Citizens' Assembly in Ireland, *Irish Political Studies*, 2019, 34, 1, p. 115.

[46] Unrestricted abortion up to 12 weeks of pregnancy (besides a number of special contingencies).

and political involvement in Ireland. The issue of marriage equality was, also, a socially salient and at the same time focused, demarcated issue of deeply human concern. The result was also consequential and tangible: same-sex couples can now get married in Ireland.[47]

The previously discussed cases of Iceland, Belgium, the Netherlands, and British Columbia, Canada, were not so consequential. I already pointed out the lack of effective couplings to the authorizing environment in these cases. At this point, I may add that the topic link was not conducive to high efficaciousness either: citizens were asked to outline electoral-system reform in British Columbia and the Netherlands, constitutional reform in Iceland, and a national agenda for the future in Belgium. To varying degrees, all lacked the deeply human, focused, and demarcated quality of the Irish abortion issue (as well as the same-sex marriage issue earlier). This did not render efficaciousness entirely impossible; but it did not help in a situation where the democratic design was not conducive to making effective links either.

Capitalizing on systematization?—resilience and counterbalance

Citizens' Assemblies are often recommended as a deep investment in democracy. Beyond the temporary benefits of organizing open and deliberative debate about a current issue, a Citizens' assembly is said to improve democracy in a more fundamental and systematic way. In actual fact, however, many Citizens' Assemblies have been incidental events, without long-term systematic effects.

The Irish case is distinguished by a level of systematization not found in other cases. On a range of issues, Citizens' Assemblies have developed recommendations. The Citizens' Assembly plus referendum on abortion—the focus of attention here—was inspired by a similar process targeted at marriage equality and was followed by a similar process on gender equality.[48] Ireland seems to have developed a taste for working in new and, according to many, innovative, citizen-responsive ways. The more systematized the democratic innovation, arguably, the more systematic effects get a 'chance to build up'; Ireland, with its comparatively high level of systematization, is in this sense

---

[47] For more on the marriage equality referendum, see: Elkink, J.A., D.M. Farrell, S. Marien, T. Reidy, and J. Suiter, The Death of Conservative Ireland? The 2018 Abortion Referendum, *Electoral Studies*, 2020, 65, pp. 1–11.

[48] Issues like these are enshrined in the Irish constitution, and changes therein require a mandatory referendum. Constitutional legislation and cumulating experience provide a set of regulations and rules of thumb for politicians and citizens alike.

well-placed. On the other hand, it should be noted that systematization is still a fairly recent phenomenon; systematic effects have had relatively little 'time to build up' even in the Irish case.

Theoretically, I distinguish between system-level benefits in terms of democratic resilience (impact on the political opportunity structure and civic culture conducive to a steady state of collective self-rule) and counter-balance (impact on the countervailing institutions and counter-democratic culture conducive to a checked and balanced system). Relatedly, I distinguish between systematic effects on provisions (institutionalized opportunities, rights) and perceptions (generalized trust, perceived civic efficacy). At the present stage of systematization of the Irish model, and research into this, it is more feasible to pinpoint systematic effects on provisions than on perceptions.

In terms of provisions, the hybrid of a deliberative mini-public and a follow-up referendum, connected to moments of political authorization, creates a significant addition to the institutional capacity for collective action as well as corrective contestation. It extends the repertoire of the Irish constitution, and this cannot be wiped away now that it has been activated on more than one occasion. The hybrid format is a political opportunity structure for initiating social change as well as challenging existing rules. Although the follow-up referendums on abortion and same-sex marriage were formally mandatory constitutional referendums, ultimately dependent upon top-down political authorization, the link with preceding mini-publics also gave them a bottom-up, citizen-initiated dynamic. In the cases of abortion and same-sex marriage, already existing constitutional rules were evidently challenged by recommendations from Citizens' Assemblies. Following the same route, using the Citizens' Assembly as an intermediate step towards a constitutional referendum, it is possible to bring about constitutional change, although political backing would then also be required.

Compared to provisions such as the citizen-initiated veto referendum or the popular initiative (not provided in Ireland, unlike in Switzerland and various states in the USA), the hybrid of a preparatory Citizens' Assembly and a follow-up constitutional referendum renders citizens less scope for popular self-rule independent of political authorization. Compared to the stand-alone Citizens' Assembly, however, the Irish hybrid offers civil society more access to formal procedure and follow-up action.

How the systematization of the Irish model has affected systematic perceptions, such as generalized trust in democratic governance and perceived civic efficacy, is less clear at the time of writing. Although the Irish model of democratic innovation is among the best documented, this particular relationship has not yet been specifically excavated. There are (very) general statistics on satisfaction with democratic governance and trust in political institutions and actors, which suggest a moderately positive development of such perceptions after 2008 when the appreciation of democratic governance in Ireland was at a low and the perceived need for democratic innovation at a high.[49] Although positive developments have not led to levels of appreciation higher than values for 2006, a few years before the fiscal and economic crisis hit Ireland and its political system badly, some would argue that vital trust and satisfaction statistics have at least bounced back after the plunge of 2008.[50] However, underlying survey research was not specifically targeted at the public's perception of democratic innovations in Ireland, to which trends in general trust and satisfaction can thus not be easily attributed.[51] While some contribution to the trend in these statistics is plausible considering the previous analysis, we do not presently know the weight of the contribution of the democratic innovations of the 2010s, separate from other explanatory and intervening factors (like economic recovery). It would take the next batch of Irish innovation and specifically tailored social survey research to properly tease out this statistical relationship.

Using the Irish National Election Survey of 2020, Walsh and Elkink zoomed-in on the public support for and willingness to participate in Citizens' Assemblies as well as some other formats.[52] The Election Survey revealed that 78 per cent of respondents (strongly) agreed with the statement: 'Politics in Ireland would benefit from more Citizens' Assemblies' (agree 46 per cent, strongly agree 32 per cent). Walsh and Elkink found that support for and willingness to participate in CAs are driven by citizens who are either

---

[49] Trust in the country's parliament (ESS) fell from 4.83 in 2006 to 3.86 in 2008 and remained at this low level until it moderately rose in the 2010s to 4.52 in 2016 and 4.73 in 2018. Satisfaction with how democracy works (ESS) shows a similar pattern at a slightly higher level, falling from 5.95 in 2006 to 4.48 in 2008, slowly ascending in the 2010s to a level of 5.42 in 2016 and 5.67 in 2018. Satisfaction with national government (ESS) also shows a similar, though more pronounced pattern, taking a deeper plunge from 5.32 in 2006 to 2.8 in 2008, steadily ascending in the 2010s to a level of 4.52 in 2016 and 4.73 in 2018. Thanks to Take Sipma for assistance with and advice on the ESS database.

[50] For politicians as a group, Philip O'Connell reports a slightly bigger bounce-back than for institutions such as government, Parliament, and democracy in general. As reported in his research on *Trust in Politics, Politicians and Institutions*. See O'Connell, P., Trust in Politics, Politicians and Institutions, *Public Policy*, <https://publicpolicy.ie/papers/trust-in-politics-politicians-and-institutions/>, 30 January 2020, p. 4.

[51] For political-efficacy statistics the connection is even more precarious. ISS has values for this in Ireland only for 2014, 2016, and 2018; with values for 2014 on a scale of 0–10 and values for 2016 and 2018 on a scale of 1–5. 'Confidence in own ability to participate in politics' is 3.9 in 2014 (0–10 scale); 2.17 in 2016; 2.32 in 2018 (1–5 scale). 'Political system allows people to have a say in what government does is 3.23 in 2014 (0–10 scale); 2.14 in 2016; 2.37 in 2019 (1–5 scale). Although tempting for those who like to see a positive trend, it would be statistically dubious to simply double the 2016 and 2018 scores (on a 1–5 scale) and compare them to the 2014 scores (on a 0–10 scale). Thanks to Take Sipma for assistance with and advice on the ESS database.

[52] Walsh, C.D. and J.A. Elkink, The Dissatisfied and the Engaged: Citizen Support for Citizens' Assemblies and their Willingness to Participate, *Irish Political Studies*, 2021, 36, 4, pp. 647–666.

dissatisfied with the regime or highly likely to be politically engaged. The latter are particularly attracted to more deliberative modes of innovation. The former tend to support various types of political reform: deliberative as well as plebiscitary.[53] Walsh and Elkink conclude: 'Dissatisfied citizens want change, but this does not specifically mean CAs.'[54] It could just as well mean CAs and referendums combined, which might also be supported by the politically engaged. Unfortunately, the Election Survey did not ask about the combination of formats.

In conclusion: Mixing models, winning the day

The combination of a preparatory Citizens' Assembly and a follow-up referendum, effectively linked to one another and to the relevant political realm, helped to break the stalemate on the abortion issue in Ireland; the hybrid format demonstrated an efficaciousness not often found in stand-alone Citizens' Assemblies, nor stand-alone referendums. In terms of inclusiveness and appropriateness, it exhibited the advantages of a Citizens' Assembly, added to the advantages of a referendum. The hybrid format catered to different audiences, with different participation preferences and inclinations. At the level of resilience and counterbalance—deep investments in the democratic system—the Citizens' Assembly-plus-referendum as developed in the Irish context distinguishes itself positively from less systematized and more ephemeral formats of democratic innovation.

This is not to say that we have localized the perfect democratic innovation here. Chapter 6 underscored that no such thing exists in the real world of democratic innovation. We may say, however, that the Irish case discussed in this chapter presents a comparatively successful democratic innovation. Different values (or goods) of democratic-governance innovation could be satisfied remarkably well because of the mixed and balanced design of the process that we came across here. David Farrell, a strong supporter of the potential of Citizens' Assemblies, has over time become critical of the excessive use of this one instrument by central government in Ireland, leading to many—too many—recommendations that have been 'ignored, rejected, or left to gather dust'.[55] Interestingly, his criticism does not extend to the

---

[53] Including the right to petition for a referendum, which in the aggregate is agreed by 39 per cent plus strongly agreed by 41 per cent of respondents

[54] Walsh, C.D. and J.A. Elkink, The Dissatisfied and the Engaged: Citizen Support for Citizens' Assemblies and their Willingness to Participate, *Irish Political Studies*, 2021, p. 649.

[55] Farrell, D., We may have overdone it on citizens' assemblies, *Irish Times*, <https://www.irishtimes.com/opinion/we-may-have-overdone-it-on-citizens-assemblies-1.4803375>, 16 February 2022. Farrell is

processes that led to successful proposals and impressive breakthroughs on abortion as well as, earlier, gay marriage—both were hybrid processes that combined a preparatory Citizens' Assembly with a follow-up referendum, which helped to add clarity and closure to the process.

In the abortion case—as earlier in the gay-marriage case—the combined process helped to navigate a cultural minefield populated by groups and parties with very different worldviews and social values. Referring to the Douglasian cultural typology, the pro-choice camp tends much more toward egalitarianism and individualism (commonly conflated in this field under 'libertarianism'), while the pro-life camp tends much more toward hierarchy and atomism (commonly conflated under 'conservatism').[56] With the potential for cultural conflict as high as it is in this arena—in the USA they even speak of cultural wars, and in Ireland the actual situation was not much different—arguably the need for a mixed and balanced process is higher than ever. In the Irish situation, such a process was provided. It is highly plausible that this contributed to the levels of effectiveness and legitimacy achieved. Highly plausible is the best we can get here, as there is no way of knowing for certain what a less diversified process would have achieved in the same time and space. Given the Irish constitution, abortion legislation could not be changed without authorization by referendum, but a singular referendum on the issue, without a Citizens' Assembly clearing the path, would have been a formal possibility. In fact, Ireland had singular referendums on the issue (in 1983, 1992, and 2002), which did not settle the issue and kept the unrest festering for decades.

A referendum is not always constitutionally required, neither in Ireland nor elsewhere, which means that a Citizens' Assembly can be deployed as a mini-public without the need for alignment with the maxi-public in convincing numbers. As indicated earlier, the comparative convenience of a less demanding process comes with the considerable risk of getting mini-public recommendations that are 'ignored, rejected, or left to gather dust'— Farrell's concerns about Citizens' Assemblies being used to excess resonates far beyond the realm of Ireland.[57] Another expert sympathetic to the cause of deliberative mini-publics, Graham Smith, has voiced a similar concern.[58] Smith writes that the problem is with how deliberative mini-publics are 'coupled' with decision-making institutions such as Parliaments and city

---

particularly critical of the fact that the Citizens' Assembly is increasingly approached as an instrument of government, which interferes with the intent of shaking up representative processes from the bottom up.

[56] See Chapter 2 about the Douglasian cultural theory and typology.

[57] See Chapter 3 on the implementation and concretization deficit of deliberative mini-publics in general. See earlier in this chapter for the failings of stand-alone Citizens' Assemblies.

[58] Smith, G., *Can Democracy Safeguard the Future?*, Polity Press, 2021.

councils. Although this is certainly part of the problem—for significant structural change the consent or non-veto of the authorizing environment is usually a necessary condition—this problem is not magically solved by coupling a mini-public to a legislative institution (the former issuing recommendations to the latter). For some issues, broader evidence of sufficient public support is desired not only to make the necessary political decisions but also to see them implemented in practice. The mixed model that we came across in Ireland was able to deliver on this. The stand-alone Citizens' Assemblies deployed in the Netherlands (2006) and Belgium (2011) were not so consequential at all. Without clear evidence of additional public pressure, decision-making and policy-making institutions in these two countries found no reason to act on the given recommendations. And those doubting the very ability and authority of a deliberative mini-public to effectively represent the encompassing maxi-public were confirmed in their suspicion.

The effective coupling of a Citizens' Assembly to a referendum to a wider decision-making system is a matter of fine-tuning, dependent on design choices as well as contextual factors. This is reflected in the Irish abortion case, but also in the similar cases of British Columbia (2004–2005) and Iceland (2010–2012) where referendums following-up on Citizens' Assemblies ended less well. In both cases, recommendations by Citizens' Assemblies were seconded by majorities in follow-up referendums, but finally not seen through. In British Columbia, the big stumbling block was the required supermajority, which meant that majority support of 57 per cent in the follow-up referendum was not enough. In retrospect and compared to other countries, it seems overly demanding to require a supermajority when a bottom-up developed proposal must already achieve a double majority—in the Citizens' Assembly, and in the referendum. In Iceland, the big problem was that politicians were divorced from the process, which led to the reform Bill developed bottom-up stalled in Parliament. Icelandic Parliamentarians had the motive, the opportunity, and the means to halt its progress. The more recent Citizens' Convention on Climate in France is a special case that has, at the time of writing, not resulted in a follow-up referendum, even though this seemed to be a possibility at earlier stages of the process. The aftermath of the French CCC in terms of realized political and policy change is widely seen as problematic, or outright disappointing.[59]

---

[59] Courant, D., The Promises and Disappointments of the French Convention on Climate, *Deliberative Democracy Digest*, <https://www.publicdeliberation.net/the-promises-and-disappointments-of-the-french-citizens-convention-for-climate/>, 9 June 2021; Perthuis, C., Débat: La Convention citoyenne pour le climat … et après ?, *The Conversation*, <https://theconversation.com/debat-la-convention-citoyenne-pour-le-climat-et-apres-141891>, 6 July 2020.

The mixed model of democratic innovation that we found in the Irish abortion case worked better. Clearly, this was not the result of one stroke of brilliant design, but rather of a fortunate coincidence of design options and reform motivations available in the same time span and social arena: deliberative Citizens' Assemblies coming to the fore in a political context that continued to necessitate binary referendums on particular issues; binding constitutional referendums that continued to require political handling and thus systemic connection; politicians and citizens pressured long and hard enough to try out new ways of handling highly persistent social problems; a social problem, abortion, with issue characteristics—a tough but tractable, demarcated issue of deep human concern—suitable to being handled by a Citizens' Assembly and follow-up referendum. This all contributed to the successful application of this mixed model in this particular context (see Box 7.1 for more variations on the theme of mixing referendum voting and deliberative assemblies).

Box 7.1: Deliberative referendums and variations on a theme

This chapter focused on the Irish hybrid of a deliberative Citizens' Assembly and a follow-up binary referendum on abortion, widely acclaimed as a paragon at the national level of 'how deliberation can be inserted into the referendum process in a meaningful way'.[a] There are, however, more ways of coupling deliberative assemblies and referendum procedures that deserve to be acknowledged even though they cannot be analysed and assessed to the same extent here. Elsewhere, Charlotte Wagenaar and I have distinguished three generic variants of such coupling (see Figure 7.3).[b]

The Irish process is a special case of the first variant, wherein a deliberative assembly or mini-public explores a policy issue and develops a referendum proposal which thereafter is presented to the wider electorate or maxi-public. A similar sequence of connected instruments was found in British Columbia and Iceland, albeit, as indicated, in a less fortuitous design and embedding.[c]

In a second variant, a deliberative mini-public is established after a referendum question has been decided for the ballot. The assembly's core task is to dissect the referendum question and ballot alternatives, and to provide voters with objective information, relevant considerations and—optionally—voting advice. The most developed example is the citizens' initiative review (CIR), originating in the US state of Oregon in 2010.[d]

In a third variant, an elaborating citizens' assembly is set to work after a referendum has taken place and follow-up steps operationalizing the referendum result need to be reflected on. As of yet, there are few examples of this variant except the Citizens' Assembly on Brexit, a pilot project executed in the autumn of 2017.[e]

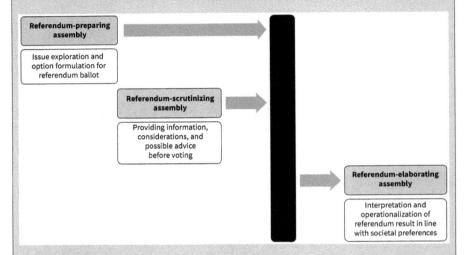

Figure 7.3 Three generic variants of coupling Citizens' Assembly and referendum

The three generic roads to hybridization depicted in Figure 7.3 depart from established models of deliberative reflection, on the other hand—the randomized citizens' assembly—and direct voting, on the one hand—the binary referendum. It should be noted that the deliberative-reflection element and the direct-voting element can be operationalized in alternative ways, and the elements may be repeated in a different order.

A pilot project that used an alternative deliberative instrument—deliberative polling—in preparation for a particular type of direct voting—the American-style Initiative—was conducted in California. In June 2011, a sample of 412 Californians was gathered to reflect on 30 proposals from a range of reform groups. Polling before and after deliberation showed considerable learning effects; six proposals that showed growing support among deliberators as well as a larger sample of Californians were combined in one ballot proposition (Prop 31), which was ultimately defeated at election time.[60]

---

[60] Fishkin, J.S., T. Kouser, R.C. Luskin, and A. Siu, Deliberative Agenda Setting: Piloting Reform of Direct Democracy in California, *Perspectives on Politics*, 2015, 13, 4, pp. 1030–42. The authors stress that the proposals actually deliberated on by the people might well have passed if not encumbered by additional elements that were not deliberated on and that drew opposition.

A so-called 'iterative public vote' took place in 2014 in two municipalities in British Columbia, Canada, considering amalgamation. After an initial referendum, which clarified that majorities in both municipalities were in favour of studying costs and benefits of amalgamation, a Citizens' Assembly was set to work and produced a positive recommendation, which was put to the maxi-public in a second referendum.[61] The second referendum returned a majority in one of the municipalities (North Cowichan) but not in the other (Duncan), where public support had already been more slight in the first referendum. Naturally, an iterative public vote, or any hybrid format for that matter, is not a magic wand for conjuring up majorities; the people may still be unconvinced, but then, if processes are sequenced properly, on a considerably stronger footing.

Beyond the use of formal referendums, there are other ways of connecting the deliberative reflections of a mini-public to the aggregated preferences of a wider maxi-public. The agenda of the deliberative G1000 in Belgium, held in 2011, was set by looking at the most frequently posed questions on the related website, and at three core themes that amassed the highest number of votes on the website. At a later moment, the instigator of the Belgian G1000, David van Reybrouck, suggested adding an element of aggregative voting (of sorts) at the end of the deliberative process by way of a follow-up multi-option survey or 'preferendum'.[62]

[a] Farrell, D.M., J. Suiter, and C. Harris, Systematizing' Constitutional Deliberation: The 2016–18 Citizens' Assembly in Ireland, *Irish Political Studies*, 2019, 34, 1, p. 120.
[b] Hendriks, F. and C. Wagenaar, The Deliberative Referendum: An Idea Whose Time Has Come? *Administration & Society*, 2023, online first.
[c] In France, the option of a follow-up referendum on particular recommendations of the Citizens' Convention on Climate (CCC) was at some point mentioned by the French president, but as of the time of writing not yet actualized.
[d] See previous remarks about the CIR in Chapter 4; Gastil, J., R.C. Richards, and K.R. Knobloch, Vicarious Deliberation: How the Oregon Citizens' Initiative Review Influenced Deliberation in Mass Elections, *International Journal of Communication*, 2014, 8, pp. 62–89; Gastil, J., G.F. Johnson, S. Han, and J. Rountree, *Assessment of the 2016 Oregon Citizens' Initiative Review on Measure 97*, State College, Pennsylvania State University, 2017.
[e] Renwick, A. and McKee, R., *The Citizens' Assembly on Brexit (I): Design and Purpose*. London, University College London, 2017; Renwick, A., Allan, S., Jennings, W., McKee, R., Russell, M., and Smith, G., *The Report of the Citizens' Assembly on Brexit*. London, University College of London, 2017; Renwick, A., Allan, S., Jennings, W., McKee, R., Russell, M., and Smith, G., What Kind of Brexit do Voters Want? Lessons from the Citizens' Assembly on Brexit. *The Political Quarterly*, 2018, 4, 649–58.

---

[61] McKay, S., Building a Better Referendum: Linking Mini-Publics and Mass Publics in Popular Votes, *Journal of Public Deliberation*, 2019, 15, 1. Processes with two consecutive referendums—but without a specifically deployed deliberative instrument in between the two steps—were organized in New Zealand on electoral reform (1992–1993) and a possible new flag (2015–2016).
[62] NRC, Geef burgers echte invloed op het klimaatbeleid met het preferendum, *NRC Nieuws*, <https://www.nrc.nl/nieuws/2021/10/08/geef-burgers-echte-invloed-op-het-klimaatbeleid-met-het-preferendum-a4061204>, 8 October 2020.

8

Participatory Budgeting-new style

Reflections on a local-level hybrid

There is a second realm where new practices of dispersed plebiscitary voting and intensive deliberative reflection have become increasingly entangled. This is the realm of 'Participatory Budgeting-new style', which distinguishes itself by an increased emphasis on large-scale voting—often using the opportunities of broadband internet and smart devices that became widely available in the 2010s—combined with continued attention to deliberative participation as an ideal emphasized in earlier incarnations of Participatory Budgeting (PB).[1] Compared to the one we encountered in Chapter 7, this is altogether a different realm—a realm with multiple spending decisions on local and urban projects, of matching many specific propositions to always limited budgetary resources. PB-ns is examined in particular through the lens of Antwerp, a Belgian town with a reputation for creative design in this field. In view of the values framework, Antwerp's Citizens' Budget is evaluated as a relatively multifunctional instrument that largely—although not perfectly—does what it is expected to do in the local context.

Participatory budgeting meets mass voting

The Brazilian city of Porto Alegre may be the archetype and best-known example of PB worldwide; it is not, however, an ideal illustration of PB-ns.[2]

---

[1] On the general phenomenon, see Ganuza, E. and G. Baiocchi, The Power of Ambiguity: How Participatory Budgeting Travels the Globe, *Journal of Public Deliberation*, 2012, 8, 2, pp. 1–12; Ganuza, E. and G. Baiocchi, The Long Journey of Participatory Budgeting, in S. Elstub and O. Escobar (eds), *Handbook of Democratic Innovation and Governance*, Edward Elgar, 2019, pp. 77–98; Sintomer, Y., A. Röcke, and C. Herzberg, *Participatory Budgeting in Europe: Democracy and Public Governance*, Routledge, 2016; Iasulaitis, S., C. Pineda Nebot, E. Carneiro da Silva. and R. Cardoso Sampaio, Interactivity and Policy Cycle within Electronic Participatory Budgeting: A Comparative Analysis, *Revista Administração Pública*, November/December 2019, 53, 6, pp. 1091–115; Laruelle, A., Voting to Select Projects in PB, *European Journal of Operational Research*, 2021, 288, 2, pp. 598–604.

[2] For contemporary contributions on Participatory Budgeting in Porto Alegre, see Wampler, B., S.L. McNulty, and M. Touchton, *Participatory Budgeting in Global Perspective*, Oxford, Oxford University Press, 2021; Wampler, B. and B. Goldfrank, *The Rise, Spread, and Decline of Brazil's Participatory Budgeting: The Arc of a Democratic Innovation*, Cham, Palgrave Macmillan, 2022; Ryan, M., *Why Citizen Participation Succeeds or Fails: A Comparative Analysis of Participatory Budgeting*, Bristol, Bristol University Press, 2021.

Rethinking Democratic Innovation. Frank Hendriks, Oxford University Press. © Frank Hendriks (2023).
DOI: 10.1093/oso/9780192848291.003.0008

PB-ns is better exemplified by metropoles and cities such as Paris, Madrid, Berlin, Chicago, New York, Fortaleza, Rosario, Reykjavik, Bristol, Amsterdam, and Antwerp—places that all invested in institutional and technological updates of PB in the 2010s. Goel and others suggest that Chicago, which added a digital voting platform to PB in its 49th ward in 2012, has triggered the spread of similar methods to other cities and towns in North America, while Reykjavik, which inserted 'open active voting' into PB in the same year, was something of a trailblazer in Europe.[3] Berlin-Lichtenberg, which has developed its own version of PB including digital voting since 2005, has influenced similar processes in the German-speaking world. In reality, however, innovations like these do not display a singular donor-to-host transmission but are typically connected to different influences with different genealogies.[4]

It is not my objective here to reconstruct PB's historical evolution and international dispersal in such a wide-ranging way. In this chapter, I wish to explore Participatory Budgeting-new style, in particular the mingling of small-scale deliberation and large-scale voting, through the lens of one particular city—Antwerp, Belgium. The Citizens' Budget or *Burgerbegroting* as developed in Antwerp is a good example of a mixed model with a closely guarded balance of deliberative and plebiscitary elements, of small-scale talking and large-scale voting. It is fascinating to see how District Antwerp is trying to maintain the balance, with conscious design thinking and rethinking that brings new challenges with every step along the way. Further down in this chapter, I elaborate and reflect on Antwerp's *Burgerbegroting*, its comparative merits, and the general idea of PB-new style.

The repeated mixing of a model—from Porto Alegre to Antwerp

To understand PB-ns in a city like Antwerp, or another city that inserts large-scale voting into Participatory Budgeting for that matter, we do need to go back briefly to where it all started in 1989—Porto Alegre, Brazil. Its

For an analysis of the enabling and inhibiting factors between the 1990s and the present, see Abers, R.N., I. Brandão, R. King, and D. Votto, Towards a More Equal City: Porto Alegre: Participatory Budgeting and the Challenges of Sustaining Transformative Change, World Resources Institute, June 2018.

[3] Goel, A., A.K. Krishnaswamy, S. Sakshuwong, and T. Aitamurto, Knapsack Voting for Participatory Budgeting, *ACM Transactions on Economics and Computation*, July 2019, 7, 2, Article 8, pp. 1–27.

[4] Schneider, S.H. and S. Busse, Participatory Budgeting in Germany—A Review of Empirical Findings, *International Journal of Public Administration*, 2018, 692, pp. 1–15; Pape, M. and C. Lim, Beyond the 'Usual Suspects'? Reimagining Democracy with Participatory Budgeting in Chicago, *Sociological Forum*, 2019, 34, pp. 861–82; Williams, D. and D. Waisanen, *Real Money, Real Power?: The Challenges with Participatory Budgeting in New York City*, Palgrave Macmillan, 2020; Laruelle, A., Voting to Select Projects in Participatory Budgeting, *European Journal of Operational Research*, 2021, 288, 2, pp. 598–604.

original model of Participatory Budgeting developed from a left-wing political and associational context. Sintomer, Röcke, and Herzberg distinguish two interlinked starting points—the need to 'reverse priorities' for the benefit of the disadvantaged, and to 'democratize democracy' via participation—and a third objective that was gradually added—the need for 'good governance' characterized by clean and transparent decision-making processes instead of political clientelism and opportunism.[5] Various studies have conveyed a largely favourable interpretation of PB in Porto Alegre up to the 2010s. Although the quest for good governance was only partially successful—party-political dynamics changed to only some extent—it is generally argued that the twin goals of widening the scope for civic participation in public spending decisions and improving the social circumstances of the less well-off were largely met.[6]

Regarding democratic design, the original Porto Alegre model of PB was already a mixed model—at least to some extent. Participatory democracy—via deliberative popular assemblies—and representative democracy—via the executive political branch in particular—were strongly connected in this model. On the other hand, sortition and referendum, favoured by many champions of deliberative and plebiscitary democracy respectively, were not so popular as devices for giving citizens an equal voice in Porto Alegre.[7] Popular assemblies decided up to about 20 per cent of the municipal budget, in a process supervised, channelled, and facilitated by participation professionals and a central planning office under the supervision of the Mayor. Popular assemblies had a real and significant influence on the process, even though they were not entirely autonomous. Executive powers in PB were delegated by the mayor who retained a formal veto on the entire budget, as did the municipal council, which could also alter the budget. City agencies could veto specific demands if they considered them technically unfeasible or economically inefficient.[8]

---

[5] Sintomer, Y., A. Röcke, and C. Herzberg, *Participatory Budgeting in Europe: Democracy and Public Governance*, Routledge, 2016.

[6] Sintomer, Y., A. Röcke, and C. Herzberg, *Participatory Budgeting in Europe: Democracy and Public Governance*, Routledge, 2016; Wampler, B., S.L. McNulty, and M. Touchton, *Participatory Budgeting in Global Perspective*, Oxford, Oxford University Press, 2021, pp. 6–11; Marquetti, A., G.A. de Campos, and R. Pires, Orçamento participativo, redistribuição e finanças municipais: a experiência de Porto Alegre entre 1989 e 2004, *Democracia participativa e redistribuição: análise de experiências de orçamento participativo*, São Paulo, Xamã, 2008, pp. 31–54; Goldfrank, B., *Deepening Local Democracy in Latin America: Participation, Decentralization, and the Left*, Penn State University Press, 2015, p. 232–3.

[7] Ryan, M., *Why Citizen Participation Succeeds or Fails: A Comparative Analysis of Participatory Budgeting*, Bristol, Bristol University Press, 2021; Gret, M. and Y. Sintomer, *The Porto Alegre Experiment, Learning Lessons for Better Democracy*, London & New York, Zed Books, 2015.

[8] Smith, G., *Democratic Innovation: Designing Institutions for Citizen Participation*, Cambridge, Cambridge University Press, 2009, p. 35, 52.

The composition of the participatory assemblies in Porto Alegre's model of PB was not based on sortition, as in randomized mini-publics, but on a mix of broad participation and election-based delegation. The original model distinguished three layers of citizen participation.[9] First, there were popular assemblies organized in each of the city's sixteen regions (each comprising different neighbourhoods). All residents showing up could participate on an equal footing in these. The popular assemblies discussed recent spending in their regions with the mayor and senior officials, selected priority issues for coming investments, elected citizens to their respective regional budget forums, the second layer of participation, and to the overall council of the participatory budget (COP), the third layer of citizen involvement in Participatory Budgeting. In 1994 a parallel process was established for thematic, not neighbourhood-specific issues such as environment, transportation, education, health, and social services. These were also first discussed in thematic popular assemblies, secondly by citizen delegates of the assemblies in thematic budget forums, and thirdly citizen representatives elected into the overall COP. Ultimately, the COP consisted of two elected councillors from each region, two from each thematic area, completed by one representative from the union of neighbourhood associations (UAMPA) and one from the civil servants' trade union (SIMPA).

From the first to the second to the third layer of the model, citizen participation gradually changed from large crowd to smaller group, from campaigning to representing, from viewing city government from a grassroots, bottom-up perspective to 'seeing like a state'—internalizing the city-wide policymakers' perspective—as Scott aptly called the phenomenon that also pertains to the local state.[10] While he recognized this trend, Smith also saw measures that circumvented the concentration of power in the hands of a new participatory elite separated from those who were meant to benefit from PB in Porto Alegre. Even though the elected delegates and councillors were more likely to be male and have a higher socio-economic status than the other participants, 'they are still on average poorer than the population as a whole and are drawn from the same neighborhoods and associations as the citizens

---

[9] The three layers of PB in Porto Alegre are extensively described and helpfully visualized in Smith, G., *Democratic Innovation: Designing Institutions for Citizen Participation*, Cambridge, Cambridge University Press, 2009. In this context, a general description suffices.

[10] Scott, J., *Seeing Like a State, How Certain Schemes to Improve the Human Condition Have Failed*, Yale University Press, 1999. In a book on Participatory Budgeting in Porto Alegre, Abers made the relevant distinction between participatory bodies that analyse proposals top-down and bodies that develop proposals bottom-up. See Abers, R.N., *Inventing Local Democracy: Grassroots Politics in Brazil*, Lynne Riener Publishers, 2000, p. 211. Also see Smith, G., *Democratic Innovation: Designing Institutions for Citizen Participation*, Cambridge, Cambridge University Press, 2009, pp. 30–71.

who have voted for them'.[11] The model of election-based delegation, super-imposed on platforms of broad participation, allowed PB to work on such a large scale—with a city of 1.3 million citizens and a financial cut of up to 20 per cent of the city budget.

There was an element of voting—for projects as well as delegates—in the original model of PB as developed in Porto Alegre, but this voting was con-strained to participants and delegates in the various assemblies. Beyond these assemblies, the general citizenry was not a party to the voting pro-cess. Although Porto Alegre added a digital platform to its PB model, it did not become a forerunner in the more recent trend of organizing large-scale voting among the wider population, often using new digital tools, in addi-tion to participation and deliberation in assemblies. In fact, many observers see PB in Porto Alegre slowly back-sliding since 2004, when the Workers' Party, a long-time champion of the model, was heavily defeated in local elec-tions. Throughout this period actors responsible for PB in Porto Alegre were, according to Sintomer, Röcke, and Herzberg 'unable to achieve any signif-icant evolution of what they considered to be "the" ultimate model, and didn't bother much to learn from other processes'.[12] In the words of Baoicchi and Ganuza 'a politically conservative coalition maintained the surface fea-tures of PB while returning the actual functioning of the administration to more traditional modes of favor-trading and the favoring of local elites'.[13] In 2017, following the process of gradual backsliding, PB was suspended by the incumbent political leadership.[14]

While PB was gradually lapsing in Porto Alegre, it came increasingly to the fore in many other cities around the world—from South America and Southern Europe to Northern Europe and North America, Africa, and most recently Asia; it is estimated that there have been more than 7,000 PB processes around the world.[15] Central elements of the original model as distinguished by Sintomer, Röcke, and Herzberg could be distinguished in the myriad local variants, although typically in different ways and to

---

[11] Smith, G., *Democratic Innovation: Designing Institutions for Citizen Participation*, Cambridge, Cambridge University Press, 2009, pp. 30–71; Abers, R.N., *Inventing Local Democracy: Grassroots Politics in Brazil*, Lynne Riener Publishers, 2000, p. 127.

[12] Sintomer, Y., A. Röcke, & C. Herzberg, *Participatory Budgeting in Europe: Democracy and Public Governance*, Routledge, 2016. |See therein 'It All Began in Porto Alegre' and text box 'The Porto Alegre Participatory Budget Following the Defeat of the Workers' Party'.

[13] Baiocchi, G. and E. Ganuza, Participatory Budgeting as if Emancipation Mattered, *Politics & Society*, 2014, 42, 1, pp. 29–50.

[14] Abers, R.N., I. Brandão, R. King, and D. Votto, Towards a More Equal City: Porto Alegre: Participatory Budgeting and the Challenges of Sustaining Transformative Change, World Resources Institute, June 2018.

[15] Cabannes, Y., The Impact of Participatory Budgeting on Basic Services: Municipal Practices and Evidence from the Field, *Environment and Urbanization*, 2015, 27, 1, pp. 257–84; Dias, N. (ed.), *Hope for Democracy: 30 Years of Participatory Budgeting World-Wide*, Epopeia Records, 2018.

varying degrees.[16] The original Porto Alegre model was transposed and transformed in a wide-ranging process of institutional variation and selection. As indicated, this chapter is not geared toward reconstructing this worldwide process of diversification from the start until now. There is already very good specialized research on this.[17]

Here, I am specifically interested in the new frontier of democratic innovation in Participatory Budgeting: the addition of large-scale plebiscitary voting to already developed practices of group deliberation on budgetary matters. Although I point to various cities that experiment with Participatory Budgeting-new style, as I prefer to call it, a full-fledged comparative analysis is not what I am after here. Similar to Chapter 7, which took the Irish case of the deliberative referendum as a central case around which further reflections were built, this chapter will take one special case, the case of PB-ns in District Antwerp, to unpack, elaborate, and reflect on PB-ns as a design challenge.

Participatory Budgeting-new style in District Antwerp (2014 and beyond)

Antwerp presents a good example of PB-new style for at least three reasons. First, the design of Antwerp's Citizens' Budget—or *Burgerbegroting* as they call it in this Belgian town, displays a relatively balanced mix of deliberative and plebiscitary elements—which is the result of a conscious, though never easy balancing act. Second, the Citizens' Budget is not a short-lived phenomenon in Antwerp but has been developed since its launch in 2014 into a robust institution, widely supported in the relevant political and social realms. Between 2014 and 2022 it survived two reversals of executive political leadership. Third, studies and observations of the conception, implementation, evaluation, and further development of Antwerp's Citizens' Budget are accessible, while key actors and observers are also open for research purposes.[18]

---

[16] Regarding the three starting points mentioned earlier—based on Sintomer, Y., A. Röcke, and C. Herzberg, *Participatory Budgeting in Europe: Democracy and Public Governance*, Routledge, 2016—most cities continued to stress the need for more citizen participation, not only as a substantial goal in itself but increasingly also as a means to an end: bolstering governmental decision-making. Some cities retained the left-wing focus on reversing priorities for disadvantaged groups evident in the original model; other cities developed their versions of PB with a less pronounced left-leaning agenda, stressing the scope for more economy, efficiency, and effectiveness in public decision-making. This also implied a broader idea of good governance, including political, legal, economic, and managerial perspectives on the matter.

[17] See previous references in this section (footnote 2).

[18] I am grateful to the alderman Femke Meeusen and her staff, Inge van Nieuwenhuyze first and foremost, for opening-up Antwerp's citizens' budgetary process to my curious eyes. Access and the information provided were highly illuminating, as was retrospective insight gained from Joop Hofman and Hanne Bastiaensen who were closely involved in process evaluation and (re)design.

The Citizens' Budget in Antwerp was initiated and championed by Willem-Frederik Schiltz, erstwhile alderman (*schepen*) responsible for citizen participation in District Antwerp, a highly visible politician of the conservative-liberal party Open-VLD (after District Antwerp he became Open VLD-leader in the Flemisch Parliament). None of the political parties in Antwerp's District Council have actively opposed the Citizens' Budget. Choices following from the citizens' budgetary process are habitually seconded by the District Council, which makes it a de facto decisive instrument (even though formally this is a matter of political pre-commitment). In this sense, Antwerps' *Burgerbegroting* aligns with Participatory Budgeting in cities like Paris and Madrid, and diverges from common practice in German cities, for instance, where it is stressed that politicians make the final decisions, and where citizens' budgeting is both formally and de facto a consultative process.[19]

Like so many cities, Antwerp initially embarked on citizens' budgeting with an ethos of deliberative participation, and an explicit preference for face-to-face, on-site get-togethers, and deliberations. In 2018, however, the Citizens' Budget was opened-up to online participation and voting, which initiated something of a quantum leap. Antwerp was not the frontrunner in this development—cities like Reykjavik, Amsterdam, Paris, and Madrid opened up their PB-processes to online voting to a larger extent and with higher resulting numbers—yet, in its first year, 2018, online participation in Antwerp's *Burgerbegroting* already jumped to the level of offline participation, which had been growing incrementally since 2014; in its second year, 2019, online participation was almost four times as large as offline participation, mainly due to online voting in the process.[20] In an evaluation report submitted to District Antwerp in 2021, the final vote on projects is described as an 'online voting battle', sometimes even 'to the point that undesirable recruiting behaviour occurs and unequal resources are used (paying for ads, special websites, calling in an advertising agency)'.[21]

[19] Röcke, A., *Framing Citizen Participation: Participatory Budgeting in France, Germany and the United Kingdom*, Palgrave Macmillan, 2014; Wolf, E., S. Rys, and W. van Dooren, Naar een Vlaamse Burgerbegroting? Lessen uit de binnenlandse en buitenlandse praktijk, Universiteit Antwerpen, 2018.

[20] In 2018, numbers were 702 live participants and 728 online participants; the latter rose quickly to 3,051 in 2019 and 7,348 in 2020 (primarily participating in online voting). Live participation on the other hand stabilized in 2019 at 771 and dropped to 343 in 2000; the latter was undoubtedly influenced by Covid-19 circumstances, but even if pre-Covid numbers had continued along the previous growth path such numbers would have been much smaller than the growing numbers reported in online participation. Hofman, J., H. Bastiaensen, and M. Nuytemans, *Evaluatierapport van de Burgerbegroting District Antwerpen*, Deventer, Rode Wouw, <https://burgerbegroting.be/evaluatie-burgerbegroting>, 2021, p. 26.

[21] Translated from: Hofman, J., H. Bastiaensen, and M. Nuytemans, *Evaluatierapport van de Burgerbegroting District Antwerpen*, Deventer, Rode Wouw, <https://burgerbegroting.be/evaluatie-burgerbegroting>, 2021, p. 14. One example is a pizza-delivery firm offering one euro discount in return for the registrations number needed for voting.

In the final analysis, the evaluators and District Antwerp were worried about the excesses of online voting, but also remained confident that, when done properly, online voting could still supplement deliberation in the citizens' budgetary process. Hence, the improvement strategy for 2022 onwards came down to a rebalancing of plebiscitary and deliberative components. In previous years, deliberative choice had been given more weight in the selection process than plebiscitary voting, but, with public interest moving strongly towards the latter, the District felt that further depreciating the online vote was not the way to go—as it still appreciated broad participation, besides meaningful deliberation.[22] Instead, the District opted for 'more fair play by counteracting undesirable behaviour in online voting through regulations and voting method' and for increasing the participation of voting individuals vis-à-vis voters mobilized en bloc by associations with a stake in the competition.[23] On the deliberative side, the District opted to reinvigorate and reconnect the pre-application steps of the process—selecting themes and dividing the budget over themes—which were originally meant to be moments of civic-minded reflection and discussion about priorities and civic needs at large. In these steps, the District wanted to see more significant deliberation, as well as more individual citizens participating vis-à-vis mobilized group members. Additionally, the District promised to put extra effort into mobilizing citizens from a particular neighbourhood (named *Luchtbal*).

With such relatively modest tweaks and rebalancing measures, Antwerp's Citizens' Budget as of 2022 proceeds in four steps, after formal triggering and authorization by the local government (see Figure 8.1 and Box 8.1). The process centrally depends on political goodwill and assumes the existence of local demands and popular energy, which feed into the budgetary process (dispersed over two years, with year one of each new budgetary cycle overlapping with year two of the previous cycle).

---

[22] The original idea was: offline scores determine 80 per cent of the aggregated score, online scores 20 per cent. The redesigned procedure takes a 50/50 ratio as a benchmark.

[23] See District Antwerp, *Visienota Burgerbegroting—Evaluatie en bijsturing 2021*, <https://burgerbegroting.be/evaluatie-burgerbegroting>, 2021, pp. 1–4. This document seconds the strategy set out in the evaluation of Hofman et al.: 'We are not going to rewrite the Citizens' Budget. ... We follow the existing approach and improve it yearly.' See Hofman, J., H. Bastiaensen, and M. Nuytemans, *Evaluatierapport van de Burgerbegroting District Antwerpen*, Deventer, Rode Wouw, <https://burgerbegroting.be/evaluatie-burgerbegroting>, 2021, p. 17.

Figure 8.1   The hybrid process of the Citizens' Budget in District Antwerp (2022)[a]

[a] In this figure—as in Figure 7.2 on the Irish process earlier—crucial moments of deliberative reflection and plebiscitary voting are accentuated with light-grey and dark-grey respectively. Other than in the Irish process, with clearly demarcated deliberative (CA) and plebiscitary (referendum) stages, smaller-group deliberation and larger-group voting are combined in Step 1 as well as Step 3 of Antwerp's Citizens' Budgetary process, which are therefore depicted in mixed shading. These steps are embedded in a wider process, in which representatives of District Antwerp also play their role, as indicated.

Box 8.1:   General objectives and core principles of Antwerp's Citizens' Budget

Antwerp's *Burgerbegroting* is inspired by a fairly stable set of general objectives and core principles. In 2013, prior to the start of the Citizens' Budget, the following general objectives were formulated:

- 'Residents develop mutual understanding, and learn that there are other points of view. Residents need to interact with each other for this. The process is important.
- The district distributes its resources in a participatory way.
- The district spends its resources as efficiently as possible, in a way that is most beneficial to citizens.
- We create support for the spending of resources, a district-wide prioritization of policy themes. The goal is consensus.
- Residents' satisfaction with participation is to increase.
- The neighbourhood committee and district administration learn.'

In the years after 2014, the core principles have been refined and reconfirmed as follows. They are the proclaimed backbone of Antwerp's *Burgerbegroting*. When evaluating and renovating the Citizens' Budget, they serve as points of reference in District Antwerp.

- 'The Citizens' Budget is a deliberative project. Central to it is that people meet, engage in dialogue, exchange ideas and opinions.
- The Citizens' Budget is decisive (not advisory): the power really lies with the citizens. What they decide is immediately clear and is also immediately communicated in a transparent manner.

- The Citizens' Budget intends to reach as many people as possible, across all divisions. The general approach is therefore as accessible as possible, and extra efforts are made to reach people who find it more difficult to find their way to us, by cooperating with associations and reaching out to the neighbourhoods.
- There are no barriers to participation: residents can participate in one step or all steps, both online and physically.
- Everyone can have a say in the whole of the Antwerp district.
- Residents can propose projects to be carried out themselves or to be realized by the district.'[a]

The stated principles and objectives thus have strongly deliberative, communitarian, and egalitarian overtones. Partly by design and partly by circumstance, as described, more plebiscitary, competitive, and individualistic ingredients have gradually been added to the institutional design of Antwerp's Citizens' Budget.

[a] Core principles and general objectives listed in: Hofman, J., H. Bastiaensen, and M. Nuytemans, Evaluatierapport van de Burgerbegroting District Antwerpen, Deventer, Rode Wouw, <https://burgerbegroting.be/evaluatie-burgerbegroting>, 2021, p. 2.

Step one is 'selecting themes and allocating budget'.[24] On a Sunday afternoon in the early spring of year one of each citizens' budgetary cycle, citizens of District Antwerp are invited to learn about the thirty themes on which the District already spends 90 per cent of its budget, and to decide about the remaining 10 per cent, roughly 1.4 million euro. Participating citizens divide this portion of the budget over five priority themes, which they choose from a list of thirty themes.[25] At the offline start of the event ('with cake!' as it is advertised), participants share within smaller groups what they consider important in the various theme areas and, after weighing them against each

[24] Before the relatively modest institutional reforms of 2022, these were two more separated steps in the procedure of Antwerp's *burgerbegroting*, which at the time consisted of five steps. For a description of the full process, as of Spring 2022, see District Antwerp, *Wat is de Burgerbegroting?*, <https://burgerbegroting.be/wat-is-de-burgerbegroting>, 2022.

[25] In earlier years, they selected 12 themes from a list of 68. See District Antwerp, *Burgerbegroting 2021*, <https://issuu.com/districtantwerpen1/docs/burgerbegroting_brochure_2021_online>, n.d. From 2022 onwards 5 themes from a list of 30. The 30 themes are explained at the offline event and include: better pavements, traffic calming measures, safe travelling to school, bicycle-friendly streets, residents with talent, local theme markets and festivals, neighbourhood concerts and festivals, more and better sports grounds, get your neighbourhood moving, incentives for physical activity in the public space, more attractive streets and squares, child-friendly streets and squares, accessible streets and squares, more trees, softening, neighbourhood-oriented climate and environment projects, garden areas and experimental green space, green in streets and squares, place to study, everybody belongs, connecting projects, sharing, giving and exchange ideas, better communication, more participation, strengthening of associations, support for volunteers and digital innovation. See District Antwerp, *30 thema's van de Burgerbegroting*, <https://burgerbegroting.be/30-thema-s>, 2022.

other, allocate points to the respective themes. The five themes that collect the highest number of points become the selected themes.[26] The next task is to allocate the available budget (1.4 million) across the themes.[27] Participants are grouped at tables of five citizens, who each have ten 'poker chips' (each worth 20,000 euro) to divide between themes. Participants need to seek some level of coordination because at least three others in the group should be willing to put money into the same theme, and each theme should be awarded at least 120,000 euro or more. The same procedure is followed in a number of neighbourhood meetings with special attention to groups that tend to be underrepresented at events, such as the 'kick-off' event (the elderly, the young, the less well-off).

All citizens of District Antwerp can also choose to participate online in this step, first selecting five themes and then allocating the available budget individually on their smartphones or other web-connected devices. All scores—collected offline and online—are aggregated to decide which portions of the available budget are allocated to the selected five themes. It is a matter of principle in Antwerp that the offline scores, assigned after some group deliberation, count more than the online scores, even though the exact aggregation formula has changed somewhat throughout the years. Before the coronavirus hit Antwerp's Citizens' Budget, and without a lot of experience with online participation in the Citizens' Budget, an 80/20 ratio was initially trialled; this was subsequently dropped as being too skewed against online participants. In 2020 and 2021 virtually all participation was online due to the corona crisis. The redesigned procedure for 2022 onwards aims at a 50/50 ratio (offline scores and online scores both determining half of the aggregated score), but in view of corona-related uncertainties, possible alternatives are being considered.[28]

Step two is 'submitting projects'. In relation to the chosen themes, individuals or groups can submit projects with (claimed) added value to the district and its inhabitants, to be implemented by District Antwerp or by the submitting individual or group. Projects need to be focused on District Antwerp, but submissions may in theory come from everywhere. The District offers help in the formulation of a clear proposal and budget statement, and screens

[26] The name of the game is 'Model 35', as this is the maximum number of points that can be awarded. See Hofman, J., H. Bastiaensen & M. Nuytemans, *Evaluatierapport van de Burgerbegroting District Antwerpen*, Deventer, Rode Wouw, <https://burgerbegroting.be/evaluatie-burgerbegroting>, 2021, p. 22.
[27] Before 2022, this was a separate step. As of 2022, the idea is to integrate selecting themes and allocating budget in a more integrative and deliberative way.
[28] For instance, if offline participation continues to be scant, giving this a 50 per cent weight seems overdone. An alternative (used at the 'kick-off' meeting of 27 March 2022) is to count each offline participant as two, and each online participant as one.

all submitted proposals in two stages. First, proposals are purged that reach beyond the functional scope of District Antwerp, or that relate to a 'negative list' containing foreign travel, commercial activities, fundraising, and the like. Secondly, the initiators of the remaining proposals are contacted by District professionals who may ask for additional information and who may suggest tweaks, technical specifications, or label changes. The written procedure underscores that this is done 'in dialogue' between submitters and professionals and 'based on the philosophy of the Citizens' Budget and experience with previous editions'.[29] The focus is not on elevating the rejection rate (the orientation of some academic journals), but on elevating rough ideas to the level of feasible propositions, with special attention to people who for whatever reason need more help than others in the process (for instance, Syrian newcomers or African mothers with plans for after-school remedial teaching).

Step three is 'choosing projects'. In September of year one of each citizens' budgetary cycle, all citizens can participate, online or offline, in selecting the projects that will be implemented in year two within the budget constraints of the year. Citizens contribute to the final selection in a number of ways. Primarily, at the *Burgerbegrotingsfestival*, the offline citizens' budget festival, citizens can discuss and choose projects in a series of selection rounds. Each round takes two hours and focuses on the projects submitted in two theme areas. This is to assure that all participants see at least one other theme in addition to the theme for which they have specifically come to the meeting. Participants in each selection round meet at tables of five citizens, who ultimately select five projects for each theme. Secondly, citizens can discuss and choose projects online in essentially the same way: groups of five citizens meet (now online) and ultimately select (also online) five projects per theme.[30] Thirdly, online participants can individually push forward their selected projects.[31] To mitigate the effect of voter mobilization campaigns for single projects, resulting in an 'online voting battle', the rule in Antwerp is that each individual online voter needs to select at least three projects—the compulsory-multiple vote as they call it in Antwerp.

It is a matter of principle in Antwerp that votes for projects acquired after group exchanges (both offline and online group exchanges) should have more

---

[29] District Antwerp, Stap 2: dien ideeën in, <https://burgerbegroting.be/ronde-3>, 2022.

[30] This option was developed in the corona-years; it may or may not survive the post-corona situation.

[31] A combination of online voting and offline voting is found in other cities experimenting with PB-ns, for instance in New York where there are pop-up voting booths in addition to online voting in its fourth phase of participatory budgeting. See Williams, D. and D. Waisanen, *Real Money, Real Power?: The Challenges with Participatory Budgeting in New York City*, Palgrave Macmillan, 2020, p. 35.

weighting than scores acquired from individual participants voting online without a group exchange. This is done by limiting the weight of the latter, who are usually more numerous than those engaging in a group exchange, again aiming at a 50/50 ratio.[32] Projects are then ranked according to their final score. From top-ranked to lowest-ranked, the projects' requested budgets are subtracted from the available budgets in all theme areas until the Citizens' Budget is depleted.[33] In the developing practice of the *Burgerbegroting*, it is not uncommon to see about 80–90 projects surviving the selection process—from a total number of submissions two to three times larger. Before the existence of Antwerp's citizens' budget, said projects would have been selected more traditionally, in an administrative process under political supervision. In comparison, the selection process in Antwerp's Citizens' Budget is significantly opened-up and democratized, with a considerable number of citizens contributing to the final selection of projects. At the same time, a professional working for the District's participation team is realistic when she remarks: 'if we have 10,000 citizens participating in this it is still a small portion of the total population'[34]—indeed: no more than 5 per cent.

Finally, step four is 'realization of favoured projects'. This always runs in year two of the citizens' budgetary cycle (when, parallel to this, year one of the next citizens' budgetary cycle starts up again). Projects can be implemented by the District of Antwerp, but project realization can also be taken up by the citizens or groups that submitted the projects.[35] Examples include organizing after-school activities, rainwater recuperation, neighbourhood cinema for all, a community launderette, a music festival or graffiti workshop (civil society implementation), planting trees, refurbishing public squares, bituminizing streets, constructing bicycle-storage facilities (District implementation). For its implementation, District Antwerp relies on its own staff and deconcentrated personnel of central divisions of the larger, amalgamated municipality of Antwerp.

---

[32] Even though the general principle is fixed, the exact aggregation is not set in stone, and may be tweaked e.g., when Covid-19-related uncertainties demand it. The procedure for 2022 onwards aims at a 50/50 ratio, which means that the score for each project is: 0.5 * all votes in favour acquired after group exchange plus 0.5 * all votes in favour without group exchange. However, at the initial meeting of 27 March 2022, the first large meeting after the lifting of Covid restrictions, a simpler rule was used: each deliberative choice counted double compared to each non-deliberative vote.

[33] It may happen in a particular theme area, that e.g. projects ranked first and second fit the budget, while a project ranked third or fourth is too large to fit in, and thus a project ranked lower—but with a more modest budget—is awarded the remaining budget space. In this way, the very popular and the somewhat less popular get both awarded.

[34] Interview with closely involved participation professional, 21 February 2022.

[35] In that case, the implementing group enters into a contract with the District, specifying milestones and disbursement periods, so that realization can be monitored.

Comparative merits of Antwerp's Participatory Budgeting-new style

In Chapter 7, I confronted the Irish case, a national-level hybrid, with the key values of democratic innovation distinguished in Chapter 6. I will do the same now for the Antwerp case, a local-level hybrid.

The heart of the matter—inclusiveness and appropriateness

Crucially important and closely related values in Antwerp's Citizens' Budget are inclusiveness—understood as broad and diverse participation—and appropriateness—understood as open and deliberative process design. Design thinking and available evaluative research on the *Burgerbegroting* in Antwerp is first and foremost focused on these values, habitually acknowledging the fact that, however much they are preferred as complementary values, there is also tension between them.

On the one hand, the Citizens' Budget is inspired by an open-door participatory policy, attempting to include as many participating citizens as possible, offline and online. While some would rather see a deliberative mini-public (of the type used in the Irish case) in place, politicians in Antwerp have repeatedly stressed that everyone who wants to participate should be allowed and helped to participate. Growing numbers of participants were desired and to some extent achieved, especially in the project-selection stage of the process, most prominently after digital voting for projects was facilitated. In 2020, a total of 6,638 citizens participated in online voting on submitted projects (step 4)—in absolute numbers not the typical mini-public, but in relative numbers also far from the maxi-public (4.1 per cent of the Antwerp citizenry to be precise).[36] To further elevate the numbers, Antwerp is looking at a number of Dutch towns that have been able to engage 10–25 per cent of their citizens, mostly online, via assertive policies of invitation and facilitation (a.o. personal invitation letters, unique personal codes for online voting, making participation easy and user-friendly).[37]

Those involved in design thinking and evaluation gladly report a relatively inclusive pattern of participation, with a remarkably even distribution over age groups (with e.g. the 10–19 age group participating no less than the 50–59 age group), with slightly more women participating than men

[36] Hofman, J., H. Bastiaensen, and M. Nuytemans, *Evaluatierapport van de Burgerbegroting District Antwerpen*, Deventer, Rode Wouw, <https://burgerbegroting.be/evaluatie-burgerbegroting>, 2021, p. 5.
[37] See Hofman, J., H. Bastiaensen, and M. Nuytemans, *Evaluatierapport van de Burgerbegroting District Antwerpen*, Deventer, Rode Wouw, <https://burgerbegroting.be/evaluatie-burgerbegroting>, 2021, p. 18.

(which is often the other way around in other democratic innovations). Of six involved postal areas, three are more involved in the voting stage; three others are not absent but are the cause of some concern, especially the area called 'Luchtbal'.[38] It seems, however, that the social-economic status (SES) of the involved neighbourhoods is less of a determining factor than the presence of organizations with mobilizing strength.[39]

The pattern of relatively diverse and broad participation may pertain to Antwerp's Citizens' Budget as a whole, but not to all specific steps in the process. Early steps in the process, selecting themes and allocating the available budget, have shown dwindling interest, related to '(the perception of) limited impact of the choices made here, as well as the demanding attention span of the full process'.[40] This led to some interventions—already discussed—that should make participation in these steps more attractive and meaningful. In 2019, pre-interventions, a relatively small group of 134 participants deliberated about themes and 258 about general budgetary divisions.[41]

In Antwerp's design thinking about the Citizens' Budget, an appropriate process is first and foremost a reflectively open and deliberative process. Compared to other cities that have also made the step to large-scale digital voting within Participatory Budgeting, Antwerp distinguishes itself by the intention to give, and continue to give, deliberative process at least as much weight as plebiscitary voting. Satisfaction with the quality of deliberating was rather high among participants who looked back at the process in 2019.[42] Participation professionals guiding the process, on the other hand, are not always satisfied with the actual group deliberation at the roundtables,

---

[38] See Graph 5.7 in the Appendix of Hofman, J., H. Bastiaensen, and M. Nuytemans, *Evalutierapport van de Burgerbegroting District Antwerpen*, Deventer, Rode Wouw, <https://burgerbegroting.be/evaluatie-burgerbegroting>, 2021, p. 30.

[39] 'The fact that a neighbourhood like 2060, with many socially and economically weaker residents, does score well in the Citizens' Budget reinforces the idea that the presence of organisations is a more important factor than the profile of the residents.' See Hofman, J., H. Bastiaensen, and M. Nuytemans, *Evaluatierapport van de Burgerbegroting District Antwerpen*, Deventer, Rode Wouw, <https://burgerbegroting.be/evaluatie-burgerbegroting>, 2021, p. 8.

[40] Hofman, J., H. Bastiaensen, and M. Nuytemans, *Evaluatierapport van de Burgerbegroting District Antwerpen*, Deventer, Rode Wouw, <https://burgerbegroting.be/evaluatie-burgerbegroting>, 2021, p. 7.

[41] See Graph 2.3 in the Appendix of Hofman, J., H. Bastiaensen, and M. Nuytemans, *Evalutierapport van de Burgerbegroting District Antwerpen*, Deventer, Rode Wouw, <https://burgerbegroting.be/evaluatie-burgerbegroting>, 2021, pp. 26–7.

[42] See Hofman, J., H. Bastiaensen, and M. Nuytemans, *Evaluatierapport van de Burgerbegroting District Antwerpen*, Deventer, Rode Wouw, <https://burgerbegroting.be/evaluatie-burgerbegroting>, 2021, p. 25, Table 3 (a survey of 375 participants in the 2019 *begrotingsfestival*, an event that concluded the process of theme, budget, and project selection). There was (strong) agreement with the statement I could voice my opinion (97.4 per cent), I was listened to (95.7 per cent), I had as much influence as anyone else (93 per cent), I could agree with the end result at my table 96 per cent). There was no (strong) support for reverse statements such as I felt that other participants had made deals about voting (23.7 per cent felt that way), I felt that large organizations had more influence than me (23.5 per cent felt that way).

particularly in the early stages of the process.[43] However, they realize (some more grudgingly than others) that maximizing the quality of the deliberative process is virtually impossible in a design that is fundamentally hybrid, with competitive and plebiscitary elements also featuring prominently in the mix.

It is part and parcel of the *Burgerbegroting*'s design that citizens also compete for project approval, and for tokens of support to get their favoured projects accepted and implemented. This gives colour and energy to the process, and Antwerp's strategy is to facilitate this as long as the 'battle' for votes and projects adheres to basic rules of appropriateness (unlike the pizza-delivery firm that offered one euro discount in return for voting registration numbers) and can still be combined with the desired level of group deliberation. New measures to keep competitive and plebiscitary dynamics in check express a refined sense of procedural justice and fairness, although as a flipside of this they run the risk of losing out in terms of clarity and traceability. For an average participant it is not easy to grasp how votes are exactly weighted and counted in Antwerp's Citizens' Budget (unlike the abortion referendum in Ireland: one man one vote, and the camp with the most votes wins). Nevertheless, the process has not been seriously called into question.[44]

Modest by design—efficaciousness

'Impact' is recognized as one of the benchmarks of Antwerp's Citizens' Budget, together with 'deliberation' and participatory 'reach'. It is presented as 'impact/say' (*impact/zeggenschap* in Dutch-Flemish), which implicates a focus on political impact—being able to determine political decisions on 10 per cent of the District's budget that is called the Citizens' Budget. Practically speaking, the political impact is real; decisions following the citizens' budgetary process are decisive in the sense that politicians have committed themselves to adopt them (in formal-legal terms politicians retain budgetary powers, but these are habitually bracketed in the context of the *Burgerbegroting*). This is more than politicians in some other contexts of Participatory Budgeting commit to. For instance, in most German cities with PB,

[43] The early stage of the process is when people are supposed to meet, in the broad sense of the word, listen to, and learn about the perspectives of fellow citizens (as a former project leader of the *burgerbegroting* explained, interview 10 March 2022). High expectations that are not easily met in a process of citizens' budgeting (nor necessarily shared by the actual participants, who were, overall, satisfied with the quality of the process, as indicated).
[44] This is also because those with questions about the exact aggregation procedure are given full insight into the underlying excel-sheets that are used.

it is common to stress the consultative nature of the process and the final decision-making role of politicians.

Political impact (on decisions) is one thing, social impact (on real-life circumstances) is another thing—generally more difficult to achieve. The (self-)evaluation studies of Antwerp's Citizens' Budget are less conclusive at this level of achievement. As indicated, the Citizens' Budget in Antwerp churns out yearly 80–90 projects, to be implemented the following year. These are relatively small-scale, short-cyclical projects in the areas of social work and spatial management. Large-scale, longer-term societal transformation of the type that the original Porto Alegre model boasted is neither designed into the Antwerp model nor delivered by it. The focus on efficiency and effectiveness that marks for instance the German interpretation of PB—aspiring to get better projects, more value for money—is also less pronounced in Antwerp.

One may wonder whether the 80–90 projects mentioned, the yearly outputs of the *Burgerbegroting*, are somehow more efficacious than those subsidized projects that flowed from the traditional, administrative process of selection prior to 2014—more creative, more fitting, less expensive, less intrusive? A former project leader of the Citizens' Budget calls this question hard to answer and even irrelevant.[45] She remarks that the quality of the process and the weight of citizens' input into this was always more important to Antwerp's Citizens' Budget than improved efficaciousness in measurable terms. This is not to say that the latter is non-existent. Absence of evidence is not necessarily evidence of absence. The former project leader and other observers of Antwerp's Citizens' Budget point to meaningful small-scale wins such as the granting of after-school support and of bicycle storage facilities—both against the grain of official policy at the time. They remark that citizens collaborating on some of the small-scale social work projects required less public resources than commissioned professionals, and that silos of the central administration worked better together on some of the spatial projects when the pressure of the Citizens' Budget was on.[46] They admit that a full-fledged cost–benefit analysis is missing, and also not sought, stressing that some wins are real even though they are immeasurable—the gratifying feeling of doing projects together with one's peers.[47] Small wins in objective terms can be big wins in subjective terms, they argue.

---

[45] Interview with former project leader, 10 March 2022.
[46] See also Wolf, E., S. Rys, and W. van Dooren, *Naar een Vlaamse Burgerbegroting? Lessen uit de binnenlandse en buitenlandse praktijk*, Universiteit Antwerpen, 2018, p. 25.
[47] The example is mentioned of youngsters jumping up and down, high-fiving each other at the final event, when their project turns out to be successful.

Obviously, efficaciousness is a relative concept. Compared to erstwhile PB in Porto Alegre, citizens' budgeting in Antwerp reaped comparatively modest social impact (as almost any other city engaging in PA, old or new style). However, compared to some other talk-oriented democratic innovations results of the *Burgerbegroting* in Antwerp are emphatically tangible and concrete in real-life terms. There is a substantial, middle-range, budget that directly feeds into real-life action. Rainwater recuperation facilities are actually installed and public squares are visibly redecorated following Citizens' Budget decisions, to mention just a few examples. Decision-making and real-life actions are part and parcel of the same process. Some talk-oriented democratic innovations—not all, but quite some—result in recommendations and statements that never see the light of day.

Investing in robust citizenship—resilience before counterbalance

Champions of Antwerp's *Burgerbegroting* like to see it as a systematized, deep investment in local democratic citizenship; a democratic innovation that has survived two reversals of executive political leadership, and that is widely accepted and appreciated. In its first nine years of existence, the Citizens' Budget seems to have become an entrenched part of District Antwerp's governance system. As indicated previously (Chapter 7), system-level benefits are potentially observable in terms of institutionalized resilience (the systemic expression of collective self-rule) and counterbalance (the systematic expression of countervailing power), and relatedly in terms of institutionalized provisions (opportunities, rights) and perceptions (generalized trust, political efficacy).

While forging institutional counterweight to potentially corrupt politicians was an important part of the original model of Participatory Budgeting, Porto Alegre style, this element is far less emphasized, hardly ever mentioned, in Antwerp's model of Participatory Budgeting-new style. Here, systemic benefits are sought more strongly in terms of developing a robust civic culture, with citizens and civic groups willing and able to learn and work together on projects for the common good on a recurring basis. As described, various provisions are in place to support active citizenship systematically. Yearly, there is a substantial, middle-range, Citizens' Budget available; rights and possibilities to share in this budget and in bottom-up decision-making about it are clearly demarcated, and habitually activated. The systemic scope of the instrument is clear and simple: the Citizens' Budget facilitates concrete action in the social and the spatial life world; more abstract legislation and regulation is not its remit.

On institutionalized perceptions, available data are scarce. Evaluations commissioned by District Antwerp suggest that the Citizens' Budget is largely appreciated: 'A neighbourhood survey in 2019 showed that the Citizens' Budget was positively received in all neighbourhoods; 81 per cent of surveyed residents in the 2021 online evaluation are rather or completely positive about the Citizens' Budget in general.'[48] There seems to be good brand recognition, as it is called in one piece of research, among majorities in all age groups; groups under 50 display above 70 per cent recognition of the *Burgerbegroting* as a public label or 'brand'; however, there seems to also be a fair deal of indifference among those: 70 per cent of citizens who claim to know the Citizens' Budget are neither satisfied nor dissatisfied with it; 21 per cent are (very) satisfied versus 9.5 per cent (very) dissatisfied.[49]

The wish to institutionalize a learning place for democratic citizenship has accompanied Antwerp's Citizens' Budget since its inception. Willem-Frederik Schiltz, the district alderman who initiated the *Burgerbegroting*, spoke of it as 'civic education-light'—'learning from each other's perspective, each other's environment, the development of mutual understanding. That is also what we are trying to achieve through the Citizens' Budget.'[50] Does the Citizens' Budget of Antwerp indeed turn out more civically-oriented, 'better citizens'? Tibaut Renson, a Flemish researcher, posed this question and gave a largely affirmative answer. Comparing arguments before and after deliberation, Renson concluded that after 1.5 hours of effective deliberation in the early stages of the process, participants were able to present their argumentats in less individualistic and more public terms and to better appreciate the argumentats of others. Male and more highly educated participants were on average more adept in this type of social learning. Participants were not followed long enough to know whether this social learning continued in the long term, and thus amounted to deep learning of civic skills, or whether this reflected a temporal effect on socially desirable speech.

In conclusion: Hybrid design serving different publics

The Citizens' Budget as developed in District Antwerp is not a perfect instrument. This is not the reason for presenting this case here, nor can it be. As earlier explained in Chapter 6 and illustrated in Chapter 7, perfect

[48] Hofman, J., H. Bastiaensen, and M. Nuytemans, *Evaluatierapport van de Burgerbegroting District Antwerpen*, Deventer, Rode Wouw, <https://burgerbegroting.be/evaluatie-burgerbegroting>, 2021, p. 3.

[49] Hofman, J., H. Bastiaensen, and M. Nuytemans, *Evaluatierapport van de Burgerbegroting District Antwerpen*, Deventer, Rode Wouw, <https://burgerbegroting.be/evaluatie-burgerbegroting>, 2021, pp. 31–2.

[50] Quote taken and translated from Renson, T., Baart Antwerpse Burgerbegroting betere burgers?, *Sampol*, 2018, 2, p. 58.

instruments with maximum scores on all relevant values, do not exist in the real world of democratic innovation. There are always trade-offs between values, which need to be weighed in situated conversation about the design and possible redesign of the instrument.

Based on the previous assessment, however, we can say that Antwerp's *Burgerbegroting* is a relatively multifunctional instrument that largely— although not perfectly—does what it is expected to do. At the level of system values, institutionalized counter-corruption was never defined as a priority in the social and political context of Antwerp's *Burgerbegroting*, while investing in recurring active citizenship was. The general picture is moderately positive in this respect. Long-term societal transformation of the type that the original Porto Alegre model boasted was neither designed into Antwerp's Citizens' Budget nor achieved by it; nevertheless, its *Burgerbegroting* exhibits a steady stream of projects that are actualized in real-life, locally visible, and appreciated.[51] Inclusive input and deliberative process are clearly prioritized in Antwerp's design thinking, and largely achieved in the practice of the Citizens' Budget. Attention to small-scale deliberation is combined with the facilitation of relatively large-scale participation, mainly through digital voting. In this way, the Citizens' Budget caters to different publics that exhibit different ways of engaging in the public realm.

Antwerp's *Burgerbegroting* can distinguish itself as a relatively multifunctional instrument, satisfying different publics and values, because of its mixed and balanced design. The persistent effort to mix and balance different design principles is what makes Antwerp's Citizens' Budget exemplary; not so much the total number of participants, the size of the available budget, or the effect size of one particular variable. PB-processes in cities such as Paris, Madrid, and Reykjavik reach larger numbers of participants and reserve more budget per capita.[52] To some extent, these cities also present examples of PB-ns, with plebiscitary elements markedly added to deliberative foundations. Antwerp's version of it, however, is more illuminating when it comes to mixing and balancing competing design principles and dealing with the tensions that inevitably come with this.

If one aspires to facilitate small-scale deliberation as well as large-scale voting, one needs to bring together different, to some extent opposing styles of thought and action. The distinction between thinking slow, reflectively, and

---

[51] And behind the projects sometimes new associations develop, which later receive more structural funding elsewhere (such as a community centre, an association of Syrian newcomers or a climate platform).

[52] Wolf, E., S. Rys, and W. van Dooren, *Naar een Vlaamse Burgerbegroting? Lessen uit de binnenlandse en buitenlandse praktijk*, Universiteit Antwerpen, 2018, p. 24.

thinking fast, reflexively, model 1 and model 2 in terms of Kahneman, is only one aspect of the opposition.[53] Referring to the Douglasian cultural biases introduced in Chapter 2, the plebiscitary element of Antwerp's *Burgerbegroting* fosters a culture of competition and individualism, while the deliberative element resonates with a culture of egalitarianism and communitarianism. Most citizens participating in the Citizens' Budget appear to be attracted to the plebiscitary element, and to the competition and individualism that it fosters. Competition for votes and resources between initiators of projects, with some winning and others losing, is largely accepted and widely recognized as 'part of the game'. Steps two and three of the Citizens' Budgetary process, in which applications become concrete and people seek support and votes for their favourite projects, are evidently more popular than step one of the process in which people are expected to deliberate about general priorities and budget allocations (previously two separate steps). Institutional guardians of the Citizens' Budget tend to accept this as a fact of modern life, in addition to being a practical way of getting the desired growth in numbers of participants, as long as the 'voting battle' can be checked and balanced by various measures.

Measures taken are basically counter-majoritarian and egalitarian in nature. In step one and step three of the process, budgetary choices made after group deliberation are given more weight to balance the higher number of individual and digital votes cast. Disadvantaged and less-connected groups who might stay away from deliberative meetings like the central 'kick-off' meeting or budget festival are visited by participation professionals in neighbourhood venues; their deliberative choices also get a higher weight. In the intermediate step two, submitting projects, participation professionals of District Antwerp are available for special help and remedial teaching in developing project statements and budgets. The idea is that not only large voluntary associations should be able to submit projects, but that individual citizens also get a fighting chance to pitch their projects. The market logic, with suppliers of projects competing for votes and resources, is not taken out of Antwerp's *Burgerbegroting* but rather kept in check. The normative base for doing this is remarkably stable.[54]

The practice of mixing and balancing large-scale voting with small-scale deliberation—adding plebiscitary elements to a deliberative core—extends two other dualities that characterize PB in the urban realm, particularly in Antwerp. First, citizen participation is not merely geared at reaching a public

---

[53] Kahneman, D., *Thinking Fast, Thinking Slow*, New York, Farrar, Straus & Giroux, 2011.
[54] See Box 8.1. Also: District Antwerp, *Visienota Burgerbegroting—Evaluatie en bijsturing 2021*, <https://burgerbegroting.be/evaluatie-burgerbegroting>, 2021, p. 2.

verdict or general policy statement; it is directly linked to visible, practical action. The focus of attention is first and foremost on real-life interventions in the local public domain. The municipality may implement these interventions, but Antwerp's *Burgerbegroting* is also, and emphatically, designed to assist societal organization and hitherto unorganized citizens in self-implementing projects. In this way, an element of do-it-ourselves democracy or do-ocracy is added to the mix.

Second, Antwerp's model of citizens' budgeting (like almost all Participatory Budgeting in cities around the world) is closely connected to the established system of representative democracy and its administrative apparatus. It is not an institution that dissociates itself from the established system, in the way the Icelandic Constitutional Council, for instance, distanced itself (see Chapter 7). It mobilizes bottom-up initiative and decision-making by citizens, supported and facilitated by participation professionals in close proximity, commissioned and authorized by local politicians at arm's length. Some may call it 'a celebration of direct democracy', but it is clearly taking place under the wings of representative democracy.[55] As said, this particular element is not new to PB; it was already a distinctive characteristic of the original Porto Alegre version.

Not characteristic of the original model, and propelled by changes in the techno-cultural environment of the 2010s, is the addition of large-scale plebiscitary voting beyond the realm of citizens participating in deliberative forums and councils. This addition, foregrounded in this chapter on PB-ns, is in a way—albeit in a different way, and at a different level—akin to the addition of a referendum vote to a deliberative assembly as we saw in Chapter 7 on the 'deliberative referendum' and variations thereof (see Box 8.2 for variations on the theme of 'PB-new style' that are also connecting plebiscitary, mostly digital voting to deliberative, mostly open-invitation platforms).

Box 8.2: *Participatory Budgeting-new style and variations on a theme*

In this chapter, I looked at the addition of large-scale popular voting (not through referendum voting as in Chapter 7 but through digital voting) to already developed practices of small-scale group deliberation (not through randomized CAs as in Chapter 7 but through largely open, round-table platforms as developed in the

---

[55] At the initiating meeting on 27 March 2022 one of the civil servants who organize the Citizens' Budget for District Antwerp welcomed all participants to this 'celebration of direct democracy' ('feest van directe democratie').

context of PB). The Citizens' Budget as developed with and within the District of Antwerp was presented as a case in point. But there is plenty of variation on the same theme to be acknowledged even though it cannot be presented in as much detail as the Antwerp case.

As indicated, the integration of voting among the wider involved citizenry into contemporary models of PB is also evident in places such as Paris, Madrid, Berlin, Chicago, New York, Reykjavik, Amsterdam, and many more cities around the world. The arrangement and balance of popular voting versus group deliberation vary in such models, as does the relation between (bottom-up) public involvement versus (top-down) political decision-making. Antwerp's design thinking is special because of its inherent effort to straddle such oppositions. Other places stand out with other elements. German cities, for instance, are commonly reluctant to develop PB (new-style no different than old-style) into a decisive instrument (neither *de jure* nor *de facto*). At the same time, various German towns have added a citizens' jury to the proceedings (often, though not always a randomized jury). For instance, the district of Berlin-Lichtenberg combines active discussion forums with quarterly votes on proposals in PB, as well as a citizens' jury active in the screening of proposals for the district.[a]

Some cities have designed digital platforms for deliberation and for voting on proposals, partly coupled to and partly uncoupled from PB-ns. As a frontrunner in this field, the city of Barcelona has developed an integrated digital platform called *Decidim*, which is used to support PB-ns in the various districts of Barcelona, but is also used as a platform for monitoring public policy, initiation, deliberation, and voting on proposals outside of PB, for instance on the city-wide urban plan. The general motto in Catalan is '*seguin, proposing i decideixin*' (monitoring, proposing, and deciding). *Decidim* is designed to do this at different levels, from the smaller scale of neighbourhoods to the larger scale of the encompassing city, and in different ways, straddling notions of deliberative exchange and plebiscitary voting.[b]

Amsterdam exemplifies a city in which platforms for PB-ns and for more generic ideas competition operate side-by-side in its various districts. In Amsterdam-West, for instance, citizens can participate in a Neighborhood Budget that resembles the Citizens' Budget of District Antwerp, but also in an annex called *De Stem van West* (The Voice of West) that allows (groups) of citizens to promote and defend proposals, and to collect the declarations of support needed for implementation.[c] The annex is more reminiscent of the platform *Frankfurt Fragt Mich* (FFM) introduced in Chapter 4 when discussing new plebiscitary practices. FFM is entirely disconnected from PB (which was in fact discontinued in Frankfurt altogether), and on the whole more plebiscitary in its operation than the combined plebiscitary-deliberative models that were developed in Amsterdam, Barcelona, and certainly Antwerp. Nevertheless, the potential for dialogue and reflection is not entirely missing and might in time even grow; an in-depth analysis of the longest string of comments on a proposal in FFM indicated that the deliberative quality was surprisingly high.[d]

Hybridization of digital voting and group deliberation of the sort discussed here takes root more often at the local level—particularly the digitized urban arena—as compared to the national level. A notable exception is the hybrid model of vTaiwan discussed in Chapter 5. As specified there, civic hackers engaged by Taiwan's national government developed vTaiwan as a platform for advanced public polling—using the digital technology of *Pol.is* that is also used by cities such as Madrid to sound out the citizenry—in addition to collaborative governance formats such as hackatons and round-tables with cognitively diverse participation. In vTaiwan, the counters' perspective and the talkers' perspective on pooled democracy, the plebiscitary and the deliberative, have been brought together in a notable way.[e]

[a] Bürgerhaushalt Lichtenberg, Startseite, <https://www.buergerhaushalt-lichtenberg.de>, n.d.; Sintomer, Y., C. Herzberg, and A. Röcke, Participatory Budgeting in Europe: Potentials and Challenges, *International Journal of Urban and Regional Research*, 2008, 32, 1, p. 172; Wolf, E., S. Rys, and W. van Dooren, *Naar een Vlaamse Burgerbegroting? Lessen uit de binnenlandse en buitenlandse praktijk*, Universiteit Antwerpen, 2018, p. 35.

[b] Francesca Bria, Barcelona's Chief Technology and Digital Innovation Office, calls it 'a hybrid of online and offline participatory democracy'. See Graham, T., Barcelona is leading the fightback against small city surveillance, Wired, <https://www.wired.co.uk/article/barcelona-decidim-ada-colau-francesca-bria-decode>, 18 May 2018. On Decidim, see also Decidim, Features, <https://decidim.org/features>, n.d.; Decidim, Pressupostos participatius de Barcelona, <https://www.decidim.barcelona/processes/PressupostosParticipatius>, n.d.; Ajuntament de Barcelona, Citizens to decide how to improve neighbourhoods with the first participatory budget, <https://ajuntament.barcelona.cat/bombers/en/noticia/citizens-to-decide-how-to-improve-neighbourhoods-with-the-first-participatory-budget_911307>, 2020. On the Barcelona case, see also: Blanco, I., Y. Salazar, and I. Bianchi, Urban governance and political change under a radical left government: The case of Barcelona, *Journal of Urban Affairs*, 2020, 42, 1, pp. 18–38; Calzada, I., (Smart) Citizens from Data Providers to Decision-Makers? The Case Study of Barcelona, *Sustainability*, 2018, 10, 3252.

[c] Gemeente Amsterdam, West Begroot, <https://www.amsterdam.nl/stadsdelen/west/westbegroot/>, n.d.; Gemeente Amsterdam, Buurtbudget, <https://buurtbudget.amsterdam.nl/>, n.d.; Gemeente Amsterdam, West Begroot 2023, <https://westbegroot.amsterdam.nl/toetsingscriteria>, n.d.; Gemeente Amsterdam, Meedenken, meepraten en meedoen, <https://www.amsterdam.nl/bestuur-organisatie/invloed/?utm_source=amsterdam.nl&utm_medium=internet&utm_campaign=bestuur-en-organisatie/meedenken-meepraten-en-meedoen&utm_content=redirect#h16eb617a-ce7d-402f-b075-d4393c7be240>, n.d. For facts and figures about Neighborhood Budgeting in another neighborhood of Amsterdam (East) see Radboud University/KU Leuven, Burgerbegroting Amsterdam OOD-Oost [Infographic], <https://soc.kuleuven.be/centre-for-political-research/demoinno/files/infographic-adam-oud-oost.pdf>, December 2020.

[d] Pieper, A.K. and M. Pieper, Political participation via social media: a case study of deliberative quality in the public online budgeting process of Frankfurt/Main, Germany 2013, Universal Access in the Information Society, 2015, 14, pp. 487–503. For more on FFM, see Chapters 4–5.

[e] For more on V-Taiwan, see Chapter 5.

9

Conclusion

On the hybrid-innovations hypothesis

The chapters of this book have essentially dealt with two issues: first, how to understand the struggle between different ideas of democratic innovation and, relatedly, democratic reform (Part I); secondly, it has explored ways to use the struggle between competing ideas that are value-rich, creative, as well as realistic (Part II). One overarching conclusion of the book is that a perfect democratic design that will end all polishing of democratic governance cannot exist. Ever-changing circumstances, fundamental value diversity, and perpetual cultural dynamics will prevent this from becoming a reality. Returning to the metaphor used as a preliminary step to understanding the dynamics of democratic innovation, we might say that the democratic reform cake (Chapter 1) is based on self-raising flour. Ideas of democratic betterment are bound to respond to each other, which will keep the debate going, both in theory and practice (Chapters 2–5). Another overarching conclusion is that the recurring feedback—both positive and negative—is not necessarily wasteful ('here we go again'), but potentially fertile depending on the way in which democratic revitalization is being pursued. Some ways are more fertile than others, and with good sense we may be able to see and make the difference (Chapters 6–9). In the course of this book, I explored the idea and practice of hybrid innovation, which capitalizes on the tensions between opposites in potentially beneficial ways. In this chapter, I will formulate some final reflections on such hybrid democratic innovations, which feed into the hybrid-innovations hypothesis that closes off this book—although not the debate.

Hybrid democratic innovations

The previous chapters describe an important development in the realm of democratic innovations—a development toward hybrid innovations in which competing opposites are combined without erasing their distinctiveness. The advanced form of hybridization that I found in the

Rethinking Democratic Innovation. Frank Hendriks, Oxford University Press. © Frank Hendriks (2023).
DOI: 10.1093/oso/9780192848291.003.0009

national-level case of Ireland (Chapter 7) and the local-level case of Antwerp (Chapter 8) takes a significant step beyond simpler forms of hybridization found elsewhere, such as microscopic deliberation followed by a vote within the same deliberative mini-public, or a binary referendum vote surrounded by spontaneous, non-incentivized deliberation. In the Irish case, the Citizens' Assembly and the referendum were equivalent, separately activated yet complementary, parts of a broader democratic process. In Antwerp's Citizens' Budget, deliberation on the smaller scale was paired and balanced with voting on the larger scale. In both cases, direct voting on the matters at hand was not confined to a vote among the deliberating mini-publics, but was extended with voting at the level of the involved maxi-public (respectively the Irish citizenry and the citizenry of District Antwerp). By matching the 'square peg of direct democracy' to the 'round hole of deliberative democracy', to paraphrase LeDuc,[1] and by embedding this in representative democracy, the analysed Irish and Antwerp cases push back the frontier of democratic innovation; in Box 7.2 and Box 8.2 variations on the same themes have been explored (Chapters 7 and 8).

Hybrid democratic innovation is presented here as a form of innovation geared to the tying together of competing opposites, with the plebiscitary versus deliberative contrast in the foreground; and the citizens-oriented versus representatives-oriented dichotomy intertwined with this in the background—much as we saw in the Ireland and Antwerp case studies. In the Irish case, the combined mini- and maxi-publics that deliberated and voted on abortion exerted combined bottom-up pressure for change on representative politics, which remained involved in the process at strategic moments. Without strong and aligned social pressure from below, real change would have been unlikely and, without political action on the other side, it would have been impossible to carry real change through. In the Antwerp case, the combined mini- and maxi-publics delivered concrete plans for changes in the spatial and social fabric of the District through connected deliberative and plebiscitary instruments, in a democratic process in which local government was closely involved from front to back. Interestingly, in the Antwerp case, public participation was not merely talk- and text-based, but even more so oriented on concrete action, part of it based on self-implementation.[2]

Advanced hybrid innovations combine diverging forms of bottom-up democratic pressure, and keep representative democracy connected and on its toes. Coupling antipodes in this manner is no sine cure. Effort and creativity are required to overcome cultural blocks against the mixing and

---

[1] Leduc, L., Referendums and Deliberative Democracy, *Electoral Studies*, 2015, 38, p. 147.
[2] In this way, an element of do-it-ourselves democracy or do-ocracy was added to the mix of citizen-oriented, and government-supplementing democracy, see Chapter 8.

mingling of democratic formats as described and explained in the first part of this book (Chapters 1–5), institutionalizing the productive tensions as explored and ultimately advanced in the second part of the book (Chapters 6–9). For the purpose of this volume, I looked principally at the generation of bottom-up democratic pressure on behalf of the *demos*, the grassroots of civil society. In this arena, expectations often run high of a single deliberative or plebiscitary instrument, and the urge to combine instruments is not always at the forefront of people's minds. In fact, adherents of plebiscitary and deliberative instruments tend to be suspicious or uncaring of the other side of the spectrum. Ways of approaching the field of democracy and styles of playing the democratic game are profoundly different, the more so at both ends of the spectrum. Yet, there is also great potential in bringing diverging approaches and playing styles together, overcoming subcutaneous allergies.

This book is about the field of democracy, but in other fields similar arguments have been made. A personal favourite, stemming from the world of sports, is the Dutch national football team that at the World Cup of 1974 astonished the world with innovative 'total football'. The two most successful Dutch football clubs at the time—Feyenoord-Rotterdam and Ajax-Amsterdam—combined forces in this team, despite the great animosity between the two clubs and cities. Many of their fans would not have voluntarily chosen to get together, but the players assembled showed how innovative the combination was.[3] The analogy obviously has its limitations (like all analogies: behind some telling similarities field-specific idiosyncrasies loom large), but an additional likeness here is that for a good match of football there is a counterpart required that also needs to keep its game up to par.[4]

The counterpart in the field of democracy—viewed from the perspective of the *demos* and its varied set of bottom-up instruments—is the established system of representative democracy. In recent democratic-innovations research,

---

[3] For other examples beyond the world of democracy one could think of various bands in pop music (The Beatles, The Stones, The Smiths) that brought together very different, yet complementary characters and musical skills. Or, in the world of technology, the iPad and tablet that combined and synergized the strengths of the mobile telephone with those of the personal computer (previously disconnected tools). Obviously, such analogies have limitations, operating in very different fields as they do.

[4] In the example mentioned, the other team that had to keep up with the Dutch was the German national team, which in the end even won the 1974 World Cup against the expectations of most pundits at the time, in turn creating an everlasting motivation in Dutch football to do better next time. What works well in this analogy is the idea of keeping the other side on its toes by working hard and trying to be as innovative as possible (an idea also central to the Red Queen-effect, which is discussed later in this Chapter, referring to Acemoglu, D. and J.A. Robinson, *The Narrow Corridor: States, Societies, and the Fate of Liberty*, Penguin Press, 2019). What does not work so well—all analogies are flawed—is the idea of a competitive match that can be won by one side and lost by the other. The hybrid-innovations hypothesis developed here assumes (as the more general Red Queen-effect underscored by Acemoglu and Robinson) that both sides can win, and improve their game (even when it happens that temporarily one side scores more points against the other).

focused as it is on instruments of citizen participation, less attention has been paid to this side of the democratic field than in earlier democratic-reform studies (see Chapter 1). Yet, this side also needs due attention. Participatory Budgeting-new style in Antwerp functions relatively well not only because of the delicate balance between deliberation and voting in the bottom-up process of social involvement, but certainly also because of the continuous, active, learning involvement of local government and politics. One of the explanations for why the combination of the Citizens' Assembly and the follow-up referendum was more successful in Ireland than in Iceland lies in the connection (Ireland) versus the disconnection (Iceland) of the established system of representative democracy. In Iceland, politicians were in many ways divorced from the process, which led to the constitutional reform Bill (developed in a bottom-up process that in and of itself contained some innovative elements) being stalled in Parliament. Icelandic Parliamentarians were provided with the motive, the opportunity, and the means to put the brakes on it. In the Irish process, conversely, politicians found out that there were good reasons, openings, and instruments to engage with the bottom-up process, and to make it work (Chapter 7).

Earlier democratic-reform research has shown that the institutions of representative democracy are open and amenable to changes only up to a certain—limited—point (Chapter 1). Against this background, it is not incomprehensible that subsequent democratic-innovations research has focused on the bottom-up processes that can be changed and influenced to a larger extent. Yet, working only bottom-up in rethinking democratic innovations, would be a mistake—particularly if more than symbolic or paper results are sought.[5]

That it is crucial to mobilize and connect forces bottom-up, in civil society, without looking away from the realities and capacities of government and politics, is a message that runs through recent work by the

---

[5] Some researchers focusing on bottom-up democratic innovations have kept a keen eye on the representative system. Examples include Hendriks, C.M., Coupling Citizens and Elites in Deliberative Systems, *European Journal of Political Research*, 2016, 55, pp. 43–60; Hendriks, C.M. and A. Kay, From 'Opening Up' to Democratic Renewal: Deepening Public Engagement in Legislative Committees, *Government and Opposition*, 2019, 54, 1, pp. 25–51; Setälä, M., Connecting Deliberative Mini-Publics to Representative Decision Making, *European Journal of Political Research*, 2017, 56, 4, pp. 846–63; Neblo, M., K. Esterling, and D. Lazer, *Politics with the People: Building a Directly Representative Democracy*, Cambridge, Cambridge University Press, 2018. More often, however, the representative system is something of an afterthought in developing and advancing bottom-up democratic innovations—a ceiling to screw the plug in when the deliberative or participatory light needs to be hung somewhere, without too much care for the neighbours on the other side of the ceiling. In the governance-innovations literature, the anchorage of governance networks in representative systems has received more systematic attention. See Sørensen, E. and Torfing, J., The Democratic Anchorage of Governance Networks. *Scandinavian Political Studies*, 2005, 28, 3, pp. 195–218.

political-economists Acemoglu and Robinson in a more generic sense.[6] In *The Narrow Corridor* they stress that all states, including states listed as representative democracies, have a Janus-face, with a dangerous side that should be checked at all times, and a more benevolent side that could be of use to all when pushed and pulled by a strong society in the right way. What is needed is a shackled, yet capable state, on the one hand, and, on the other hand, a plural, well-equipped society that maintains both the shackles and capabilities of the state. If this works well we get what Acemoglu and Robinson call the 'Red Queen effect', loosely based on Lewis Carroll's book *Through the Looking-Glass, and What Alice Found There*, in which two characters, Alice and the Red Queen, run a race against each other, both trying their hardest to top the other, but continuously remaining at the same height. While running hard they keep each other in balance. In Carroll's book, Alice and the Red Queen do not get ahead either, but this is not how Acemoglu and Robinson would have it for a strong society and a capable state running together. This would keep each of them sharp and focused and it would make both perform better together.

Acemoglu and Robinson do not deal specifically with democratic innovations—they focus more generally on developing and maintaining free societies with capable states—but their thesis nonetheless resonates clearly with the argument developed here. The Red Queen effect hinges on a pluralistic civil society, which can express itself in a variety of ways and can thus put effective pressure on the inevitable state. I have examined democratic innovations that may contribute to this, and my argument is that they work better as a mixed bag from which fitting combinations are developed as and when required, rather than as a single keg from which variants of the same theme are drawn time and again. The *demos* must be enabled to exert pressure on public decision-making in both deliberative and plebiscitary ways, microscopic as well as macroscopic, engaging different publics with different backgrounds, perspectives, and preferences for participation. Developing democratic innovations in this fashion is bound to be more forceful and authoritative in the eyes of both citizens and policymakers.

This calls for intelligent democratic design, sensitive to the relationship between different instruments that help the demos to exert pressure, but also to the relationship with the system on which the pressure is exerted. Democratic innovations that are internally well-ordered but externally not well-connected often end up disappointing on important points, especially

---

[6] Acemoglu, D. and J.A. Robinson, *The Narrow Corridor: States, Societies, and the Fate of Liberty*, Penguin Press, 2019, p. 41.

in terms of getting things changed on the ground. In addition to the already mentioned failure of the Icelandic case versus the success of the Irish case (a CA-plus-referendum comparatively well-embedded in the Irish case, and not so well-embedded in the Icelandic case), I can contrast Antwerp's Citizens' Budget (balanced in mixing deliberative reflection and plebiscitary voting, anchored in the established system of District Antwerp), to some Dutch cities that copied the democratic toolbox from Antwerp but failed to plug it into the power socket with the same level of success and consequentiality.[7]

In other words, for advanced hybrid innovations, the system of representative democracy, politics and leadership still matters.[8] As said, however, the necessary maintenance and possible reform of representative democracy are currently not central to democratic-innovations discourse. It has become the bottom layer of the reform cake (Chapter 1), which is considerably less in view than the top layer of innovations aimed at encouraging citizen participation. Curiously, reforms geared at rearranging or reorienting democratic politics and leadership in the representative system fall outside influential definitions and conceptualizations of what is democratically innovative; such reforms are being studied, but mostly in separate fields that are not sufficiently connected to the democratic-innovations debate (Chapters 1, 5). For this debate, bringing representative democracy, politics, and leadership back in, and working on its connection to bottom-up innovations in democracy, remains an important challenge.

This does not mean that a preoccupation with citizen-oriented democratic innovations should be exchanged for a fixation on reforms of political leadership and electoral systems. At the very least it should mean, however, sharper attention to factors and actors in representative democracy that appear to be important for the success of democratic innovations. Bottom-up innovations need to be developed with a realistic eye to the systemic context in which they have to work, including the feedback mechanisms—institutionalized sympathies and antipathies—to be expected there. Structural reform of representative institutions is not always necessary for achieving better interactions between civil society and the political system. In some places, however, structural reform is badly needed, even though it is often hard to actually accomplish, and likely to raise all kinds of frustrations.

---

[7] The biggest contrast is with the city of Breda, which attempted to copy-and-paste PB from Antwerp but failed to integrate it into the established system of representative democracy. See Hendriks, F., Leidende principes voor bestuurlijke innovatie: naar een robuust referentiekader, *Bestuurswetenschappen*, 2018, 72, 1, pp. 46–63.

[8] Ruscio, K.P., *The Leadership Dilemma in Modern Democracy*, Edward Elgar, 2008; Kane, J., H. Patapan, and P. 't Hart (eds), *Dispersed Democratic Leadership: Origins, Dynamics, and Implications*, Oxford University Press, 2009; Rhodes, R.A.W. and P. 't Hart (eds), *Oxford Handbook of Political Leadership*, Oxford University Press, 2014.

However understandable the tendency may be, those dedicated to democratic innovations cannot then look away and be satisfied with the study of microscopic or isolated innovations only.

The systemic turn in the study of deliberative democracy was an important step in the right direction, although it is still a limited step.[9] With the focus shifting to encompassing 'deliberative systems'—as opposed to isolated deliberative instruments such as mini-publics—the bigger picture of democratic governance comes into better view. The adjective—'deliberative'—underscores that more deliberative quality is still the central objective here, albeit now at the overall system level. It is an important insight that promoting deliberation at the system level does not necessarily require that all institutions within the system are deliberative. Deliberative-systems thinkers accept that there might be a place for plebiscitary institutions in deliberative systems, as long as they do not become too prominent and in the final analysis contribute to the deliberative system. The question remains, however, why a 'deliberative' democratic system should be the ultimate goal. And why not, for instance, an 'efficacious' democratic system, for which there is at least as much to be said (Chapter 6)—unless one adheres to the strong claim, as yet unproven, that a deliberative system is automatically an efficacious system. In addition to maintaining high-quality deliberative reflection, a democratic system must also be judged on its ability to deliver efficacious action in a stable and reliable manner.[10] It is exactly on this point that non-democratic systems of the Chinese or the Singaporean variant challenge democratic systems, which cannot defend their case merely by brushing up on the deliberative qualities of the democratic system. Alternatively, I would propose a broader framing of the ambition as fittingly mixed systems resulting from and honed by hybrid innovations.

The hybrid-innovations hypothesis

Hybrid innovations can be understood as well as advanced in connection to the general typology of democratic reform (outlined in Chapter 2; further specified in Chapter 5), which facilitates thinking in terms of competing

[9] Mansbridge, J., J. Bohman, S. Chambers, T. Christiano, A. Fung, J. Parkinson, D.F. Thompson, and M.E. Warren, A Systemic Approach to Deliberative Democracy, in J. Parkinson and J. Mansbridge (eds), *Deliberative Systems: Deliberative Democracy at the Large Scale*, Cambridge, Cambridge University Press, 2012. See earlier arguments about deliberative systems thinking in Chapters 3 and 6 particularly.

[10] Although deliberative-systems theory acknowledges the latter in the abstract, it does not assign high priority to it. More attention to delivering efficacious action in a stable and reliable manner in e.g. Diamond, L., *In Search of Democracy*, London, Routledge, 2016; Ringen, S., *Nation of Devils: Democratic Leadership and the Problem of Obedience*, New Haven, Yale University Press, 2013.

opposites. Principally, this book looked into the antithesis of deliberative versus plebiscitary democratic innovations and on the possibility of making the tension between such integrative versus aggregative approaches—the horizontal axis of the typology—productive through connective democratic innovations (such as deliberative referendums, Participatory Budgeting-new style, and other variations on the theme of hybrid innovation, see Chapters 7–8).

In exploring the tensions and complementarities along the horizontal axis, the vertical axis of the typology—describing the opposition between democracy from below, driven by direct citizen participation, and democracy from above, driven by representative politics and leadership—inevitably came into view as well. As did the issue of how hybrid democratic innovations that combine pressures from below could be anchored in wider systems of representative democracy. The Ireland and Antwerp case studies proved empirically that it is possible to develop a working relationship and that something resembling the aforementioned Red Queen effect can actually be achieved, with a comparatively virtuous push and pull going on between civil society on the one hand and the established system on the other (Chapters 7–8).

Thus, while a large part of this book deals with democratic innovations that organize civic participation in diverging ways, representative democracy and developments therein remain an important context and area of attention. Figure 4.1 underscores this schematically: plebiscitary and deliberative formats of democratic innovation are institutional additions—essentially rivalling, potentially synergistic—in the context of established systems of electoral, representative democracy. This three-part diagram can be mirrored with the three-part diagram that Dalton et al. sketched some twenty years ago, although they named and framed their three spheres differently.[11] In addition to the hard core of representative democracy, they saw two alternative spheres growing strongly. First, a sphere of what they called 'advocacy democracy', in which politics remains responsible and is informed and influenced to some extent by social groups and parties. Nowadays it would be subsumed under 'network governance', 'interactive governance', or other concepts used to describe basically the same phenomenon. Second, a growing

---

[11] Dalton, R.J., B.E. Cain, and S.E. Scarrow, New Forms of Democracy?, in B.E. Cain, R.J. Dalton, and S.E. Scarrow (eds), *Democracy Transformed*, Oxford, Oxford University Press, 2003, pp. 9–11; Dalton, R.J., B.E. Cain, and S.E. Scarrow, Democratic Publics and Democratic Institution, in B.E. Cain, R.J. Dalton, and S.E. Scarrow (eds), *Democracy Transformed*, Oxford, Oxford University Press, 2003, pp. 252–6.

sphere of 'direct democracy', in their conceptualization not only a collection of direct-voting practices but also deliberative and participatory practices (Chapter 1). Although these developments are still relevant, in my conceptualization of present-day innovative practices that complement and challenge representative democracy, I chose to distinguish more sharply between plebiscitary (or more generally: aggregative) and deliberative (or more generally: integrative) formats. My alternative conceptualization is informed by developments in current practice together with theoretical considerations as outlined in Part I of this book (Chapters 2–5).

New plebiscitary and deliberative practices draw on distinctive models of democracy, which are consonant with distinctive types of culture. Figure 5.1 indicates schematically how new plebiscitary formats feed mostly on aggregative models of democracy that share a culture of competition and adversarialism. The strongest tie is with voter democracy (oriented on efficient direct voting on issues), but pendulum democracy (oriented on competitive leadership) is, to a more limited extent, also a source of inspiration. Innovations that centralize deep deliberation among citizens draw on integrative models of democracy that share a culture of cooperation and communitarianism. The strongest link here is with the general model and ethos of participatory democracy (oriented on the engagement and gathering of citizens in groups), even though consensus democracy (oriented on the organization of representation in round-table settings) is to a more limited extent also of some influence here (Chapters 3, 4, 5).

The democratic-cum-cultural theoretical framework applied in this book not only helps to understand the positive and negative feedback mechanisms between different ideas of polishing and rinsing democracy. It also supports theorizing about polyrational—more versatile, connective, and potentially more rewarding—democratic redesign. The rethinking of democratic innovation culminates here in the hybrid-innovations hypothesis, which posits that more versatile and connective democratic innovations are more likely to perform better—on balance, considering a wider set of democratic-governance values—than democratic innovations that fall short of these qualities.

The hybrid-innovations hypothesis is theoretically an extension of the polyrational-solutions hypothesis, which has been confirmed in a series of empirical studies that have shown that policy solutions become more promising, in terms of perceived legitimacy and effectiveness, to the extent that monorational solutions—culturally biased solutions, drawing on a single corner of the cultural spectrum—are avoided and polyrational solutions—mobilizing and connecting multiple cultural outlooks—are actualized.[12] The central point is that different policy cultures—outlooks on specific policy fields—have varying strengths and weaknesses, which should not be kept away from each other but should in fact collide. From the perspective of those who advocate monorational solutions, polyrational policy solutions are not tidy, elegant, or pure—logical elaborations from a dominant theme—but they are unpure, clumsy, or messy—patchworks of different logics. However, in policy domains in which different values are important such polyrational solutions tend to have advantages over monorational solutions.

The hybrid-innovations hypothesis takes the polyrational-solutions hypothesis one level up in Elinor Ostrom's three-worlds-of-choice model, which distinguishes operational choice, collective choice, and at the highest level constitutional choice.[13] The original polyrational-solutions hypothesis is focused on the enactment and formulation of working plans and action strategies in Ostrom's worlds of operational choice and collective choice—in actual policy fields such as urban traffic, local housing, regional energy, national debt, immigration, pensions, etc. In the hybrid-innovations hypothesis, the attention is extended, or rather elevated, to Ostrom's world of constitutional choice. This type of choice is partly but emphatically not only about the specification of constitutional legislation that steers the organization of the state. It is also about the design and redesign of institutions—national, regional, local—that in other durable ways—not necessarily codified in the formal constitution—channel processes of collective and operational choice in the public arena.

Following Ostrom, democratic (re)design is a matter of constitutional choice par excellence. Decisions on the democratic (re)design of PB-ns in Antwerp typically belong to her world of constitutional choice, as do decisions on the CA-plus-referendum process that led to new abortion legislation in Ireland (Chapters 7–8). The same goes for design choices establishing a Citizens' Initiative Review, a G1000 with preparatory voting, an Iterative Public Vote, vTaiwan, Decidim Barcelona, and other variations on the theme of hybrid innovation (Boxes 7.2, 8.2).

---

[12] There are studies in a range of policy fields in Verweij, M. and M. Thompson (eds), *Clumsy Solutions for a Complex World: Governance, Politics and Plural Perceptions*, Basingstoke, Palgrave Macmillan, 2006. See also: Hendriks, F., *Public Policy and Political Institutions: The Role of Culture in Traffic Policy*, Edward Elgar, 1999; Verweij, M., *Clumsy Solutions for a Wicked World*, Palgrave Macmillan, 2011; Hartmann, T., *Clumsy Floodplains: Responsive Land Policy for Extreme Floods*, Routledge, 2016; Gyawali, D., M. Thompson, and M. Verweij (eds), *Aid, Technology and Development*, London, Routledge, 2016.

[13] Ostrom, E. (ed.), *Strategies of Political Inquiry*, Beverly Hills, Sage, 1982; Ostrom, E., *Governing the Commons*, Cambridge, Cambridge University Press, 1990.

It is clear that all formats for democratic betterment—whether framed as democratic innovations or reforms—have their particular strengths and weaknesses. Deliberative mini-publics can lead relatively diverse microcosms to respectfully reflect on public issues resulting in relatively nuanced verdicts; however, only small groups can participate, and larger maxi-publics, as well as political elites, do not always take notice. Binary referendums on the other side give large groups of citizens the opportunity to transmit a loud and clear signal to the powers that be; however, there is also a real risk of polarization, simplification, and jumping to conclusions in public affairs. Other talk-oriented and voting-oriented innovations in bottom-up democracy also have their peculiar strengths and weaknesses. And reforms of representative democracy, focused on the other side of the fence so to speak, are equally limited in what they can and cannot bring about (Chapters 2–5).

The hybrid-innovations hypothesis hinges on the central idea that connecting opposing formats of democratic betterment can bolster the merits and compensate for the vulnerabilities of the connected formats. In a single format of democratic betterment, the associated vulnerabilities may prevail, while in a hybrid construction the combined forces may lead to an overall more advantageous situation. The hypothesis thus elevates and extends initiatives to improve policy learning through one particular type of democratic innovation, for instance through more deliberation.[14] Following this hypothesis, the challenge of democratic revitalization is to develop creative combinations of democracy from below (straddling the dichotomy of plebiscitary versus deliberative democratic formats) and to effectively match this to the encompassing system of representative democracy (straddling the dichotomy of democracy from below, driven by civic participation, and democracy from above, driven by representative leadership). Those who do not care for the adjective 'hybrid' are welcome to rename this the 'blended', 'mixed', or 'matched' innovation hypothesis, as long as the idea of connecting competing opposites remains central to it.

On the basis of the hybrid-innovations hypothesis, we should expect more versatile and connective democratic innovations to have net advantages as regards the wider set of democratic-governance values over innovations that fall short of these qualities. The integrative values framework elaborated in this book brings together five core values or expectations with respect to democratic governance and innovation. Ideally, democratic innovations

---

[14] Lodge, M., The Public Management of Risk: The Case for Deliberating among Worldviews, *Review of Policy Research*, 2009, 26, 4, pp. 395–408; Ney, S. and M. Verweij, Exploring the Contributions of Cultural Theory for Improving Public Deliberation about Complex Policy Problems, *The Policy Studies Journal*, 2014, 42, 4, pp. 620–43.

promote inclusiveness on the input side, efficaciousness on the output side, appropriateness throughout the process, resilience as well as counterbalance on the system level. In reality, however, democratic innovations tend to be specialized in particular performance areas, which means that scoring patterns displaying bulges and dents are always to be expected (Chapter 6). Maximum scores on all core values cannot be expected from hybrid democratic innovations either. The hybrid-innovations thesis does not presume such an ultimate (unrealistic) level of success. It simply states that the chance of positive net benefits is systematically greater for hybrid innovations than for non-hybrid innovations.

It seems that democratic values are so diverse and simultaneously crucial that democratic innovations almost have to be advanced hybrids most of the time. Support for this idea is emerging in theory and practice, but it must be acknowledged that the hybrid-innovations hypothesis is at this point a general hypothesis that requires further probing and testing.[15] Hybrid innovation in the realm of democracy is an emerging phenomenon, which needs to be tracked and scrutinized over a longer period of time in order to understand better what it entails and what it actually brings in terms of democratic values. More cases need to be followed and examined in-depth and in-situ. This is likely to lead to further specification and refinement. Potentially damaging to the hybrid-innovations hypothesis would be empirical studies that clearly show that non-hybrid innovations systematically outperform hybrid innovations in relation to the comprehensive set of democratic-governance values. This is not what I would expect for democratic innovations attempted in real-life settings (as opposed to artificial lab treatments), and in relation to the wider set of values (as opposed to performance on singular values), but the discovery of a systematically superior non-hybrid innovation (the democratic variant of the 'killer app' that overshadows all other apps) cannot be ruled out in advance. To date, however, I have not seen convincing evidence for the existence of systematically superior non-hybrid innovations.

Considering developments in theory and practice, as I have done here, the hybrid innovation of democracy seems to be an idea whose time has come. It comes, however, with challenges and questions that theorists and practitioners have only just begun to tackle and answer. One of the biggest difficulties harks back to the point that 'mixophobia' (fear of institutional pollution) is a primary reflex to reckon with here, while 'heterophilia' (love for the institutionally different) is a precious feature requiring special effort (Chapters 2–5).

---

[15] In an ongoing research project named REDRESS, a network of researchers including myself as principal investigator is looking into the deficits of singular democratic innovations and the scope for neutralizing such deficiencies through combined innovations, see <https://redressproject.nl/en/>

This is particularly evident along the plebiscitary–deliberative divide that I have highlighted in this book. People who are enthusiastic about deliberative formats tend to be suspicious of plebiscitary formats, and the other way around. To further add to the challenge, people who are passionate about furthering bottom-up democracy, often run up against people who are equally adamant about not undermining representative politics and leadership.

Reaching out to the other side does not come naturally here. At least one element in a hybrid design tends to be approached with reserve and suspicion. ('Why add an unruly referendum process if we have a tidy deliberative mini-public on offer?'; 'Why resort to cumbersome talk by a mini-public if we can get a clear vote from the encompassing maxi-public?'; 'Why acknowledge representative democracy if we want to take control ourselves?'; 'Why engage other citizens if we can have our representatives selected, and potentially deselected?). Such reservations and suspicions are bracketed in emerging practices of hybrid design that I have explored in this book, illustrating the high-effort–high-reward potential of such practices. Hybrid innovation requires more effort, it goes against the grain in more than one way, but it also promises a higher return on a broader spectrum—if and when mixing and matching are done with practical wisdom, which can be facilitated by multi-faceted research but not replaced by it (Chapter 6).

For all the research done on democratic innovations, we should realize that this is ultimately a field depending on practical wisdom. In the Aristotelian tradition, practical wisdom—*phronesis*—is a matter of operating wisely within a situational context in which values have to be weighed against each other and in which the truest or best option cannot be indicated beforehand. Practical wisdom should be distinguished from the epistemic wisdom—*episteme*—that science aspires to produce, on the one hand, and from the technical know-how—*techné*—that experts may bring to bear on a social challenge like democratic innovation, on the other hand.[16] How to organize a digital platform that reliably collects and aggregates scores of digital voters is a question that technical experts may answer. The degree to which stakeholders are satisfied with a democratic innovation in relation to a particular value (say inclusiveness) is a question that can be answered using the scientific method. But how to combine democratic formats in a way that is acutely sensitive to the likely advantages and disadvantages of the combined formats in a specific time and place is a question that

---

[16] On acknowledging practical wisdom, *phronesis*, also called *mētis*, in public affairs generally: Flyvbjerg, B., *Making Social Science Matter: Why Social Inquiry Fails and How It Can Succeed Again*, Cambridge, Cambridge University Press, 2001; Scott, J., *Seeing Like a State, How Certain Schemes to Improve the Human Condition Have Failed*, Yale University Press, 1999.

requires a great deal of practical wisdom. It will inevitably involve creative action, bricolage, and recombination, and cannot rely on mono-rational blueprints or copy-and-pasting of hybrids that have proven to work elsewhere (Chapters 6, 7, 8).

Ultimately, the important work of democratic innovation needs to be done by reflective practitioners, whose work cannot be replaced by research, although it should be informed and can be inspired by it. It is my hope that this book contributes—even if only indirectly—to asking the right questions and getting the right conversations going in the practice of democratic innovation, in addition to the science of it.

Bibliography

Abers, R.N., *Inventing Local Democracy: Grassroots Politics in Brazil*, Lynne Riener Publishers, 2000.

Abers, R.N., I. Brandão, R. King, and D. Votto, Towards a More Equal City: Porto Alegre: Participatory Budgeting and the Challenges of Sustaining Transformative Change, *World Resources Institute*, June 2018.

Acemoglu, D. and J.A. Robinson, *The Narrow Corridor: States, Societies, and the Fate of Liberty*, Penguin Press, 2019.

Ahmed, A., K. Rogers, and J. Ernst, How the Mighty Caravan Became a Trump Election Strategy, *New York Times*, <www.nytimes.com/2018/10/24/world/americas/migrant-caravan-trump.html>, 24 October 2018.

Aitamurto, T., H. Landemore, and J. Saldivar Galli, Unmasking the Crowd: Participants' Motivation Factors, Expectations, and Profile in a Crowdsourced Law Reform, *Information, Communication & Society*, 2017, 20, 8, pp.1239–60.

Ajuntament de Barcelona, *Citizens to decide how to improve neighbourhoods with the first participatory budget*, <https://ajuntament.barcelona.cat/bombers/en/noticia/citizens-to-decide-how-to-improve-neighbourhoods-with-the-first-participatory-budget_911307>, 2020.

Alexander, L., *Constitutionalism: Philosophical Foundations*, Cambridge, Cambridge University Press, 2001.

Almond, G.A. and S. Verba, *The Civic Culture Revisited*, Boston, Little, Brown & Company, 1980.

Altman, D., *Direct Democracy Worldwide*, Cambridge, Cambridge University Press, 2011.

Altman, D., The Potential of Direct Democracy: A Global Measure (1900–2014), *Social Indicators Research*, 2017, 133, 3, pp.1207–27.

Andrews, M., Good Government Means Different Things in Different Countries, *Governance*, 2010, 23, 1, pp.7–35.

Ansell, C. and A. Gash, Collaborative Governance in Theory and Practice, *Journal of Public Administration Research and Theory*, 2008, 18, 4, pp.543–71.

Ansell, C., C. Doberstein, H. Henderson, S. Siddiki, and P. 't Hart, Understanding Inclusion in Collaborative Governance: A Mixed-Methods Approach, *Policy and Society*, 2020, 39, 4, pp.570–91.

Arendt, H., *The Origins of Totalitarianism*, Berlin, Schocken Books, 1951.

Atlee, T., *Empowering Public Wisdom: A Practical Vision of Citizen-led Politics*, Berkeley, North Atlantic Books, 2012.

Bächtiger, A., J. Dryzek, J. Mansbridge, and M.E. Warren (eds), *The Oxford Handbook of Deliberative Democracy*, Oxford, Oxford University Press, 2018.

Bächtiger, A., S. Niemeyer, M. Neblo, M.R. Steenbergen, and J. Steiner, Disentangling Diversity in Deliberative Democracy: Competing Theories, Their Empirical Blind-Spots, and Complementarities, *Journal of Political Philosophy*, 2010, 18, 1, pp.32–63.

Bächtiger, A., S. Shikano, S. Pedrini, and M. Ryser, *Measuring Deliberation 2.0: Standards, Discourse Types, and Sequenzialization*. Paper presented at ECPR General Conference, Potsdam, 5–12 September 2009.

Baiocchi, G. and E. Ganuza, Participatory Budgeting as if Emancipation Mattered, *Politics & Society*, 2014, 42, 1, pp.29–50.

Baiocchi, G. and E. Ganuza, *Popular Democracy: The Paradox of Participation*, Stanford, Stanford University Press, 2016.

Barber, B.R., *Strong Democracy: Participatory Politics for a New Age*, Berkeley, University of California Press, 2004 (originally 1984).

Bardi, L., S. Bartolini, and A. Trechsel, Party Adaptation and Change and the Crisis of Democracy, *Party Politics*, 2014, 20, 2, pp.151–9.

Bardon, S., Attorney General says Eight Amendment should be replaced if it is repealed, *The Irish Times*, <https://www.irishtimes.com/news/politics/attorney-general-says-Eight-amendment-should-be-replaced-if-it-is-repealed-1.3374059>, 30 January 2018.

Barry, L., *Taiwan: Public Participation Methods on the Cyberpunk Frontier of Democracy*, Civic Hall, Civicist, <https://civichall.org/civicist/vtaiwan-democracy-frontier/>, 11 August 2016.

BBC News, *'Boaty McBoatface' Polar Ship Named after Attenborough*, <https://www.bbc.co.uk/news/uk-3622565>, 6 May 2016.

Beauvais, E. and M.E. Warren, What can Deliberative Mini-Publics Contribute to Democratic Systems?, *European Journal of Political Research*, 2019, 58, 3, pp.893–914.

Beetham, D., Key Principles and Indices for a Democratic Audit, D. Beetham (ed), *Definining and Measuring Democracy*, London, Sage, 1994, pp.25–43.

Beetham, D., Evaluating New vs Old Forms of Citizen Engagement and Participation, in B. Geissel and K. Newton (eds), *Evaluating Democratic Innovations: Curing the Democratic Malaise?*, London, Routledge, 2012, pp.56–67.

Bekkers, V. and A. Edwards, Legitimacy and Democracy: A Conceptual Framework for Assessing Governance Practices, in V. Bekkers, G. Dijkstra, A. Edwards, and M. Fenger (eds), *Governance and the Democratic Deficit*, Aldershot, Ashgate, 2007, pp.35–60.

Berry, J., K. Portney, and K. Thomson, *The Rebirth of Urban Democracy*, Washington, DC, The Brookings Institution, 1993.

Bergsson, B.T., The Constitution as a Political Tool in Iceland, in P. Blokker (ed), *Constitutional Acceleration within the EU and Beyond*, London, Routledge, 2018, pp.155–74.

Bernholz, L., H. Landemore, and R. Reich (eds), *Digital Technology and Democratic Theory*, Chicago, Chicago University Press, 2021.

Bevir, M., *Democratic Governance*, Princeton, Princeton University Press, 2010.

Bignell, J., *An Introduction to Television Studies*, London, Routledge, 2012.

Bishop, G., *The Illusion of Public Opinion*, New York, Rowman & Littlefield, 2005.

Blanco, I., Y. Salazar, and I. Bianchi, Urban Governance and Political Change under a Radical Left Government: The Case of Barcelona, *Journal of Urban Affairs*, 2020, 42, 1, pp.18–38.

Bossetta, M., A. Dutceac Segesten, and H.J. Trenz, Political Participation on Facebook during Brexit: Does User Engagement on Media Pages Stimulate Engagement with Campaigns?, *Journal of Language and Politics*, 2017, 17, 2.

Boswell, J., R. Dean, and G. Smith, Integrating Citizen Deliberation into Climate Governance: Lessons on Robust Design from Six Climate Assemblies, *Public Administration*, 2022, pp.1–19.

Bovaird, T. and E. Löffler, Evaluating the Quality of Public Governance: Indicators, Models and Methodologies, *International Review of Administrative Sciences*, 2003, 69, pp.313–28.

Box, R.C., *Citizen Governance*, Thousand Oaks, Sage, 1998.

Brändle, V.K., C. Galpin, and H.J. Trenz, Brexit as 'Politics of Division': Social Media Campaigning after the Referendum, *Social Movement Studies*, 2022, 21, 1-2, pp.234–53.

Brennan, J., *Against Democracy*, Princeton, Princeton University Press, 2016.

Browne K. and S. Caulkin (eds), *After Repeal: Rethinking Abortion Politics*, London, Zed Books, 2020.

Brugué, Q. and R. Gallego, A Democratic Public Administration?, *Public Management Review*, 2010, 5, 3, pp.425–47.

Bruun, H.H., *Science, Values and Politics in Max Weber's Methodology*, Aldershot, Ashgate, 2012.

Bryson, J.M, K.S. Quick, C. Schively Slotterbak, and B.C. Crosby, Designing Public Participation Processes, *Public Administration Review*, 2012, 73, 1, pp.23–34.

Bühlmann, M. and H. Kriesi, Models for Democracy, in H. Kriesi, S. Lavenex, F. Esser, J. Matthes, M. Bühlmann, and D. Bochsler (eds), *Democracy in the Age of Globalization and Mediatization*, Basingstoke, Palgrave Macmillan, 2013, pp.44–69.

Bürgerhaushalt Lichtenberg, *Startseite*, <https://www.buergerhaushalt-lichtenberg.de>, n.d.

Burke, P., *Cultural Hybridity*, Polity Press, 2010.

C2D—Centre for Research on Direct Democracy, *About this project*, <www.c2d.ch>, 2018.

Cabannes, Y., The Impact of Participatory Budgeting on Basic Services: Municipal Practices and Evidence from the Field, *Environment and Urbanization*, 2015, 27, 1, pp.257–84.

Cain, B.E., R.J. Dalton, and S.E. Scarrow (eds), *Democracy Transformed: Expanding Political Opportunities in Advanced Industrial Democracies*, Oxford, Oxford University Press, 2003.

Caluwaerts, D. and M. Reuchamps, Strengthening Democracy through Bottom-up Deliberation: An Assessment of the Internal Legitimacy of the G1000 Project, *Acta Politica*, 2015, 50, 2, pp.151–70.

Calzada, I., (Smart) Citizens from Data Providers to Decision-Makers? The Case Study of Barcelona, *Sustainability*, 2018, 10, 3252.

Campbell, M., O. Escobar, C. Fenton, and P. Craig, The Impact of Participatory Budgeting on Health and Wellbeing: A Scoping Review of Evaluations, *BMC Public Health*, 2018, 18, Article 822.

Caramani, D. and Y. Mény (eds), *Challenges to Consensual Politics: Democracy, Identity, and Populist Protest in the Alpine Region*, New York, Peter Lang, 2005.

Chambers, S., Rhetoric and the Public Sphere: Has Deliberative Democracy Abandoned Mass Democracy?, *Political Theory*, 2009, 2, 3, pp.323–50.

Chan, H.S. and J. Gao, Can the Same Key Open Different Locks?, *Public Administration*, 2012, 91, 2, pp.366–80.

Chandra, Y. and R.M. Walker, How Does a Seminal Article in Public Administration Diffuse and Influence the Field? Bibliometric Methods and the Case of Hood's 'A Public Management For All Seasons?', *International Public Management Journal*, 2019, 22, 5, pp.712–42.

Chappel, Z., *Deliberative Democracy: A Critical Introduction*, Basingstoke, Palgrave, 2012.

Cheneval, F. and A. el-Wakil, The Institutional Design of Referendums: Bottom-Up and Binding, *Swiss Political Science Review*, 2018, 24, 3, pp.294–304.

Chwalisz, C., *The Populist Signal: Why Politics and Democracy Need to Change*, London, Rowman & Littlefield, 2015.

Chwalisz, C., *The People's Verdict: Adding Informed Citizen Voice to Public Decision-Making*, London, Rowman & Littlefield, 2017.

The Citizens' Assembly, *First Report and Recommendations of the Citizens' Assembly, The 8th Amendment of the Constitution*, 9 June 2017.

Conservatives, *AV Sports Day* [Video], Youtube, <https://www.youtube.com/watch?v=9cmvl3tikUA>, 18 April 2011.

Courant, D., The Promises and Disappointments of the French Convention on Climate, *Deliberative Democracy Digest*, <https://www.publicdeliberation.net/the-promises-and-disappointments-of-the-french-citizens-convention-for-climate/>, 9 June 2021.

Craglia, M. and L. Shanley, Data Democracy: Increased Supply of Geospatial Information and Expanded Participatory Processes in the Production of Data, *International Journal of Digital Earth*, 2015, 8, 9, pp.679–93.

Cronin, T.E., *Direct Democracy: The Politics of Initiative, Referendum and Recall*, Cambridge, MA, Harvard University Press, 1989.

Curato, N. and S. Niemeyer, Reaching out to Overcome Political Apathy: Building Participatory Capacity through Deliberative Engagement, *Politics and Policy*, 2013, 41, 3, pp.355–83.

Dahl, R.A., A Democratic Dilemma: System Effectiveness versus Citizen Participation, *Political Science Quarterly*, 1994, 109, 1, pp.3–34.

Dahl, R.A., *On Democracy*, New Haven, Yale University Press, 2000.

Dalton, R.J., B.E. Cain, and S.E. Scarrow, New Forms of Democracy?, in B.E. Cain, R.J. Dalton, and S.E. Scarrow (eds), *Democracy Transformed*, Oxford, Oxford University Press, 2003, pp.1–22.

Dalton, R.J., B.E. Cain, and S.E. Scarrow, Democratic Publics and Democratic Institution, in B.E. Cain, R.J. Dalton, and S.E. Scarrow (eds), *Democracy Transformed*, Oxford, Oxford University Press, 2003, pp.250–75.

de Graaf, P., Eindhoven leent zich voor experimenten, *Volkskrant*, <https://www.volkskrant.nl/nieuws-achtergrond/eindhoven-leent-zich-voor-%09experimenten~b1a668cd/%20>, 1 June 2016.

Davies, W., *Nervous States: Democracy and the Decline of Reason*, London, Norton, 2018.

Dean, R.J., Counter-Governance: Citizen Participation beyond Collaboration, *Politics and Governance*, 2018, 6, 1, pp.180–8.

Decidim, *Features*, <https://decidim.org/features>, n.d.

Decidim, *Pressupostos participatius de Barcelona*, <https://www.decidim.barcelona/processes/PressupostosParticipatius>, n.d.

Della Porta, D., *Can Democracy Be Saved? Participation, Deliberation and Social Movements*, Cambridge, Polity Press, 2013.

Deschouwer, K., From Consociation to Federation: How the Belgian Parties Won, in K.R. Luther and K. Deschouwer (eds), *Party Elites in Divided Societies*, London, Routledge, 1999, pp.74–100.

de Vries, M., J. Nemec, and D. Špaček (eds), *International Trends in Participatory Budgeting: Between Trivial Pursuits and Best Practices*, Basingstoke, Palgrave Macmillan, 2021.

Diamond, L., *In Search of Democracy*, London, Routledge, 2016.

Diamond, L. and M.F. Plattner (eds), *Electoral Systems and Democracy*, Baltimore, The Johns Hopkins University Press, 2006.

Diamond, L. and M.F. Plattner (eds), *Democracy in Decline?*, Baltimore, John Hopkins University Press, 2016.

Dias, N. (ed), *Hope for democracy: 30 years of participatory budgeting world-wide*, Epopeia Records, 2018.

Direct Democracy Navigator, *Welcome to the navigator to direct democracy*, <https://www.direct-democracy-navigator.org/>, 2022.

District Antwerp, *Visienota Burgerbegroting—Evaluatie en bijsturing 2021*, <https://burgerbegroting.be/evaluatie-burgerbegroting>, 2021, pp.1–4.

District Antwerp, *30 thema's van de Burgerbegroting*, <https://burgerbegroting.be/30-themas>, 2022.

District Antwerp, *Stap 2: dien ideeën in*, <https://burgerbegroting.be/ronde-3>, 2022.

District Antwerp, *Wat is de Burgerbegroting?*, <https://burgerbegroting.be/wat-is-de-burgerbegroting>, 2022.

Douglas, M., *Purity and Danger*, London, Routledge & Kegan Paul, 1966.

Douglas, M., *Natural Symbols*, London, Berrie & Rockliff, 1970.

Douglas, M., *Cultural Bias*, London, Royal Antropological Institute, 1978.

Douglas, M., *How Institutions Think*, Syracuse, Syracuse University Press, 1986.

Douglas, M., *Leviticus as Literature*, Oxford, Oxford University Press, 1999.

Douglas, M., *Risk and Blame: Essays in the Sociology of Perception*, New York, Routledge, 1992.

Douglas, M., *Thought Styles: Critical Essays on Good Taste*, New York, Sage, 1996.

Douglas, M., Being Fair to Hierarchists, *University of Pennsylvania Law Review*, 2003, 151, pp.1349–70.

Douglas, M., *A history of grid and group cultural theory*, <https://fliphtml5.com/lxsr/vpej/basic>, 2006.

Douglas, M. and S. Ney, *Missing Persons: A Critique of Personhood in the Social Sciences*, Berkeley, University of California Press, 1998.

Douglas, M. and A.B. Wildavsky, *Risk and Culture: An Essay on the Selection of Technical and Environmental Dangers*, Berkeley, University of California Press, 1982.

Dreyfuss, E., Alert: Don't Believe Everything You Read About the Migrant Caravan, *Wired*, <www.wired.com/story/mexico-migrant-caravan-misinformation-alert>, 23 October 2018.

Dryzek, J.S., *Deliberative Democracy and beyond: Liberals, Critics, Contestations*, Oxford, Oxford University Press, 2000.

Dryzek, J.S., Theory, Evidence and the Task of Deliberation, in S.W. Rosenberg (ed), *Deliberation, Participation and Democracy: Can the People Govern?*, New York, Palgrave Macmillan, 2007, pp.237–50.

Dryzek, J.S., Democratization as Deliberative Capacity Building, *Comparative Political Studies*, 2009, 42, 11, pp.1379–402.

Dunleavy, P., H. Margetts, S. Bastow, and J. Tinkler, New Public Management is Dead: Long Live Digital-Era Governance, *Journal of Public Administration Research and Theory*, 2005, 16, 3, pp.467–94.

Easton, D., *A Systems Analysis of Political Life*, New York, Wiley, 1965.

The Economist, *Referendumania: Plebiscites in Europe*, <https://www.economist.com/europe/2016/05/19/referendumania>, 21 May 2016.

The Economist, *Almost there—Australian voters approve gay marriage*, <https://www.economist.com/asia/2017/11/15/australian-voters-approve-gay-marriage>, 16 November 2017.

The Economist, *Amateurs to the rescue, Politicians should take Citizens' Assembly's seriously*, <https://www.economist.com/leaders/2020/09/17/politicians-should-take-citizens-assemblies-seriously>, 17 September 2020.

The Economist, *The mathematical method that could offer a fairer way to vote*, <https://www.economist.com/christmas-specials/2021/12/18/the-mathematical-method-that-could-offer-a-fairer-way-to-vote>, 18 December 2021.

Economist Intelligence Unit, *Democracy Index 2020: In Sickness and in Health*, <www.eiu.com>, n.d.

Economist Intelligence Unit, *Democracy Index*, <https://www.eiu.com/n/campaigns/democracy-index-2021/>, n.d.

Elkink, J.A., D.M. Farrell, S. Marien, T. Reidy, and J. Suiter, The Death of Conservative Ireland? The 2018 Abortion Referendum, *Electoral Studies*, 2020, 65, 102142, pp.1–11.

Elkink, J.A., D.M. Farrell, T. Reidy, and J. Suiter, Understanding the 2015 Marriage Referendum in Ireland: Context, Campaign, and Conservative Ireland, *Irish Political Studies*, 2017, 32, 3, pp.361–81.

Ellis, R.J., *Democratic Delusions: The Initiative Process in America*, Lawrence, University of Kansas Press, 2002.

Elster, J., Introduction, in J. Elster (ed), *Deliberative Democracy*, Cambridge, Cambridge University Press, 1998, pp.1–18.

Elster, J. and H. Landemore (eds), *Collective Wisdom: Principles and Mechanisms*, Cambridge, Cambridge University Press, 2012.

Elstub, S., Mini-Publics: Issues and Cases, in S. Elstub and P. MacLaverty (eds), *Deliberative Democracy: Issues and Cases*, Edinburgh, Edinburgh University Press, 2014, pp.166–88.

Elstub, S. and O. Escobar, Defining and Typologising Democratic Innovations, in S. Elstub and O. Escobar (eds), *Handbook of Democratic Innovation and Governance*, Cheltenham, Edward Elgar, 2019, pp.11–31.

Elstub, S., S.A. Ercan, and R.F. Mendonça (eds), *Deliberative Systems in Theory and Practice*, London, Routledge, 2018.

El-Wakil, A., Democratic Theory: The Deliberative Potential of Facultative Referendums, *Democratic Theory*, 2017, 4, 1, pp.59–78.

Emerson, K. and T. Nabatchi, *Collaborative Governance Regimes*, Washington, DC, Georgetown University Press, 2015.

Emerson, K., T. Nabatchi, and S. Balogh, An Integrative Framework for Collaborative Governance, *Journal of Public Administration Research and Theory*, 2012, 22, 1, pp.1–29.

EP—European Parliamentary Research Service, *Prospects for E-democracy in Europe: Part II: Case Studies*, Brussels, European Parliament, 2018.

Ercan, S.A. and J.P. Gagnon, Crisis of Democracy: Which Crisis? Which Democracy?, *Democratic Theory*, 2014, 1, 2, pp.1–10.

Escobar, O., Scripting Deliberative Policy-Making: Dramaturgic Policy Analysis and Engagement Know-How, *Journal of Comparative Policy Analysis: Research and Practice*, 2015, 17, 3, pp.269–85.

Fardon, R., *Mary Douglas: An Intellectual Biography*, London, Routledge, 1999.

Farrell, D.M., We may have overdone it on citizens' assemblies, *Irish Times*, <https://www.irishtimes.com/opinion/we-may-have-overdone-it-on-citizens-assemblies-1.4803375>, 16 February 2022.

Farrell, D.M., J. Suiter, and C. Harris, Systematizing' Constitutional Deliberation: The 2016–18 Citizens' Assembly in Ireland, *Irish Political Studies*, 2019, 34, 1, pp.113–23.

Farrell, D.M., J. Suiter, K. Cunningham, and C. Harris, When Mini-Publics and Maxi-Publics Coincide: Ireland's National Debate on Abortion, *Representation*, 2020.

Farrell, D.M., J. Suiter, and C. Harris, The Effects of Mixed Memberships in a Deliberative Forum: The Irish Constitutional Convention of 2012–201, *Political Studies*, 2020, 68, 1, pp.54–73.

Felicetti, A., Learning from Democratic Practices: New Perspectives on Institutional Design, *The Journal of Politics*, 2021, 83, 4, pp.1589–601.

Felicetti, A., Casting a New Light on the Democratic Spectator, *Democratization*, 2022.

Fishkin, J., *Democracy and Deliberation: New Directions for Democratic Reform*, New Haven, Yale University Press, 1991.

Fishkin, J., *When the People Speak: Deliberative Democracy and Public Consultation*, Oxford, Oxford University Press, 2009.

Fishkin, J., *Democracy When the People are Thinking*, Oxford, Oxford University Press, 2018.

Fishkin, J.S., T. Kouser, R.C. Luskin, and A. Siu, Deliberative Agenda Setting: Piloting Reform of Direct Democracy in California, *Perspectives on Politics*, 2015, 13, 4, pp.1030–42.

Flinders, M., *Delegated Governance and the British State: Walking without Order*, Oxford, Oxford University Press, 2008.

Flinders, M., The Problem with Democracy, *Parliamentary Affairs*, 2015, 69, 1, pp.181–203.

Flyvbjerg, B., *Making Social Science Matter: Why Social Inquiry Fails and How It Can Succeed Again*, Cambridge, Cambridge University Press, 2001.

Foa, R.S. and Y. Mounk, The Democratic Disconnect, *Journal of Democracy*, 2016, 27, 3, pp.5–17.

Font J., S. Pasadas del Amo, and G. Smith, Tracing the Impact of Proposals from Participatory Processes: Methodological Challenges and Substantive Lessons, *Journal of Public Deliberation*, 2016, 12, 1.

Foucault, M., *Archeology of Knowledge*, London, Routledge, 1969.

Fournier, P., H. van der Kolk, R.K. Carty, A. Blais, and J. Rose, *When Citizens Decide: Lessons from Citizens' Assemblies on Electoral Reform*, Oxford, Oxford University Press, 2011.

Franzosi, P., F. Marone, and E. Salvati, Populism and Euroscepticism in the Italian Five Star Movement, *The International Spectator*, 2015, 50, 2, pp.109–24.

Fukumoto, E. and B. Bozeman, Public Values Theory: What is Missing?, *American Review of Public Administration*, 2019, 49, 6, pp.635–48.

Fung, A., *Empowered Participation: Reinventing Urban Democracy*, Princeton, Princeton University Press, 2004.

Fung, A., Varieties of Participation in Complex Governance, *Public Administration Review*, 2006, 66, 1, pp.66–75.

Ganuza, E. and G. Baiocchi, The Long Journey of Participatory Budgeting, in S. Elstub and O. Escobar (eds), *Handbook of Democratic Innovation and Governance*, Cheltenham, Edward Elgar, 2019, pp.77–98.

Ganuza, E. and G. Baiocchi, The Power of Ambiguity: How Participatory Budgeting Travels the Globe, *Journal of Public Deliberation*, 2012, 8, 2.

Ganuza, E., H. Nez, and E. Morales, The Struggle for a Voice: Tensions between Associations and Citizens in Participatory Budgeting, *International Journal of Urban and Regional Research*, 2014, 38, pp.2274–91.

Gastil, J., *Democracy in Small Groups: Participation, Decision Making, and Communication*, State College, PA, Efficacy Press, 2014, 2nd Edition (originally 1993).

Gastil, J. and K. Knobloch, *Hope for Democracy: How Citizens Can Bring Reason Back into Politics*, Oxford, Oxford University Press, 2020.

Gastil, J. and P. Levine (eds), *The Deliberative Democracy Handbook*, San Francisco, Jossey-Bass, 2005.

Gastil, J. and R. Richards, Making Direct Democracy Deliberative through Random Assemblies, *Politics & Society*, 2013, 41, 2, pp.253–81.

Gastil, J., G.F. Johnson, S. Han, and J. Rountree, *Assessment of the 2016 Oregon Citizens' Initiative Review on Measure 97*, State College, Pennsylvania State University, 2017.

Gastil, J., K.R. Knobloch, J. Reedy, M. Henkels, and K. Cramer, Assessing the Electoral Impact of the 2010 Oregon Citizens' Initiative Review, *American Politics Research*, 2017, 46, 3, pp.534–63.

Gastil, J., R.C. Richards, and K.R. Knobloch, Vicarious Deliberation: How the Oregon Citizens' Initiative Review Influenced Deliberation in Mass Elections, *International Journal of Communication*, 2014, 8, pp.62–89.

Gaus, G., What Might Democratic Self-Governance in a Complex Social World Look Like?, *San Diego Law Review*, 2019, 56, 967.

Geissel, B. and K. Newton (eds), *Evaluating Democratic Innovations: Curing the Democratic Malaise?*, Abingdon, Routledge, 2012.

Geissel, B. and M. Jaos (eds), *Participatory Democratic Innovations in Europe: Improving the Quality of Democracy?*, Barbara Budrich Verlag, 2013.

Gemeente Amsterdam, *West Begroot*, <https://www.amsterdam.nl/stadsdelen/west/west-begroot/>, n.d.

Gemeente Amsterdam, *Buurtbudget*, <https://buurtbudget.amsterdam.nl/>, n.d.

Gemeente Amsterdam, *West Begroot 2023*, <https://westbegroot.amsterdam.nl/toetsingscriteria>, n.d.

Gemeente Amsterdam, *Meedenken, meepraten en meedoen*, <https://www.amsterdam.nl/bestuur-organisatie/invloed/?utm_source=amsterdam.nl&utm_medium=internet&utm_campaign=bestuur-en-organisatie/meedenken-meepraten-en-meedoen&utm_content=redirect#h16eb617a-ce7d-402f-b075-d4393c7be240>, n.d.

George, A.L. and A. Bennett, *Case Studies and Theory Development in the Social Sciences*, Cambridge, MA, MIT Press, 2005.

Gerbaudo, P., Are Digital Parties more Democratic than Traditional Parties? Evaluating Podemos and Movimento 5 Stelle's Online Decision-Making Platforms, *Party Politics*, 2021, 27, 4, pp.730–42.

Geurtz, C., Immune to reform? Understanding democratic reform in three consensus democracies: the Netherlands compared with Germany and Austria, PhD dissertation, Tilburg University, 2012.

Giest, S., Big Data for Policymaking: Fad or Fasttrack?, *Policy Sciences*, 2017, 50, 3, pp.367–82.

Goel, A., A.K. Krishnaswamy, S. Sakshuwong, and T. Aitamurto, Knapsack Voting for Participatory Budgeting, *ACM Transactions on Economics and Computation*, July 2019, 7, 2, Article 8, pp.1–27.

Goldfrank, B., *Deepening Local Democracy in Latin America: Participation, Decentralization, and the Left*, Penn State University Press, 2015.

Goodin, R.E., *The Theory of Institutional Design, Theories of Institutional Design*, Cambridge: Cambridge University Press, 1998.

Goodin, R.E., *Innovating Democracy: Democratic Theory and Practice after the Deliberative Turn*, Oxford, Oxford University Press, 2008.

Goslinga, H., Het referendum deugt van geen kanten, *Trouw*, <https://www.trouw.nl/nieuws/het-referendum-deugt-van-geen-kant~b0096128/>, 3 April 2016.

Graham, T., Barcelona is Leading the Fightback against Small City Surveillance, *Wired*, <https://www.wired.co.uk/article/barcelona-decidim-ada-colau-francesca-bria-decode>, 18 May 2018.

Green, J.E., *The Eyes of the People: Democracy in an Age of Spectatorship*, Oxford, Oxford University Press, 2010.

Green, J.E., Analysing Legislative Performance: A Plebeian Perspective, *Democratization*, 2013, 20, 3, pp.417–37.

Gret, M. and Y. Sintomer, *The Porto Alegre Experiment, Learning Lessons for Better Democracy*, London & New York, Zed Books, 2015.

Grindle, M.S., Good Enough Governance Revisited, *Development Policy Review*, 2007, 235, 5, pp.533–74.

Grönlund, K. and Setälä, M. Political Trust,Satisfaction and Voter Turnout, *Comparative European Politics*, 2007, 5, pp.400–22.

Gutmann, A. and D. Thompson. *Why Deliberative Democracy?*, Princeton University Press, 2003.

Gyawali, D., M. Thompson, and M. Verweij (eds), *Aid, Technology and Development*, London, Routledge, 2016.

Habermas, J., *Theorie des kommunikativen Handelns*, Frankfurt, Suhrkamp Verlag, 1981.

Halupka, M., Clicktivism: A Systematic Heuristic, *Policy & Internet*, 2014, 6, 2, pp.115–32.

Harari, Y.N., *Homo Deus: A Brief History of Tomorrow*, London, Vintage, 2017.

Hartley, J., E. Sørensen, and J. Torfing, Collaborative Innovation: A Viable Alternative to Market Competition and Organizational Entrepreneurship, *Public Administration Review*, 2013, 73, 6, pp.821–30.

Hartmann, T., *Clumsy Floodplains: Responsive Land Policy for Extreme Floods*, Routledge, 2016.

Heijstek-Ziemann, K., Exploring the Impact of Mass Cultural Changes on the Patterns of Democratic Reform, *Democratization*, 2014, 21, 5, pp.888–911.

Heinelt, H., D. Sweeting, and P. Gemitis (eds), *Legitimacy and Urban Governance*, London, Routledge, 2006.

Helms, L., Democracy and Innovation: From Institutions to Agency and Leadership, *Democratization*, 2015, 23, 3, pp.459–77.

Hendriks, C.M., Coupling Citizens and Elites in Deliberative Systems, *European Journal of Political Research*, 2016, 55, pp.43–60.

Hendriks, C.M. and A. Kay, From 'Opening Up' to Democratic Renewal: Deepening Public Engagement in Legislative Committees, *Government and Opposition*, 2019, 54, 1, pp.25–51.

Hendriks, C.M., S.A. Ercan, and J. Boswell, *Mending Democracy: Democratic Repair in Disconnected Times*, Oxford, Oxford University Press, 2020.

Hendriks, F., *Public Policy and Political Institutions: The Role of Culture in Traffic Policy*, Aldershot, Edward Elgar, 1999.

Hendriks, F., Democratic Reform between the Extreme Makeover and the Reinvention of Tradition: The Case of the Netherlands, *Democratization*, 2009, 12, 2, pp.243–68.

Hendriks, F., *Vital Democracy: A Theory of Democracy in Action*, Oxford, Oxford University Press, 2010.

Hendriks, F., Purity and Democracy: Beauty Ideals and Pollution Reduction in Democratic Reform, *Administrative Theory & Praxis*, 2011, 33, 1, pp.45–62.

Hendriks, F., Understanding Good Urban Governance: Essentials, Shifts, and Values, *Urban Affairs Review*, 2014, 50, 4, pp.553–76.

Hendriks, F., Leidende principes voor bestuurlijke innovatie: naar een robuust referentiekader, *Bestuurswetenschappen*, 2018, 72, 1, pp.46–63.

Hendriks, F., Democratic Innovation Beyond Deliberative Reflection, *Democratization*, 2019, 26, 3, pp.444–64.

Hendriks, F., Selection: The Key to Studying Democracy and Innovation, *The Loop*, <https://theloop.ecpr.eu/selection-the-key-to-studying-democracy/>, 24 January 2022.

Hendriks, F., Unravelling the New Plebiscitary Democracy: Towards a Research Agenda, *Government & Opposition*, 2021, 56, 4, pp.615–39.

Hendriks, F. and M. Bovens, Pacificatie en polarisatie: Kentering en continuïteit in politiek en bestuur in Nederland post 2002, *Bestuurskunde*, 2008, 17, 3, pp.56–63.

Hendriks, F. and G. Drosterij (eds), *De Zucht naar Goed Bestuur in de Stad*, The Hague, Boom/Lemma, 2012.

Hendriks, F. and A. Michels, Democracy Transformed? Reforms in Britain and the Netherlands (1990–2010), *International Journal of Public Administration*, 2011, 34, 5, pp.307–17.

Hendriks, F. and Th.A.J. Toonen (eds), *Polder Politics: The Re-Invention of Consensus Democracy in the Netherlands*, Aldershot, Ashgate, 2001.

Hendriks, F. and C. Wagenaar, The Deliberative Referendum: An Idea whose Time has Come? *Administration & Society*, 2023, 55, 3, pp.569–90.

Hendriks, F. and P.W. Tops, Everyday Fixers as Local Heroes, *Local Government Studies*, 2005, 31, 4, pp.475–91.

Hendriks, F., K. Jacobs, and A. Michels, *Nationale burgerfora: verkenning van nationale burgerfora als democratisch gereedschap*, Den Haag, Ministerie van Binnenlandse Zaken en Koninkrijksrelaties, 2021.

Hendriks, F., K. van der Krieken, and C. Wagenaar, *Democratische zegen of vloek? Aantekeningen bij het referendum*, Amsterdam University Press, 2017.

Hibbing, J.R. and E. Theiss-Morse, *Stealth Democracy: Americans' Beliefs About How Government Should Work*, Cambridge, Cambridge University Press, 2002.

Hilgers, D. and C. Ihl, Citizensourcing: Applying the Concept of Open Innovation to the Public Sector, *International Journal of Public Participation*, 2010, 4, 1, pp.67–88.

Hill, S., *Digital Revolutions: Activism in the Internet Age*, Oxford, New Internationalist Publications, 2013.

Hofman, J., H. Bastiaensen, and M. Nuytemans, *Evaluierapport van de Burgerbegroting District Antwerpen*, Deventer, Rode Wouw, <https://burgerbegroting.be/evaluatie-burgerbegroting>, 2021.

Hollander, S., *The Politics of Referendum Use in European Democracies*, London, Palgrave, 2019.

Holtkamp, L. (ed), *Direktdemokratische Hochburgen in Deutschland*, Wiesbaden, Springer, 2016.

Holtz-Bacha, C. and J. Strömbäck, *Opinion Polls and the Media: Reflecting and Shaping Public Opinion*, New York, Palgrave, 2012.

Hood, C., A Public Management for All Seasons?, *Public Administration*, 1991, 69, 1, pp.267–82.

Hood, C., *The Art of the State: Culture, Rhetoric, and Public Management*, Oxford, Oxford University Press, 1998.

Hood, C. and M. Jackson, *Administrative Argument*, Aldershot, Dartmouth, 1991.

Hood, C. and G. Peters, The Middle Aging of New Public Management: Into the Age of Paradox?, *Journal of Public Administration Research and Theory*, 2004, 14, 3, pp.267–82.

Hornblower, S., Creation and Development of Democratic Institutions in Ancient Greece, in J. Dunn (ed), *Democracy: The Unfinished Journey 508 BC to AD 1993*, Oxford, Oxford University Press, 1992, pp.1–13.

Howard, E., How 'Clicktivism' Has Changed the Face of Political Campaigns, *The Guardian*, <www.theguardian.com/society/2014/sep/24/clicktivism-changed-political-campaigns-38-degrees-change>, 24 September 2014.

Iasulaitis, S., C. Pineda Nebot, E. Carneiro da Silva, and R. Cardoso Sampaio, Interactivity and Policy Cycle within Electronic Participatory Budgeting: A Comparative Analysis, *Revista Administração Pública*, November/December 2019, 53, 6, pp.1091–115.

Inglehart, R., *Culture Shift in Advanced Industrial Society*, Princeton, Princeton University Press, 1990.

Jacobs, K. and M. Leyenaar, A Conceptual Framework for Major, Minor and Technical Electoral Reform, *West European Politics*, 2011, 34, 3, pp.495–513.

Jacquet, V., Explaining Non-Participation in Deliberative Mini-Publics, *European Journal of Political Research*, 2017, 563, pp.640–59.

Jacquet V. and R. van der Does, Deliberation and Policy-Making: Three Ways to Think About Minipublics' Consequences, *Administration & Society*, 2021, 53, 3, pp.468–87.

Jeffares, S., *Interpreting Hashtag Politics: Policy Ideas in an Era of Social Media*, London, Palgrave, 2014.

Jørgensen, T.B. and B. Bozeman, Public Values: An Inventory, *Administration & Society*, 2007, 39, 3, pp.354–81.

Kahneman, D., *Thinking Fast, Thinking Slow*, New York, Farrar, Straus & Giroux, 2011.

Kane, A., L. Kennedy, and M. O'Boyle (Directors) and A. Maher (Producer), *The 8th* [Film; online video], <https://the8thfilm.com/>, 28 May 2020.

Kane, J., H. Patapan, and P. 't Hart (eds), *Dispersed Democratic Leadership: Origins, Dynamics, and Implications*, Oxford, Oxford University Press, 2009.

Karner, A., K.B. Brown, R. Marcantonio, and L.G. Alcorn, The View From the Top of Arnstein's Ladder, *Journal of the American Planning Association*, 2019, 85, 3, pp.236–54.

Keane, J., *The Life and Death of Democracy*, London, Simon & Schuster, 2009.

Keen, A., *The Cult of the Amateur*, New York, Doubleday, 2007.

Kernaghan, K., Integrating Values into Public Service, *Public Administration Review*, 2003, 63, 6, pp.711–19.

Kjaer, A.M., *Governance*, Cambridge, Polity, 2004.

Klijn, E.H. and C. Skelcher, Democracy and Governance Networks: Compatible or Not?, *Public Administration*, 2007, 85, 3, pp.587–608.

Knight, J. and J. Johnson, Aggregation and Deliberation: On the Possibility of Democratic Legitimacy, *Political Theory*, 1994, 22, 2, pp.277–96.

Knoght, J. and J. Johnson, Aggregation and Deliberation: On the Possibility of Democratic Legitimacy, *Political Theory*, 1994, 22, 2, p. 277–96.

Kriesi, H., The Populist Challenge, *West European Politics*, 2014, 37, 2, pp.361–78.

Kriesi, H. and A.H. Trechsel, *The Politics of Switzerland*, Cambridge, Cambridge University Press, 2008.

Kriesi, H. and D. Wisler, The Impact of Social Movements on Political Institutions: A Comparison of the Introduction of Direct Legislation in Switzerland and the United States, in M. Giugni, D. McAdam, and C. Tilly (eds), *How Social Movements Matter*, Minneapolis, University of Minnesota Press, 1999, pp.42–65.

Labrie, A., Purity and Danger in fin-de-siècle Culture, *Psychoanalytische Perspectieven*, 2002, 20, 2, pp.261–74.

Landemore, H., Collective Wisdom: Old and New, in J. Elster and H. Landemore (eds), *Collective Wisdom: Principles and Mechanisms*, Cambridge, Cambridge University Press, 2012, pp.1–20.

Landemore, H., Democratic Reason: The Mechanisms of Collective Intelligence in Politics, Elster, J. and H. Landemore (eds) *Collective Wisdom: Principles and Mechanisms*, Cambridge, Cambridge University Press, 2012, pp.251–89.

Landemore, H., *Democratic Reason: Politics, Collective Intelligence, and the Rule of the Many*, Princeton University Press, 2017.

Landemore, H., Debate: Referendums are Never Merely Referendum: On the Need to Make Popular, Vote Processes More Deliberative, *Swiss Political Science Review*, 2018, 24, 3, pp.320–27.

Landemore, H., *Open Democracy: Reinventing Popular Rule for the Twenty-First Century*, Princeton, Princeton University Press, 2020.

Lang, A., But is it for Real? The British Columbia Citizens' Assembly as a Model of State-Sponsored Citizen Empowerment, *Politics and Society*, 2007, 35, 1, pp.35–70.

Laruelle, A., Voting to Select Projects in Participatory Budgeting, *European Journal of Operational Research*, 2021, 288, 2, pp.598–604.

Leahy, P., Who Exactly are the Citizens in the Citizens' Assembly?, *The Irish Times*, <https://www.irishtimes.com/news/politics/who-exactly-are-the-citizens-in-the-%09citizens-assembly-1.3059708>, 24 April 2017.

LeDuc, L., Referendums and Deliberative Democracy, *Electoral Studies*, 2015, 38, pp.139–48.

Lee, C.W., *Do-It-Yourself Democracy: The Rise of the Public Engagement Industry*, Oxford, Oxford University Press, 2015.

Leow, A., Celebrities Take to Social Media to say #ImWithHer or Just Get out the Vote, *Straits Times*, <www.straitstimes.com/world/united-states/celebrities-take-to-social-media-to-say-imwithher-or-just-get-out-the-vote>, 20 November 2016.

Lepore, J., *These Truths: A History of the United States*, New York, W.W. Norton, 2018.

Lerner, J., *Everyone Counts: Could 'Participatory Budgeting' Change Democracy?*, Cornell Selects, Cornell University Press, 2014.

Levisky S. and D. Ziblatt, *How Democracties Die*, New York, Crown, 2018.

Levy, R., Deliberative Voting: Reforming Constitutional Referendum Democracy, Public Law, July 2013, pp.555–74.

Leydesdorff, L. and H. Etzkowitz, The Triple Helix as a Model for Innovation Studies, *Science and Public Policy*, 1998, 25, 3, pp.195–203.

Leyenaar, M. and R. Hazan, Reconceptualizing Electoral Reform, *West European Politics*, 2011, 34, 3, pp.437–55.

Lijphart, A., *Patterns of Democracy: Government Forms and Performance in Thirty-Six Countries*, New Haven, Yale University Press, 1999.

Lijphart, A., The Evolution of Consociational Theory and Consociational Practices, 1965-2000, Acta Politica, Spring/Summer 2002, 37, pp.7–140.

Lilleker D.G., D. Jackson, and A. Veneti, The UK: The Post-Brexit, Ghost Election, in J. Haßler, M. Magin, U. Russmann, and V. Fenoll (eds), *Campaigning on Facebook in the 2019 European Parliament Election, Political Campaigning and Communication*, Cham, Palgrave Macmillan, 2017, pp.233–48.

Lindgren, S., The Work of Audiences in the Age of Clicktivism; On the Ins and Outs of Distributed Participation, *Media Fields Journal*, 2015, 10, pp.1–6.

Lipset, M. and S. Rokkan (eds), *Party Systems and Voter Alignments: Cross-National Perspectives*, New York, The Free Press, 1967.

Lodge, M., The Public Management of Risk: The Case for Deliberating among Worldviews, *Review of Policy Research*, 2009, 26, 4, pp.395–408.

Loughlin, J., F. Hendriks, and A. Lidström (eds), *The Oxford Handbook of Local and Regional Democracy in Europe*, Oxford, Oxford University Press, 2010.

Lowndes, V. and C. Skelcher, The Dynamics of Multi-Organizational Partnerships: An Analysis of Changing Modes of Governance, *Public Administration*, 1998, 76, 2, pp.313–33.

Lucardie, P., *Democratic Extremism in Theory and Practice*, London, Routledge, 2014.

McKay, S., Building a Better Referendum: Linking Mini-Publics and Mass Publics in Popular Votes, *Journal of Public Deliberation*, 2019, 15, 1.

Mann, M., *The Dark Side of Democracy: Explaining Ethnic Cleansing*, Cambridge, Cambridge University Press, 2005.

Mansbridge, J., *Beyond Adversary Democracy*, New York, Basic Books, 1980.

Mansbridge, J., *Beyond Adversarial Democracy*, Chicago, Chicago University Press, 1983.

Mansbridge, J., J. Bohman, S. Chambers, T. Christiano, A. Fung, J. Parkinson, D.F. Thompson, and M.E. Warren, A Systemic Approach to Deliberative Democracy, in J. Parkinson, and J. Mansbridge (eds), *Deliberative Systems: Deliberative Democracy at the Large Scale*, Cambridge, Cambridge University Press, 2012, pp.1–26.

March, J.G. and J.P. Olsen, Organizing Political Life: What Administrative Reorganization Tells us about Government, *American Political Science Review*, 1983, 77, pp.281–96.

Marcos, J., Podemos' Pablo Iglesias Calls Leadership Vote in Response to Country House Scandal, *El País*, <https://elpais.com/elpais/2018/05/21/inenglish/1526892734_555474.html>, 21 May 2019.

Marquetti, A., G.A. de Campos, and R. Pires, Orçamento participativo, redistribuição e finanças municipais: a experiência de Porto Alegre entre 1989 e 2004, *Democracia participativa e redistribuição: análise de experiências de orçamento participativo*, São Paulo, Xamã, 2008, pp.31–54.

Matsusaka, J., *Let the People Rule: How Direct Democracy Can Meet the Populist Challenge*, Princeton University Press, 2020.

Meijer, A., R. van der Veer, A. Faber, and J. Penning de Vries, Political Innovation as Ideal and Strategy: The Case of Aleatoric Democracy in the City of Utrecht, *Public Management Review*, 2017, 19, 1, pp.20–36.

Mendonça, R.F and E.M. Cunha, Can the Claim to Foster Broad Participation Hinder Deliberation?, *Critical Policy Studies*, 2014, 8, 1, pp.78–100.

Menser, M., *We Decide! Theories and Cases in Participatory Democracy Michael*, Philadelphia, Temple University Press, 2018.

Michels, A., Debating Democracy: The Dutch Case, *Acta Politica*, 2008, 43, 4, pp.472–92.

Michels, A.M.B., Innovations in Democratic Governance: How Does Citizen Participation Contribute to a Better Democracy, *International Review of Administrative Sciences*, 2011, 77, 2, pp.275–93.

Michels, A., Participation in Citizens' Summits and Public Engagement, *International Review of Administrative Sciences*, 2019, 85, 2, pp.211–27.

Michels, A. and H. Binnema, Assessing the Impact of Deliberative Democratic Initiatives at the Local Level: A Framework for Analysis, *Administration & Society*, 2019, 51, 5, pp.749–69.

Miller, C., *Taiwan is making democracy work again. It's time we paid attention*, Wired, <https://www.wired.co.uk/article/taiwan-democracy-social-media>, 26 November 2019.

Moore, M., *Creating Public Value: Strategic Management in Government*, Cambridge, MA, Harvard University Press, 1997.

Morel, L. and M. Qvortrup (eds), *The Routledge Handbook to Referendums and Direct Democracy*, Abingdon, Routledge, 2018.

Mounk, Y., *The People vs Democracy: Why Our Freedom is in Danger and How to Save it*, Cambridge, MA, Harvard University Press, 2018.

Mudde, C., The Populist Zeitgeist, *Government and Opposition*, 2004, 39, 3, pp.541–63.

Mulgan, G., *Big Mind: How Collective Intelligence Can Change our World*, Princeton, Princeton University Press, 2018.

Mulish, H., *The Discovery of Heaven*, London, Penguin Books, 1996.

Müller, J.W., *Democracy Rules*, Penguin Books, 2021.

Müller, J.W., *What is Populism?*, Philadelphia, University of Pennsylvania Press, 2016.

Mutz, D.C., *Hearing the Other Side: Deliberative Versus Participatory Democracy*, Cambridge, Cambridge University Press, 2006.

Nabatchi, T., Public Values Frames in Administration and Governance, *Perspectives on Public Management and Governance*, 2017, 1, 1, pp.59–72.

Nabatchi, T. and M. Leighninger, *Public Participation for 21st Century Democracy*, New York, Jossey Bass, 2015.

Nabatchi, T., A. Sancino, and M. Sicilia, Varieties of Participation in Public Services: The Who, When, and What of Coproduction, *Public Administration Review*, 2017, 77, 5, pp.766–76.

Nagle, A., *Kill All Normies: Online Culture Wars from 4chan and Tumblr to Trump and the Alt-Right*, London, Zero Books, 2017.

Neblo, M., K. Esterling, and D. Lazer, *Politics with the People: Building a Directly Representative Democracy*, Cambridge Studies in Public Opinion and Political Psychology, Cambridge, Cambridge University Press, 2018.

Newton, K., Curing the Democratic Malaise with Democratic Innovations, B. Geissel and K. Newton (eds), *Evaluating Democratic Innovations: Curing the Democratic Malaise?*, London, Routledge, 2012, pp.3–20.

Ney, S. and M. Verweij, Exploring the Contributions of Cultural Theory for Improving Public Deliberation about Complex Policy Problems, *The Policy Studies Journal*, 2014, 42, 4, pp.620–43.

Norris, P. and R. Inglehart, *Cultural Backlash: Trump, Brexit and Authoritarian Populism*, Cambridge, Cambridge University Press, 2019.

Noveck, B., *Wiki Government: How Technology Can Make Government Better, Democracy Stronger, and Citizens More Powerful*, Washington, DC, Brookings Institution Press, 2009.

Noveck, B., Five Hacks for Digital Democracy, *Nature*, 2017, 544, 7650, pp.287–9.

Noveck, B., *Smart Citizens, Smarter State: The Technologies of Expertise and the Future of Governing*, Cambridge, MA, Harvard University Press, 2015.

NRC, Geef burgers echte invloed op het klimaatbeleid met het preferendum, *NRC Nieuws*, <https://www.nrc.nl/nieuws/2021/10/08/geef-burgers-echte-invloed-op-het-klimaatbeleid-met-het-preferendum-a4061204>, 8 October 2020.

O'Connell, P., Trust in Politics, Politicians and Institutions, *Public Policy*, <https://publicpolicy.ie/papers/trust-in-politics-politicians-and-institutions/>, 30 January 2020.

OECD, *Innovative Citizen Participation and New Democratic Institutions: Catching the Deliberative Wave*, Paris, OECD Publishing, 2020.

O'Flynn, I., Democratic Innovations and Theories of Democracy, in S. Elstub and O. Escobar (eds), *Democratic Innovation and Governance*, Cheltenham, Edward Elgar, 2019, pp.32–44.

O'Flynn, I. and G. Sood, What Would Dahl Say? An Appraisal of the Democratic Credentials of Deliberative Polls and other Mini-Publics, K. Grönlund, A. Bächtiger, and M. Setälä (eds), *Deliberative Mini-Publics, Involving Citizens in the Democratic Process*, Colchester, ECPR Press, 2014, pp.41–81.

Olsen, E.D.H., and H.J. Trenz, From Citizens' Deliberation to Popular Will Formation? Generating Democratic Legitimacy in Transnational Deliberative Polling, *Political Studies*, 2014, 62, 1, pp.117–33.

Olsen, J.P., Change and Continuity: An Institutional Approach to Institutions of Democratic Government, *European Political Science Review*, 2009, 1, 1, pp.3–32.

Olsen, M., *The Rise and Decline of Nations*, New York, Yale University Press, 1982.

Ostrom, E. (ed), *Strategies of Political Inquiry*, Beverly Hills, Sage, 1982.

Ostrom, E., *Governing the Commons*, Cambridge, Cambridge University Press, 1990.

Ostrom, V., A Forgotten Tradition: The Constitutional Level of Analysis, in J.A. Gillespie and D.A. Zinnes (eds), *Missing Elements in Political Inquiry*, New York, Sage, 1982, pp.237–52.

Owen, D. and G. Smith, Survey Article: Deliberation, Democracy, and the Systemic Turn, *Journal of Political Philosophy*, 2015, 23, 2, pp.213–34.

Oxford Dictionary, *concretize*, <https://www.lexico.com/definition/concretize>, n.d.

Page, B.I. and R.Y. Shapiro, *The Rational Public: Fifty Years of Trends in Americans' Policy Preferences*, University of Chicago Press, 1992.

Page, S.E., *The Difference: How the Power of Diversity Creates Better Groups, Firms, Schools, and Societies*, Princeton University Press, 2007.

Papadopoulos, Y., *Democracy in Crisis?*, Basinstoke, Palgrave Macmillan, 2013.

Papadopoulos, Y. and P. Warin, Are Innovative, Participatory and Deliberative Procedures in Policy Making Democratic and Effective?, *European Journal of Political Research*, 2007, 46, 4, pp.445–72.

Pape, M. and C. Lim, Beyond the 'Usual Suspects'? Reimagining Democracy with Participatory Budgeting in Chicago, *Sociol Forum*, 2019, 34, pp.861–82.

Parker, S., *Taking Power Back: Putting People in Charge of Politics*, Policy Press, 2015.

Parkinson, J., Legitimacy Problems in Deliberative Democracy, *Political Studies*, 2003, 51, 1, pp.180–96.

Parkinson, J., Why Deliberate? The Encounter Between Deliberation and New Public Managers, *Public Administration*, 2004, 82, 2, pp.377–95.

Parkinson, J., Deliberative Systems, in A. Bächtiger, J. Dryzek, J. Mansbridge, and M.E. Warren (eds), *The Oxford Handbook of Deliberative Democracy*, Oxford, Oxford University Press, 2018, pp.432–46.

Parkinson, M., The Roles of Referendums in Deliberative Systems, *Representation*, 2020, 56, 4, pp.485–500.

Participedia, *Method*, <https://participedia.net/method/4682>, n.d.

Participedia, *The Irish Citizens' Assembly*, <https://participedia.net/case/5316?lang=en>, n.d.

Pateman, C., *Participation and Democratic Theory*, Cambridge, Cambridge University Press, 1970.

Pateman, C., Participatory Democracy Revisited, *Perspectives on Politics*, 2012, 10, 1, pp.7–19.

Peixoto, T., F.M. Sjoberg, and J. Mellon, A Get-Out-the-Vote Experiment on the World's Largest Participatory Budgeting Vote in Brazil, *British Journal of Political Science*, 2017, 50, 1, pp.1–9.

Pellikaan, H., S. De Lange, and T. van der Meer, The Centre Does Not Hold: Coalition Politics and Party System Change in the Netherlands, 2002–12, *Government and Opposition*, 2018, 53, 2, pp.231–55.

Pennings, P. and H. Keman, The Changing Landscape of Dutch Politics since the 1970s, *Acta Politica*, 2008, 43, 2-3, pp.154–79.

Perthuis, C., Débat: La Convention citoyenne pour le climat . . . et après ?, *The Conversation*, <https://theconversation.com/debat-la-convention-citoyenne-pour-le-climat-et-apres-141891>, 6 July 2020.

Perri 6, Institutional Viability: A Neo-Durkheimian Theory, *Innovation: The European Journal of Social Science Research*, 2003, 16, pp.395–415.

Peters, B.G., *Strategies for Comparative Research in Political Science*, London, Palgrave Macmillan, 2013.

Peters, B.G., J. Pierre, E. Sørensen, and J. Torfing, Bringing Political Science back into Public Administration Research, *Governance*, 2022, pp.1–22.

Pettigrew, E., How Facebook Saw Trump Coming When No One Else Did, *Medium*, <https://medium.com/@erinpettigrew/how-facebook-saw-trump-coming-when-no-one-else-did-84cd6b4e0d8e>, 9 November 2016.

Pieper, A.K. and M. Pieper, Political Participation via Social Media: A Case Study of Deliberative Quality in the Public Online Budgeting Process of Frankfurt/Main, Germany 2013, *Universal Access in the Information Society*, 2015, 14, pp.487–503.

Pierre, J. (ed), *Debating Governance: Authority, Steering and Democracy*, Oxford, Oxford University Press, 2000.

Pierre, J., Reinventing Governance, Reinventing Democracy?, *Policy & Politics*, 2009, 37, 4, pp.591–609.

Pogrebinschi, T. and M. Ryan, Moving Beyond Input Legitimacy: When Do Democratic Innovations Affect Policy Making, *European Journal of Political Research*, 2017, 57, 1, pp.135–52.

Pol.is, *Mission and Values*, <https://pol.is/company>, 17 July 2014.

Pol.is, *Pol.is Explainer and Demo* [Video], Youtube, <https://www.youtube.com/watch?v=FrIin_omVn4>, 9 September 2016.

Pol.is, *Input Crowd, Output Meaning*, <https://pol.is/home>, 2022.

Popper, K., *The Open Society Society and Its Enemies*, Princeton, Princeton University Press, 1945.

Posner, E.A. and G.W. Weyl, *Radical Markets: Uprooting Capitalism and Democracy for a Just Society*, Princeton University Press, 2018.

Powell, G.B., *Elections as Instruments of Democracy: Majoritarian and Proportional Visions*, Cambridge, MA, Harvard University Press, 2000.

Public Voice, *Polis*, <https://www.publicvoice.co.nz/online-engagement-tools/entry/194/>, 3 October 2016.

Putnam, R.D., *Making Democracy Work: Civic Traditions in Modern Italy*, Princeton, Princeton University Press, 1993.

Pyun, H.O. and C. Edey Gamassou, Looking for Public Administration Theories?, *Public Organization Review*, 2018, 18, pp.245–61.

Qvortrup, M. (ed), *Referendums Around the World: The Continued Growth of Direct Democracy*, Houndmills, Palgrave Macmillan, 2017.

Qvortrup, M., Referendums in Western Europe, in M. Qvortrup (ed), *Referendums around the World*, Houndmills, Palgrave Macmillan, 2017, pp.19–45.

Qvortrup, M., *Death by a Thousand Cuts: The Slow Demise of Democracy*, De Gruyter, 2021.

Qvortrup, M., B. O'Leary, and R. Wintrobe, Explaining the Paradox of Plebiscites, Government and Opposition, 2020, 55, 2, pp.202–19.

Raadschelders, J., *Public Administration: The Interdisciplinary Study of Government*, Oxford, Oxford University Press, 2011.

Radboud University/KU Leuven, *Burgerbegroting Amsterdam OOD-Oost* [Infographic], <https://soc.kuleuven.be/centre-for-political-research/demoinno/files/infographic-adam-oud-oost.pdf>, December 2020.

Rahat, G., *The Politics of Regime Structure Reform in Democracies*, New York, State University of New York, 2008.

Rahat, G. and R.Y. Hazan, The Barriers to Electoral System Reform: A Synthesis of Alternative Approaches, *West European Politics*, 2011, 34, 3, pp.478–94.

Ratner, R.S., British Columbia Citizens' Assembly: The Learning Phase, *Canadian Parliamentary Review*, 2004, 27, 2, pp.20–6.

Real Truth Exposed, *Muslims ravage through US neighborhood*, <https://www.facebook.com/1121413461303246/posts/muslims-ravage-through-us-neighborhoodreal-truth-exposed-againheadlines-mob-of-2/1126824964095429/>, 30 January 2017.

Reinisch, C. and J. Parkinson, *Swiss Landsgemeinden: A Deliberative Democratic Evaluation of Two Outdoor Parliaments*, Helsinki, ECPR Joint Sessions, 2007.

Renson, T., Baart Antwerpse Burgerbegroting betere burgers?, *Sampol*, 2018, 2, pp.58–66.

Renwick, A., *The Politics of Electoral Reform: Changing the Rules of Democracy*, Cambridge, Cambridge University Press, 2010.

Renwick, A. and R. McKee, *The Citizens' Assembly on Brexit (I): Design and Purpose*, London, University College London, 2017.

Renwick, A., S. Allan, W. Jennings, R. McKee, M. Russell, and G. Smith, *The Report of the Citizens' Assembly on Brexit*, London, University College of London, 2017.

Renwick, A., S. Allan, W. Jennings, R. McKee, M. Russell, and G. Smith, What Kind of Brexit do Voters Want? Lessons from the Citizens' Assembly on Brexit, *The Political Quarterly*, 2018, 4, pp.649–58.

Rhodes, R.A.W., *Understanding Governance: Policy Networks, Governance, Reflexivity and Accountability*, London, Open University Press, 1997.

Rhodes, R.A.W. and P. 't Hart (eds), *Oxford Handbook of Political Leadership*, Oxford, Oxford University Press, 2014.

Ringen, S., *Nation of Devils: Democratic Leadership and the of Obedience*, New Haven, Yale University Press, 2013.

Roamresearch, *Pol.is method*, <https://roamresearch.com/#/app/polis-methods/page/EK79EAAcB>, n.d.

Röcke, A., *Framing Citizen Participation: Participatory Budgeting in France, Germany and the United Kingdom*, Palgrave Macmillan, 2014.

Rosanvallon, P., *Counter-Demcoracy: Politics in an Age of Distrust*, Cambridge, Cambridge University Press, 2008.

Rosanvallon, P., *Good Government: Democracy Beyond Elections*, Cambridge, MA, Harvard University Press, 2015.

Ross, S.M., *Beyond the Box: Television and the Internet*, Oxford, Blackwell, 2008.

Rothstein, B. and J. Teorell, What is Quality of Government? A Theory of Impartial Government Institutions, *Governance*, 2008, 21, 2, pp.165–90.

Rowe, G. and L.J. Frewer, Public Participation Methods: A Framework for Evaluation, *Science, Technology & Human Values*, 2000, 25, 1, pp.3–29.

Rowe, G. and L.J. Frewer, A Typology of Public Engagement Mechanisms, *Science, Technology & Human Values*, 2005, 30, 2, pp.251–90.

Runciman, D., *How Democracy Ends*, Profile Books, 2018.

Rural Alliance, *Skills Plotting Tool Version 4*, n.d., retrieved 1 April 2019.

Ruscio, K.P., *The Leadership Dilemma in Modern Democracy*, Edward Elgar, 2008.

Ryan, M., *Why Citizen Participation Succeeds or Fails: A Comparative Analysis of Participatory Budgeting*, Bristol, Bristol University Press, 2021.

Ryan, M. and G. Smith, Defining Mini-Publics, in K. Grönlund, A. Bächtiger, and M. Setälä (eds), *Deliberative Mini-Publics*, London, ECPR Press, 2014, pp.9–26.

Sandri, G. and A. Seddone (eds), *Party Primaries in Comparative Perspective*, Routledge, 2016.

Sartori, G., *Parties and Party Systems: A Framework for Analysis*, Cambridge, Cambridge University Press, 2016 (originally 1976).

Saward, M., *The Terms of Democracy*, Cambridge, Polity Press, 1998.

Saward, M., Making Democratic Connections: Political Equality, Deliberation and Direct Democracy, *Acta Politica*, 2001, 36, pp.361–79.

Saward, M., *The Representative Claim*, Oxford, Oxford University Press, 2010.

Saward, M., *Democratic Design*, Oxford, Oxford University Press, 2021.

Schaap, L. and J. van Ostaaijen, Good Multi-Level Governance: Brainport-Eindhoven, in L. van den Dool, F. Hendriks, A. Gianoli, and L. Schaap (eds), *The Quest for Good Urban Governance*, Wiesbaden, Springer VS, 2015, pp.147–64.

Schama, S., *The Embarrassment of Riches: An Interpretation of Dutch Culture in the Golden Age*, Berkeley, University of California Press, 1987.

Scharpf, F.W., *Governing in Europe: Effective and Democratic?*, Oxford, Oxford University Press, 1999.

Scharpf, F.W., The Joint-Decision Trap Revisited, *Journal of Common Market Studies*, 2006, 44, 4, pp.845–64.

Schenk, M., *Muslim figure: 'We must have pork-free menus or we will leave US' What's your response?*, <https://leadstories.com/hoax-alert/2019/03/fake-news-muslim-figure-we-must-have-pork-free-menus-or-we-will-leave-us-how-would-you-respond-this.html>, 10 March 2019.

Schmidt, V.A., Democracy and Legitimacy in the European Union Revisited: Input, Output and 'Throughput', *Political Studies*, 2013, 61, 1, pp.2–22.

Schneider, S. H. and S. Busse, Participatory Budgeting in Germany—A Review of Empirical Findings, *International Journal of Public Administration*, 2018, 692, pp.1–15.

Scott, J., *Seeing Like a State, How Certain Schemes to Improve the Human Condition Have Failed*, Yale University Press, 1999.

Scurr, R., *Fatal Purity: Robespierre and the French Revolution*, New York, Metropolitan Books, 2006.

Setälä, M., Connecting Deliberative Mini-Publics to Representative Decision Making, *European Journal of Political Research*, 2017, 56, 4, pp.846–63.

Setälä, M., K. Grönlund, and K. Herne, Citizen Deliberation on Nuclear Power: A Comparison of Two Decision-Making Methods, *Political Studies*, 2010, 58, 4, pp.688–714.

Shapiro, I., Enough of Deliberation: Politics is about Interests and Power, in S. Macedo (ed), *Deliberative Politics*, Oxford, Oxford University Press, 1999, pp.28–38.

Sintomer, Y., Random Selection, Republican Self-Government, and Deliberative Democracy, *Constellations*, 2010, 17, 3, pp.472–87.

Sintomer, Y., C. Herzberg, and A. Röcke, Participatory Budgeting in Europe: Potentials and Challenges, *International Journal of Urban and Regional Research*, 2008, 32, 1, pp.164–78.

Sintomer, Y., A. Röcke, and C. Herzberg, *Participatory Budgeting in Europe: Democracy and Public Governance*, Routledge, 2016.

Smith, G., *Democratic Innovation: Designing Institutions for Citizen Participation*, Cambridge, Cambridge University Press, 2009.

Smith, G., Review of 'When the People Speak', *Perspectives on Politics*, 2010, 8, 3, pp.908–09.

Smith, G., Reflections on the Theory and Practice of Democratic Innovations, in S. Elstub and O. Escobar (eds), *Democratic Innovation and Governance*, Cheltenham, Edward Elgar, 2019, pp.572–82.

Smith, G., *Can Democracy Safeguard the Future?*, Polity Press, 2021.

Smith, T.W., The First Straw A Study of the Origins of Election Polls, *Public Opinion Quarterly*, 1990, 54, 1, pp.21–33.

Sørensen, E. and J. Torfing, The Democratic Anchorage of Governance Networks. *Scandinavian Political Studies*, 2005, 28, 3, pp.195–218.

Sørensen, E. and J. Torfing, Making Governance Networks Effective and Democratic Through Metagovernance, *Public Administration*, 2009, 87, 2, pp.234–58.

Stadt Frankfurt am Main, *Bürgerbeteiligung leicht gemacht*, <https://www.ffm.de/frankfurt/de/home>, n.d.

Steiner, J. and T. Ertman, Consociationalism and Corporatism in Western Europe: Still the Politics of Accomodation?, *Acta Politica*, Spring/Summer 2002, 37, pp.7–140.

Stoker, G., Regime Theory and Urban Politics, in D. Judge, G. Stoker, and H. Wolman (eds), *Theories of Urban Politics*, London, Sage, 1995.

Stoker, G., Governance as Theory: Five Propositions, *International Social Science Journal*, 1998, 68, 2, pp.15–24.

Stone, C.N., *Regime Politics: Governing Atlanta 1946–1988*, Lawrence, University Press of Kansas, 1989.

Stone, C.N., Power, Reform and Urban Regime Analysis, *City & Community*, 2006, 5, 1, pp.23–38.

Strebel, M.A., D. Kübler, and F. Marcinkowski, The Importance of Input and Output Legitimacy in Democratic Governance, *European Journal of Political Research*, 2019, 58, pp.488–513.

Suiter, J. and T. Reidy, Does Deliberation Help Deliver Informed Electorates: Evidence from Irish Referendum Votes, *Representation*, 2020, 56, 4, pp.539–57.

Suiter, J., D. Farrell, and C. Harris, Ireland's Evolving Constitution, in P. Blokker (ed), *Constitutional Acceleration within the European Union and Beyond*, London, Routledge, 2018, pp.142–54.

Sunstein, C., The Law of Group Polarization, *Journal of Political Philosophy*, 2002, 10, 2, pp.175–95.

Sunstein, C., *Infotopia: How Many Minds Produce Knowledge*, Oxford, Oxford University Press, 2008.

Sunstein, C., #Republic: Divided Democracy in the Age of Social Media, Princeton, Princeton University Press, 2017.

Surowiecki, J., The Wisdom of Crowds: Whay the Many are Smarter than the Few, New York, Doubleday, 2004.

Susskind, J., Future Politics: Living Together in a World Transformed by Tech, Oxford, Oxford University Press, 2018.

Talpin, J., Qualitative Approaches to Democratic Innovations, in S. Elstub and O. Escobar (eds), Democratic Innovation and Governance, Cheltenham, Edward Elgar, 2019, pp.486–500.

Tanasoca, A., Against Bot Democracy: The Dangers of Epistemic Double-Counting, Perspectives on Politics, 2019, pp.1–15.

TEDx Talk, Digital Social Innovation to Empower Democracy | Audrey Tang | TEDxVictoriaGasteinz [Video], YouTube, <https://www.youtube.com/watch?v=LscTx6DHh9I>, 8 May 2019.

Teisman, G.R. and E.H. Klijn, Complexity Theory and Public Management: An Introduction, Public Management Review, 2008, 10, 3, pp.287–97.

Thomas, G., A Typology for the Case Study in Social Science, Qualitative Inquiry, 2011, 17, 6, pp.511–21.

Thomas, J.C., Public Participation in Public Decisions, San Francisco, Jossey-Bass Publishers, 1995.

Thompson, M., Man and Nature as a Single but Complex System, in T. Munn (ed), Encyclopedia of Global Environmental Change, Chichester, John Wiley, 2002, 5, pp.384–93.

Thompson, M., Organising and Disorganising: A Dynamic and Non-Linear Theory of Institutional Emergence and its Implications, Devon, Triarcy Press, 2008.

Thompson, M., R. Ellis, and A. Wildavsky, Cultural Theory, Boulder, Westview Press, 1990.

Thompson, M., G. Grendstad, and P. Selle (eds), Cultural Theory as Political Science, London, Routledge, 1999.

Tierney, S., Using Electoral Law to Construct a Deliberative Referendum: Moving beyond the Democratic Paradox, Election Law Journal, 2013, 12, 4, pp.508–23.

Toonen, Th.A.J., Networks, Management and Institutions: Public Administration as 'Normal Science', Public Administration, 1998, 76, 2, pp.229–52.

Toonen, Th.A.J., Administrative Reform: Analytics, in B.G. Peters and J. Pierre (eds), Handbook of Public Administration, New York, Sage, 2003, pp.467–76.

Toonen, Th.A.J., Resilience in Public Administration: The Work of Elinor and Vincent Ostrom from a Public Administration Perspective, Public Administration Review, 2010, 70, 2, pp.193–202.

Torfing, J. and P. Triantafillou (eds), Enhancing Public Innovation by Transforming Public Governance, Cambridge, Cambridge University Press, 2016.

Torfing, J., L.B. Anderson, C. Greve, and K. Klausen, Public Governance Paradigms: Competing and Co-Existing, Cheltenham, Edward Elgar, 2020.

Torfing, J., G. Peters, J. Piere, and E. Sørensen, Interactive Governance, Oxford, Oxford University Press, 2012.

Tormey, S., The End of Representative Politics, Cambridge, Polity Press, 2015.

Torney, D., Deliberative Mini-Publics and the European Green Deal in Turbulent Times: The Irish and French Climate Assemblies, Politics and Governance, 2021, 9, 3, pp.380–90.

Tsebelis, G., Veto Players: How Political Institutions Work, Princeton University Press, 2002.

Tyler, T. and Y.J. Huo, Trust in the Law: Encouraging Public Cooperation with the Police and Courts, New York, Russell Sage Foundation, 2002.

Tyler, T.R., Governing amid Diversity: The Effect of Fair Decisionmaking Procedures on the Legitimacy of Government, Law and Society Review, 1994, 28, 4, pp.809–32.

van Beek, U. (eds), *Democracy under Threat: A Crisis of Legitimacy*, Palgrave Macmillan, 2019.

van Biezen, I., P. Mair, and T. Poguntke, Going, Going . . . Gone? The Decline of Party Membership in Contemporary Europe, *European Journal of Political Research*, 2012, 51, 1, pp.24–56.

van den Dool, L., F. Hendriks, A. Gianoli, and L. Schaap (eds), *The Quest for Good Urban Governance: Theoretical Reflection and International Practices*, Wiesbaden, Springer, 2015.

van der Kolk, H., *Kiezen voor een nieuw kiesstelsel*, Enschede, Universiteit Twente, <https://www.utwente.nl/en/bms/pa/staff/kolk/bf_verslag_deel_2_versie_4.pdf>, 1 February 2008.

van der Lans, J. and P. Hilhorst, *Sociaal doe-het-zelven*, Amsterdam, Atlas Contact, 2013.

van der Meer, T., PoliticalTrust and the 'Crisis of Democracy', *Oxford Research Encyclopedia of Politics*, <https://oxfordre.com/politics/view/10.1093/acrefore/9780190228637.001.0001/acrefore-9780190228637-e-77>, 25 January 2017.

van der Meer, T. and A. Hakhverdian, Political Trust as the Evaluation of Process and Performance: A Cross-National Study of 42 European Countries, *Political Studies*, 2017, 65, 1, pp.81–102.

van der Meer, T., C.C.L. Wagenaar, and K. Jacobs, The Rise and Fall of the Dutch Referendum Law (2015–2018): Initiation, Use and Abolition of the Corrective, Citizen-Initiated and Non-binding Referendum, *Acta Politica*, 2020.

van de Wijdeven, T., Bewonerscoöperatie Biest-Houtakker: 'Iedereen kan iets', in T. van de Wijdeven and L. de Graaf (eds), *Kernkracht: over doe-democratie in het landelijk gebied*, Tilburg, Tilburg University Reports, 2014, pp.43–60.

van de Wijdeven, T. and F. Hendriks, A Little Less Conversation, a Little More Action: Real-Life Expressions of Vital Citizenship, in J.W. Duyvendak, F. Hendriks, and M. van Niekerk (eds), *City in Sight*, Amsterdam, Amsterdam University Press, 2009, pp.121–141.

van Dongen, M., *Het success can GeenPeil in 12 lessen*, <https://www.volkskrant.nl/nieuws-achtergrond/het-succes-van-geenpeil-in-12-lessen~b25cfda5/>, 31 March 2016.

van Hulst, M.J., L. de Graaf, and G. van den Brink, The Work of Exemplary Practitioners in Neighborhood Governance, *Critical Policy Studies*, 2012, 6, 4, pp.433–50.

van Loon, A., Social Media Predicted Trump's Win, *We Are Social*, <https://wearesocial.com/blog/2016/11/social-media-predicted-trumps-win.>, 26 November 2016.

van Reybrouck, D., *Against Elections: The Case for Democracy*, London, Penguin Random House, 2013.

van Vos, L.H. (eds), *Petitions in Social History*, Cambridge University Press, 2002.

van Vree, W., *Meetings, Manners and Civilization*, Leicester, Leicester University Press, 1999.

Vatter, A., M. Flinders, and J. Bernauer, A Global Trend Toward Democratic Convergence? A Lijphartian Analysis of Advanced Democracies, *Comparative Political Studies*, 2014, 47, 6, pp.903–29.

V-Dem, *Democracy Reports*, <https://www.v-dem.net/democracy_reports.html>, n.d.

Verweij, M., *Clumsy Solutions for a Wicked World*, Palgrave Macmillan, 2011.

Verweij, M. and M. Thompson (eds), *Clumsy Solutions for a Complex World: Governance, Politics and Plural Perceptions*, Basingstoke, Palgrave Macmillan, 2006.

Verweij, M., M. Douglas, R. Ellis, C. Engel, F. Hendriks, S. Lohman, S. Ney, S. Rayner, and M. Thompson, Clumsy Solutions for a Complex World: The Case of Climate Change, *Public Administration*, 2006, 84, 4, pp.817–43.

Voorberg, W.H., V.J.J.M. Bekkers, and L.G. Tummers, A Systematic Review of Co-Creation and Co-Production: Embarking on the Social Innovation Journey, *Public Management Review*, 2014, 17, 9, pp.1333–57.

Vrydagh, J., Measuring the Impact of Consultative Citizen Participation: Reviewing the Congruency Approaches for Assessing the Uptake of Citizen Ideas, *Policy Sciences*, 2022, 55, 1, pp.65–88.

Walsh, C.D. and J.A. Elkink, The Dissatisfied and the Engaged: Citizen Support for Citizens' Assemblies and their Willingness to Participate, *Irish Political Studies*, 2021, 36, 4, pp.647–66.

Wampler, B. and B. Goldfrank, *The Rise, Spread, and Decline of Brazil's Participatory Budgeting: The Arc of a Democratic Innovation*, Cham, Palgrave Macmillan, 2022.

Wampler, B., S.L. McNulty, and M. Touchton, *Participatory Budgeting in Global Perspective*, Oxford, Oxford University Press, 2021.

Warren, M.E., A Problem-Based Approach to Democratic Theory, *American Political Science Review*, 2017, 111, 1, pp.39–53.

Warren, M. and A. Lang, Supplementary Democracy? Democratic Deficits and Citizens' Assemblies, in P. Lenard and R. Simeon (eds), *Imperfect Democracies*, Vancouver, University of British Columbia Press, 2012, pp.291–314.

Warren, M.E. and H. Pearse, *Designing Deliberative Democracy: The British Columbia Citizens' Assembly*, New York, Cambridge University Press, 2008.

Watkins, A. and I. Straitens, *Crowdocracy: The End of Politics*, Rochester, Urbane Publications, 2016.

Weber, M., *Economy and Society: An Outline of Interpretive Sociology*, New York, Bedminster Press, 1968 (originally 1922).

Wikipedia, *Votation*, <https://en.wiktionary.org/wiki/votation>, 28 October 2019.

Wildavsky, A., Democracy as a Coalition of Cultures, *Society*, 1993, 31, pp.80–3.

Wilkinson, C., J. Briggs, K. Salt, J. Vines, and E. Flynn, In Participatory Budgeting We Trust? Fairness, Tactics and (In)accessibility in Participatory Governance, *Local Government Studies*, 2019, 45, 6, pp.1001–20.

Williams, D. and D. Waisanen, *Real Money, Real Power?: The Challenges with Participatory Budgeting in New York City*, Palgrave Macmillan, 2020.

Wojciechowska, M., Towards Intersectional Democratic Innovations, *Political Studies*, 2019, 67, 4, pp.895–911.

Wolf, E., S. Rys, and W. van Dooren, *Naar een Vlaamse Burgerbegroting? Lessen uit de binnenlandse en buitenlandse praktijk*, Universiteit Antwerpen, 2018.

Yin, R.K., *Applications of Case Study Research*, Los Angeles, Sage, 2012.

Young, I., *Inclusion and Democracy*, Oxford, Oxford University Press, 2000.

Zakaria, F., *The Future of Freedom: Illiberal Democracy at Home and Abroad*, New York, Norton, 2003.

Zieman, K., Exploring the Impact of Mass Cultural Changes on the Patterns of Democratic Reform, *Democratization*, 2013, 21, 5, pp.888–911.

Zieman, K., *Democratic Reforms and Legitimacy in Established Western Democracies*, PhD Thesis, Leiden University, 2014.

Zimmerman, J.F., *The New England Town Meeting: Democracy in Action*, Westport, Praeger, 1999.

Zuboff, S., *The Age of Surveillance Capitalism: The Fight for a Human Future at the New Frontier of Power*, London, Profile Books, 2019.

Zuiderveen Borgesius, F.J., J. Möller, S. Kruikjemeier, R. Fathaigh, K. Irion, T. Dobber, B. Bodo, and C. de Vreese, Online Political Microtargeting: Promises and Threats for Democracy, *Utrecht Law Review*, 2018, 14, 1, pp.82–96.

Index

For the benefit of digital users, indexed terms that span two pages (e.g., 52–53) may, on occasion, appear on only one of those pages.